WITHDRAWN FROM
TSC LIBRARY
TALLAHASSEE
LIBRARY
COMMUNITY COLLEGE

D1552857

BEATRICE W. SHAW FLORIDA
COLLECTION
Tallahassee Community College
Library
Tallahassee, Florida
Presented by
Mabel Shaw

"A Rogue's Paradise"

"A Rogue's Paradise"

Crime and Punishment in Antebellum Florida, 1821–1861

James M. Denham

The University of Alabama Press
Tuscaloosa and London

Tuscaloosa, Alabama 34587–0380

Manufactured in the United States of America
∞
The paper on which this book is printed meets the minimum requirements of American National Standard for Information Science–Permanence of Paper for Printed Library Materials, ANSI Z39.48-1984.

Library of Congress Cataloging-in-Publication Data

Denham, James M.
"A rogue's paradise" : crime and punishment in Antebellum Florida, 1821–1861 / James M. Denham.
p. cm.
Includes bibliographical references (p.) and index.
ISBN 0-8173-0847-4 (cloth : alk. paper)
1. Crime—Florida—History—19th century. 2. Criminal justice, Administration of—Florida—History—19th century. 3. Florida—History—1821–1865. I. Title.
HV6793.F6D46 1997
364.9759'09'034—dc20 96-24837

British Library Cataloguing-in-Publication Data available

For Jim Denham
and
in memory of Emma Denham

Contents

Contents

Preface

This book traces the patterns of crime and punishment in antebellum Florida from 1821 to 1861. The manner in which each criminal was captured, tried, and incarcerated offers vital ingredients to this story. Crimes are categorized as crimes against person, crimes against property, and crimes against public order and morality. This work also examines collective criminal behavior (outlaw gangs); evaluates the criminal jurisdiction of the courts; explores the duties and responsibilities of law enforcement officials; details the catching of criminals; records jail conditions and escapes; and analyzes patterns of punishment (both legal and extralegal). Finally, this study also explores how crime affected ordinary Floridians—whites and blacks, perpetrators, victims, and enforcers—and the world they lived in.

The territory and state developed a criminal justice system that, by more enlightened twentieth-century standards, might seem primitive and even haphazard. Insufficient funding, a sometimes ambivalent general public, and always a sparsely settled, dangerous frontier that made travel difficult and frequently impossible—these often thwarted the system. And yet it functioned surprisingly well through the persistent efforts of judges, sheriffs, and various other lawmen.

Few have investigated significant aspects of Florida's antebellum social life. Studies that exist mainly explore slavery, politics, military issues, and Seminole Indian life. Little is known about the everyday life of Floridians, black or white, male or female. A number of scholars who have written about social aspects of Southern society in the first half of the nineteenth century have chosen to ignore Florida, claiming that sources do not exist or that this sparsely populated region is unworthy of notice.[1] But the sources, although sometimes difficult to obtain, are available. Though the present work is not modeled after any particular work or methodology, various works related to the subject have informed my writing. I have benefited from a number of excellent recent works pertinent to the history of crime and punishment in the South, or the nation as a whole.[2]

I must mention from the outset that my main objective is to write a readable narrative history of the subject. When it comes to numbers, some basic statistics are useful and will be brought to bear when appropriate, but the emphasis is on *narrative,* not *numbers*. Moreover, issues such as class, race, gender, and their relationship to crime and punishment are laden with controversy. Probably no other combination of subjects is as ready-made for promoting agendas or for proving or disproving hypotheses. Using a history of crime and punishment in antebellum Florida for the purpose of descending into extensive polemical debates on these issues is not the purpose here. Still, I think studying such an important aspect of the state's history can provide a perspective that is so often lacking in today's society. This approach will please some and frustrate others, but it coincides with my primary goal of reaching an audience beyond just the academic community. Finally, though I recognize the impossibility of writing "value-free" history, I believe that objectivity, though difficult to reach, is a goal worth striving for.

My decision to refer to Florida as a "rogue's paradise" perhaps needs some explanation. Many will find the title a bit strange, and others will argue that such a pejorative reference could better be ascribed to Texas, which was perhaps better known both then and now as an escape hatch for runaway rascals of various sorts. The phrase "Gone to Texas" says it all. And yet not only did the title come from a territorial editor's description of Florida, but it is also my contention that Florida and Texas shared a number of similarities that make the appellation appropriate. Both experienced land booms in the 1830s and 1840s. Both had large frontiers. Both had reputations as lands of lawlessness and opportunity. Both became states at roughly the same time (1845). And during Texas's fight for independence from Mexico (1835–36), a number of Floridians migrated to Texas. Indeed, movement of settlers back and forth between the Republic of Texas and the Territory of Florida was common; and a number of Florida's most illustrious citizens eventually migrated to Texas—Judge James Webb and Gov. William P. DuVal are two who come immediately to mind.[3]

But it was mainly Florida's vast frontier that, like Texas, made the territory and the state attractive to fleeing debtors, thieves, and criminals of various descriptions. This does not mean, however, that antebellum Florida was peopled entirely by this sort of folk—far from it. Middle Florida's well-heeled, aristocratic settlers certainly contradict this tendency, as do several substantial migrants in other regions of the state. But the key to understanding Florida during its antebellum years is to recognize not only its diversity but also its vast frontier, which determined much of its economic history, its social history, and certainly its criminal history.

If settlement in Middle Florida was relatively dense, it was so sparse in other regions that law enforcement in the traditional sense was practically impossible. Thus it often occurred that crooks, thieves, and other criminals could find safe haven in Florida's vast wilderness, at least for a time. In such cases they could either live undetected or perhaps even change their identity and assume a new life.

In summary, the purpose of this book is to examine and consider the patterns, specific instances, and effects of lawbreaking on Florida's antebellum frontier. At the same time, matters entailing administration, such as the role of law enforcement officials, the accommodation of criminals in jails and in the courts, the patterns of punishment, and the public's attitude toward lawbreakers, are considered. These findings may lead the way to a better understanding of society and culture in antebellum Florida and the South.

Over the course of the research and writing of this book I have accumulated a number of debts, and it now gives me pleasure to acknowledge the various individuals and institutions that have assisted me along the way. For reading, criticizing, and offering suggestions, I thank John Roberson, Keith Huneycutt, Ben Anderson, Jonathan Lawrence, and especially Canter Brown, whose critical eye and extensive knowledge of Florida history offered constant support and advice. I also thank David Coles at the Florida State Archives, whose special friendship I value even more than his skills as an archivist and historian. Andrew Pearson, Director of Roux Library, Florida Southern College, with his expert knowledge of computers, helped me construct the tables in appendix 4. I would also like to thank those whose special friendship offered me support along the way: Leland Hawes, William Rogers Jr., Charles Thomas, Tom Thomson, Mac Wicht, Lewis N. Wynne, Brian R. Rucker, Risdon Slate, Francis Hodges, John Santosuosso, Pat Anderson, Edwin Plowman, Randall MacDonald, Bob and Andrea Norgard, Sharon Masters, Barbara Giles, and Rose Lamm. Finally, I would like to thank Lane Goodson, like myself a fifth-generation Floridian, for sharing his knowledge of our native state's flora and fauna as we have explored its many lakes and rivers.

I acknowledge assistance and encouragement from superiors at Limestone College and Florida Southern College: John Fincher, Dan Champion, Richard Burnette, Ben Wade, and Tom Reuschling. I also thank Walter B. Edgar and his staff at the Institute of Southern Studies at the University of South Carolina for providing an ideal setting on the "Horseshoe" for research and writing during the summer of 1990. And finally to William W. Rogers at Florida State University, a mentor and a model in every sense of the word, whose patience, encouragement, and kind words gave me the confidence to pursue this study, I express my gratitude.

One of the great joys of writing a book of this kind is doing research in Florida's county courthouses, whose sizes and characteristics vary so widely that they are indeed a good representation of Florida's diverse physical and demographic landscape. From the massive Hillsborough County courthouse in Tampa and its annex in Brandon to the tiny Jefferson County courthouse in Monticello, each had a character of its own. The staffs of these courthouses, though often puzzled at the requests to see old records, always cheerfully acquiesced and surrendered their treasures. Escambia, St. Johns, and Hillsborough Counties are models in the preservation of old court records, but other counties also accomplish this important objective—each in its own way. I also wish to thank Rebecca Piskura (Hillsborough), Janice Mahaffey (Putnam), Karl Goodwin (Orange), and Eleanor Hawkins (Jefferson), as well as the staffs at Monroe, Madison, Manatee, Leon, Marion, Clay, Jackson, Volusia, and Gadsden Counties.

I also thank the late Dorothy Dodd of the State Library of Florida; Elizabeth Alexander of the P. K. Yonge Library of Florida History, University of Florida; Paul Camp at the University of South Florida Library; James Servies at the Pace Library at the University of West Florida; Taryn Rodriguez-Boette and Dot Lyons at the St. Augustine Historical Society Library; Tom Hambright at the Key West Public Library; Nancy Dobson at the Florida Supreme Court; and finally, the staff at the Manning Strozier Library, Florida State University.

Finally, I owe my deepest debt of gratitude to my parents, Jim and Donnajo Denham; to my wife, Patty, who makes our house a home; and to my two children, Maggie and Jim, who make my life worth living.

“A Rogue’s Paradise”

One

Crime, the Law, and Society

All kinds of ingenious rascality seem to have been perpetrated at some time or other in Florida & one would almost believe that Florida could equal Texas in such interesting specimens of civilization.

—Bishop Henry Whipple (1844)

In 1828, when James Webb first arrived in Key West, he was appalled to find the island in veritable anarchy. As the first federal judge of the newly created Southern District of Florida, Webb's charge was similar to that of other federal appointees in Florida—and indeed all other American territories: to establish respect for Anglo-American concepts of law and order. This task would be difficult, for, as he explained to authorities in Washington, the population was "composed of a heterogenous mass, congregated from various parts of the world, many of whom were unacquainted with the operation of our laws, and had for several years been living in a state of unrestrained, and indeed licentious freedom."[1] If Judge Webb's situation was trying, his experiences were not unlike those of other federal appointees who struggled to establish orderly civil government in new American acquisitions. In Florida this process would not be easy because of a number of factors—not the least of which was the territory's vast, unsettled regions, which made travel and communication difficult and dangerous. Indeed, Florida remained a frontier long after the Civil War.

Florida's early experiences with crime and punishment closely parallel its settlement history. As white settlers poured in from all parts of the Union, one of their first concerns was to construct "civilization" as they had experienced it in other American possessions. Most would have contended that the legal system—and above all the courts—was the starting point, promising as it did the protection of life and property from mobile disorderly elements that always plagued frontiers.

In any thoughtful investigation of crime and punishment in antebellum Florida, a number of obvious questions arise. What did contemporary observers think was the cause of crime? Which crimes were the most fre-

James Webb served as judge of the Southern Judicial District from 1828 to 1839. (Courtesy of the Archives Division, Texas State Library, Austin, Texas)

quently prosecuted? Which were the least prosecuted? What kinds of crimes did society find most reprehensible? Which offenses drew the harshest and which the most lenient punishment? Were there regional variations on these themes? What role did race and gender play in the equation? These questions are far easier to ask than to answer, but the student of crime and punishment is obliged to use available evidence to search for clues. Because of the complex nature of human emotions, definitive answers to these questions are as difficult to obtain now as they were at the time and can probably never be established with any degree of certainty; but the search is revealing in itself. Some answers can be found by a simple tabulation of indictments and successful and unsuccessful prosecutions of crimes in surviving court records. Other clues can be found in the statements of those involved in the criminal justice system itself. The laws themselves, those who made them, and the provisions for punishments are crucial elements of these questions.

A basic familiarity with Florida's geographical and demographic features are also important if we are to understand the state's handling of crime and punishment. In the antebellum decades, Florida's population stood at approximately 35,000 in 1830, 55,000 in 1840, 88,000 in 1850, and 140,000 in 1860. At all times whites made up slightly more than half of the total population. Throughout the antebellum period population was most concentrated in Middle Florida, between the Apalachicola and Suwannee Rivers. The Census of 1860 revealed that Gadsden, Jefferson, and Leon Counties in Middle Florida, and Alachua and Marion Counties in East Florida, had black majorities, the vast majority of whom were slaves. Florida had no "cities," but three towns (Pensacola, Key West, and Jacksonville) had populations in excess of two thousand. Tallahassee, St. Augustine, and Apalachicola fell within a hundred of that total, while Milton, Fernandina, and Monticello numbered at least a thousand.[2]

Fundamental to an understanding of any aspect of antebellum Florida—especially crime and law enforcement—is the pervasive influence of the frontier. Recently a number of scholars have noted that many parts of Florida, particularly the eastern and southern regions of the state, remained extremely isolated well after the Civil War and even into the twentieth century.[3]

The difficulties of travel, the danger of Indian uprisings, and, of course, the problems of holding courts that could prosecute criminals held important ramifications for the way Floridians organized their criminal justice system. The frontier shaped the way people thought, acted, and responded to emergencies. "Judgements about crime," writes Lawrence Friedman, "and what to do about it, come out of a specific time and place. . . . [T]he system . . . is not accidental or random or 'historical'—and is definitely not shaped by some intellectual or philosophical tradition." What matters is the way "society is organized. . . . [S]ocial *norms* (peoples' ideas, customs, habits, and attitudes) . . . interact chemically with the context, and with what is happening in the world—with the specific events and situations; for example, the sheer size of the country, its climate and geography, its natural resources; plagues, depressions, and wars."[4] Working in unison with the frontier in this "chemical" reaction were the pervasive influences of honor (a fundamental concept that defined relationships among Southerners) and, of course, slavery. Thus Florida's experience is as much the story of crime in the antebellum South as it is the story of crime on the frontier in transition. I will further examine these issues later.

If the effects of the frontier, of honor, and of slavery are fundamental to an understanding of Florida's early antebellum society, Friedman's notion of a "culture of mobility" and its "spatial meaning" are also relevant to any discussion of the state's criminal justice system.[5] The irony is perhaps that, on the surface at least, Florida's antebellum settlers would seem to have been relatively static—made so by the frontier, the sparsely inhabited areas, and the difficulty of movement. But the very circumstance of isolation made travel absolutely necessary. Whether Floridians traveled by foot, horseback, wagons, or boats, their culture was a culture of mobility: farmers transported goods to towns or herded livestock through the woods; immigrants traversed through vast tracts of territory searching for fertile homesteads; military personnel moved from frontier outpost to outpost, policing the Indian boundary and regulating white–red contacts. Stage routes tied inland communities to river, Gulf, and sea ports. By the 1850s passenger and freight traffic operated in full swing on the Apalachicola and St. Johns Rivers, while a whole host of lesser streams were in use on a smaller scale. If inland maritime travel was extensive, merchants, planters, and government officials found the coastal traffic indispensable. Regular service linking the state's coastal ports of Pensacola, Apalachicola, St. Marks, Tampa, Key West, St. Augustine, and Jacksonville gave Floridians access to all the major ports in the United States as well as the world.

But this "culture of mobility" was also significant for Florida's criminal justice system. Crime itself was a sort of stimulant to movement, since criminals often fled after breaking the law. Sheriffs, sometimes supported by citizens, chased fugitives through the Florida frontier or transported them back and forth from jail to trial. Judges and lawyers rode circuit, and sheriffs sought out and served summons to witnesses. Travel and its hardships were a constant theme for antebellum Floridians, as they were for all Americans.

Samuel Walker, Edward Ayers, and others have noted that court weeks were significant days in the lives of rural communities.[6] The criminal justice system brought an isolated people together. Courthouse days were a time for socializing, doing business, meeting new settlers, catching up on local news, and listening to politicians, or a time for settlers to validate their citizenship by serving as jurors. Officers of the court not only adjudicated disagreements, they also interpreted the laws that the citizens, at least in the-

5
Crime, the Law, and Society

Antebellum Florida, ca. 1850–60

ory, made to govern themselves. But above all, the system was participatory to a far greater degree than today, and this tended to legitimize the supremacy of the people by engaging them in the criminal justice system at all levels. It was the citizens themselves who served as jurors, helped guard and capture prisoners, and ultimately approved or disapproved of judicial decisions by their actions.

But who were "the people"? In the first half of the nineteenth century, "the people" were primarily white males, which meant that blacks, Indians, and women were excluded from participating in the legal process as equals.

They were, of course, "subjected" to the laws; yet they played no role in making, executing, and interpreting laws. But to dwell on the aspect of inequality alone is to forget that early-nineteenth-century American society was the most "representative" on earth at that time. Floridians continually prided themselves on this fact, and this pride was reflected in legislative and court records. For the most part, legislative and judicial officers took their responsibilities seriously, knowing full well that their judgment was as imperfect as the society they represented.

Similar to that of other states in the nineteenth century, the focus of Florida's criminal justice system was geared more toward the resolution of disputes than the prevention of crime: it was reactive rather than proactive. This was observable primarily in the handling of crimes against person and property. When an assault or theft occurred, the aggrieved party reported the crime to a justice of the peace, who directed the sheriff to summon both the accused and witnesses to swear under oath as to the facts of the case. On the strength of these affidavits, the accused was either released or bound over for trial, and pertinent records about the case were given over to a prosecutor, who presented them to a grand jury at the next term of the court. If the grand jury found a "true bill" of indictment, the case was tried in superior or circuit court. Witnesses were summoned, a petit jury was called, and guilt or innocence was determined. If innocent, the accused was released immediately; if guilty, the culprit was fined, whipped, placed on the pillory, or sentenced to a short jail term (rarely more than one year) and compelled to pay the costs of his prosecution.

Florida's first criminal laws were a product of the territorial legislative council, which was appointed by the president until 1826, when the territorial inhabitants themselves selected delegates. The members were chosen from a variety of backgrounds. Several were close associates of Andrew Jackson; others, such as Joseph Hernandez, John de la Rua, and Joseph Noriga, were selected because they were well respected among the Spanish residents. Also of great significance in the formation of the territory's first criminal laws was territorial governor William P. DuVal of Kentucky. Replacing Andrew Jackson in 1822, DuVal was present at each meeting of the territorial legislative council from that year until 1834.

Probably the most knowledgeable in the law of those who served on the first territorial council was Henry M. Brackenridge, who had considerable experience as a district judge in the Orleans (Louisiana) Territory. Though he resigned his post to become judge of the Western Judicial District of Florida, Brackenridge remained on hand in an advisory role. He suggested that the legislators take up a digest of the Missouri territorial laws as a guide. The circumstances of Missouri were similar to Florida at that time, because, as Brackenridge stated, "it was settled by citizens of the United States, habituated to English and American Legislation. The volume . . . was the result of fifteen years experience in that state, and yet contained for the greater part, little more than the adaptation of the joint labors of Jefferson, Wythe, and Madison, and some of the Pennsylvania Legislators, to the circumstances of the country."[7] When it came to civil law, the first council also adopted the common and statute law of England prior to July 4, 1776, provided these laws did not conflict with the Constitution. It was specifically provided, however, that none of the British statutes respecting crimes, misdemeanors, and punishments would apply to Florida.[8]

The 1820s were a time of legislative chaos in Florida. Laws were frequently passed and repealed with each successive session so that there was significant doubt as to what the law was at any given time. Citizens, judges, juries, and public officials constantly complained of this uncertainty—so much so that it seems that the early laws of the territory were as confusing to Floridians at the time as they are now to historians. As Judge Brackenridge explained in 1831 to the Jackson County Grand Jury, "Since 1822 the whole body of the law, criminal as well as civil, not even excepting the fundamental act which adopted the common and statute law of England, has since been repeatedly repealed and re-enacted, and partial alterations have been made by which they have been rendered vague and uncertain." Every succeeding session, the legislative council "presented us with a new code, which was repealed before the people had time to become acquainted with it; reminding one of the web of Penelope, who undid at night what she had woven in the day time."[9]

A basic familiarity with the ethnic and cultural makeup of those who inhabited Florida is necessary if we are to assess the state's crime and law enforcement history. Today's "natives" of Florida often deplore the fact that everybody in Florida comes from somewhere else. Yet, given Spain's general policy of restricting American immigration, this circumstance was also literally the case in Florida's antebellum years. Before 1821 the region was almost entirely free of Anglo-American influence. Certainly, some Americans lived in Florida during Spain's Second Period (1783–1821), but the vast majority migrated after Spain relinquished the Floridas in 1821. Criminals, lawmen, judges, and those who served on juries, as well as political leaders, all came from somewhere else.

Life in antebellum Florida was a close replica of that experienced in neighboring states, but the state was unique in a number of ways. Spanish Creoles who stayed after the transfer of flags in 1821 helped shape the so-

Henry Marie Brackenridge served as judge of the Western Judicial District from 1822 to 1832. (Courtesy of the Florida State Archives, Tallahassee, Florida)

cial, economic, and political affairs of the new society. By the 1850s the port cities of Pensacola, Apalachicola, Jacksonville, Key West, and Tampa served as entry points for ships from the United States and the world. Because of its extended coastline, Florida received large numbers of immigrants and interlopers from the West Indies. Florida's close proximity to Spain's Latin American colonies encouraged trade with the Caribbean. Newspapers, court records, and accounts of local inhabitants in Florida's southern ports indicate that inhabitants of Spain's Caribbean colonies lived in Florida at least part of the year.

Florida's antebellum population was also far more cosmopolitan than one might expect. Florida circuit court minutes reveal naturalization proceedings for immigrants from England, France, Austria, Spain, Portugal, the German and Italian states, and even as far away as Sweden, Denmark, Poland, and Russia. State census takers in 1855 estimated that nearly three thousand of Florida's inhabitants had been born abroad.[10] The relatively large military presence in Florida (many of whom were either foreign- or Northern-born) also added to the diversity. Even so, antebellum Florida's social and economic life most resembled its sister slave states.

The appointive nature of many of Florida's important administrative posts during its territorial years (1821–45) also had an important role in giving Florida's professional population a particular political stamp. These years coincided with national political struggles between the Democrats and the Whigs. In a sense, party battles at the national level often played themselves out in Florida. Kermit Hall has demonstrated that the presidential appointment of judges often reflected as much the whims of party politics as the real administrative needs of the territory.[11] But the same was true of governors, district attorneys, marshals, and a whole host of lesser officials. Regardless of their tenure in office, federal appointees left a lasting imprint on the state because many of these same individuals were elected to similar posts after 1845. Federal appointees, no matter where they came from, played a crucial role in shaping the criminal justice system because they were the ones who interpreted and executed the laws during Florida's territorial years.

The origins and backgrounds of Florida's antebellum residents ultimately affected its criminal justice system at all levels. Most of those who settled in Florida during the antebellum decades migrated from Georgia, South Carolina, North Carolina, and Virginia. But they also came from the border states of Kentucky and Maryland. These newcomers, along with migrants from the North, made up a large share of Florida's professional ranks. Lawyers, editors, schoolteachers, merchants, cotton factors, doctors, and ministers of the gospel formed an educated elite that came to dominate economic and political affairs. These folk also supplemented their income by pursuing the South and Florida's most honorable as well as profitable profession, planting.

Florida also experienced some immigration from free states. Newcomers from the North soon conformed to the prevailing ethics and values of the majority, sometimes becoming leading advocates and defenders of Southern values. It simply was not in the cards for them to do otherwise. Migrating required adjustment, and migrants understood the realities of adaptation before they came south. But no matter the origin of the newcomers, migrating to Florida's frontier offered not only opportunity, but also immense challenges.

By far the most numerous immigrants into Florida after the transfer of flags were those whites—mostly of Scotch-Irish extraction—who drifted over the boundary seeking fertile land and a better life. Frank L. Owsley's "plain folk," W. J. Cash's "men in the middle," and Grady McWhiney's "crackers" were drawn to Florida by the fertility and availability of public land, particularly in East Florida, where wild hogs and cattle were in abundance.[12] Their livelihood consisted mainly of growing staples like corn for subsistence. Hunting and fishing supplemented their diets, but many in this group also herded cattle and hogs on the open range. This group's tendency toward extreme mobility brought them ultimately into contact, sometimes violently, with Indians, surveyors, military officials, and even lawful purchasers of lands they squatted on. Florida's "plain folk," like their kinsmen in other Southern states, shared a strong adherence to popular democracy, a hatred of Indians, and a strong sense of racial superiority over blacks, whom they believed were fit only for slavery. Their strong sense of individualism and resolve came from living on the isolated frontier. They usually acted on their own authority, often showing little respect for governmental or judicial authority. And yet these folk participated in Florida's criminal justice system at all levels. They were the criminals, the victims, and, in some cases, the lawmen. They also served on juries, swore out complaints, or were the subjects of the complaints themselves. They captured fugitives and collected rewards based on gubernatorial or private proclamations. They served as hastily deputized guards hired to attend to dangerous prisoners or to transport them across sparsely inhabited tracts of the Florida frontier. Finally, they made up posses that fulfilled or exceeded their specified duties.

Perhaps the most striking characteristic of antebellum Florida was its diversity (both human and geographical), which was reflected not only in its sizable black population but also in the enforcement of the laws that regulated that population. Blacks made up nearly half of Florida's antebellum population, and most of them were slaves.

The institution of chattel slavery influenced the minds, values, and beliefs of antebellum Southerners in ways that historians are still exploring. Scholars studying any aspect of the Old South cannot ignore the impact of slavery on the Southern mind and culture. Thus the relationship of blacks to Florida's criminal justice system is an important component of the state's history of crime and punishment. Florida's experience with the peculiar institution both duplicated and differed from that of other slave states. In Middle Florida, bounded by the Apalachicola and Suwannee Rivers, a thriving plantation economy emerged that created a society similar to the "black belt" of Alabama and Mississippi. Yet in sparsely settled West and East

Florida, slavery existed on a more limited scale. In East Florida fewer settlers were scattered over a larger region. These settlers, who faced hostile Indians, built an economy based less on cotton and more on subsistence farming, herded livestock on the open range, and had relatively few large plantations. All of this permitted the emergence of a society that was less rigid, less restrictive, and less regimented. There were fewer slaves, and gradations of wealth were not as dramatic. In some respects economic and social life in East and West Florida differed so markedly from life in Middle Florida that some residents favored a formal division of the territory into separate political entities. These regional variations are important, because the way Floridians dealt with lawbreaking and lawbreakers depended on both culture and the physical environment.

The vast majority of Florida's blacks migrated to the territory with their masters, but some free blacks remained in the old Spanish towns of St. Augustine and Pensacola after the transfer of flags. The peculiar legal and cultural heritage of Spain set these towns apart, at least for a decade or so, from the prevailing traditions and customs of the Anglo-Americans. The recent research of Jane Landers, Canter Brown, Susan Parker, and Daniel Schafer has uncovered a cultural tradition in East Florida that provided for a far less rigid system of servitude.[13] Blacks everywhere, however, ultimately fell under the sway of statutory restrictions instituted by the politically powerful Middle Florida planter establishment. The model for racial control was established in Middle Florida, where most of Florida's antebellum population, white and black, was concentrated. This region became the most prosperous, politically influential, and, for blacks, oppressive. There, plantation-based agriculture, a carbon copy of that which emerged simultaneously in the black belt of Mississippi and Alabama, prevailed. The principal economic pursuit was using slave labor to grow cotton. The entire society was organized around the sustainment of a well-managed workforce, which became the basis of the cotton culture.[14] Laws were by necessity oppressive and restrictive, and they were enforced in a much more stringent way than in East Florida. In a sense, the slave codes were written by and for the benefit of Middle Florida planters. Because of its population, wealth, and overall sophistication, Middle Florida gave many in the region the tendency to think that their interests *were* the interests of Florida. Recent research has shown that many of East Florida's most substantial whites, at least when it came to personal decisions like manumission, resisted the slave code's harshest sanctions, but they were successful in doing so only to a point. Of primary importance, however, is that repressive slave statutes were in force and had currency in all regions of Florida, where they could be either enforced or ignored.

Two

Crime and Its Causes

> Not a mail arrives but brings several journals noticing the alarming increase of crime. The demoralization of the country is going on at a rate calculated to create the most serious & alarming apprehensions in the honest and virtuous. Crime is coming on the land like "pestilence."
>
> —*Tallahassee Floridian,* May 22, 1841

What did Floridians think were the causes of crime in antebellum Florida? Almost everyone—politicians, newspaper editors, judges, travelers—held an opinion. Most understood that excessive drinking, gambling, and a Southern penchant for "hot blood" (a condition made even more dangerous by Florida's open frontier), both separately and together, were causes of violence and crime in the state. Some laid the cause to the lack of jails and to insufficient funds directed toward law enforcement, deficiencies that induced outlaws to immigrate and thus made Florida a kind of "rogue's paradise." Others pointed to a general decline in national morality as well as to the deficient moral character of those who inhabited the state.

Especially in the territorial era, which lasted from 1821 to 1845, fugitives from other states found Florida's sparsely settled frontier a safe haven. The territory contained many vast, remote, and unsettled places where fleeing felons could hide undetected after making their way overland from Alabama and Georgia or easily traveling by ocean or river routes.

A few Floridians, overwhelmed by the criminal influx, divined causation in the secret machinations of other nations. Elias Gould of the *St. Augustine Florida Herald* noted in 1833 the difficulties Northern cities had with "excessive emigration of the lower classes from foreign countries" and saw a conspiracy. The British government, he asserted, sent out "transport ships with cargoes of paupers, with a view that they may ultimately find their way to the United States." Gould believed that other nations were carrying out similar policies. Many, however, saw immigration as a boon rather than a curse. Bishop Henry Whipple in 1843 described East Florida—the peninsular region east of the Suwannee River—as "common ground for Southern blacklegs and desperadoes." Still, he argued that because of "continued influx of new settlers, . . . course, rough, backwoods crackerisms are giving place to refinement & Civilization."[1]

Some residents merely acknowledged Florida's reputation for attracting undesirables and hoped for the best. One stoical man hoped "these hot-blooded fellows perhaps will kill each other off after a while and make room for a more peaceable population."[2] The *Pensacola Gazette*'s William Hasell Hunt saw a glimmer of hope in a marshal's work toward providing a district jail. If similar vigilance was practiced in other areas, he declared, "Florida will no longer be a Paradise for Rogues."[3] Sadly, fourteen years later the paper still found too many "refugees from Alabama" who chose to "locate themselves among us." The editor opined, "They have but to cross the 31st degree north latitude and they are safe."[4]

And yet a number of Floridians could be found who insisted that the state's bad reputation was unearned. Less attractive districts, they suggested, jealous of Florida's growing popularity, simply hashed up negative reports to redirect immigration. In 1834 a Tallahassee editor offered a case in point. The *Baptist Register* had claimed that the territory was a modern-day Sodom and Gomorrah. Gambling, horse racing, and intemperance, the article insisted, "are matters of constant occurrence" and "common to all ranks from the beggar on the dunghill to the official dispenser of public justice." In turn, the editor denounced the slander. The offending article was as "foul a perversion of truth as ever originated in the ignorant and besotted fanaticism of the darkest ages." Furthermore, the writer was a "lying hypocrite."[5]

Florida's reputation as a rogue's paradise could be debated, but few doubted that overindulgence in alcohol figured prominently as a cause of most crimes. Floridians, like other Americans, used every excuse to indulge. An antidote to boredom, drinking increased when crowds gathered. To a rural, isolated people, public gatherings prompted celebration, including a degree of alcoholic indulgence that led directly to violent crime. Court days, militia musters, Fourth of July celebrations, horse-racing weeks, land sales, political campaigns, and election days offered popular occasions for imbibing. Funerals, births, and marriage ceremonies did the same. Scholars have estimated that drunkenness among Americans reached a peak in the antebellum period.[6]

The levels of drunkenness cannot be documented statistically, but natives and outsiders often were shocked at commonplace practices. The Comte de Castelnau, a French naturalist who visited in 1838, thought that, "of all vices" he found, "intemperance is the most common." He added, "It is often that men of responsible position are found rolling drunk in the streets."[7] Editor Hunt similarly concluded that drunkenness was the "prevailing vice among great numbers of the young and old men," and at Pensacola it existed to an "abominable degree." Many "do not . . . always get sloppily drunk, as to make *zig zags*," he asserted, "but they are daily more or less affected by incessant tippling, from the time they rise in the morning until falling in bed at night."[8] Excessive drunkenness often was cited as a cause of early death. Moral abandonment, ill health, a life of crime, and perhaps suicide, many believed, were in store for those who overly indulged.

Lawmakers, appreciating the link between drunkenness and lawbreaking, passed territorial, state, and local ordinances to regulate the whiskey trade. Since thirsty Floridians were determined to obtain strong drink, however, the statutes met with limited success.[9] Despite licensing requirements imposed on retailers, an underground traffic flourished. Superior and circuit court minute books are filled with indictments for that and other liquor-related offenses.

Commentators and grand juries pointed an accusing finger at local grog establishments as places of origin for petty burglaries, misbehavior among the slave population, and scenes of vice. Typically, in 1833 the Duval County Grand Jury condemned the "great magnitude of tippling shops interspersed through the County, which are resorted to by the idle and dissolute." Such establishments "become the hotbeds from which spring the great majority of crimes and misdemeanors which infest our county."[10] Escambia County authorities were convinced that "crimes in every part of our county is to be traced" to grogshops and other sources of the whiskey trade. They proposed limiting the number of saloons, increasing license fees, and securing "satisfactory evidence . . . of the good character of the applicant."[11] Yet efforts at control were usually ineffective.

Apalachicola River settlements particularly were "whiskey soaked." After Charles Hentz graduated from the University of Louisville Medical School in 1848 he located at Port Jackson, east of Marianna. Hentz remembered the wide-open river town as one of the worst whiskey-drinking, fighting, horse-racing, gambling communities to be found this side of Texas. "In those days rectified whiskey only cost about 27 and a half cents a gallon, by the barrel—and it was abundant," he recalled. Locals resorted to two notorious groggeries, one "about half mile back from the Ferry kept by a great fat beast of a man named Friday that was always filled with tipplers—and another by a man named Bob Crawford; which was a resort to all riff raff of the country; where all day and night was spent in soaking with whiskey and playing cards."[12]

If grog establishments were labeled as centers of criminal activity, most critics nonetheless realized that the key issue was how drunkenness affected the individual. Few failed to notice the connection between excessive drinking and crime. "Nearly all criminal cases," claimed the Gadsden County Grand Jury in 1850, "seem to have their origin in too free use of ardent spirits. There is scarcely an exception to this and in one instance death has been the result." The grand jury called for a total end to the sale of liquor and hoped the legislature would "banish . . . this most demoralizing vice upon the land."[13] Though facing an uphill fight against alcohol, some communities and religious groups organized to combat the evil. A few respectable citizens joined the temperance movement, which grew in the North beginning in the Age of Jackson. At one such meeting in Tallahassee, prominent lawyer James Westcott cited personal and professional experience to buttress claims that excessive drinking resulted in violent crime. In twenty years of practice, he commented, he had been involved in sixty-three cases of homicide. He concluded that at least four-fifths of the cases could be traced "directly or indirectly to the besetting and besotting influence of intemperance." The lawyer noted that the same pattern held in a host of lesser cases.[14]

Many newspaper editors and public officials joined the struggle against intemperance and warned against the hazards of the vice. The *Pensacola Gazette*'s Hunt published in 1829 an address by Judge Henry M. Brackenridge to town drunk and condemned killer Andrew Crail. The remarks, Hunt hoped, would "have a salutary effect by checking crime and its prolific cause—INTOXICATION."[15] A quarter century later Hillsborough County Judge Simon Turman acknowledged that the fight was not being won. He condemned the legislature's failure to regulate the traffic in liquor. "We have had a large supply of whiskey shipped to Tampa this year and I look for a large harvest by way of inquisitions," he declared. "Those who profit by the traffic should pay for burying their own dead *as they are licensed to kill*."[16] As one commentator observed, every community of Florida contained "some turbulent spirits, who are disposed, especially when under the influence of John Barleycorn, to carry everything by force."[17]

Closely associated with excessive drinking as a cause of crime was gambling. Floridians wagered on the turn of a card, the gait of a horse, the ferocity of a dog or a cock, the roll of dice, or the eventual resting place of a roulette wheel. A sampling of court minute books suggests that gambling was one of antebellum Floridian's most popular forms of entertainment, and many would have agreed with the Comte de Castelnau's assertion that it was responsible for many of the "murders so frequent."[18] Editor

Hunt, thought the most moralistic of antebellum newspapermen, struck a chord when he declared that the "wretched vice" of gambling was "a passion which if not restrained in time, almost always leads to drunkenness, ruin, desperation, and dishonesty, and not infrequently to suicide."[19] Hunt was not alone in his belief. Others refused to accept the notion that gambling was a respectable form of gentlemen's entertainment. An Apalachicola man denied that outlawing the custom was undue meddling in the private affairs of free individuals. Instead, he claimed, gambling "is ruinous to a community," adding that "there is perhaps no evil in existence . . . so baneful upon the morals of society." Thus it was the duty of society to exclude all gamblers from "all social intercourse."[20]

The availability of concealed arms often encouraged bloody assaults, especially when mixed with intemperance and gambling. The Comte de Castelnau thought the practice of carrying weapons was "universal." He observed, "Every man has constantly on him a bowie knife, and when he is on horseback he has a long rifle in his hand."[21] The frontier was a dangerous place, and strapping on firearms and knives came natural to men who lived there. Not surprisingly, in the light of those circumstances antebellum Floridians insisted that the federal Constitution guaranteed them the right to bear arms. Section twenty-one, article one of the Florida State Constitution (1838) essentially restated the Second Amendment. But section one of that document declared that all white Floridians possessed "certain inherent . . . rights . . . of enjoying and defending liberty; of acquiring possessing, and protecting property and reputation; and of pursuing their own happiness." Not a few Floridians would have argued that ball and powder and cold, hard steel, rather than words, were the surest means of protecting life, liberty, property, and, of course, reputation.

Lawmakers, jurists, and many others, however, drew the line at concealed weapons.[22] The practice of carrying the "disgraceful and unmanly weapon" of a bowie knife, complained an Apalachicolan, "has become of such general use that many gentlemen seem to look upon it a material part of their wardrobe." Such miscreants, he declared, seemed to think that they were "not in suitable garb even to pay their respects to the fair" unless armed to the teeth.[23]

Numbered among those most outspoken against the practice of carrying concealed weapons were members of Florida's judicial fraternity, who continually drew a connection between carrying concealed weapons and violent crime. Judge Samuel Douglas recalled witnessing tragic scenes of "bloodshed and crime" that could be "traced to the vicious practice of wearing these instruments of death."[24] Judge Robert Raymond Reid similarly called possession of weapons a "remnant of barbarism [that] . . . should be discountenanced by opinion as well as positive enactment."[25] Judge Thomas Randall agreed: carrying secret arms was a sign of a "lurking malignancy of heart."[26]

The relationship between homicide and carrying concealed weapons was so strong that some judicial officers demanded reinterpretation of the laws regarding manslaughter to address the problem. In 1828 Judge Randall explained to one jury that any man who tramps about with "murderous arms secretly prepared and habitually worn [and] causes the death of another" should never be able to claim that his violent act was "not premeditated [or] accidental. . . . This very possession of deadly weapons, gives in the eye of the law, a new colour to the act—it is deemed to be the evidence of a settled rancorous malice—and thereby converts the offense into the odious crime of murder."[27] The legislative council agreed and attempted to prohibit the carrying of concealed weapons of all descriptions. A Jacksonville newspaperman correctly predicted continuance of the practice unless honest citizens would visit "such offenders with public contempt and disgrace and either drive them from our borders or coerce them into obedience to the laws." Yet both legal and social proscriptions were ineffective until late in the antebellum period.[28]

Other perceived causes aside, the emotion of anger loomed as the single most popular cause of violent crime among Southerners. Commentators, both Northern and Southern, termed this characteristic "hot blood." Few travelers failed to notice the white Southerner's touchiness to insult, his hair-trigger temper, which often resulted in outbursts of physical force. One student of crime in antebellum South Carolina, in words applicable as well to Florida, concluded that "hot-blooded" retaliation in reaction to any perceived imputation of honor was "part and parcel of virile manhood," a theme subsequently pursued by other scholars to a degree that the concept now is placed at the center of our understanding of social relations among Southerners. It was a fundamental ethic that shaped a great part of public and private behavior. By extension, some have argued that the code of honor became the single most important cause of violent crime among Southerners and, presumably, Floridians. These themes will be developed further in chapter 5.[29]

Violence resulting from dueling is distinguishable from violence arising from "hot blood." The institution of dueling (though for the most part beyond the scope of this study) enjoyed popularity and a fashionable status among the upper classes. It served as a formal way of settling disputes relating to honor. Death might well result, but it was not a sudden act of "hot blood."[30] Defenders of dueling claimed that the practice actually forestalled violence since it took the combatants out of the immediate situation and handed the dispute over to arbitrators, who often arranged a peaceful settlement.

The duel offered one of two methods to adjudge matters of honor. First, issues could be litigated in courts under the laws of libel and slander. In such cases attorneys mediated under statutory provisions. The other potential forum was the "field of honor." There a combatant was represented by a trusted friend, or second, whose main purpose was to see that an honorable adjustment of the issue was arranged. Since the laws made little provision for honor, many men preferred their "particular friend" acting in their interest as the only honorable alternative. A judge or a jury was too unreliable when honor was at stake.

While resort to the duel was not uncommon, many prominent and influential Floridians deplored the practice. As early as 1828 the Leon County Grand Jury noticed that society's peaceful light was often "darkened by the occurrence of personal dissensions" that "seem to have arisen from the sudden heat of blood or false notions of honor." During that same session Judge Randall deplored the "dangerous maxim . . . that every gentleman should be the guardian of his own honor & the avenger of his own wrongs."[31] Through the antebellum period, protests against dueling mounted, but despite its illegality the practice remained popular until the 1850s.[32]

Anger and honor provoked violence, but so too did economic troubles and the tensions they created. The collapse of Florida's banking system in the late 1830s led many to fear outbreaks of violent crime among debtors and creditors. The Gadsden County grand jurors asked citizens to avoid "*lawless violence*" and encouraged those with monetary disputes to follow "patterns of prudent and assiduous industry, frugality, and economy." They warned, "Instead of rapacious enforcement of power on the one hand, or illegal resistance on the other, all should bear and forbear."[33]

The idealized relationship between debtors and creditors hoped for by the Gadsden County jurors was rarely achieved. Predictions of violent outcomes, though often exaggerated, were widespread. In one year of extreme financial calamities, their Leon County counterparts "expressed apprehension" over the "potential lawlessness on the part of the debtor portion of our community." A local editor objected, insisting the jury had "mistaken the temper of our community." The editor added, "Though a few, overburdened by pecuniary misfortune, may have imagined a result like that apprehended, the mass will be found in favor of the law."[34]

Bank failures of the late 1830s marked the beginning of economic collapse and were attended by urban disorder in Tallahassee and surrounding Middle Florida areas. Violent confrontations between Democrats and Whigs culminated in U.S. Marshal Leigh Read's murder by Willis Alston in 1841. Much of the trouble came from the mix of politics and banking. Democrats charged that Whig policies had resulted in the territory's economic woes. Whigs resented the Democrats' strength. Demagogic charges among party leaders translated themselves into violent street confrontations. Duels were fought. Riots and violent public disturbances erupted continually. Previous differences took on economic significance, and violent crimes increased.

The linkage of politics and violence was not forged in the late 1830s. Even before the economic depression, partisan conflict frequently resulted in violent crime. Historians have noted the antebellum era's political partisanship and the degree to which Americans participated in it. But if campaigns and elections were reaffirmations of faith in democratic institutions, they often took undemocratic forms. Florida did not differ from the rest of the nation. Many observers noticed how partisan politics often led to violence among individual candidates and their followers. One Leon County judicial panel referred in 1828 to "party Spirit" as the "bane of social life." It lamented that "it had so deeply interwoven itself with the ordinary transactions of society, that those who have zealously interested themselves in the behalf of any of the conflicting parties have arrayed themselves against the peace of society."[35] Jefferson County jurors added that officers of the law "shielded political friends *on party grounds*" and concluded, "If the minister of the Law is not worthy of confidence and respect in like degree will the law be [held in] contempt and disregarded." In this instance there was even evidence that some prisoners had been allowed to escape.[36]

As suggested by the Jefferson County findings, the period's volatile nature put law enforcement officials themselves at the center of political turbulence. An anonymous petitioner deplored the electioneering of St. Johns County Sheriff Bennett Dell during a 1822 congressional delegate race between John Bronough and Richard K. Call. The sheriff, according to the petitioner, "brought up with him to the Cowford [Jacksonville] a number of his neighbors, who had never before heard the name of Dr Bronough." He continued, "The sheriff's business at a poll, when he attends one, is to keep the peace and promote good order—not to be instrumental in disturbing the peace, much less to put himself at the head of a riotous gang, and encourage and protect their disorderly conduct."[37]

The time-honored custom of "treating" by candidates made violent outbreaks inevitable. Voters expected office seekers to supply liquor at political gatherings, where local distillers always had many customers. Concerned Jefferson County citizens in 1837 petitioned against "the demoralizing practice of candidates for office treating during the canvass of an Election."[38] Madison County residents appealed to the "purity, virtue, integrity, and permanence of our Republican institutions" in opposition to "this *monstrous* practice . . . of treating voters to intoxicating drinks."[39] Treating continued nonetheless, and, so long as settlers used political campaigns as entertainment, few candidates could afford to ignore custom.

Political customs and other circumstances prompted crime and violence. Still, when newspapermen, politicians, and ministers commented on the lawbreaker and his crime, they usually pointed to the culprit's abandonment of morals. To them crime resulted from moral deficiency. They rarely laid the cause to poverty, broken families, a lack of education, or other causes cited by modern-day commentators. Contemporary observers usually noted that society itself was suffering from a kind of moral sickness. As proof, they pointed to an increase in murders, drunkenness, swearing, Sabbath-breaking, and—worst of all—public apathy.

In response to the apparent pestilence of crime, judges also took official note of the close connection between moral depravity and crime and called for a moral rebirth. In a charge to the Franklin County Grand Jury in 1831, for instance, Judge David L. White warned his listeners against the evil results of swearing. "Of all the vices the wickedness and ingenuity of man have been able to invent," he warned, "there is none that furnishes a more melancholy evidence of moral degradation and depravity of mind than the practice of profane swearing in common conversation." Abandoned moral behavior, claimed White, would lead to crime. "Profanity leads to lying, and the practice of lying is the high road to perjury."[40]

The threatening tide appeared ready to overwhelm some residents. "The land seems flooded with crime," declared one St. Augustine man, "and we turn in vain for a spot upon which the eye may repose in quiet and enjoy the luxury of a guileless people." He added, "Rogues and Rascals seem striding with an equal pace, and cheek by chowl [*sic*], the progress of intellect and march of villainy are found throughout the land."[41] What caused the moral tailspin? Did the fault lie with laws and the system's "uncertainty of punishment," or in the "chances of escape which its loopholes afford"? Was it partisan politics "which look more frequently to the triumph" of "party attachments than support of the law"? All these factors were at play with our St. Augustinian, but equally culpable was the activity of the "press which teems with murders and robberies committed in many instances without an apparent motive, and with scarce a prospect of escape; serving up almost daily some fresh commission of crime, some new device in the ways of wickedness."[42]

Echoing the St. Augustinian's remarks, some editors attributed the increase in crime to its sensational newspaper coverage. In doing so, they anticipated present-day arguments. Editor Elias Gould of the *St. Augustine East Florida Herald* announced that "from Principle we have never noticed the many accounts of duels and fisty [*sic*] cuffs which so frequently meet our eye in the public press."[43] The *Pensacola Gazette* claimed that printing shocking stories of violence without "accompanying remarks intending to discourage these practices, has in itself a tendency to harden the feelings and destroy the human sensibilities of the readers." Eventually, its editor claimed, the reader "becomes callous and hardened and in time may be brought to see and witness those very scenes, not only without the feeling of horror but with pleasure."[44]

One expert claimed that the press could even make a certain crime "come into vogue." As he explained, "Almost every year there is one crime peculiar to it; a sort of annual which overruns the country but does not bloom again." The man continued, "Unquestionably the press has a great deal to do with these epidemics. Let a newspaper give an account of some out of the way atrocity that has the charm of being novel, and certain depraved minds fasten to it like leeches. They brood over it and revolve it: the idea grows up a horrid phantasmalian monomania; and all of a sudden in a hundred different places, the one seed sown by the leaded types, springs into foul flowering."[45] Accordingly, appeals for a crime-reporting gag rule were voiced repeatedly. Little evidence exists, however, that a majority of Florida newspapermen ever endorsed these sentiments.

The aftereffects of the Panic of 1837 stirred enhanced concerns, and leading men seemingly endured painful self-appraisal. Many Southern commentators considered the bank failures and subsequent economic disorder a just reward for a dishonest financial system. Banking had created an atmosphere of fraud and corruption. Naturally, the question of morality rose to the forefront. One critic claimed that the system had "vicious influences . . . tainting the fountain of public morals, and setting an example of open defiance to the laws of honesty, justice, and morality." Another added that "secret fraud, . . . open ruffianism, . . . mercenary falsehood, and cowardly murder, with unblushing avowals of *financering* [*sic*] and roguery . . . by the rich" had created an atmosphere in which the honest poor were led astray.[46]

Perhaps to ease a difficult or impossible journey of self-examination, scores of leading figures directed Southerners to turn inward and ignore the North, which was in a worse state of moral depravity. So long as the South successfully warded off the evils to which the North had succumbed, hope survived.

Typically, an editor in close-by Mobile, Alabama, most likely spoke for his brethren in Florida when he contended that, even worse than the South's problems were cases of violent crime in the North that had greed as their cause. Southern victims fell in "open and manly combat," but in the North the motivation for "cold blooded murder" was economic gain. "We do not defend our duels, much less our street affrays with pistol and bowie knife," the Alabamian proclaimed, "but they indicate less depravity in society than the diabolical class of crimes so common in the North."[47] Thus did Southern—and Florida—editors counter Northern criticism. If the South was barbarous, the North was money-mad. Motives for crime, by this logic, had a geographical base. They hoped the message was clear. Southerners sometimes were forced to break the law for honorable purposes, while crimes of Northerners held darker, more sinister implications. The message was that there was more honor among Southern criminals.

By the 1830s, Floridians had joined other Southern states in decrying increasing Northern influence in their internal affairs. It was as though Southerners had developed a different sense of right and wrong, good and evil, and, of course, legality and illegality. As politics, economics, and social affairs began to divide South from North, so did attitudes toward crime and how to deal with it. The fundamental disagreement fell not with the specific crimes themselves but with which ones were the most destructive to society and which ones should be prosecuted in the most determined fashion. Southerners—and, for that matter, Floridians—were willing to accept that their section had its share of criminals. Yet they insisted that the whole of their society was far superior to Northern society in morals and virtue.

The Northern threat aside, Florida's leaders advanced plans to make the state freer of crime. In circumstances not dissimilar to those of the later Progressive Era, some suggested a closer adherence to Christian principles, while others recommended stricter laws against drunkenness, gambling, Sabbath-breaking, and adultery. Those hostile to the "new political process" and its excesses predicted that the nation would suffer the "penalties of demoralizing reaction."[48] Some sought ways to protect the state from fugitives and, especially, from money-grubbing Yankees. Others called for stricter adherence to existing law and greater support of law enforcement officials. They believed that more jails and perhaps a state penitentiary would act as deterrents to lawbreakers. Editor Gould was not a Mason, but he commended their work and that of other fraternal organizations in setting good examples, observing that "in the newly established settlements of the South" such orders might "prove beneficial in checking and frowning down the brutal ruffianism of the age."[49]

Similar comments deploring the decline in morals, the increase in crime, and the pervasive influence of alcohol, guns, and gambling could be read in nearly every newspaper in antebellum America. But as several historians have suggested, much of this contemporary commentary reflects a pessimistic view of mankind that was even more typical of nineteenth-century Southerners, namely, that when left unrestrained by law, religious morality, social convention, or some other counterbalancing force, men's and women's brutal, lustful, and sinful nature would predominate.[50] The law and its faithful enforcement and support by an enlightened public opinion would be the only remedy. If this was the solution, few predicted that it was possible.

These observations suggest another theme: when antebellum Americans had to choose between social stability and individual rights, they usually sided with stability. In the context of nineteenth-century American notions of freedom and liberty, especially when it came to alcohol, guns, and gambling, or on such issues as lifestyle, liberty did not automatically translate to license.[51]

Did this commentary influence public opinion and, more importantly, the formation of criminal law? These questions are far easier to ask than to answer, but it is likely that the commentary had a measure of importance. Given the fact that these remarks emanated primarily from the same groups that made and enforced the laws, the statements probably strengthened views already held. For the majority of lawbreakers, however, these comments were as ineffective in controlling crime then as they are today. Yet for those who read newspapers and were in a position to provide effective support to lawmakers or enforcers, this commentary probably had some impact by raising the level of public awareness.

But the criminal justice system ultimately relied on the courts as the final arbiter of its actions. Before specific instances of criminal activity can be discussed, it now becomes necessary to set up the institutional framework of the courts. A basic familiarity with the law officers, prosecutors, judges, and the world they lived in is essential to an understanding of how crimes were detected and prosecuted. Thus what follows is a description of antebellum Florida's courts, judges, and law enforcement personnel.

Three

Courts, Judges, and Law Enforcement Officers

> There can be nothing more delightful, in the sight of God and man, than a well governed, and regulated community. Where violence and crimes are repressed; where peace dwells in its borders, and where SAFETY TO PERSON, PROPERTY, AND REPUTATION, ARE SECURED TO ITS INHABITANTS.
>
> —Judge Henry Marie Brackenridge (1831)

During Florida's territorial period (1821–45), the national government in Washington provided Florida with its judicial and law enforcement officers. Presidents Monroe, Adams, Jackson, Van Buren, Harrison, Tyler, and Polk served in the White House, and each appointed federal judges, district attorneys, and marshals for the judicial districts. In 1822 Congress divided the territory at the Suwannee River into two judicial districts. Superior courts, organized primarily at the county level, began functioning immediately. Thereafter judicial districts were created as population growth required. In 1824, for example, a Middle Judicial District, encompassing the area between the Apalachicola and Suwannee Rivers, was added to the existent Eastern and Western Districts. A Southern District followed in 1828. A decade later Congress created the Apalachicola District, which provided for meetings of superior courts in Washington, Jackson, Franklin, and Calhoun Counties.[1]

Florida statute set the meeting place and times of each county's superior or circuit court, but often the whims of judges, the vagaries of travel and weather, the number of pending cases, and even the outbreak of disease altered court schedules and meeting places.[2] Most, but not all, counties had their own superior or circuit courts, but sometimes sparse population or a lack of adequate facilities meant that some settlers attended court in adjacent counties.

Not all counties had their own superior courts. For example, during most of the territorial period, settlers in Marion, Hillsborough, Columbia, Hernando, and Levy Counties attended court at Newnansville (north of present-day Alachua). St. Augustine served as a court site, not only for St. Johns residents, but also temporarily for those in St. Lucie and Mosquito, and in Monroe until 1828. During most of the 1820s and 1830s, citizens of Nassau County attended court in Duval County. Likewise, settlers in Madison and Hamilton Counties, both created in 1827, did not have their own superior courts until later. They traveled to Monticello in Jefferson County. Even after Florida became a state in 1845, many counties lacked their own circuit courts. For example, residents of St. Lucie, Volusia, and Brevard Counties attended court at the Orange County seat of Mellonville (Sanford) and later Orlando by 1857.[3]

Though the "judiciary of the Florida territory operated under federal authority," writes legal scholar Kermit Hall, it "more closely resembled a state court." This was so because it had jurisdiction over criminal, property, and some probate and contract cases—matters that traditionally are the perusal of state courts.[4] Congress vested Florida's superior courts with a variety of powers. They possessed original jurisdiction in criminal matters and in controversies involving $100 or more. Superior courts also adjudicated controversies arising under federal law. One of the court's most arduous tasks was adjudicating the conflicting land claims between private citizens and the federal government dating from the Spanish period. Superior courts sat for spring and fall terms, which meant that judges, district attorneys, marshals, and lawyers rode circuit twice within the district each year. Superior courts possessed appellate jurisdiction over the lower courts. A court of appeals, composed of the district judges sitting together, heard cases under review from superior courts.[5]

Below the superior courts, county courts handled cases in equity below $100 along with other civil and probate matters. Before Florida became a state, three-man county courts also served as a kind of county commission. County courts had no criminal jurisdiction, but they were empowered, like justices of the peace, to take affidavits, commit suspects to jail, and supervise police and patrols in their respective counties. They appointed constables and were responsible for constructing and maintaining roads, bridges, and public buildings such as courthouses and jails. County courts had local tax-assessing powers, and they also laid out districts for justices of the peace within each county.[6] Justices of the peace and county judges were appointed by the governor. One year before Florida became a state, these positions became elective.[7]

Of all institutions of territorial government, county courts were probably the most criticized. Local citizens often complained that their tax-assessing powers were unfair and their decisions arbitrary. One citizen of St. Johns County proclaimed that all his fellow citizens in East Florida shared his sentiments that all the officers of the county courts were incompetent, irresponsible, and indolent. Another man charged that the root problem was in Tallahassee, where officials wanted influence in local communities and "were willing to purchase it by . . . corrupt patronage." Others argued that county courts were an expensive, unnecessary layer of bureaucracy between the superior courts and the justices of the peace.[8] But most of the criticism was directed against the county courts' tax-assessing powers. Citizens in Escambia County complained of "enormous taxes," while residents in Gadsden County insisted that the very fact that they were being taxed by those they had not chosen to represent them was "unconstitutional" and not within the "Rights of Republicans."[9]

When it came to law enforcement in the territorial period, U.S. marshals exercised broad power over their respective judicial districts. Sheriffs, functioning on the county level, operated more or less at the service of marshals as deputies. They executed writs, summoned jurors and witnesses, opened and closed court, sequestered property, and administered punishment to prisoners. Sheriffs also fulfilled many civil responsibilities, including tax collecting.

Divisions of authority between sheriffs and U.S. marshals remained vague. Yet when it came to enforcing federal law and attending to federal prisoners, marshals were in charge. One suspects that superior court judges and district attorneys were always available to arbitrate jurisdiction disputes between marshals and sheriffs. Both sheriffs and marshals executed edicts of the superior courts, and despite apparent overlap in their authority, there seem to have been few instances of conflict or friction. Marshals were entitled to $200 annually, as well as fees for services they performed. Sheriffs received no salaries and, like justices of the peace and other functionaries of lower courts, were remunerated for their services by fees. After statehood the authority of federal marshals was more clearly circumscribed. They attended federal courts only. In 1845 the general assembly organized the circuit courts to serve the state's criminal and civil needs, and designated sheriffs as the chief executive of these courts.

Larry Ball has written that "as a concession to inhabitants of each judicial district, marshals were often appointed from among residents of the area. Appointees to higher office were persons of national consequence."[10] The experiences of Florida both confirmed and contradicted this statement. Since there were few "natives" in the early years of the territory, almost all marshals came from the outside, but by the 1840s Washington tended to look for local leaders to fill these posts. This was particularly evident in Middle Florida, where Thomas E. Randolph of the prominent Virginia Randolphs was appointed in 1831. By the late 1830s, however, Samuel H. Duval, Leigh Read, and Minor Walker—all local leaders of consequence—were appointed. But in 1841, when political turmoil and violence culminating in the assassination of Leigh Read rocked the district, Pres. William Henry Harrison selected Indianan John G. Camp to replace Walker. Not only was Camp a loyal Whig from Harrison's own Indiana, but it was expected that the public would view the appointment of an outsider as a positive step toward an unbiased enforcement of the law.[11]

If presidents catered to the desires of local communities in the appointment of marshals, it was often the case that the partisan nature of these communities meant that some were pleased and others were outraged. The appointment of Leigh Read and Joseph Sanchez of the Eastern District, both Democrats, are cases in point. In 1840 one prominent Democrat joined Leon County Whigs in deploring Read's appointment, claiming that Read was "never a man of business" and possessed neither the "capacity" nor the "common sense sufficient to learn his duties." Read was most unfit, however, because he was a "man of violent passions and prejudices—and incapable of acting with the impartiality that the office demands."[12] That same year a St. Augustine newspaper castigated Joseph Sanchez's reappointment because he was a "loco-foco" and a "*notoriously partisan prostituted office holder* of the late Van Buren party . . . and a man who on every occasion openly manifested a *total disregard for the rule laid down by the present Administration for the regulation of officeholders*." This outburst may have had some impact. Within a year Sanchez was replaced with John Beard.[13]

When it came to judges, the need for absolute impartiality meant that presidents *always* appointed from outside the territory. (The appointment of district attorneys also followed this pattern, though not absolutely.) This circumstance changed, however, when the federal courts were organized after statehood. Isaac Bronson and William Marvin, for example, both superior court judges when Florida became a state, served as the first two judges of the newly created federal Northern and Southern District of Florida.

The first territorial judiciary represented some of the best legal talent in the nation. Henry Marie Brackenridge (Western District, 1823–32), a native of Pennsylvania, had experience as a district judge and attorney general in the Orleans Territory before joining Andrew Jackson as a translator in Pensacola in 1822. By 1820 he had achieved a reputation as one of the great men of American letters.[14] Augustus Woodward, the first judge of the

Middle District, was a graduate of Columbia University. At the time of his appointment in 1824, he had already served nineteen years as superior court judge of the Michigan Territory, where he contributed so extensively to Michigan territorial statutes that they are sometimes referred to as the "Woodward Code." Joseph Smith of Connecticut studied at Yale and replaced William P. DuVal of the Eastern District, who became governor in 1822. Serving until 1832, Smith had experience as a trial lawyer in Litchfield, Connecticut.[15]

Though judicial appointments became more and more politicized as the years went by, Florida continued to receive excellent judges. Among these was Robert Raymond Reid, a graduate of South Carolina College who spent most of his legal career in Georgia. Before his appointment to the Eastern District in 1832, Reid had served as circuit judge, U.S. congressman, and mayor of Augusta, Georgia. In 1839 Pres. Martin Van Buren appointed him governor. Another talented judge was Virginia-born James Webb, who was the first to preside over the Southern District, created in 1828. Webb came to Florida from Georgia and later left the territory to become attorney general and secretary of state for the Republic of Texas. Webb was replaced in the Southern District by William Marvin of New York. Marvin became a national authority of maritime law, writing *A Treatise on Wreck and Salvage* in 1858.[16]

Though presidents selected judges from all over the nation, Florida's territorial judiciary was composed mainly of natives of Southern states: Reid and Richard C. Allen (Apalachicola District, 1832–38) were born in South Carolina; Webb, DuVal, Samuel Douglas (Middle District, 1842–45), and John A. Cameron (Western District, 1832–38) were born in Virginia; Alfred Balch (Middle District, 1840–41) and David Carmack (Apalachicola District, 1841–45) came to Florida from Tennessee. Dillon Jordan (Western District, 1838–45) was a native of North Carolina. If Thomas Randall (Middle District, 1827–40) of Maryland is counted as a Southerner, that means ten out of fifteen territorial judges hailed from states south of the Mason-Dixon Line. Of the Northern states, New York was the best represented, having contributed Judges Woodward, Marvin, and Isaac Bronson (Eastern District, 1840–45). Brackenridge and Smith put the number of Northern judges at five.

There is little evidence that Northern judges had difficulty adjusting to Florida's peculiar characteristics, especially in the early years of the territory. Woodward died in 1827 before sectional tensions reached their peak. In 1831 Brackenridge left little doubt that he was determined to enforce the legal mandates of the slave system in remarks he made to the Jackson

Robert Raymond Reid served as judge of the Eastern Judicial District from 1832 to 1840, when he became governor. (Courtesy of the Florida State Archives, Tallahassee, Florida)

County Grand Jury. The judge denounced the "circulation of inflammatory publications [lately] thrown into the Southern Country, by incendiaries, actuated by fanatic zeal." He announced his determination to enforce what laws were on the books regarding these issues and suggested that even more legislation on these matters might be necessary.[17]

William Marvin remembered facing some hostility on account of his

William Marvin served as district attorney from 1835 to 1839 and as judge of the Southern Judicial District from 1839 to 1845. (Courtesy of the Florida State Archives, Tallahassee, Florida)

Northern birth when he served in the legislative council in 1837.[18] A Unionist when Florida seceded in 1861, Marvin sat out the war in New York, but he returned in 1865 when Pres. Andrew Johnson appointed him provisional governor. Both Marvin and fellow New Yorker Isaac Bronson seem to have adjusted well to the South. By all accounts Joseph Smith was a man of intense energy, passion, short temper, and even volatility. He was often involved in confrontations with other federal officials, members of the bar, and private citizens. One official complaint lodged against him addressed to Pres. Andrew Jackson charged him with being a "bully among the people." Other opponents of the judge referred to him as a "tyrant."[19] Whether the judge's outbursts were motivated by disagreements over the law, politics, personalities, or North/South conflicts is difficult to determine. Still, Smith had little patience with the tendency of Southerners to criticize Northerners in his presence. Judge Robert Reid remembered Smith's agitation at a dinner party both attended in St. Augustine when Reid told Smith that he had enjoyed Achille Murat's latest book and asked his opinion, whereupon Smith responded, "You don't expect me to agree to that, do you?" "I had forgotten," noted Reid in his diary, "the Ex-Prince had abused the Yankees." But Reid was relieved that when Smith proposed to put the existence of sea serpents up to a vote, "every native" at the table "voted with him."[20] The irony is that Smith was the father of Confederate Gen. Edmund Kirby Smith.

The rigors of riding circuit during Florida's territorial days wore many a good man down. Nevertheless, Judge Henry Brackenridge seemed to enjoy the experience and kept his wife in Pennsylvania constantly abreast of his activities. In the spring of 1830 he informed her that he would hold court in Pensacola, Alaqua, and Marianna (Chipola). "I shall start . . . my little wagon, and will have a resting place at my own little house at Alaqua, half way to Chipola, where I shall have plenty of good milk and no mosquitos."[21] In 1832 John Cameron replaced Brackenridge as judge of the Western District. After four years on the circuit, Cameron complained to authorities in Washington that his responsibilities were unreasonably arduous and his pay inadequate. "Pray, cast your eyes upon the Map of Florida & look at my district! I have to hold Courts in five Counties, twice a year, besides one yearly term of the Court of Appeals: my travelling is more than 2,000 Miles in the year. I am from home, on my official duties, more than 6 Months in the year: from the nature of the Country & the distance of my Courts, my traveling is not only great & fatiguing, but my health and even life are often hazarded. And yet, for this I receive the salary of $1,800 only, without any perquisites or allowances."[22]

Even before the 1840s some Floridians chafed under what they called the "political whims of Washington." Many called for the right to select their own judiciary. In one instance, a select committee of the legislative council authored a resolution for the election of a governor and judiciary by the people of the territory, claiming that selecting one's own rulers is the "foundation of every Republican Government." The present circumstances, they complained, rendered Florida citizens more the "subjects of Colonial vassalage, than the citizens of a free republic."[23] This kind of rhetoric increased, especially after the St. Joseph Convention in 1838, when political considerations seemed to keep Florida out of the Union.

As the territorial period wound down, frustration with the political nature of judicial appointments mounted. The election of William Henry Harrison in 1840 brought the Whigs to power, but his sudden death and the elevation of John Tyler sent the appointment process heading in a different direction. This confusion brought even more uncertainty to citizens of

Florida. Complaints like these voiced by the Gadsden County Grand Jury were common: "Our state of Territorial dependence and vassalage is degrading and galling to American freemen. We are denied participation in political rights and privileges of the great body of American citizens." The system had created a kind of "arrogance of power" that produces a "forgetfulness" of who are the "*servants*" and who are the "*masters*." "History will record the narrative, to the shame of the National Legislature. The officers of the local government are totally irresponsible to us—are sent hither to rule over us, without our having any voice in their selection. They have been often without any community of feeling or interests with us [and are] not identified with us in sentiment."[24]

The quality of the appointments also came under criticism. Some referred to them as the president's "needy friends," while others called them "second rate and broken down politicians of other states, troublesome and cringing office seekers, who fly to Florida as a place of refuge, the same as Convicts fly to Texas."[25] The Whigs, of course, charged that these allegations were leveled by disgruntled Democrats who were disappointed at having their own party replaced. The partisanship was the most intense in the Middle District, where the new administration brought in an entire slate of Whig appointees.[26] Preceding Judge Samuel Douglas's first sessions of court were bank failures, violent bankruptcy hearings, and political rioting. Not surprisingly, Douglas's first session through the district was a stormy one. Though he refused to be deflected from holding court, he did receive criticism—primarily from Democrats. "President Tyler's sending him hither to dispense law and justice to the people of this District," charged the *Tallahassee Floridian,* "makes him one of the *Territorial* Government. But he will discover ere long that his is a government every true-hearted Floridian despises and contempts from the bottom of his soul—a Government degrading alike to those who continue it, and to those who are constrained to obey it."[27] Judge Douglas, however, soon won the respect of his district. At the conclusion of the December 1841 term, the Leon County Grand Jury congratulated him for the "impartial, dignified manner in which . . . he has discharged his duties."[28] Economic improvements lessened the political partisanship. By 1845 passions had cooled.

When Florida became a state in 1845, the role of the federal government in Florida's judicial affairs diminished considerably. Home rule meant that Florida was immediately granted both jurisdiction and monetary responsibility over its own criminal affairs. The superior courts, renamed circuit courts, functioned essentially as they had before, though with some important differences. The legislative assembly elected a judge and "solicitor" for

Samuel J. Douglas served as judge of the Middle Judicial District from 1841 to 1845. (Courtesy of the Florida Supreme Court, Tallahassee, Florida)

each judicial circuit until 1853, when a state constitutional amendment provided that judges and solicitors would be popularly elected.[29]

After statehood the county courts were abolished, and most of their civil responsibilities, such as the maintenance of roads, jails, militia, and patrol matters, were given over to the board of county commissioners. As one contemporary source summarized their responsibilities, "They exercise all powers, and perform all duties of county courts (under the territorial laws) while sitting for county purposes," and they sit for two sessions per year and "other such times as the judge of probate, or any two members may require."[30] Florida's highest court was modeled after the old territorial court of appeals, since it was provided that circuit judges, sitting together, would constitute the Supreme Court of Florida, with the judge of the case under consideration being disqualified in the appeal. In 1850 the general assembly elected separate supreme court judges. Soon thereafter it was decided that supreme court judges would serve six-year terms and be elected by the people.

After 1845 the role of the federal government in the state's judicial affairs changed dramatically. Congress created two federal districts, the Northern (1846) and Southern (1847) Districts of Florida, and Pres. James K. Polk appointed Judges Isaac Bronson and William Marvin to the new federal posts. The primary concerns of these courts involved issues in which the federal government was a party, such as land claims and maritime commerce. The courts also adjudicated alleged violations of federal criminal law. It had original jurisdiction over such federal crimes as piracy, slave smuggling, mail robbery, counterfeiting, violation of military and Indian reservations, cutting live oak timber on public lands, and malfeasance of public officials.[31] But it is Florida's state courts that are of primary relevance.

The transferal from superior (federal) to circuit (state) went smoothly. As one commentator noted late in 1845, the "courts are now organized, will administer the same laws, under the same forms, and be governed by the same rules as the late U.S. Courts."[32] In nearly all instances the judges and solicitors either remained in their old jobs or assumed new positions based on their experience in the old system. For example, when William Marvin declined his legislative appointment to the Southern Circuit, Gov. William Moseley appointed George W. Macrea. Macrea had previously served as district attorney of the Southern District. George S. Hawkins, who had been U.S. District Attorney of the abolished Apalachicola District, became judge of the Western Circuit. Thomas Douglas, who replaced Judge Bronson as judge of the Eastern Circuit, had been U.S. District Attorney for the Eastern District since 1826. Only Thomas Baltzell, selected to preside over the Middle Circuit, had no previous experience as judge or district attorney in the old system. Selected as solicitors for the new circuits were Caraway Smith (Western), Thomas Heir (Middle), Felix Livingston (Eastern), and R. W. Brantly (Southern).[33]

An added feature of the new post-territorial judicial structure was the "alternating system." This arrangement provided that circuit judges, despite their appointment to specific circuits, attend court in all the circuits on a rotating basis. The proponents of this system contended that this would ensure impartiality and prevent any favoritism toward or biases against any specific group. From the very beginning, however, the difficulties of travel—especially in the Southern Circuit, where all the meeting places had to be reached by water—placed excessive hardships on judges. Early on Gov. William Moseley urged the legislative assembly to consider abolishing the system and at least exclude the Southern Circuit from the process.[34]

Many saw the implicit hardships in the alternating system. Just as the system was about to be implemented, a correspondent to the *Tallahassee Floridian* reminded the public that as far as the Southern Circuit was concerned, a "judge in time must become a practical sailor, and egad, a *bold* one; for many is the man who would face a cannon or meet his particular friend at ten paces, without the slightest tremor of nerves, but would still falter and hesitate at making a trip to Key West, in a sail boat with an inexperienced crew." Finally the dour critic recommended that the legislative assembly appropriate money for "Life Preservers" instead of a "Law Library," and clothe judges in "Indian Rubber" rather than "ermine."[35]

By 1846 nearly everyone was calling for the system's repeal. Citizens in the Southern Circuit were particularly vocal. In November 1845, for example, citizens in Key West petitioned the legislative assembly to repeal the system, claiming that judges attending courts in Hillsborough, Benton, Monroe, and Dade Counties had to "travel more than fifteen hundred miles by sea, besides considerable distance by land." Times for holding court could not be guaranteed "unless judges were provided with a vessel of suitable size to make their voyage." The petitioners estimated that it would cost $1,200 to hire such a vessel to operate for four months during the spring and fall terms. The petitioners also complained that the plan would keep judges "almost constantly from home so as to prevent applications for orders at chambers."[36]

Yet the alternating system operated for two years. When the first circuit court met at Tampa on April 17, 1846, Judge Thomas Baltzell of the Middle Circuit presided. Thomas Douglas of the Eastern Circuit presided in the fall term, followed finally by Southern Circuit Judge George Macrea, who arrived in April 1847. The rotation was complete in October of that year when Western Circuit Judge George S. Hawkins presided over the fall term.[37] By that time a large number of citizens were complaining that the difficulties of water travel and communication destroy "all certainty of the sessions." Interested parties "must await the arrival of judges" and must be "necessarily subjected to great loss of time, and pecuniary sacrifices." By 1847 the complaints against "circular judges" had become so general, even from Northern constituents, that the legislative assembly abolished the alternating system.[38]

The brief experience with the alternating system was probably positive in the long run because it highlighted the difficulties of travel throughout the state. As judges, solicitors, and their entourages rode circuit on horseback, wagons, or boats far and wide throughout the Florida frontier, it became immediately necessary to provide easier access to these isolated areas by building more roads and improving the ones that already existed. This no doubt stimulated demand for better stage and water travel.

After 1848 judges held court in their own districts. The circuits changed little from during the territorial period, except that places of holding court were added as new counties were created. In Florida's remaining antebellum years, Holmes County (1848) was added to the Western Circuit; Liberty (1855), Taylor (1856), and Lafayette (1856) Counties joined the Middle Circuit; Putnam (1849), Sumter (1853), Volusia (1854), and Clay (1858) Counties were added to the Eastern Circuit; and Brevard and Manatee Counties (1855) became stops on the Southern Circuit. The creation of New River and Suwannee Counties in 1858 stimulated proposals to create a circuit in the Suwannee River region. One year later the legislative assembly peeled away Nassau, Alachua, Levy, Lafayette, and Columbia Counties from the Eastern Circuit and added New River and Suwannee Counties to create the Suwannee Circuit. The new circuit completed its first term just one year before Florida seceded from the Union.[39]

In order to understand the social context in which these courts functioned, it now becomes necessary to examine the social milieu of the districts themselves. Florida was diverse, and this diversity was reflected in the social, economic, and political characteristics of the state's antebellum judicial circuits. Though the social and economic characteristics of these districts differed, all shared the difficulty of bringing law and order to the frontier.

Four

Receptacles of Crime
Florida's Judicial Circuits

> When I took office, there were neither books, forms nor any thing else! Two books are used—one for *all* the dockets and the other for the minutes of court. I want several other books, but am unable to learn the proper person to apply to for them. I had to rent an office and furnish it entirely with desks, tables, etc. which I understood the law makes no provision for and I never have received any laws until recently, and being entirely unacquainted with the routine of such matters—errors in form are unavoidable at the outset. I made out my a/c [accounts] under the instruction of the judge and solicitor, and if you think it necessary to curtail it you must do it—though as the duties were performed therein charged I should think it rather hard upon an officer, whose office is by no means a sinecure one. I made out the sheriff's a/c for him from his a/c to which he made an oath. . . . There was no law books nor advice to be queried by which will in measure account for the looseness manifested in making out the accounts.
>
> —E. A. Ware to N. P. Bemis (1846)

These words, set down to the state comptroller from Hillsborough County's first clerk of the circuit court, would have been typical of similar administrative officials as they struggled to extend the American system of jurisprudence to Florida's new frontier. Ware's narrative speaks to a number of themes common to the experience: rapid growth in a sparsely populated frontier, difficulties of travel, limited resources, and little direction or assistance from superiors in Tallahassee. In such primitive environments, judges, lawmen, and court officials had to be resourceful.

Local differences also played a key role. Throughout its antebellum decades, Florida remained one of the South's and America's most diverse states. This diversity was reflected in Florida's geographical regions, its population, and its outlook. Of all Floridians, judges, perhaps because they were constantly on the move, recognized this diversity. Robert Raymond Reid, judge of the Eastern District from 1832 to 1839, recognized this fact on his numerous travels from St. Augustine to Tallahassee. After returning from a trip to the territorial capital in 1835, he expressed his frustrations with regional divisions within the territory. "There is an Eastern, and Western, and Middle Party," as well as parties reflecting personalities—"the whole community from the point of the Peninsula to the St. Mary's and Pensacola split into bits. . . . No body can tell when we shall get into the Union but 'tis to be regretted that there are not separate Governments for East and West Florida."[1]

Florida's population was so scattered, and travel so difficult, that at times any kind of unity seemed beyond anyone's grasp. If there was a unifying feature in the territory and state, it was the courts. Florida's judicial system served as a kind of agent for unity. As they brought law and order and civil authority to outlying settlements, judges and other members of Florida's criminal justice system represented one of the state's most positive forces for unity.

To understand how society and the courts responded to crime and violence, the state's regional differences must be taken into account. So too must the differing social and economic patterns. The institution of slavery, of course, was of fundamental importance. Everywhere slavery existed, but in the Eastern and Western Districts it was less stringent. In these districts—unlike Florida's plantation-rich Middle District—settlement was sparse and the lands were more suited to cattle raising and subsistence agriculture. But everywhere—except in the most densely populated plantation-belt counties in the north—the frontier, with all its implicit dangers, prevailed. Florida's port towns of Pensacola, Tampa, and Key West also added to the diversity. Here native Southerners came into contact with Northerners, Europeans, and subjects of Spain's Caribbean colonies. Cultures fused but sometimes clashed.

Western Judicial Circuit

The natural boundary of the Apalachicola River formed the eastern boundary of Florida's Western Judicial District. In 1850 West Florida contained roughly twenty-five thousand inhabitants, about two-thirds of them white. West Florida's westernmost settlement was the old Spanish town of Pensacola. When Presbyterian missionary David Preston visited there in 1829, it boasted a population of roughly two thousand. In his journal he recorded that he found the building styles and ways of doing business un-

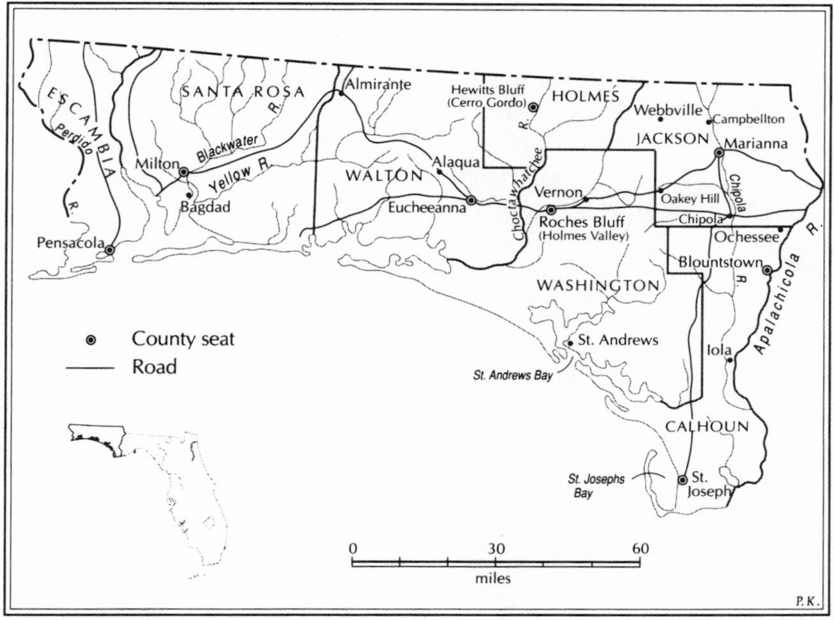

Western Judicial Circuit of Florida, ca. 1850–60

familiar—more Spanish than American. Indeed, many Creoles remained after the transfer of flags in 1821, and despite periodic clashes with the American newcomers, they became actively engaged in civic, economic, and political affairs. Because of its exposed position on the Gulf coast, Pensacola was vulnerable, as a local editor warned in 1838, to "itinerant gamblers and other rogues."[2]

Urban activity in Pensacola revolved around the inner city and dock areas, Cantonment Clinch, and the naval yard at Warrenton. The military posts remained at full strength throughout the antebellum period, and their presence contributed both to the city treasury and to urban tumult. Biennial visits of the U.S. West India Squadron especially signaled festivities and fisticuffs between community members and rowdy sailors. One typical outbreak of violence led to bloodshed in 1849 when sailors on liberty from the *Raritan* clashed with the barkeepers of Mr. Pons's public house. Shots were fired and a sailor was hit, causing a number of his comrades to break into the house and continue the mayhem. Five years earlier a sailor from the French corvette *La Brilliant* killed a fellow crew member in a knife fight. In 1853 an affray among sailors and townspeople forced one Major Sierra, a local lawman, to kill a sailor while suffering serious injury himself.[3] Just who had jurisdiction—civil or military tribunals—in such matters is often confusing and was often dependent on personalities, whims, or cooperation or lack of cooperation of the officials on the scene. Usually, however, especially in the territorial period, such disturbances were prosecuted in the superior courts. In 1827, for example, when Pvt. Benjamin Donica murdered his commanding officer in Pensacola, he was sentenced to hang by the Escambia County Superior Court although the military seems to have been heavily involved in his trial and incarceration. One suspects that some military commanders were often more than willing to turn troublesome subordinates over to the civil courts. The experiences in Key West, Tampa, and St. Augustine—all towns with sizable military contingents—bear this out.[4]

Bostonian Samuel Keep, who supervised construction of the naval yard in 1827, viewed Pensacola as a scene of unremitting violence. He frequently had trouble with his own workers, some of whom threatened him. Because of the possible danger, he was "obliged . . . not . . . to step out of doors without both my pistols Loaded." Keep was a difficult taskmaster, but his encounters illustrate the violent nature of the naval yard and those who toiled there, a situation that continued throughout the antebellum period. At the March term of the U.S. District Court in 1860, federal prosecutor Chandler Cox Yonge tried a number of cases involving violence at the yard. Yonge's personal accounts listed six prosecutions for assault and battery, three for assault with intent to kill, one for cruel and unusual punishment of a soldier, another for attempted rape, and yet another for larceny.[5]

Although favored with one of the best harbors on the Gulf, Pensacola had no major river linking it to the interior. Moreover, land to the north was less favorable to planting than land found north of Apalachicola, in Middle Florida, or in the area south of Jacksonville along the St. Johns. Accordingly, as Florida's other ports increased in size, Pensacola's growth leveled off about 1845. Nonetheless, Pensacola and the surrounding area exploited the region's rich timber sources. Mills and brickyards quickened life in such communities as Milton and Bagdad. By 1849, Milton, situated on the Blackwater River in Santa Rosa County, supported two stores, two churches, a sawmill, a shipyard, a courthouse, a jail, and a tavern.[6]

Other communities in West Florida grew as well. East of the Blackwater stood Alaqua, a convenient day's ride from Milton. The settlement was a midway point between Pensacola and the Choctawhatchee and Chipola River settlements of LaGrange, Ucheeanna, Mt. Vernon, Webbville, and Marianna. The origins of their inhabitants, realities of river travel, and difficulties of moving overland caused these communities to forge stronger social and commercial ties with south Alabama than with Middle Florida.

The lands bounded by the Chipola, Apalachicola, and Chattahoochee River systems were some of the most fertile in Florida. Jackson County, west of the Apalachicola, possessed the circuit's richest planting region. The county's most important town, Marianna, was located on the upper Chipola and was a regular stop on the Western Circuit. Marianna began its existence as a turbulent frontier metropolis, but by 1841 the village reportedly had undergone a most "saluatory [*sic*] change" in morals. Now there was "little or no drinking, gambling, and carousing, and all was peaceable and quiet."[7] In 1853 prosperous Marianna boasted eight stores, three churches, and two academies. That year a traveler visited the Jackson County Circuit Court and noted that Judge Jessee Finley "preside[d] with dignity." But Finley was also a little too "affable to the bar—a circumstance which sometimes is regarded as license to wraggle and procrastinate."[8] Thoroughly Whig by 1840, the county contributed several prominent political and judicial leaders, including Whigs George Hawkins and Chandler Cox Yonge and Democrat John Milton.

South of Marianna along the left bank of the Apalachicola rested the villages of Ochesee, Blountstown, Iola, and Apalachicola, Florida's most important port on the Gulf. The Chattahoochee River system, which included the Apalachicola, the Flint, and the Chattahoochee, linked these settlements with some of the richest planting regions in Alabama and Georgia. As early as 1830 a vigorous steamboat traffic facilitated commerce and regular travel with such upriver towns as Bainbridge, Irwinton (Eufala), and Columbus.[9]

On the Apalachicola's eastern bank near the confluence of the Chattahoochee and Flint nestled the community of Chattahoochee, the first important landing in Florida. Below lay Aspalaga, and approximately eight miles further south on the opposite bank was Ocheesee. The location was an important crossing point, and by the early 1820s a regular ferry had been established. The community was projected as the county seat for both ill-fated Fayette County and Calhoun County, created in 1838. By 1853 Ocheesee contained a "steamboat landing, a very fine hotel, saw and grist mill, warehouse, and cotton gin."[10]

Apalachicola, at the river's mouth, showed promise as a major commercial center. As the outlet for commerce flowing down the river and as county seat for Franklin County, Apalachicola factorage and merchant houses tied upriver planters to establishments in Savannah, Charleston, New York, and faraway Liverpool and London. But Apalachicola merchants

George S. Hawkins served as district attorney of the Apalachicola Judicial District from 1842 to 1845 and as judge of the Western Judicial Circuit from 1845 to 1853. (Courtesy of the Florida Supreme Court, Tallahassee, Florida)

depended on upriver agriculture for their livelihood. Downturns in output could send factors reeling. Despite seasonal fluctuations, Apalachicola was a seaport center that attracted shrewd businessmen throughout the antebellum decades. The city also diverted upriver planters, sailors, or other frontier flotsam who sought to blow off steam. Gambling and excessive drinking tempted many of the town's transients, making Apalachicola a center of vice and immorality. In 1846 the county grand jury remarked that civilized graces had improved, but recalled the time only a few years earlier when "the peaceful and unoffending citizen was continually jostled, in the legitimate walks and avocations of life, by the violent and licentious—when our streets were the scenes of continual outrage and turbulence—laws inoperative and justice silenced." Four years previously, the county clerk had reported judgments in twenty criminal indictments over the last three terms of court. Included were six for assault and battery, three for murder, one for gaming, two for keeping a disorderly house, two for receiving money from a slave, and one for malpractice—all for fines and costs totaling $1,162.[11]

Middle Judicial Circuit

Many newcomers among the first rush of settlers into territorial Florida were attracted to the fertile lands surrounding the new territorial capital of Tallahassee. Most were quick to appreciate the uses to which the Apalachicola, Ochlockonee, Econfina, Wakulla, and St. Marks Rivers could be put as transportation and commercial links to the outside world.

Judge Henry M. Brackenridge of the Western District described the area in the late 1820s. "It is a great pleasure to see this fine country after leaving the dreadful sterility of Pensacola," he recorded. "The forests are very beautiful, and the general surface of the country which is hilly is pleasing. It is a pleasure to cultivate such a soil as they have here." By 1850 Middle Florida's population had risen to approximately thirty-eight thousand, with blacks outnumbering whites by about seven thousand.[12]

Moving east across the Apalachicola River, the first stop on Florida's Middle Judicial Circuit was Quincy. By 1850 Gadsden County's seat had more than a thousand inhabitants and contained a courthouse, two well-kept hotels, two academies, and Presbyterian, Methodist, and Episcopal churches. Quincy's educational establishments, temperance society, and respected newspapers (literary as well as political) prompted one visitor to label it the "Athens of Florida." Even so, it possessed backsliders. Methodist minister Simon Richardson recalled arduous duty beginning in 1848. His greatest challenge was the county sheriff, who "owned a grog shop . . . thoroughly organized for every evil work." As the preacher noted, the sheriff "was very strongly fortified . . . was rich . . . and connected to some of the best families" in his congregation. When confronted, the sheriff warned Richardson that he had come by his license legally and had a right to do business. He further advised the minister to attend to his "preaching and

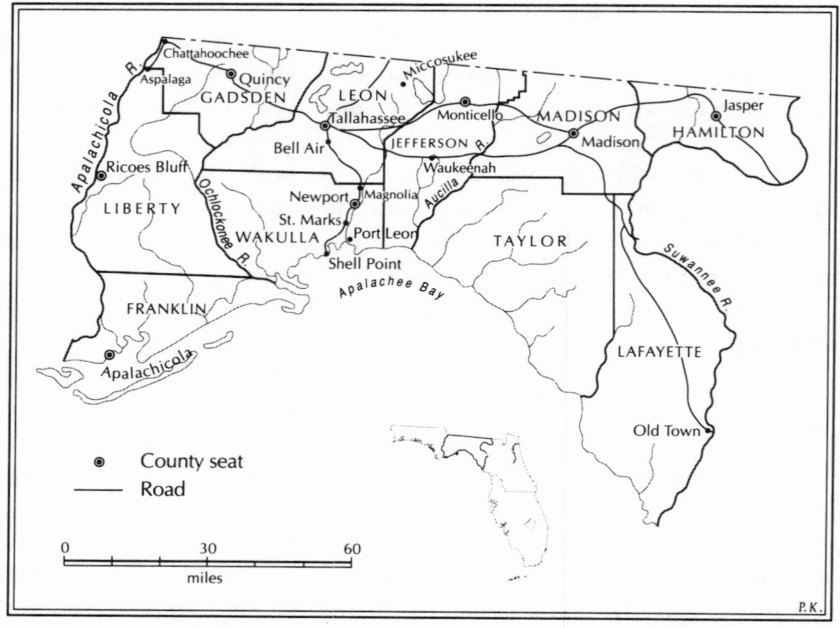

Middle Judicial Circuit of Florida, ca. 1850–60

quit meddling with other people's business." Standing to the challenge, Richardson converted the reprobate.[13]

Even with its educational and religious accomplishments, Quincy was still a violent frontier settlement. The personal accounts of James D. Westcott, U.S. Attorney for the Middle District, show eighteen prosecutions for assault and battery and three prosecutions for riot and affray before the 1834 superior court. Even as late as the eve of the Civil War, Gadsden County continued to suffer from sporadic outbreaks of violence, but one grand jury in the 1850s had congratulated local citizens on the "gradual moral progress of the community as is witnessed by the very few ordinary breaches of the peace."[14]

Tallahassee rested about twenty-five miles east of Quincy. Founded in 1824 as the territorial capital, it contained approximately a thousand inhabitants in 1829. Situated in Middle Florida's red hill country, Tallahassee by then contained two churches, one academy, two private schools, three public houses of entertainment, several boardinghouses, nine stores, two groceries, and several grogshops. Substantial planters settled rich cotton growing lands nearby. In the 1850s, Reverend Richardson boasted that "Tallahassee, like Quincy, was made up of the very best society from the old states."[15]

As Tallahassee grew, its relative prosperity, land office, and legislature attracted a number of undesirable "extraneous appendages." A St. Augustine editor, for example, counted fifty "blacklegs" when he visited the town in 1839. The total included gamblers, thieves, sharpers, and others usually attracted to new frontier settlements. An 1842 newspaper report of a typical session of the Leon County Superior Court attested to the disorderly element's exploits: "A Sailor was tried for murder and found guilty of manslaughter and sentenced to three months imprisonment. Another defendant was convicted of keeping a faro-table and fined $300 and [sentenced to] 12 days in prison but escaped. Another was fined $100 for carrying arms secretly and fighting. Another was put on the pillory one hour for stealing or (as his lawyers contended) *borrowing* his horse. Another was fined 6 and one half cents for fighting, and two were acquitted of assault and battery."[16]

The town's population multiplied in the winter when the legislature was in session, and along with judges and legislators came gamblers and loafers. Parties, balls, social-political gatherings—all made Tallahassee a lively place during the legislative season. "We have had a number of dancing parties in Tallahassee and neighborhoods, much fun and amusement," noted a local man in 1840. He added, "[I saw] many newcomers [Democrats] in the political world and more oddities than I have ever seen."[17] The winter in which that account was written preceded Tallahassee's most turbulent summer. Disagreements over banking policy, the conduct of the Seminole War, and ultrapartisan elections fueled conflicts that erupted into violence. The issues divided the community into opposing political factions, each finding support from a partisan press. Some thought violent political upheavals encouraged citizens' apathy toward violence and crime. A close examination of superior court records and other documentation reveals that 1838–42 was Tallahassee's most crime-ridden period.

Travel accounts, even with allowance for exaggeration, described social disorder that local inhabitants either accepted or ignored. The Comte de Castelnau, a French naturalist who made his rounds in 1838, reported that a dead man was found one morning in the streets; next to the body was a bowie knife recognized as belonging to an influential planter. The man "immediately left the city and withdrew to his home where he was never disturbed." Charles Hutchinson, a bank clerk from 1839 to 1843, wrote relatives that "I never saw politics run so high as here every day or two somebody gets a broken head—Two days since one man shot another thru the abdomen without any cause—the man has since died. Nobody takes any notice of it—People here look upon such things as a matter of course. The laws are not executed at all. They do not even have a gaol or prison or any other place where they could keep a man if arrested." Hutchinson further averred that with normal law enforcement facilities at a standstill, Gov. Robert R. Reid was forced to call out the "militia to protect two or three rascally fellows who deserved a thrashing."[18]

Such scenes continued to plague the territorial capital. After Florida became a state, though, Tallahassee's reputation for bloodshed diminished, and by the 1850s society had become more settled. Former "scenes of horror," claimed Simon Richardson, "passed away and peace and prosperity, religion, and morality had taken their place." As an 1828 grand jury had predicted, the time had arrived when "Dirks and Pistols" were "no longer . . . the appendage of a gentlemen" but were "laid aside and harmony and peace shed abroad those elevated sentiments which distinguish liberal minds."[19]

Directly east from Tallahassee and some thirty miles on the St. Augustine Road lay Monticello, the seat of justice for Jefferson County. Economic and social activity there closely resembled life in Leon County, except that Monticello and neighboring communities of Waukeenah and Miccosukee had an even greater reputation for violence, and the courts sometimes were compelled to operate under difficult circumstances. In 1838, for instance, the Comte de Castelnau found Judge Thomas Randall "holding court in a log house, and rain had come so that the judge was for two hours exposed to the water that poured in abundantly between the improperly joined beams." Castelnau also noted that Monticello was "famous for the quarrelsome nature of its inhabitants," and he discovered from Judge Randall that in two years eleven men had been murdered in the marketplace. The Frenchman reported that in one day he witnessed "several fights and saw several heads bruised." Bloody noses "were so ordinary that one might have considered them universal." The entire village seemed to be fighting. "Here two drunken men were dragging themselves along to attack each other," he recalled, "farther on young men were blaming each other for the murder of a relative, and murderous weapons gleamed immediately in their hands. Finally night put an end to all these horrors, and I was glad to leave that cursed place the next morning."[20]

Careful analysis of existing court records verifies Jefferson County's dubious distinction as one of Florida's most violent frontier counties. From 1828 to 1861 (records are missing from 1841 to 1845), county prosecution of whites included 13 cases of murder, 191 cases of assault and battery, and 17 cases of assault with intent to kill. The only other counties with more indictments for these offenses were Escambia (302), which had no missing court records, and Leon (356), which had a much larger population. Court records also indicate that indictments were difficult to sustain in Jefferson County. For example, of the 221 indictments for violent crime, only 94 reached a verdict: 73 were guilty and 21 were not guilty.

In 1835 the grand jury laid the cause of Jefferson County's excessive violent crime at the feet of an inept civil authority that was unwilling to enforce the law. More stringent law enforcement and a strict fine system, they hoped, promised a more peaceful society.[21] The county's reputation for bloody conflicts among its citizens continued throughout the antebellum period.

Crossing the Aucilla River west to east on the St. Augustine Road, the traveler entered Madison County, created in 1827. The county contained fifty-five hundred inhabitants in 1850, a total that doubled in the next five years. Most of the newcomers came from Georgia and, particularly, South Carolina. By the middle 1840s the village of Madison had become a regular stop on the Middle Circuit. On a "flying visit" in 1846 one editor attended the court and noted that the onlookers "possess[ed] intelligent countenances, healthy complexions and cheerful faces." By 1853 Madison had two schools, a hotel, a shoe factory, and a cotton mill. Though a growing, prosperous community, Madison predictably faced recurrent crime and violent disorder. In 1851 the grand jury complained that "at no period in our short history have vice and crime more unblushingly developed themselves than the present." The body recognized many commonly cited causes of lawbreaking, including intemperance, gambling, an increase in party spirit, and slipshod management of slaves.[22]

Directly east of Madison stood Jasper. The Hamilton County seat was the last major settlement before the Suwannee River, the border of the Middle and Eastern Judicial Circuits. Serving the villages between Madison and Jasper were the St. Marks, Wakulla, Wacissa, and Aucilla Rivers. The Middle Florida streams connected upper-tier planting communities to the settlements of St. Marks, Port Leon, Magnolia, and Newport, all of which could be reached from Apalachee Bay. Each of the four villages struggled to monopolize river traffic. Commercial rivalry was keen; conflict started as early as 1828 between St. Marks, site of a crumbling Spanish fort at the confluence of the St. Marks and Wakulla Rivers, and Magnolia, a town founded by the Hamlins, three brothers from Maine long experienced in mercantile trade. Regular shipping service soon linked Apalachee Bay with New Orleans, New York, and other Northern ports.[23]

By the 1830s a railroad linked Tallahassee to Port Leon, a community just three miles south of St. Marks. In 1841, when New Yorker John S. Tappan visited the town, he found about twenty structures of the "meanest kind." For Tappan the inhabitants of Port Leon resembled its physical appearance: "The people oh my! The 'ruff scuff' of civilization, and as to the Law, they don't know what it means for Law and Justice are not in their vocabularies." Tappan further commented that there was no church in Port Leon, and the Sabbaths there were usually "spent in playing billiards, drinking, swearing, smoking etc."[24] When a hurricane demolished the community in 1843, several local merchants selected Newport, further up the St. Marks River, as a new center for commerce. The new town became the county seat for Wakulla County, created in 1845, and a system of trails and roads soon linked Newport with the Jefferson and Madison County settlements.

Transportation routes through the interior were exceedingly dangerous. Robbers, desperadoes, and runaways lurked in dense undergrowth, often preying on travelers going through the isolated paths on their way to Newport. Several murder cases were tried in the first session of the Wakulla County Circuit Court. In December 1846 the grand jury announced that "our County is still stained with blood. . . . One of our fellow citizens has fallen by the hand of violence, and others have been cut and otherwise maltreated." The body urged greater support of law officers so that the county might "escape the further evil of individuals or bodies of men taking the law into their own hands, as has unfortunately been the case in some parts of our state."[25]

Eastern Judicial Circuit

As the Middle Florida plantation belt grew and prospered, shrewd observers also recognized the fertility of portions of the area bounded to the west by the Suwannee and to the south by the Withlacoochee. These tracts, located within the Eastern Judicial District, soon attracted settlers from Georgia and South Carolina. Before the outbreak of the Second Seminole War (1835), numerous settlements were established.

The Second Seminole War, which continued until 1842, both aided and impeded settlement in Florida's Eastern Judicial District. It devastated existing settlements along the St. Johns and Withlacoochee Rivers. But the conflict also spurred immigration; it prompted congressional passage of the Armed Occupation Act to encourage settlement of the area by whites as a way to speed Indian removal. Early settlement attempts had been costly, but by the 1840s newcomers were using the St. Johns and other routes to

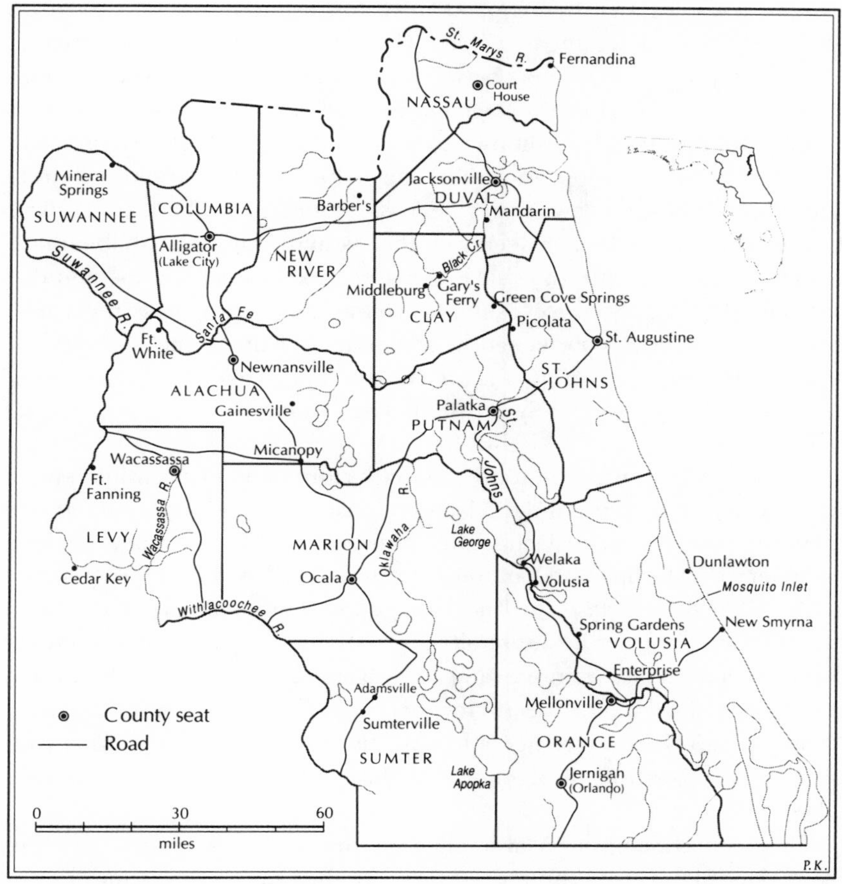

Eastern Judicial Circuit of Florida, ca. 1850–60

penetrate central Florida. Marion, Orange, Volusia, Hillsborough, St. Lucie, and Hernando Counties were organized. Soon steamboat traffic linked the upper St. Johns settlements of Enterprise and Mellonville with Palatka, Picolata, Black Creek, Mandarin, Jacksonville, and points to the north. Once the last remaining Seminoles had withdrawn into the Everglades, substantial migration from across the Union began anew.

By 1850 the district of East Florida was the fastest-growing section of Florida. It contained approximately twenty-six thousand inhabitants, about one-third of them black slaves. Most travelers coming into the area from lower Georgia crossed the Suwannee River at Mineral Springs, a village in

Columbia (Suwannee by 1859) County. More important as a town than Mineral Springs was Alligator (Lake City), the Columbia County seat and a major stopover for travelers between Jacksonville and the Middle Florida settlements. In 1860 the town contained seven dry goods stores, thirty-three dwellings, two print shops, two livery stables, two bars, two grogshops, two hotels, a jewelry shop, an eating house, three schools, and two churches. There were also five law offices near the courthouse. Though Columbia County court records have been lost, the testimony of local inhabitants and travelers alike indicates that Lake City often experienced crime and disorder. On May 19, 1860, for example, young Washington Ives recorded in his diary that he was awakened in the middle of the night by gunfire. He learned the next morning that a ruckus had broken out among eight men who were subsequently arrested. The schoolboy asserted that "everybody . . . in town wants to fight."[26]

Leaving Alligator to the south, a circuit-riding jurist next would encounter Newnansville (present-day Alachua), East Florida's largest inland settlement. Sometimes called Dell's, the frontier outpost was situated near the boundary of Alachua and Columbia Counties and had a superior court by 1828. Ellen Brown described her village in 1839 as "an isolated city containing about 15 hundred inhabitants . . . built of logs and surrounded by a dull monotonous, uninteresting pine barren." Newnansville's combination of log houses, pine trees, crackers, pigs, and dogs stirred her to add, "Now mix up these ingredients in any and every possible way, add a little of some preparation of alcohol and the result will always be Newnansville."[27]

The Second Seminole War swelled Newnansville's population with pioneers flooding in from threatened farms to the safety and shelter of nearby Fort Gilliland. The town was soon overrun with refugees, and the crowding and war-related tensions often provoked conflict. In response, by 1843 county authorities had erected a jail. Labeled by one visitor as a "wolf trap," the structure consisted of "hewn logs with an opening at the top into which they drop the prisoner & thus render his escape impossible." Previously the judge had been "compelled to fasten culprits on rail fences" because there were "no other means of punishment."[28]

Unlike the antebellum experiences of towns such as Tallahassee, time was not kind to Newnansville. The local legacy for violence, for one thing, continued unabated. As resident Jessee Barnard noted in 1852, "I have witnessed more dissipation in the last few weeks than I ever saw before. Drunken brawls are common." Further, several factors soon combined to make the "fine city of logs" a ghost town. As Marion, Columbia, and Hillsborough Counties grew large enough to sustain their own circuit court, Newnansville's usefulness declined. Then, seeking a more central location to hold court, Alachua County authorities relocated the new county seat to Gainesville. Finally, in 1859 the railroad bypassed Newnansville, also in favor of Gainesville. Thus from the late 1850s onward, Gainesville replaced Newnansville as Alachua County's most important settlement. By 1860 Gainesville contained a courthouse, three stores, one grogshop, two hotels, and a two-story jail. Below Gainesville and a short distance across Payne's Prairie lay Micanopy, one of the oldest inland settlements in East Florida. This town grew less rapidly than Gainesville to the north or Fort King (Ocala) to the south. In 1860 Micanopy boasted several stores, a drinking establishment, and a hotel.[29]

St. Augustine, originally founded as a Spanish city in 1565, remained the most important settlement in East Florida until Jacksonville finally surpassed it in the 1850s. The town's, and indeed Florida's, most recognizable landmark was its ancient Spanish fortification, the Castillo de San Marcos. Built by the Spaniards in the eighteenth century, the coquina structure had various uses. Renamed Fort Marion, it served as a garrison for troops, a stockade for captured Seminoles, and a prison for regional prisoners. Throughout most of the antebellum period, the U.S. marshal and sheriffs from outlying counties brought in prisoners from all over East Florida because few of the district's counties had adequate jails.

St. Augustine usually charmed its visitors and seasonal residents. Army engineer Capt. John Mackay described the Ancient City in 1838 as "prettily situated [with] an appearance of comfort, cleanliness and stability not often seen in southern towns." The captain was less pleased with the town's eighteen hundred residents, terming them an "idle and contented set." Eastern Judicial District Judge Isaac Bronson's young protégé George Fairbanks reported to relatives in New York in 1840 that St. Augustine "resembles Montreal more than any place I have ever seen; the same narrow streets." Sometimes teeming streets and docks fostered their share of crimes. After visiting Judge Bronson's court in 1843, Bishop Henry Whipple offered up a general appraisal of Florida's criminal justice system. "Law is a rather hard commodity here. . . . Murder costs about 2 years imprisonment or $1,000 fine." Whipple's praise for the Florida judiciary was high, but not so for its residents. "Such juries as they have here are beyond any man's control." They "look as if made up of scant materials where all the stock on hand was worked in. A more motley group I have never seen than today in the jury room. Such an assortment of characters," he wagered, "could only be found in Florida." While the court was in recess Whipple witnessed an example of the area's fighting spirit. A juror noticed his son fighting with another boy in the front yard of the courthouse. When the conflict concluded, the man took his son aside and gave him a lesson in personal warfare. "Now you little devil," the juror declared, "if you catch him down again bite him, chaw his lip or you never'll be a man."[30]

With a sizable military presence, a relatively large slave and free black population, and a regular inflow of county visitors doing business in town, St. Augustine had more than its share of drunken disturbances. Strains arising out of the Second Seminole War also caused serious problems. In 1838 a concerned citizen complained that the cessation of army operations had "let loose" upon the city a "set of men" determined to violate the "peace and privacy of the inhabitants of this city." The town council thereafter made it "unlawful for any person to be seen in the streets of the city, in a state of drunkenness, or behaving in a disorderly manner." The ordinance enjoined the marshal and his patrol to "take up all drunkards" and confine them in the county jail until the mayor saw fit to liberate them.[31]

St. Augustine, like other Florida towns, passed ordinances to curb disorder, but enactment did not mean enforcement. Turbulent spirits, facing insults from perceived enemies, seldom consulted city code books before reacting violently. By way of illustration, a bloody affray erupted in 1845 between local newspaperman Albert Nunes, his brothers-in-law, Charles and William Wing Loring, and the Mackay brothers. The ruckus occurred at a dry goods store when William Loring advanced toward a Mackay, who drew a gun and warned, "I know of your threats and intentions and if you advance, I'll fire!" Charles Loring also advanced and exclaimed, "Fire and be d—d to you!" All three men shot simultaneously. Two guns misfired, and another missed. Nunes and the other Mackay aided their respective friends, and a desperate struggle ensued. When the shooting and slashing concluded, William Loring had a bullet in the shoulder, and both his brother and Nunes had knife gashes in the abdomen. The Mackays escaped unharmed. Two justices of the peace ordered the men arrested, and all were released on bail. In the June 1846 circuit court term the five men were jointly indicted. The cause was continued to the next term, when Solicitor Felix Livingston dismissed all charges upon the payment of costs.[32]

A Tallahassee friend of Nunes recorded in response to the affray that despite this unfortunate incident, Nunes was a "good fellow—somewhat unique in manners, and sturdy in opinion but those disturb not the *man* and the *heart*." Besides, "we all have to elbow a little now and then to get onward."[33] Many St. Augustine residents felt the same way about William W. Loring: that same year they awarded him a seat in the state legislature. From St. Augustine, judges and lawyers often traveled westward to the St. Johns River, which they crossed at Picolata. The route was only eighteen miles, but the tedious ride lasted "four & a half hours," for, as a veteran of the road recollected, "all running horses [are] strictly prohibited on this line." Steamboats connected Picolata with Palatka to the south and with Black Creek and Mandarin to the north.

Jacksonville, located strategically atop the St. Johns River system, was poised to act as a funnel for goods moving in and out of Florida. The settlement grew faster after the Second Seminole War than did any other town in East Florida. Business activity quickened, and so did the steamboat traffic. St. Augustine editor Elias Gould praised Jacksonville's "true Southern Hospitality," but his witness of a brutal slaying dimmed his image of the town. The killings were the result of the "baneful, foolish practice of carrying secret arms." Both local and territorial statutes forbade the practice, but the public seemed unwilling to enforce them. Gould found some comfort in the fact that the combatants were not permanent Jacksonville residents. "Two of them are natives of Maine," he reported, "and the third was brought up in Middle Florida, where the bowie knife system has been much in vogue."[34]

In 1840 the Duval County Grand Jury decried outbreaks of violence and added that crime was on the increase. The problems its members saw were not peculiar to Duval County, and contemporary observers throughout the territory repeatedly made the same points. The jurors focused some blame on the Indian hostilities for "a laxity of morals" and the "increase of crime as an almost inevitable result." On every side, the jurors lamented, "we witness this truth. In a distressed and unsettled state of this country, the incentives to crime are many and the restraints few." Thorough investigations had revealed that justices of the peace and other officers had not done their duty in enforcing the law. Armed men paraded Jacksonville's streets, violent threats went unchecked, and the absence of a jail hampered adequate law enforcement. Either criminals remained at large or officers were compelled to muster a large force to transport them to Fort Marion.[35]

The northernmost settlement in East Florida was the seaport community of Fernandina. Located on Amelia Island near the mouth of the St. Marys River, Fernandina served area planters as a commercial center. Several miles inland and near the center of Nassau County was Nassau Court House, which a visitor described in 1843 as the "emporium of fashion" for the county. The traveler noted that the largest structure in town was the courthouse, a "small two story building roughly boarded up, with neither ceiling or plastering, with two windows of glass & a half a dozen others with shutters."[36]

When Florida achieved statehood in 1845, officials in the lower East Florida counties of Benton (later Hernando), Mosquito (later Volusia, St. Lucie, Orange, and Brevard), and Marion assumed full responsibilities of civil government. With the Seminoles removed or pushed into the Everglades, white settlement and immigration proceeded apace. In 1845 nearly fifteen hundred settlers lived in Marion County and more than five hundred in Benton County, which officials attached to the Southern Circuit.[37] The organization of county government proceeded only with difficulty, however. Jails and courthouses had to be built, criminals had to be prosecuted, and sheriffs, judges, and other civil authorities worked under primitive conditions.

Southern Judicial Circuit

Under the circumstances, members of Benton County's first grand jury congratulated themselves on the few criminal cases they had to consider. "It is highly gratifying," the panel remarked, "when it is recollected that we are inhabiting a new country in which migration is daily and numerously filling up with an intelligent population in a section heretofore so sparsely settled and where more crime might have existed." The body insisted on strict enforcement of the laws and ordered the county commissioners to begin plans for the construction of a courthouse and a jail.[38]

Hillsborough County, established in 1845, also struggled to meet its administrative and judicial responsibilities. Hillsborough County authorities moved briskly, if not always smoothly. The scene in and around Tampa Bay was often a raucous one. In 1846 the grand jury inveighed against the number of vagrants living among the citizens "without visible means of support" and recommended their expulsion. The jurors suspected the vagrants, who were holdovers from the recent war against the Seminoles, of engaging in gambling, committing petty burglary, and carrying on an underground traffic with slaves.[39] Fort Brooke, the local military establishment, also presented problems. It remained following the Second Seminole War, and, while a continual source of revenue, its presence permitted friction between military personnel and local citizens.

Congress created the Southern Judicial District in 1828, primarily because of extensive admiralty operations taking place at Key West. The island city then possessed a population of only six hundred persons, but it was surrounded by dangerous waters. Accordingly, the town was a center for

55
Florida's Judicial Circuits

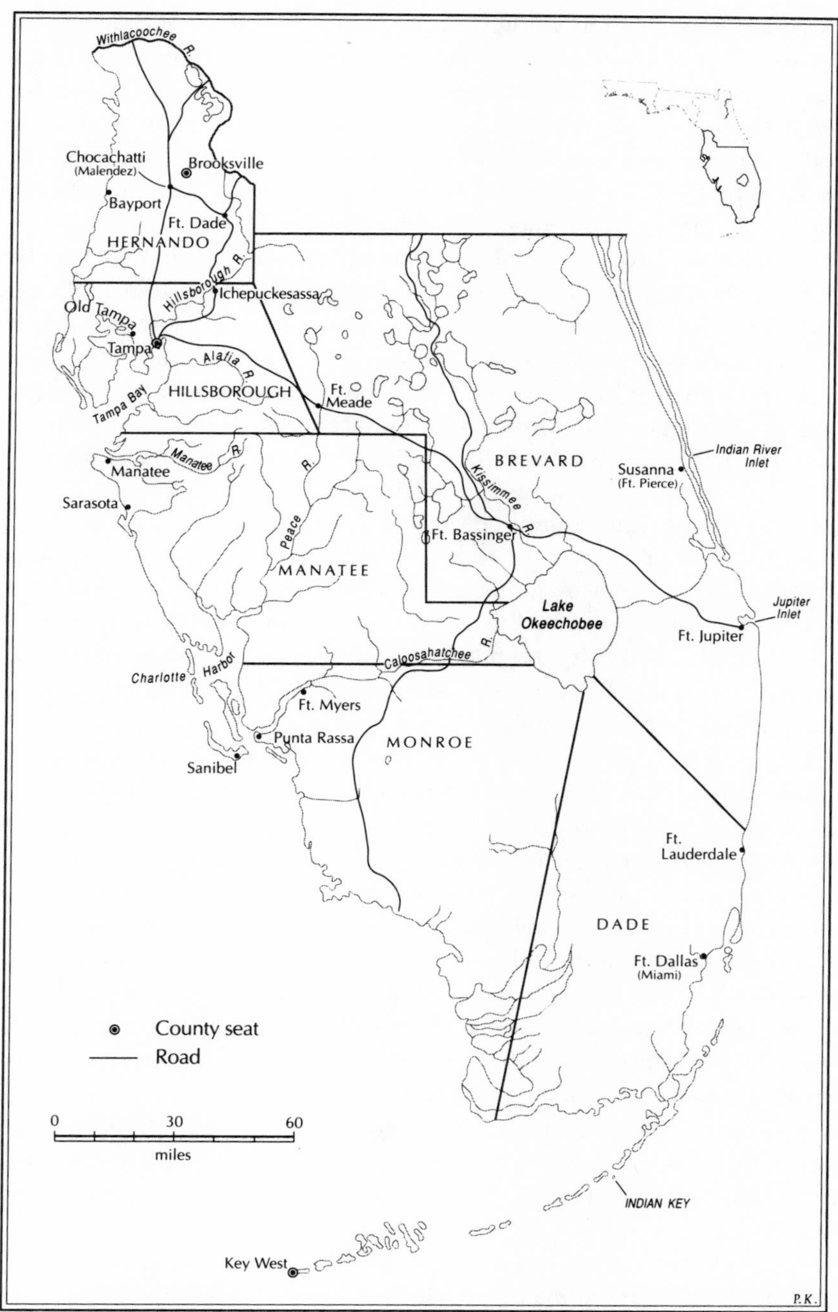

Southern Judicial Circuit of Florida, ca. 1850–60

extensive wrecking and salvage activity, and the commerce required close regulation. Key West's exposed position atop the Caribbean dictated the vigorous enforcement of U.S. authority. An incoming criminal element also required immediate attention, and, through most of the 1820s, law and order was conspicuous by its absence. Murderers and other felons often escaped punishment because they, and witnesses against them, had to be transported to St. Augustine for prosecution.

Concern for proper law enforcement commanded the immediate attention of newly appointed Judge James Webb upon his arrival in 1828. In an early letter, the judge informed congressional delegate Joseph M. White that a company of troops would be necessary to enforce the civil authority. Webb reminded White, "The population of this place, will always in great degree be composed of foreigners from various Governments, and as such are but little acquainted with our habits & customs & usually form very erroneous & imperfect ideas of liberty as found in our Country. . . . Many of these people," he continued, "are of the opinion that as soon as they land on our shores, they are at liberty to do as they please & it is difficult to learn them except by punishments." Webb reported that preparations were under way to convert the marine hospital into a suitable courthouse. A jail was also necessary, he noted, because no house on the island was a suitable substitute. U.S. Marshal Henry Wilson joined Webb in an appeal for federal assistance in building a jail.[40]

One year later Key West's needs still were unmet, and the situation had grown critical. The town, Webb assured Treasury Secretary Richard Rush, occupied "a spot, more than two hundred miles from which the smallest aid could be procured, surrounded by a sea infested with pirates and other depredators. . . . Unless some provision be made for their protection the Islanders and much valuable property must remain in a cruelly exposed situation." Webb then recalled an incident that occurred one year before in which a "piratical vessel, manned by upwards of one hundred desperadoes, came to our coast, took a Sloop and compelled the master to pilot them to such places as they directed." He also noted that, within the past week, the crew of a sinking Spanish ship had been rescued and brought to Key West. The next night the crew tried to seize the same vessel that had saved them. Webb reported that the men were "now at large on the Island, and must remain ungarded [*sic*], until an opportunity can be had of sending them to Cuba."[41]

Key West authorities also were concerned about the increasing number of grogshops. In 1835 one report claimed that a "multitude of these establishments are springing up in every part of the Town." The report continued, "The sober and quiet part of the community will doubtless have their peace and comfort often interrupted from these sources [catering to] the dram and revel loving bloods." The grand jury also complained about coffeehouses and billiard rooms that remained open on Sunday, encouraging the "idle and prolifigate [*sic*]" to commit various crimes.[42]

By the 1850s Key West had become a major seaport, military station, and commercial center. A traveler noted in 1852 that it had become Florida's largest city, totaling more than three thousand permanent residents. He recorded 650 houses, 26 stores, 10 warehouses, 4 churches, a courthouse, a jail, a customs house, a marine hospital, and large military barracks. Just offshore he found twenty-seven wrecking, coasting, and fishing vessels in the harbor.[43]

Key West and Tampa remained the only sizable settlements in the Southern District, but in 1836 the territorial legislative council created Dade County on the mainland, and Indian Key was selected as the county seat. Many insisted that the decision to locate a superior court there was premature. Petitioners opposing the move contended that only "*four families* and ten white men" lived on the island and that the county's residents were wreckers "afloat with no fixed habitation."[44] Because of its sparse population, Dade had difficulty in getting sufficient numbers to attend courts. As one man noted, "It is utterly impossible to obtain a Legal Grand and Petit Jury to convict even for a Petty misdemeanor."[45] Indian Key's small population was not the only reason that the "administration of the law [in Dade County] . . . was worse than a farce." Matters were further complicated by Jacob Housmann, Indian Key's owner, whose economic influence had enabled him to seize "control of all power both judicial and executive." Housmann owned the largest wrecking operation in South Florida and employed practically all the island's permanent inhabitants. He could and did arrange to have his own men appointed to positions of authority in the county. In turn, they "belong to him and dare do no official act which he does not sanction." The petitioners argued that all men in the area were his "tools."

Under Housmann's virtual dictatorship, normal administration of justice could hardly proceed. "The payments of simple matters of debt and accounts cannot be enforced there except by one man," petitioners proclaimed. "The dishonorable debtor defies his confiding creditor, and there is no remedy for the evil."[46] A legislative council committee discovered that Housmann also had periodically ordered persons confined in stocks in his warehouse "at his own whim . . . without due process of law." They recommended removal of the county court until matters could be straightened out.[47] Such were the problems of the administration of justice in large, sparsely settled districts.

Other stops on the Southern Circuit were Manatee and Brevard Counties, which by 1856 essentially separated Hillsborough and Orange Counties to the north and Monroe and Dade Counties to the south. Manatee County was settled primarily by Middle Florida planters who came south to establish sugar plantations on the Manatee River. Inland settlers, however, drove large herds of cattle south along the route of the Peace River to Charlotte Harbor. By the eve of the Civil War a lucrative trade with Cuba was established.[48]

The settlement of Florida followed patterns similar to those experienced in other Southern states. Growth required systems of law enforcement. As more permanent residents moved in, they sought out the judicial system as a way of preserving their communities. Congress responded to the need for establishing federal control by creating territorial judicial districts. When Florida became a state, its leaders created a new system based on the preceding one. The judicial system faced many obstacles in the beginning, and principal among these was the frontier. As the years progressed, though, the system provided most communities with the security they had demanded. In addition to providing much-needed law and order, the judicial districts, with circuit-riding judges, clerks, and lawyers, provided Florida with an added and important benefit. The judicial apparatus promoted travel and communication within the territory, which, in turn, helped to unify the state.

Five

Crime against Person

However careful they might be to walk softly, such men as these of the South were bound to come often into conflict. And being what they were—simple, direct, and immensely personal—and their world being what it was—conflict with them could only mean immediate physical clashing, could only mean fisticuffs, the gouging ring, and knife and gunplay.
—W. J. Cash, *The Mind of the South*

In the spring of 1843, a man named Ellerby killed a man named Skiffington outside a popular Apalachicola inn. It seems both men were predisposed against each other, and when Ellerby and a friend attempted to secure lodging at the inn, Skiffington, already a resident, expelled Ellerby from the doorway, shouting that he "dare not come here to live." Ellerby soon returned with more companions and ordered Skiffington and the others to come out, if they dared. Answering the challenge, Skiffington and his friends rushed out and chased Ellerby and company down the street; then a "regular fight ensued." Both drew weapons, and Ellerby's sharp thrust to Skiffington's abdomen ended his enemy's life. Ellerby turned himself in but was released on $400 bail. Court records that would reveal Ellerby's fate have been lost, but in the hands of an attorney with any skill at all, Ellerby would have had little to fear. The circumstances of the killing had all the necessary ingredients for a plea of self-defense. The combination of insult, physical struggle, and death usually brought acquittal or, if conviction, only light punishment. On March 4, 1843, the *Apalachicola Commercial Advertiser* reported the fight, and the editor used Skiffington's murder to lecture his readers about similar crimes. It is "high time," the journalist declared, that these "cutting, stabbing, *cotton hook* affairs are end[ed]." A "rigid prosecution and punishment" should be instituted against "such outrages." That was the only way, he asserted, to extricate the "unenviable blood thirsty character upon the South." Such incidents and comments were as common to Florida as they were to other regions of the antebellum South.

Whether transacting business, socializing, or politicking, Floridians often broke the peace, and the combat ignored both person and class. The upper class assaulted the lower class, and vice versa; employers assaulted employees, and workers their employers; and husbands, wives, and other family members battled one another.

Typically, criminal cases heard in antebellum Florida's superior and circuit courts involved violent crimes, including murder, assault and battery, assault with intent to kill, and affray, riot, and mayhem. Murder was, of course, a capital offense, while the punishment for manslaughter carried up to a $1,000 fine, twelve months in jail, or thirty-nine stripes—all at the discretion of the jury. Assaults and mayhem carried up to a $1,000 fine and/or up to six months' imprisonment. Those convicted of riot or affray faced penalties of up to a $500 fine and/or twelve months in jail.[1]

Prosecutions for crimes against person far outnumbered those for violations against property. Available records reveal that out of a total of 4,648 prosecutions, 2,215, roughly half, involved personal violence.[2] Indictments for crimes against person were also difficult to sustain. Prosecutions for murder, assault and battery, and assault with intent to kill illustrate the point: only 63 of 206 were found guilty of murder or manslaughter; 478 of 1,254 were found guilty of assault and battery; and 97 of 280 were found guilty of assault with intent to kill. The unsuccessful prosecution of crimes against person in antebellum Florida also demonstrates what David Bodenhamer and others have represented as the South's tendency toward an inefficient criminal justice system.[3] This is so because the majority of these cases never reached a verdict. Of the above-listed crimes only 794 of 1,699 white Floridians were found guilty or not guilty.

Surviving records of violent encounters in antebellum Florida suggest that weapons, either concealed or worn openly, were almost always close at hand. When violently brandishing arms, Floridians often used a knife or some other sharp weapon, usually concealed underneath their clothing or strapped inside a pants leg. The numerous statutes that forbade the carrying of concealed arms were largely ignored. Many armed themselves when visiting a neighbor, tippling with cronies, listening to stump speeches, or gambling at cards. Some Floridians spent their entire lives armed. For persons living in the country, the most popular weapons were bowie knives. These could be used for skinning animals, chopping down dense undergrowth, or deciding a dispute with an antagonist. Town dwellers' knives were smaller but no less deadly. Easily concealed were spring-back knives, similar to modern-day switchblades. Moreover, fashionable Floridians walked about sporting walking sticks, which, in times of danger, might serve as weapons. The sword cane, with its blade ingeniously concealed, doubled as a saberlike weapon, enabling its owner to make or fend off attacks.

Ball and powder, though used less frequently than knives, ended many disputes—and lives. Pocket pistols could be easily concealed, but shotguns loaded with heavy charges of powder, lead, and iron projectiles were more deadly. Fired at close range, shotguns were a means of bloody murder. During the antebellum era at least three public figures met their deaths at the hands of assassins. Peter Alba Jr., former speaker of the territorial House of Representatives and a leader among Pensacola's Spanish Creoles; Leigh Read, U.S. marshal for the Middle District and general of the Florida Militia; and William Allison McRea, U.S. Attorney for the Southern District, were ambushed, each murdered by assailants using double-barreled shotguns.[4]

Floridians sometimes assaulted and killed one another with unconventional weapons. In 1828 a man named Chenney was prosecuted in Escambia County for taking after Isaac Vaughn with an "iron bolt." Twelve years later Jefferson County roughneck Jessee Holloman was indicted for assault and battery for striking John Lofton over the head with a bottle. When Lofton died twenty-three days later from the horrible gash, the charge was changed to murder. In 1851 Josiah Jacobs killed Darling Cherry with a handspike in a drunken brawl at Bemis's Distillery in Wakulla County, a crime for which Jacobs eventually was hanged. In the 1850s two Santa Rosa County men were killed by similar commonplace objects: John Wilson with a boat oar and Martin Williford with a chair.[5]

Anyone interested in crime or law and order in the antebellum South cannot overlook this Southern propensity toward violence. Were Southerners more prone to violence than their Northern brethren? And if so, why? Historians have not been remiss in pointing out causes or themes that explain violence in the South.[6]

Some writers dispute whether the South was more violent than the other parts of the Union. They view violence as an American characteristic, not a uniquely Southern one.[7] For example, Ray Allen Billington, Philip Jordan, and others attribute violence to frontier characteristics. They define the frontier as sparsely settled areas where Indians might still be present and where law enforcement and courts were in their earliest stages of development. This definition would certainly fit antebellum Florida. Billington and Jordan suggest that other frontier antebellum areas (certain parts of the trans-Mississippi West, the Far West, and the California gold fields—areas into which large numbers of newcomers were settling for the first time) were just as violent as the antebellum South.[8]

Though controversial, a consensus that the South was more violent seems to have emerged. Edward Ayers, for example, has contended that what seemed an excess of violence on the Western frontier may well have been Southern violence transplanted. Moreover, it was the culture Southerners brought with them that made for a legacy of violence. "We need to look beyond the mere setting of the frontier to explore the character of the people who lived and died there. Bloodshed was the product of a culture Southern frontiersmen brought with them, not something they found waiting in the wilderness."[9]

Violence may also have emanated from American notions of liberty and freedom from restraint that were pronounced on the frontier but were present to an even greater extent in the South. Billington contends that the man of the frontier had a "passionate faith in liberty" that "encouraged lawbreaking" and violence. "Liberty to the frontiersman," according to Billington, "meant the right to battle with bowie knives, gun down enemies, and lynch suspected wrongdoers" as well as a "license to cheat and abuse in the name of private gain."[10] Any individually imposed or government-induced restriction on such "liberties" and "freedoms" was often resisted, sometimes violently. Mississippian Reuben Davis offered his own interpretation of the values of many antebellum Southerners when he declared, "A man ought to fear God and mind his own business. He should be respectful and courteous to all women; he should love his friends and hate his enemies . . . eat when . . . hungry, drink when . . . thirsty, dance when . . . merry . . . and knock down any man who questioned his right to these privileges."[11] Of course, not all Floridians—or, for that matter, all Southerners—agreed with Davis that a life free of restraints was necessary, or even desirable. But there were enough in every community, county, or district to make regular enforcement of the law—indeed, life in general—dangerous.

The contention that the frontier alone produced violence ignores important characteristics exclusive to the antebellum South. W. J. Cash recognized that frontier characteristics were inherent causes of violence, but he insisted that those conditions were more pronounced and exaggerated in the South. Cash held that the South witnessed the slowest "development of law and government beyond the limits imposed by the tradition of the old backcountry." That was because of Southerners' "intense distrust of, and, indeed, downright aversion to, any actual exercise of authority beyond the barest minimum essential to the exercise of the social organism." Compact and effective governmental mechanisms at the local level did not exist in most communities. The South's "counties were merely huge, sprawling hunks of territory, with almost no internal principles of cohesion. And to the last day before the Civil War, the land remained by far the most poorly policed section of the nation."[12] In those areas where law enforcement was either unorganized or unreliable—and many regions of antebellum Florida fit this description—settlers had to be on constant alert. Forced to rely on themselves or their family for protection, "going to the law" in case of emergency was not the safest way to proceed. The law was uncertain and took time. Plus, the latent distrust of governmental organization may itself have contributed to violence. Few resources were committed to creating a well-run, efficient police system, and this made the frontier even more dangerous and put an already touchy people on edge. Nor did "going to the law" satisfy the Southerners' need for instant accounting for wrongdoing, a sense of personal retribution. "When confronted by a crime that aroused his anger," the Southerner often demanded "immediate satisfaction . . . now, within an hour—and not some ponderous abstract justice in a problematic tomorrow."[13]

If the Southern frontier was violent, so were the more settled areas of the plantation South. Southerners, wherever they lived, rich or poor, placed a premium on personal integrity and were not prone to take insults lightly. Cash thought that the tendency came not only from a strain of individualism but also from the need to enforce the mandates of the slave system, and John Hope Franklin considered the institution of slavery a key to the South's tendency toward violence. Franklin thought slavery instilled in Southerners a paranoia that influenced the conduct of their everyday lives. Most observers noticed a touchy, hair-trigger mentality that Franklin attributed to an apprehensiveness over attacks, from within and without, on the institution of slavery. "The prevalence of violence," claimed Franklin in *The Militant South* (1956), "was due, in part at least, to the section's peculiar social and economic institutions and to the imperfect state of its political organizations." The slave system itself was held together by a regimen of institutionalized violence. "Far from loathing violence, the man of the South was the product of his experiences as a frontiersman, Indian fighter, slaveholder, self-sufficient yeoman, poor white, and Negro. He gladly fought, even if only to preserve his reputation as a fighter." But even if slavery was a fundamental cause of the region's penchant for violence, what underlaid, and indeed undergirded, the peculiar institution was the ethic of honor. Franklin contended that among Southerners a code of honor still existed that had died out in other areas—a code that permeated all classes.[14]

It would be approximately three decades after *The Militant South* was published before the concept of Southern honor would again gain the serious attention of historians.[15] The concept was so out of accord with the nation's movement towards civil rights that few believed it had ever existed. Even historians could be blinded by present-mindedness. "For some thirty or more years," wrote Bertram Wyatt-Brown in 1982, "historians of the South, with but few exceptions, have relegated the most important aspect of antebellum ethics to the trashbin of history. Honor, the keystone of the slaveholding South's morality, has been called a chimera, one that was imposed to hide the region's guilt over race domination. The ethic was so clearly incompatible with the moral thrust of civil rights and democratic hopes that Southern-bred scholars joined with Northern students of the region's past to eliminate the ethic from serious consideration." A kind of unintentional conspiracy had occurred. For Wyatt-Brown, historians have spent too much time condemning or condoning past modes of thinking: "Recapturing the mood of the past is hard enough without indulging in should have beens." Wyatt-Brown concluded that, at bottom, the concept of honor was the root of violent action among Southerners themselves and eventually among Northerners in the Civil War. Honor was not just a system of beliefs that came into play when men fought one another; it was a whole network of values that guided a man's everyday relations with his family and all persons in the outside world.[16]

Another historian writing perceptively on the issue of violence in the antebellum South was Dickson Bruce. He also recognized that the notion of honor was an important ingredient in the culture of Southern violence. But certain modes of behavior, claimed Bruce, separated the more genteel classes from the middle and lower classes. For Bruce, the way an individual dealt with passion, an inescapable emotion in everyday life, was all-important. The display or lack of display of passion was a significant ingredient in gradations of Southern antebellum society. Bruce disagreed with the notion that most Southerners "exhibited the thoughtless readiness to fight that the region's reputation would lead one to expect." Some among the lower classes no doubt did, but those in the upper classes "tended to be highly moralistic. They saw violence as a particularly difficult moral problem, and when they had to come to terms with it, most tried to do so—to justify it or to condemn it . . . in a way that was compatible with their most strongly held values. . . . To look at antebellum violence is to find a window to some of the most powerful elements of Southern culture." As Bruce sees it, the major sources of violence in the South were the frontier, slavery, and a regional paranoia toward relationships with the North. Southerners, claimed Bruce, saw their world as a violent place and "saw violence as unavoidable, as an essential fact of human life, somehow built in, profoundly, to human relationships." But violence also emanated from a profound sense of pessimism that permeated the upper ranks of Southern society. "It was remarkable and worrisome," writes Bruce, "how many gentlemen were prepared at all times to turn a minor altercation into a killing and such preparedness could only have occurred in a community where social pessimism could so easily turn into social fear."[17]

It was left for others to argue that the cultural-ethnic antecedents of the Southerners, such as the Celtic, Scotch-Irish heritage, were the most significant cause for the region's violence. Historians Forrest McDonald and Grady McWhiney declared that when Southerners fought with outsiders or among themselves, they were merely acting out their heritage. The "usual explanations" of slavery and the frontier as causes of Southern violence, they contend, are "far too simplistic. . . . Some of the most violent parts of the South had few slaves; nor were all frontiers in America and abroad tumultuous places. The South was and still is a violent society because violence is one of the cultural traditions that Southerners brought with them to America. . . . Proud and contentious Scots, Irish, Welsh, and other Celtic people—touchy about their honor and dignity—were ever ready for either mass combat or individual duels."[18] McDonald and McWhiney agree with Wyatt-Brown and others that honor was a primary ingredient in Southern violence, but they fault all writers who fail to trace "violence and honor in southern culture to its primary source—the South's Celtic heritage."[19]

Some writers have suggested that America's and the South's peculiar legal institutions have given the nation and the region a legacy of violence. Richard Maxwell Brown, for example, notes that jurists and the courts, over the course of time and because of environmental and cultural circumstances, cast aside the English common-law dictum of "Duty to Retreat to the Wall" in the face of violence. On the contrary, the American maxim seems to have become just the opposite. This "No Duty to Retreat" doctrine had the immediate effect of expanding the use of self-defense.[20] The impact of this circumstance was felt throughout the nation, but it had wider implications in the South because that was where the ethic of honor ruled supreme. But the South also had a different legal tradition from that of the North. According to David Bodenhamer and James Ely, among the "unique dimensions" setting the South apart from the rest of the nation "has been an unusual degree of attention to matters of race and caste, a rural culture, a hierarchical society, and a pervasive localism."[21]

This overview of various interpretations of the South's violence may seem excessively long or even overdrawn, but it is essential as a beginning step toward an assessment of crime against person in antebellum Florida. Whether violence sprang from the deadly frontier, sudden anger among those with an exaggerated sense of honor, ethnic antecedents, or peculiar legal traditions, it was all too typical in antebellum Florida. When mixed with the deadly ingredient of alcohol, all four, separately and together, caused violent confrontations in Florida.

Social commentators and historians have noted that even a thoughtless remark, gesture, or facial expression could trigger rage, often deadly and uncontrollable. Insults, slights, and the questioning of a man's honesty or personal integrity could result in bloodshed, especially when weapons were close at hand. One representative instance occurred in Tallahassee, where in 1837 James Huguenin shot and killed a shopkeeper, Robert S. Miller. According to one account, Huguenin, a native of Savannah, "was led to the commission of the act by some expression of Mr. Miller implicating his honor." Another seemingly senseless, but typical, outburst of violence occurred in 1828 at Sebastian Barrio's Pensacola grogshop as Benito Blaupen was stabbed nearly to death when he refused a glass of beer from Juan Foxando. George Grouard, an eccentric newspaperman, killed Thomas Jones in 1852 at Grimes's store in Mellonville (Sanford). "Grouard was driven to this bloody deed," a witness observed, "by insults heaped upon him."[22]

Often old grudges caused violent assaults. An 1856 confrontation between Calhoun County's W. V. Stone and Willis Whaley resembled a deadly encounter more associated with the Old West than the Old South. Upon meeting, they "both drew their pistols, but Mr. Stone being the quickest, killed [Whaley] before he had time to fire." Such reflexive action indicated a predisposed hatred. Similarly, in May 1849 Benjamin Wood, described as "slow spoken, quiet, [and] inoffensive," encountered an old enemy, Elijah Jordan, at an election in Marianna. Both voted without incident, but when Jordan left town with two friends, Wood confronted them on the road with a double-barreled shotgun. Jordan jumped out of his carriage, but Wood shot and killed him instantly. Wood escaped and was never apprehended.[23]

Few antebellum Floridians would have disagreed with the idea that intoxication precipitated violent deaths. In addition to Josiah Jacobs, numerous others were hanged for killing men during drunken brawls. Yet juries rarely considered inebriation a mitigating factor. Thomas Horan, for example, admitted knocking down James Ramsey in a fit of intoxication in a Port Leon tavern, but denied to the last that he stabbed him. Nevertheless, on April 24, 1842, Horan was hanged, but only after making a desperate and almost successful escape from the Leon County jail.[24] Samuel Right, a private in the U.S. Army, was hanged for killing Sgt. John Williams. From the scaffold he acknowledged that drunkenness was the cause of his present dilemma and asked forgiveness from the large crowd assembled at St. Augustine for his 1836 execution. Reportedly, he then went to the gallows "with firmness and resignation."[25]

Similarly, drunken Norman Sherwood shot and killed John Wilson, his "friend and partner" in Key West. On the morning of July 5, 1830, Sherwood had a fight with one Jones. After they were separated Sherwood went off but returned with a fully charged flintlock pistol, "avowing his intention to kill Jones [but he was] induced to fire . . . at a mark" and withdrew. One hour later he returned with his pistol reloaded. By that time John Wilson had arrived. Wilson tried to calm his friend but was killed himself when a "scuffle ensued." Sherwood's only defense was that he had given the assembled crowd "fair notice" that he meant to kill Jones and that he would kill any man who attempted to disarm him. As Sherwood asserted, "Wilson had attempted to prevent it and he shot him, believing he had a right to do so." The jury disagreed. They found Sherwood guilty of murder, and Judge James Webb sentenced him to hang.[26]

In 1861 petitioners in Pensacola asked Gov. Madison Stark Perry to pardon condemned killer James Duggan, citing chronic alcoholism as the cause of an unfortunate mishap. Among the petitioners was U.S. Sen. Jackson Morton, who wrote, "It would be gratifying to the citizens of Pensacola if you could find it consistent with your sense of duty in the exercise of a high and responsible constitutional prerogative to extend to him Executive Clemency." The prisoner was only twenty-three and had a "countenance with no indication of the murderer or assassin." Duggan's deportment was usually good, but once intoxicated he became a "madman, disposed to assault, without discrimination every person he met on the streets. In a word," wrote Morton, "he was made a maniac by too free use of ardent spirits, which has led many before him to the gallows." The result of the appeals is unrecorded.[27]

"Plain folk society," Dickson Bruce has noted, "could readily appreciate the existence of 'fighting words,' " as it "was characterized by honesty, free-speaking, and violence." Such folk spoke their minds "and claimed to accept violence willingly as a natural concomitant of that freedom."[28] Calling a fellow Floridian a liar, a rascal, a scoundrel, or even a "drunken runaway man-of-war-man" was to court disaster. The two following examples, both disagreements emanating originally from controversies regarding fence placement, are cases in point.

In 1853 in Gadsden County, Henry Edgerton, his son, and a man named Morris asked Robert Stuckey about moving a fence that blocked access to a creek. An argument ensued, and the son later swore that he heard his father tell Stuckey that he had "taken as much from such a trifling a fellow as he had ever intended to take," to which Stuckey retorted, "If you say that sir you are a God Damned Rascal." Both men closed and struck together. One witness speculated that Edgerton would have killed Stuckey had Morris not pulled him off. Edgerton, later found guilty of assault and battery, was fined one dollar.[29]

In 1841 a Walton County man, James Mallett, lost his life in an argument over a fence. He had erected the structure on his own land, but it prevented public access to a boat landing. James C. Slocumb and a hired hand, a sailor named Robert Mellon, pulled the fence down so their wagon could pass. After dark Mallett came down with two guns and started a quarrel with Slocumb. As they were arguing Mellon appeared, armed with a gun. Mallett, noticing his clothing, said "Why do you let that drunken sailor carry a gun, he might shoot me?" When Mellon asked Mallett to repeat himself, Mallett called him a "drunken runaway man-of-war-man." Mellon replied, "You are a gentleman and I am another." Mallett then came at Mellon, exclaiming, "I will cut your throat!" Mellon stepped back and shot Mallett in the stomach. Mallett died two weeks later. By then Mellon and Slocumb had fled to Alabama.[30]

Election-day partisanship often heightened existing tensions among men, and few election days passed without a fight among some of the voters. At a Leon County election-day dinner in 1852, Benjamin F. Trippe found himself sitting across the table from Elisha McDaniel. As others debated presidential candidates Franklin Pierce and Winfield Scott, McDaniel began "good humorously teasing" Trippe, while at the same time emphasizing his statements with the point of a case knife. Incensed at being addressed in such a manner, Trippe warned McDaniel to cease immediately or be killed. McDaniel made another pass, looked down, and was about to stab his hog meat when Trippe drew a pocketknife and thrust it into McDaniel's heart. Trippe was convicted and sentenced to death, but Gov. Thomas Brown pardoned him on the condition that he "leave the state of Florida never to return."[31]

Religious controversy also led to bloodshed. Washington County authorities committed William McKinney to the Jackson County jail in 1856 for shooting and killing John Crawford. The dispute's cause was "about a church—one being a Methodist and the other being a Baptist."[32] Thin-skinned parishioners sometimes responded violently to public denunciation by religious leaders. James Piles of Ocala was convicted in 1849 of assault and battery and sentenced to pay a fine of $125. Piles insisted in mitigation that a minister had shamelessly provoked him. "Mr. Connel made a most unjust and outrageous attack on me from the pulpit which led to my unfortunate reconnoiter with him," he contended.[33]

A number of Floridians were killed in disagreements involving female family members. At an Independence Day celebration in Ocala in 1859, one man took offense at how a man named Monroe conducted himself toward the former's sisters. One then brandished a knife, one a stick, "and an affray commenced." The next day the protective brother lay dead, the victim of stab wounds to the head, neck, and side. In matters connected to defending the honor of women, the law could always be employed against evildoers. A Marion County jury convicted Monroe of manslaughter, fining him $1,000 and sentencing him to twelve months in jail.[34]

Public places were focal points for hot-blooded tragedy. Bullies, vagrants, and drunks often hung around grogshops, boardinghouses, and dry goods stores. Daniel Hundley's stereotypical image of the Southern bully has his counterpart in antebellum Florida. In October 1853 former Escambia County Sheriff Antoine Collins used a sword cane to stab and kill Charles Winters at the latter's Pensacola coffeehouse. Collins had sold a piece of property for Winters. When the proprietor received the money for the sale, he remarked while in the midst of a large group of patrons, "I don't wish to see you darken my door again." Winters attempted to eject Collins but was shoved back. Heavily armed for combat, Collins shot at Winters but missed. Winters then rushed his attacker but was killed when Collins unsheathed the blade from his sword cane and stabbed him. Those present took Winters to his house on Palofox Street, where he died. Collins, apprehended immediately, later escaped.[35]

As would be expected given the commonplace nature of violence, many antebellum Floridians killed for self-preservation. The following incident involving Cornelius Taylor, a well-known planter and hotel owner from Enterprise who blasted Theodore Hinsdale through the abdomen with a double-barreled shotgun in 1845, illustrates the complicated nature of the self-defense plea. Shortly after Hinsdale, a man named Crane, and several of their associates arrived from Mellonville by steamboat, Taylor ran out of his hotel and fired both barrels of a double-barreled shotgun at Crane. Taylor's burst missed its target, but he still pursued, yelling, "Come on you damned rascal, I have a cane yet." Taylor swung wildly at Crane, but the cane flew out of his hand. As the two struggled, Crane wrested the shotgun out of his hand and broke it over Taylor's head. Dazed but not down, Taylor took up the attack again, this time with a brickbat. Witnesses later recalled that some onlookers tried to stop the fight, but others encouraged it. "Taylor gloried in fighting," claimed one witness. All of a sudden, Taylor broke off his struggle with Crane, ran back to the hotel, got another gun, mounted a horse, and rode down to the shore where the passengers were frantically boarding the boat. When Taylor saw Hinsdale he became reenergized with rage. According to one witness, he commanded him to stop, rode up to him, "shot him down, [and] made off."

Taylor defended his violent act by claiming that Hinsdale and the others had constantly threatened him and were in league to run him out of Orange County. His first run-in with Hinsdale had occurred when he was county clerk and had quarreled with the deceased over the papers in his office. Hinsdale, he maintained, had often threatened to kill him and burn down his place. One evening when Taylor was not home, Hinsdale and a group of "banditti" had come over from Fort Mellon to "clear me out of the country." Finding Taylor absent, they warned his wife to "take her children and clear right out as they would certainly be destroyed." Taylor also offered an exculpatory version of the shooting incident. He had shot the gun merely to clean it for reloading. Crane then ran at him with a brickbat, screaming "You damned rascal—I have got you now!" Crane, Taylor alleged, struck him a violent blow to the head, causing him to black out. Taylor swore that the next thing he remembered was his wife leaning over him as he lay in his bed late that night. One witness countered the claim, however, by noting that Taylor had sought out Hinsdale, boasting only a few minutes after the shooting, "That is one of you damned rascals down." Taylor may also have been drunk. Clement Brown, a boarder at Taylor's hotel, testified that the proprietor "drank frequently during the day." Public opinion was strongly prejudiced against Taylor because he had often quarreled with others. Nevertheless, a jury eventually accepted his plea of self-defense. Convinced that he was only protecting himself and his home against intruders, they found him not guilty.[36]

Dickson Bruce has noted that the upper echelons of Southern society "sought to minimize the potential for conflict and violence through the observation of impersonal, restricted forms of expression."[37] They accomplished this by repressing the passion that often erupted into violence. Occasionally, however, emotions boiled over. Violence among Florida's professional ranks demonstrated the point. In 1859, for example, Alfred Sears, an engineer for the Florida Atlantic and Gulf Central Railroad, shot his superior, J. L. Gregg, through the heart "after tea" at Jacksonville's Judson House. Though convicted of manslaughter, Sears's case demonstrates that society was often forgiving. After serving twelve months in jail and paying a $1,000 fine—the maximum jail term and fine for manslaughter—Sears resumed his duties at the railroad.[38]

Occasionally physicians succumbed to uncontrollable rage and killed their antagonists. In the summer of 1860 a Dr. Curlee at Sulphur Springs in Hamilton County responded violently to chastisement by Richard Inge Wynne, a Fernandina lawyer. When the counselor came at Curlee with a cane, the doctor wrested it free, broke it over Wynne's head, and stabbed him with a sword. Wynne died on the spot. The *Cedar Keys Telegraph* lamented the loss. Though he possessed a volatile temperament, Wynne was "a man of first rate intellect, being a most accomplished scholar and thorough lawyer."[39]

Schoolmasters, then as now, also faced random violence. The Jefferson Academy near Monticello was the scene of two such incidents. Jessee Holloman interrupted the day's lessons when he appeared outside, threatening schoolmaster Thomas Leonard if he dared come out of the schoolhouse. Judge Budd issued a warrant for Holloman's arrest, and he was bonded to appear before the superior court to answer the charge.[40] In 1839 Clement Barrett charged into a classroom, demanded a copy of a letter, and attacked teacher Joel Groves. According to Groves, Barrett threatened to "beat [his] brains out" and proceeded to carry out his intention. Barrett struck Groves repeatedly with a stick while the teacher attempted to defend himself with a fire iron. Barrett thereupon drew a gun, "fired at some of the scholars," and withdrew, saying that "he was not done yet & would return."[41]

Violence sprang, as well, from the employer-employee relationship, and assaults were frequent. Tensions between planters and overseers often reached a boiling point. In October 1860 a "shocking murder" occurred when Thomas F. Drew, an overseer, killed his employer, William L. Tooke, "an old and highly esteemed citizen." During an argument between the two, Drew threatened to shoot Tooke's son. Instead, he drew a knife and "cut open the bowels of Mr. T[ooke] and then knocked him down in an attempt to cut his throat." Confident that the first blow had done its work, he grabbed a shotgun and disappeared on horseback. Indignant at the outrage, the Madison County community raised $2,500 reward for the fugitive's capture. The "horror" of Tooke's death was so "wide-spread," a Tallahassee newspaper predicted, that "should the murderer be arrested a strong rope and a short shrift will be his doom." After a number of days at large, Drew was apprehended near Quitman, Georgia. But what became of him is unknown.[42]

Many Floridians died in arguments over land ownership. In 1838 Hugh Duncan stabbed and killed Wildman Hines in an argument over the use of a grazing field. As a group of men were talking in front of Duncan's house in Monticello, Hines stepped up and began arguing with Daniel Mathews.

When Duncan questioned the veracity of Hines's statements, "they both caught hold of each other." Duncan ordered Hines to leave his house, Hines refused, and Duncan "collared him," saying that he could whip him if he was not sick—to which Hines, spewing forth a volley of violent oaths, scoffed that he could "whip nobody." Hines then "made at him," and Duncan pushed Hines back long enough to grab "a large butcher knife" from a nearby table. As Hines rushed forward, Duncan stabbed him.[43]

Three years later, also in Jefferson County, a similar incident arose. A gang attacked John Sandwich's house, shooting and killing his brother. Ever since Sandwich and his brother had built their house, one Henry Womble had repeatedly threatened them because he believed the house was on his land. Earlier, during some "hard talk about fighting with guns—Womble [had] challenged both men and they agreed to fight if he wished." The Sandwich brothers and friends occupied the house, armed themselves, and awaited the attack. Once it occurred, Womble and company fled after learning that they had killed one of the occupants.[44] What became of the attackers remains unknown.

Bertram Wyatt-Brown and others have noted that slavery, honor, and violence were inextricably intertwined.[45] Thus controversies over the treatment of slave property could lead to homicide. Such conflicts often involved bystanders who questioned masters' rights to punish the slaves as they chose. Outside interference suggested that the master was either morally deficient or incapable of carrying out his responsibility. To intervene was thus in essence an attack against the owner's honor. Sometimes masters who persistently mistreated their slaves were socially stigmatized and subjected to criminal prosecution.

The fear of being branded a social outcast was the reason Daniel Burleson reacted so violently when John Madison threatened to turn him in to the authorities for ill-treating his slave. While traveling on a road adjacent to Burleson's Cabbage Hammock Plantation in Marion County, Madison heard the screaming of a black woman. Soon thereafter he found Burleson and his overseer, Jessee Meadows, severely beating a slave. According to one account, the "brutes had actually caused the woman to be torn to pieces by their dogs."[46] On Madison's testimony both men were indicted for "cruelty to a slave." Seeking revenge, the shamed men "waylaid Mr. Madison near Orange Springs, as he was riding home. [They] felled him to the ground with a club, stabbed him in several places and left him for dead." Remarkably, Madison survived. Fleeing for a time, both Burleson and Meadows were captured and convicted of assault with intent to kill. The

$1,000 fine and six-month jail term the jury imposed on Burleson and Meadows reflected the seriousness of their crime.[47]

Clearly, violent personal crime was commonplace in antebellum Florida. Florida was not a land of homicidal maniacs, but the cases cited reveal a number of conditions and circumstances that caused Floridians to address threats, real or imagined, against their person or their honor. Evidence of public opinion was seen in many jury decisions. Unless it could be proven that victims had fallen in an unfair fight or that the killer or assaulter had taken some unfair advantage over the abused or the slain, juries were reluctant to convict fellow Floridians. Some simple statistics, though not as exciting as the actual facts of each case, offer their own testimony to the fact that prosecutors had a difficult time convicting men of assault and battery. Records available for Leon County indicate that of the whites indicted under this offense, only 90 of 288 were convicted. The pattern held true in other counties. For example, in Alachua County it was 11 of 52; in Escambia, 101 of 231; in Gadsden, 30 of 50; in Hamilton, 18 of 50; in Hillsborough, 21 of 56; in Jackson, 20 of 53; in Jefferson, 65 of 191; in Madison, 31 of 65; in Marion, 18 of 35; in Monroe, 27 of 90; in Orange, 5 of 16; in Putnam, 18 of 37; and in St. Johns, 13 of 24.

It might not be too far off the mark to conclude that law meant little when a man defended his person or his honor. When either was threatened, an antebellum Floridian likely would assume personally the triple role of judge, jury, and enforcer. Even if violent conduct broke the law, such behavior tended to demonstrate that a man's right to defend himself against any threat, either real or imagined, had society's tacit approval.

Six

Violating the Domestic Sphere
Women, Violence, and Crime

> You [Andrew Crail] have been tried and convicted of a crime at which the mind of Man, under the guidance of Religion and Morality revolts with horror—a crime which strikes at the very foundation of the social fabric and calls for the infliction of the highest penalty, not only for the safety of society, but as an awful example. . . . The sentence of this court is that, on Monday, the 30th of March, you are to be hung by the neck until you are dead.
>
> —Judge Henry Marie Brackenridge (1829)

Domestic violence loomed an ever-present reality for many antebellum Floridians, and it occurred at all levels of familial relationships. Brother against brother, brother against sister and mother, husband against wife, violence between in-laws—every kind of family member periodically experienced its threat. Threats from outside the family also led to violence as husbands invoked the unwritten law against men who dared to violate the sanctity of the marital bond. Violence disrupted domestic peace and also constituted an important part of Floridians' everyday relationships with the outside world. Some family members reacted to day-to-day vexations in the only way they knew. Pressure over economic disputes, unfulfilled expectations, and familial responsibilities might erupt into physical conflict. Not traceable to any single cause, familial or domestic altercations often sprang from a complex tangle of human emotions.

Journalists, religious leaders, and concerned public officials portrayed domestic disturbances as characteristic of the lower class. Deficient moral character, they believed, came from a neglectful upbringing. Some observers speculated that insufficient religious training led to moral inadequacy. Social miscreants, the critics claimed, resorted to a miscellany of immoral behavior: Sabbath breaking, intemperance, loose sexual habits, and violent inclinations.

The most distasteful cases of crimes against person involved violent acts committed by males against females. To most antebellum Americans, the female's proper sphere was the family. Her role was to marry, have children, and care for her family. The Southern female was idealized, looked upon as a divinelike being, one to be revered and protected. Such was the myth-reality of Southern womanhood. Actually, despite their "favored" position, females were subjected to violence inside and outside the familial unit. And despite their vigorous public condemnation of violence against women, males frequently attacked them. In fact, the first man hanged in the territory lost his life for the murder of a woman. In 1826 the Jackson County Superior Court convicted John Carrol of murdering Elvira Northrup.[1]

The courts usually preferred to ignore violence committed within the domestic sphere, and, when entertained at all, the issue was treated gingerly. Yet such a laissez-faire attitude was sometimes not possible; the presence of domestic violence was inescapable, and circumstances often forced law enforcement and judicial officers to intervene.

Male violence directed against female family members was not uncommon. The Mattair family in St. Johns County is a case in point. In 1829 Prisella Mattair, recently widowed, filed a complaint against her son Joseph, fearing that her and her daughters' lives were at stake. The distraught woman swore that Joseph "often . . . assaulted and beat her [and had] threatened to take her life." Constantly drunk, he had also "beaten his sisters . . . in a cruel and inhuman manner, without any just cause or provocation." The week before the complaint was filed, Joseph had chased his mother and sisters out of their house and off their property. He had come "after [Prisella] with a knife and threatened to cut her throat and set fire to the store house on the plantation." The women found temporary protection with neighbors but were afraid to return home until Mattair was in protective custody. County Judge Elias B. Gould ordered Mattair's arrest, but Mattair's violent treatment of females continued. Two years later he assaulted and battered Mary Ann Turner in Alachua County.[2]

Shortly after Mattair's attack on his mother and sisters, Judge Gould decided that the law protecting a wife from her husband's physical abuse was "flawed." Without mentioning names, he wrote in the *St. Augustine Florida Herald* of a battered wife who had gone before a magistrate asking protection from a violent and drunken husband. The civil authorities did not act because she could not, as the law required, post bond to pay the prosecution costs.[3] Enacted to prevent frivolous assault and battery prosecutions by making the complainants financially responsible for failed prosecutions, this law made it risky for anyone to issue allegations of physical abuse. Without legal control over the family's assets, beaten wives could only appeal to their fathers or brothers or seek assistance from some concerned person. In reality they had little hope of gaining relief from an abusive domestic situation.

When it came to the law, a wife was subjected entirely to the will of her husband. Under the legal principle of *feme covert,* married women could neither sue nor be sued. As legal scholar Kermit Hall explains, "The principal legal doctrine affecting women was coverture, the condition into which women passed when married. It merged two individuals into one, and the person who remained was always a man. The woman's legal existence essentially disappeared, with her property rights passing to her husband." Ironically, perhaps, this principle also could potentially shield a woman from prosecution if she could prove that she acted under the command of her husband.[4]

Absent adequate statutory protection against abuse, women at least benefited from the powerful extralegal force of Southern custom. They were to be treated as dependents, and that fact made their male counterparts responsible for their safety. Their dependent status both restrained and protected them. Given prevailing antebellum attitudes, physical abuse by a husband toward his wife was one of the lowest forms of moral degradation. Violators of the unwritten code were treated with contempt and sometimes were subjected to extralegal correction.[5] For instance, William Ward, editor of Key West's *Key of the Gulf,* regularly condemned "Wife Whipping." On March 6, 1858, he noted, "On last Saturday morning a fellow steeped in cowardice and passion gave his wife a severe beating—a wife who but for a few short months ago went forth from her father's house trustingly, joyously, a bride strong in confidence." Ward used the incident to analyze domestic violence and to emphasize a husband's marital responsibilities. According to the editor, the man had "committed a crime against society, humanity, & Heaven, in becoming a husband" because he had forsaken his "most awful of all human responsibilities—the guardianship of an immortal soul." A husband, he declared, must "love, cherish, comfort, and honor" his wife. "No matter what the provocation . . . none but a coward would raise his hand to strike a woman."

Women's dependent status required husbands to "guard" their wives and daughters against all threats—from family or society. Accordingly, physical abuse directed against females within the family threatened existing social institutions. As a mother and a wife, the Southern female was the moral guardian of all familial virtue. The female's role as "mother of the race" made her sustainment and protection the key to the South's most valued institutions. "It is an evil sign when any man in whatever position of life is so sunken morally as to be capable of laying a hand upon a woman," Ward asserted. "Murder is not so bad an omen for society as cruelty or even rudeness to the weaker sex."[6]

Ward's impassioned comments suggest that interference from the outside community often occurred. Strong communal strictures, though, forbade such meddling, which would have challenged strongly held beliefs that the male was the unquestioned ruler of his household. For outsiders to risk serious reprisals, abuse had to be long-standing, extremely violent, or life-threatening. Moreover, most antebellum Floridians equated cultural stability with the enshrined custom that permitted a husband's "moderate disciplining" of his wife. Yet such "discipline" had limits, and extreme cases could trigger intervention by neighbors or a vigilance committee. Divorce also offered relief to some wives.[7] A complainant could either bring her case before a superior or circuit court or she could petition the legislature. However, public officials discouraged divorce except in cases of extreme cruelty.

While newspapermen, politicians, and religious leaders might comment on husband-wife relationships, few admitted that physical aggression directed against wives was a widespread problem. Contemporary divorce petitions suggest the contrary. Judge Henry M. Brackenridge granted Josephine Gagnet a divorce in 1829 from the "bed and board of her husband." Louis, Mrs. Gagnet argued, was an "irreclaimable drunkard." She charged that over the two previous years, he had constantly abused his family, "beating" them with "great violence . . . threatening . . . his wife and children with great bodily harm and even death." Two years earlier, Brackenridge had concluded that Gagnet was guilty of "*extreme cruelty* toward his wife." In similar circumstances the judge had given Gagnet another chance when the husband made "promises that he would conduct himself in a proper manner."[8]

Recourse to the legislative council necessarily involved delays and introduced additional elements of uncertainty. Ellen Foster appealed to that body in 1829 for relief against her husband, Nathaniel, insisting that he had for the "last ten years [been] in the state of confined drunkenness and when in that state he most cruelly beats, and ill-treats his wife and children." On one occasion he even hit her over the head with an umbrella just after she gave birth. Despite the depositions of five others who chronicled the abuse, it was two years before the legislative council granted her a divorce. Three years later Mary Rhymes asked the same body for a divorce, in part because of her husband's "extremely harsh, cruel, and unnatural" behavior. The council complied, but Gov. William Pope DuVal, a staunch opponent of divorce, vetoed the bill.[9]

Often, when the state did punish a husband for physical abuse of his spouse, the penalty weighed just as heavily on the abused. In 1850 Newnansville's Francis Richards was fined $100 for assaulting his wife. His uncle, John Richards, made light of the affair and asked Gov. Thomas Brown to remit the fine because it unduly penalized the wife and children.[10] As the incident illustrated, criminal law was not an adequate remedy for abused wives. Public court cases could shame the culprit into temporary submission, but they failed to stop the problem of abuse.

Aggravated spousal murder often terminated a long succession of abuse. One example occurred at St. Marks in March 1843. George Everhart killed his wife, and during the trial prosecutors established "that Everhart, on various occasions used the most violent and coercive measures with his wife, frequently beating her in the most brutal and unfeeling manner." In one instance previous to the murder he actually attempted to burn her eyes out with a lamp. One source reported that the eventual murder was the work of a "cold-blooded, and inhuman monster, who satiated his thirst by intruding his hands in her blood." With such condemnatory evidence the jury took only fifteen minutes to find Everhart guilty. Judge Samuel Douglas, perhaps influenced by Everhart's "unconcerned" manner, sentenced him to hang.[11]

Numerous other Floridians murdered their wives. Some, such as James Grier of Newnansville, seemed more sensible of the errors of their ways than was Everhart. Grier "exhibited great calmness [and] fully admitted the justice" of his execution. Some murderers fled before they could be tried in a court of law. Acting Gov. John P. DuVal, for example, issued a proclamation in 1838 for the arrest of Jessee M. Goodman, accused of murdering his wife at St. Joseph. Authorities in Calhoun County suspected that he would head for Tennessee. Accused wife killer William Crawford of Hernando County also absconded. Because that county's jail was unfinished, Crawford was lodged in the Tampa lockup. The killer escaped in 1851 after being held approximately one and a half months. He was never recaptured.[12]

Even a trial and conviction did not assume punishment in a case of spousal abuse. Politics and social prominence could make a difference. One of the most remarkable instances of gubernatorial intervention against court-ordered sanctions involved Dr. William J. C. Rogers of Marion County, who, in 1856, shot and killed his wife, Emma. Rogers fled immediately, but

Marion County authorities subsequently captured him. Convicted of manslaughter, he was sentenced to nine months in jail and ordered to pay a $500 fine. For some inexplicable reason, Governor James Broome reduced the sentence to five months in jail and remitted the fine.[13]

Wives occasionally were accused of murdering their husbands. When Joseph Goldshier of Santa Rosa County was found dead in the spring of 1850, suspicion immediately fell on his wife and a friend. Eliza Goldshier and Daniel Malone subsequently were tried for murder at Milton, but they were found not guilty.[14]

Murder also occurred in households where the couple was not legally married. Henry Jourardin, an itinerant French portrait painter, shot and killed his common-law wife, Lucinda Forkner, at Iola in May 1842. The killer escaped from the Calhoun County jail but was captured three months later in Alabama. The final outcome of his case remains unknown.[15] Similarly, Ann Walker's badly beaten body was found near Pensacola's Bowie Spring in 1828. Andrew Crail, Walker's live-in companion, had shared with her a life of extreme poverty, resorting to petty crime as a livelihood. Evidence introduced at both the coroner's inquest and Crail's subsequent murder trial established that before the final beating, Crail had submitted Walker to a steady diet of abuse. The Escambia County Superior Court convicted Crail of murder, and Judge Brackenridge pronounced the sentence of death.[16]

Perhaps the most brutal case of spousal murder in antebellum Florida occurred in 1859 when James O'Conner killed his wife, Bridgett, in Apalachicola. Mrs. Rashit Mattox lived near the couple's two-room shanty. One afternoon she saw "Biddy" O'Conner running toward the Mattox household screaming for help. Just as Mrs. O'Conner was about to reach the door, her husband came up from behind and took hold of her and told her she might yell all she liked, but if she entered that house "he would finish her before tomorrow morning." Biddy then screamed, "Kill me Jim, kill me, but I'll go in!" O'Conner then dragged her back home by her hair and threw her into their house. Mrs. Mattox did not see Mrs. O'Conner until the next morning, when she helped several other ladies of the neighborhood "shroud her" for burial. A physician's postmortem found evidence of a wanton and brutal outrage. He determined the immediate cause of death was a "chop with a knife over the right eye extending from the eye brow . . . upward to about the edge of the hair." He also found "two long slashes—ten wounds in all." Further examination of the body found the "abdomen much bruised, [the] nose stricken with a heavy missile [such] as a brick, [the] neck, legs, hands and feet, and left thigh much bruised, the last as if with a boot or shoe." Mrs. Mattox, present when the dwelling was searched, saw "bed and pillows dripping with blood." A bloody knife was also recovered from the chimney. Still, O'Conner denied that he had committed the crime, but nevertheless he was found guilty of murder. Judge Jesse Finley sentenced him to hang.[17]

Females who defended themselves against male aggression broke the traditional mold of the meek, submissive lady. Sometimes women either fought off attackers or initiated combat themselves. In May 1843 a "white blackguard" assaulted two ladies in the territorial capital as they passed the cemetery. A local editor happily noted that the ladies "vanquished him . . . in a fair fight" and that their pursuer "was obliged to 'claw off' well 'clawed.' "[18] In 1847 Rachel Drew, a Jefferson County woman, burst through the door of William Ramsey's residence, where he and a group of men were meeting. She had a "musket in her hands" and threatened to "blow out [their] brains if they did not leave the premises." The men fled, but they were so concerned about the threats that they appeared before a magistrate and asked that Drew "be required to find sureties to keep the peace." A grand jury found a true bill of indictment against her, but she was found not guilty.[19]

Males who committed violence while coming to the defense of a female family member could reasonably expect that the law would look the other way. Few juries would convict a man of assault and battery in such a case; if they did, the guilty party stood a good chance of having his punishment revoked by appealing to the governor. For example, Gov. John Eaton in 1835 remitted the fine imposed on Isaac Nathans, a Jackson County man convicted of assault and battery. Eaton explained that the victim made some "provoking . . . abuse and slander of the female part of his [Nathans's] family, render[ing] his conduct and course in a degree excusable if not entirely justifiable."[20]

One exception arose in the case of marital infidelity. Many historians have recognized that antebellum Southern honor accorded a dishonored husband the right to kill his wife's seducer. The unwritten law provided that aggrieved husbands were obliged to exact personal retribution. Bertram Wyatt-Brown noted that in such cases "juries were loath to convict on even the mildest charges of manslaughter under provocation."[21] In fact, one of Florida's most celebrated murder cases was prompted by an adulterous liaison.

The scandalous affair ended on May 24, 1829, as U.S. Marshal Henry Wilson and Port Collector Algernon Thurston were talking on the piazza of the Key West Customs House. Suddenly they heard a series of shotgun blasts. Wilson abruptly terminated the conversation, moved toward the scene of the explosions, and quickly came upon Capt. Charles E. Hawkins, late of the Mexican Navy. "Major, I am your prisoner," Hawkins informed Wilson. "I surrender myself voluntarily to you and to you only. Mr. McRea has destroyed my earthly happiness. I shot him with a doubled barreled gun, loaded with buck shot. I intended to have killed him. Do with me as you think proper."[22]

The victim of the bloody assassination was William Allison McRea, just fired as U.S. Attorney for the Southern District. McRea and his killer had known each other for more than a decade and had clashed after both men served in the U.S. Navy's West India Squadron. Later they had coexisted peacefully until Hawkins became convinced that McRea was having an affair with his wife. After a physical encounter one evening, Hawkins challenged McRea, and a subsequent duel left McRea seriously wounded.[23] Hawkins, considering the matter closed, left Key West for Veracruz on business. He returned to find his wife with relatives in Nassau, where his brother had taken her after discovering that the illicit affair with McRea had resumed. Hawkins's passions were further stirred upon hearing rumors that McRea had "boasted that he had carnal communications with Mrs. Hawkins."

Most Key West residents believed that Mrs. Hawkins was to blame for the resulting murder.[24] James M. McRea, the dead man's brother, insisted that Mrs. Hawkins was a "woman of disreputable character" and that she had engaged in "criminal intercourse with more than one (before the arrival of the deceased at the island)." When her husband introduced Mrs. Hawkins to McRea, McRea's brother argued, she made a number of "indelicate advances; the woman then complained to her husband that the deceased had been rude to her and had attempted a violation of her purity." Aware that her complaint would force a duel, Mrs. Hawkins hoped that her husband would be killed. After the encounter, the brother asserted that Mrs. Hawkins was "perseveringly wicked and determined to make still stronger effort."[25]

Controversy persisted over the cold-blooded way in which Hawkins had killed McRea, but the fact of their previous duel afforded Hawkins special consideration. To many, McRea had been given a chance for an honorable solution by the first duel, but his subsequent conduct had wiped out the possibility of another such contest of honor. As one New York newspaper explained, the circumstances under which Hawkins acted "divests it of much of its atrocity. . . . We can scarcely conceive of a stronger incentive to the taking of a fellow being's life, than that under which Hawkins acted. Let his *conduct* be thought of as it may, that of McRea destroyed sympathy for his untimely fate."[26]

Vigilant defense counsel, a negligent prosecutor, and the political influence of the prisoner's brother, George S. Hawkins, eventually led to the killer's release. In February 1831, before Hawkins could be tried, news arrived at Key West that the legislative council had passed an "Act for the Relief of Charles E. Hawkins." The body had acted on a petition received from the Monroe County Grand Jury indicating that public opinion firmly supported Hawkins's act.[27] The defendant had manfully defended himself against a miscreant who had scorned the sacred bonds of matrimony. Few expressed the need to prosecute a man who salvaged his honor by taking an adulterer's blood. In the meantime, Hawkins had discarded his wife and remarried.

Beyond clear-cut cases of infidelity, a husband's groundless jealousy might also lead to violent death. In May 1827 Judge Henry Brackenridge wrote his wife, Caroline, that one John R. Watkins, "a young gentlemen of fortune," shot and killed Jessee Butler. Watkins had been married only three months to a woman devoted to him. "He appears to be a man of weak understanding," Brackenridge wrote, "but at the same time a victim of the most unaccountable and groundless jealousy." The judge continued, "Two servant women who had the management of his household . . . had determined not to be controlled by a mistress, conceived the horrid idea of working on his weak intellect to induce him to separate from his wife." They convinced Watkins that Butler and the wife were having an affair. Once Watkins felt he had sufficient "proofs," he summoned Butler to his house and shot him in the presence of his wife.

Public opinion ran strongly against Watkins. "Even a Methodist clergyman of advanced age was heard to remark," Brackenridge commented, "that he ought to be hanged without judge or jury." Cooler heads prevailed, however, and Watkins was jailed to await trial. Judge Brackenridge especially pitied Watkins: "I can not but view the evil of passion with compassion; nothing but insanity or an intellect *extremely weak,* could prompt him to commit such an act. He acted perhaps excusably if not justifiably, upon *false* premises. To his imagination it was real, his *brain* was on fire, from a belief that he was assailed by a villain in the most delicate point, and under the delirium even a stronger one would not act wisely or calmly. But it is a subject upon which persons will think differently, and the whole affair is too sad to dwell upon."[28]

Watkins's wealth afforded him outstanding legal counsel: territorial delegate Joseph M. White and Georgia's John Berrien. Still, he was convicted and sentenced to hang. Thereupon, his lawyers employed an artful series of legal maneuvers that ended in the prisoner's release on a legal technicality.[29]

Within the context of Florida and Southern culture, a woman who dishonored her family by committing adultery faced violent reprisal from her male family members. A case in point involved Thomas King, his three sons, and an aggrieved son-in-law. The men crossed the St. Marys River into Georgia in February 1835 and descended on the Caseys, whose son had eloped with King's daughter, already a married woman. The attackers were armed with dirks and, according to reports, "had the original design of taking the blood of a daughter" and her lover. Instead, they killed two and severely wounded three inhabitants of the house. After the seduction two weeks earlier, King and the others had sworn to kill both the seducer and the woman. The mother of the adulteress, no less vehement, visited the Casey household the day after the massacre and viewed the victims. The woman vowed that she "should be satisfied, if she could but wash her hands in her daughter's heart blood."[30]

If conflict festered within antebellum marital life, it also brought some brothers to battle. In 1850 David Scott shot his brother Aaron with a double-barreled shotgun in Monticello as they and two other brothers, Mitchell and Nathaniel, were "standing in the front yard" talking. Mitchell later testified that as David held a gun in his hand, "Aaron in a playful manner caught David by the suspenders and pulled him about the yard and David told him to let go which he did giving him a push . . . at which time David jumped back, cocked his gun and shot him." David soon mounted a horse and rode off, but Nathaniel pursued and overtook him. The trapped man jumped off his horse, "pointed the gun" at Nathaniel, and invited his brother to "come on as he was ready for him." Nathaniel, not willing to be his next victim, turned back to the house. Other accounts suggested pent-up emotions between rivals. The root cause of the tragedy, a lifetime of taunts, fraternal ridicule, and humiliation, ended with a deadly resolution.[31]

A husband who lived with his wife's family sometimes found life unbearable. Notwithstanding the presence of a stereotypical nagging mother-in-law, the son-in-law usually directed his pent-up aggression against his wife's father. In February 1858 Hillsborough County residents William Rushing, his son, and son-in-law Richard Vickers went to Ichepuckesassa (Plant City) to do their monthly purchasing. Their business completed, father and son wanted to return home, but Vickers was not ready. After a few "sharp words," they left him at the store. The son-in-law finally rejoined the Rushings on the road home. When he saw Vickers, "the younger Rushing remarked 'you must have rode slow; we waited for you several times.' " An account added, "When the old man asked an explanation for his conduct, insulting monosyllables were the only response. The old man approached Mr. V who was on horseback, stating that 'he could stand it no longer.' " As he finished the sentence, Vickers stabbed his father-in-law several times with a large knife. The two had probably exchanged blows before because the son did not become alarmed at the sight of physical force—that is, until he "discover[ed] the knife" and saw his "father lay[ing] before him—a corpse." The son brought the rest of the family to the scene, and Vickers "assisted in carrying the body . . . to the house." Though behaving sullenly and showing little remorse, he promised to surrender himself to the sheriff in Tampa. Nevertheless, after remaining at the house for two days, "he absconded."[32]

In 1859 a similar murder occurred in the same county when George M. Buckley killed his father-in-law, George M. Goodwin, with a gun.[33] The exact cause and manner of the killing are unknown, but Buckley had "for some time previous to the murder, entertained hostile feelings to the deceased, and threatened to kill him on one or two occasions." Judge James King's lengthy death sentence clarified the severity of the offense:

> Your crime is greatly augmented by the relation in which you stand to the deceased. He was the father of your wife, and to him you owed reverence and protection. You have deprived your mother-in-law of her husband, and caused her to be left in her old age, poor and helpless. You will soon make another widow—your own wife, whom you have but recently vowed to love and cherish—and leave her poor and desolate. A fearful weight of crime, legal and moral, is thus heaped upon you, and you must soon answer at a bar that punishes offenses both against the laws of God and man.[34]

Deadly conflict also occurred among in-laws. Brothers-in-law were the most likely to engage in such physical encounters. For example, in Marianna, not long before George Buckley killed his father-in-law, John Sharp warned Maurice Simms, his brother-in-law, to stop intruding upon his family's affairs. In a rage, as Sharp's wife testified, Simms told his enemy in-law that "he might consider himself a dead man." When Sharp reached for his revolver, Simms shot him with a rifle. As Sharp slumped to the floor, Simms, still choked with rage, uttered, "God Damn him, if he is not dead, let me get my axe, and cut his head off." A similar encounter occurred in

1856 at the Madison County courthouse. A heated argument led to a shoot-out between Joseph Morris and George Dixon. When the firing ended both brothers-in-law lay dead.[35]

Most families may not have experienced the kind of domestic violence discussed in this chapter, nor did most family members resort to thoughtless violence against one another. Yet as a major institution in Florida's antebellum social life, the family sometimes functioned in a violent, uncertain environment. Although women played a key solidifying role in families, the idealized view of the sheltered female was in fact not true. Few women could be certain of escaping violence, and, in Florida, women both were victimized by and instigators of violence.

Seven

Crime against Property

According to their morality, cowstealing is the greatest crime.
—Achille Murat, *A Moral and Political Sketch of the United States of North America* (1833)

In early January 1828 Pensacola authorities executed a search warrant at a local boardinghouse. As expected, they found a pocketbook containing $115, a writing desk, numerous articles of clothing, and a number of other items reported missing over the previous several weeks. Enoch Hoye, already suspected of larceny, was arrested. During the following court term, a jury convicted Hoye of larceny and sentenced him to pay a $50 fine, stand at the pillory for two hours, and receive ten more "stripes" than the law allowed—a total of forty-nine lashes—on the "bareback *well* put on."[1] Hoye's punishment is not interesting because it was unusual. On the contrary, it is noteworthy because it was typical.

Persons caught stealing in antebellum Florida could expect to be treated severely, which in most cases meant corporal punishment. The most hated lawbreaker among Florida frontiersmen was not the perpetrator of violent assaults but the larcenist or the burglar. The record of punishments for those convicted of crimes against property confirms that thieves were the most despised of all Florida lawbreakers. Convicted burglars or larcenists could expect to be whipped or to be shamed by being put on the pillory. Arson and slave stealing were even more serious; both carried the death penalty. Stripes, the pillory, or branding with the letters "SS" could be prescribed by juries in lieu of death.

Larceny, Burglary, and Robbery

Larceny and burglary were crimes of stealth, while robbery, at least by modern definition, involves the use or threat of force. Curiously, Florida law did not distinguish between punishment for burglary, larceny, robbery, and assault with intent to rob. At the jury's discretion, each offense carried one or a combination of the following: one hour on the pillory, a fine not exceeding $1,000, or up to thirty-nine stripes.[2] Burglars and larcenists were usually transients. Often suspected of pilfering as a livelihood, thieves dealt in stolen property and encouraged slaves to steal in exchange for liquor. Public safety demanded that such violators be dealt with severely. The goal was to force them to leave the area, but not before authorities administered a suitable corporal punishment—whipping or the pillory.

In most cases a fine was an ineffective punishment against a criminal element who stole because it possessed no money. Certainly, juries assessed fines when there was money to collect, but the most likely punishment (the whip, the pillory, or a combination of both) reflected society's attitudes toward thieves. Crime against property carried a stigma that branded violators as the most condemned of all legal offenders. Historians of Southern criminal behavior have noted that the Southern honor code placed a premium on personal honesty and frowned severely on thievery.[3] The threat of social ostracism and moral condemnation, coupled with the relative severity of punishment, was a strong deterrent against thievery. It has already been noted that larcenists, if convicted, faced the probability of stiff corporal punishment. But the odious label "hog thief" was also a deterrent. Most persons living on the Florida frontier were poor and had few personal possessions, so pilfered items could be easily traced to the thief in small, personalized communities. Transients were closely monitored, and newcomers possessing telltale marks of the whip or brand fell under close scrutiny.

Though prosecutors had a difficult time convicting persons charged with crimes against property (only 89 of 550 whites were convicted), those who were, as a rule, faced harsh corporal punishment. In Escambia County, for example, prosecutors succeeded in convicting only twenty-one out of eighty-seven accused larcenists, but of that number, fifteen received stripes or the pillory. This experience was duplicated in other counties. Monroe County prosecuted thirty-eight of its inhabitants for larceny but found only seven guilty, of whom only four received stripes or the pillory. Jackson County convicted seven of forty-one and punished six of the seven with stripes or the pillory. But what stands out most of all in these numbers is the poor conviction rates for larceny. Totals in ten counties—Leon, Jefferson, Putnam, Marion, Madison, Gadsden, Hamilton, Hillsborough, St. Johns, and Alachua—reveal that of 207 indictments of whites for larceny only 27 were convicted.

Habitual thieves often perplexed local officials. That authorities did not know how to handle repeat offenders is demonstrated by the case of Benjamin Oglesby, who was convicted and punished several times for petty larceny in Holmes County. Just after the Civil War's outbreak, Solicitor

William D. Barnes notified Gov. John Milton that Oglesby had been in jail nearly a year in default of a fine assessed against him. "He is hopelessly insolvent," Barnes wrote the governor, "and his confinement has been sufficient punishment. He is anxious to be discharged, that he may enter the service, having promised faithfully to do so." Oglesby planned to join a local unit preparing to leave, but the governor's pardon would be necessary. Barnes highly recommended Oglesby as a proper subject for forgiveness, especially since he was a "large able bodied man, and will make a good soldier, if he can be broken of stealing." Besides, asserted Barnes, "should the Federalists ever take him prisoner, he is the best man I know to break their concern, by stealing it out." Milton acquiesced and pardoned Oglesby.[4]

As this example shows, public officials often expressed a frustration with thieves that is almost comical in retrospect. The same was also true of newspaper editors. On April 15, 1829, for example, the *St. Augustine Florida Herald* recounted the escapades of one Thomas Jones, a man convicted of stealing a horse in Duval County. Jones received thirty-nine lashes, was extradited to Alachua County on another charge, "broke jail, and stole another horse . . . and has not been since heard from. So much for that!!!" exclaimed the editor.

Horse thieves were among the most hated of all robbers. Horses were easily marketable, and they certainly were mobile. Thieves could steal a mount and disappear. Even though the crime was not a capital offense in Florida as it was in many older states, apprehended thieves could expect to be punished severely. For example, John Thompson, convicted of this crime in 1829 in the Alachua County Superior Court, was given thirty stripes.[5] On the other hand, horse thieves were rarely apprehended, and most were able to convert their ill-gotten gains into cash before they were detected. Some even used false letters of introduction to obtain horses. In 1839 two such men calling themselves Alexander Towns and Abner Townsend used the confusion of the Second Seminole War to "borrow" a number of horses from farmers in Madison County. John Miller offered a $100 reward for Townsend in which he noted that the thief had shown him a "recommendation from Samuel Gillison Esq. of Beaufort District, South Carolina, which is no doubt a forgery." Miller was prepared to go as far as Mississippi to reclaim the thief or the horse.[6]

Since horse stealing was viewed as an important threat to societal order, its victims were often as concerned with capturing the thief as with recovering their horse. Rewards for capture of the thief usually equaled or exceeded those offered for the stolen property. In 1837 Tallahassee planter A. M. Gatlin offered $10 for the recovery of a stolen horse but $20 for the thief if convicted. Similarly, Henry Penny from Holmes Valley, Washington County, announced in 1834 that he suspected John Owens and Anthony Burr of stealing two of his horses. The reward specified was $50 for the thieves and $20 for the horses.[7]

Thieves preying on towns or communities usually worked alone or in pairs, and experienced larcenists used well-adapted tools and equipment. In 1842 "some villain or villains . . . armed with a large auger and chisel" attempted to enter Judge Benjamin Putnam's residence in St. Augustine. They "attacked the door and window but finally desisted." A month later the same pair failed again when they tried to break into a store owned by C. Boye. They used an auger to penetrate the weather boarding, but the "store being lined with thick yellow pine boards, they were finally thwarted in their design." The "rogues" who entered P. Bauton's dwelling in St. Augustine the previous year were "prepared with materials—they lit a candle on the mantle piece and commenced their plunder." They made off with a gold watch, a pair of diamond earrings, three pairs of pearl earrings, a gold chain, and a diamond breast pin.[8]

The list of similar incidents is long. For example, in 1860 robbers used a "couple of chisels" to pry open the back door of the Monticello post office. The culprits lit a candle and packed up "at least a bushel" of letters and left the two chisels behind. The next day a drugstore was broken open. A decade earlier in Pensacola thieves had used a "two and a half inch auger" to pry open the door of C. P. Knapp's store. They stole $200 but failed in their attempted robbery of Patterson's and Avery's store next door. In 1848 Birchett and Lindenberger's Tallahassee dry goods store also was victimized. To facilitate their entry, the thieves broke open a blacksmith shop next door, where they "procured sundry tools, a bar of iron, . . . and couple of old axes."[9]

Burglars mostly sought money, but they also stole trunks, jewelry, tools, clothing, and other items of value. When, for instance, one or more thieves entered a store in St. Augustine's North City during 1841, they took "groceries and provisions" amounting to $200. Clothing was also a popularly pilfered item. In May 1851 John Anderson of Tallahassee announced that a thief had stolen his "pantaloons and coat."[10] In 1828 Othello Jackson, a performer in the Pensacola theater, was robbed of his clothing and money. Jackson made a unique appeal for justice. He took out an advertisement in the *Pensacola Gazette* claiming that he did not wish to avenge the thief. Instead, he wanted "a favorable expression of public opinion" at his final performance, where he would perform his "usual feats of agility on the violin."[11]

Tools likewise were stolen. August Riebald, a German workman employed in Tallahassee, reported in 1844 the theft of his tool chest. His reward notice explained that the chest was of "German construction and contained many tools not usually found in this country." Even articles not easily transportable were taken. One night in 1841 "a fellow entered a window of the [St. Augustine] City Hotel and walked off with a bed." Five years earlier, when thieves entered T. D. Harlock's residence near Tallahassee, his bedroom also was the focus of their plunder. They made away with his large feather bed, nightclothes, and several other garments.[12]

Jewelry stores were special targets for thieves. One evening in 1846 Pensacola jeweler Peter Knowles was coming home from an evening at the tenpin alley, when he discovered that the door to his store was missing its lock. As Knowles went inside, a man concealed behind the counter bolted out the door. Knowles chased the thief down the street and cornered him. A fight ensued, and the thief, armed with an oyster knife, managed to break away, but a group of citizens captured him about ten miles west of town. The perpetrator, soon identified as George Walton, was convicted of larceny and sentenced to receive thirty-nine lashes.[13] The quarters of military personnel were also violated from time to time. In 1828 at Pensacola, "some consummate villain . . . with remarkably large feet" entered the hospital at the Cantonment Clinch and carried off a portable writing desk, a gold watch, and some soldier's clothing."[14]

Some robberies resembled modern-day muggings. In 1837 Henry Summer, a Charleston lawyer visiting St. Augustine, recorded that Robert Bassacre approached a South Carolina soldier, presented a pistol, drew a sword, and told him to surrender his money or be killed. Bassacre took the cash and fled but was captured. The soldier's comrades tarred and feathered Bassacre and shaved his head. Later, the robber received fifteen lashes for his crime, but that did not deter his criminal behavior. Bassacre even robbed a man who took pity on him after his tarring and feathering. Later he did the same to a drunken man. "Unless his course is checked," recorded Summer, "he will become a hardened wretch who will be stupendous in crime."[15]

Florida was largely free of bank robberies. In an area with few large towns, there were few banks, and most financial institutions that did exist were on such shaky footing that thieves could expect to find little specie. Even if robbers succeeded in breaking into the vault, banknotes could be traced easily and were so devalued that stealing them usually was worth neither the risk nor the effort. Nevertheless, in April 1844 a Tallahassee newspaper reported that "one of the most daring and outrageous attempts to commit robbery that has ever occurred in our city" had been perpetrated. "The door of the new banking house occupied by the Bank of Florida was forced open and the bank entered." The robbers, who failed to open the vault, were never identified. The ultimate disposition of the Bank of Florida's assets suggests that depositors had more to fear from bank directors than from thieves. Only a month after the botched robbery attempt, bank president James Graham absconded to New York with what remained of its specie.[16]

Some towns were plagued by gangs of skilled burglars. Tampa suffered this fate in 1858. "Our City," reported the local *Florida Peninsular,* "is now infested with light fingered individuals who are making nightly demonstrations." During the week thieves had robbed three stores and broken into the post office.[17] St. Augustine experienced its own epidemic of burglaries in 1843. On March 25 the *St. Augustine News* noted that there "are evidently a gang of vagabonds about this city." Many establishments had been robbed. A week earlier thieves had removed the door panel of the post office. Once inside they struck a light and broke open the drawers and letter cases in search of money.[18] In February the same gang of "audacious burglars" had entered a widow's house, stolen money, and destroyed bedding and clothing. The woman discovered them and ran to neighbors for help, and one of the rogues "stood at a distance, laughing, and jeering at her in the street." The mayor offered $100 reward for the gang, but they apparently escaped apprehension. In an incident perhaps related, the town council room was broken into several months later and "some evil-disposed person or persons [stole a] case containing books and papers of great value to the [city's] archives."[19]

Jacksonville likewise was a gang target. On December 24, 1852, its *Florida News* warned that "every good citizen ought to be alert to detect and punish the thieves who are now prowling about our town." During the following August the same journal announced that the town still was being treated to "midnight plunderings." In the two preceding weeks, a jewelry store had been robbed, a residence broken into, a safe in James Livingston's store blown open, and a man's pocket picked of about $150.[20]

In 1853 a theft ring headed by Samuel Piper plagued Pensacola. Its first target was a British ship lying at harbor, from which they made off with more than $1,000 in silver. On February 17, Piper's gang broke into Davis and Cox's store, burst open an iron chest with a charge of gunpowder, and carried away about $1,600 worth of gold. Though jailed temporarily, Piper and several others in his gang escaped. A week after Piper and company left the jail, the gang was suspected in the "daring Robbery of Mr. Avery's store," during which more than $100 in gold was stolen. An even greater loss was averted as "the rascals appear to have become alarmed, for they left a large bundle of sundries they had collected and tied up." Authorities also found the safe overturned and an undetonated powder canister by its side.[21]

When threatened with burglaries, citizens, prompted either by local officials or a sense of self-preservation, regularly mobilized themselves. Some communities went further than just to capture or expel thieves; many sought to punish them as well. Lake City's Washington Ives recorded in 1860 that "two burglars had broken into Mr. Daly's Store, [and] bursted open his safe by putting gunpowder underneath." The burglars then proceeded to Clement's grocery store, where they "ate some pies and oranges, took some candles, and left before they were discovered." The next day the citizens met in Ives's father's law office to "adopt means to catch the men who broke into the stores." Sheriff Thomas Mickler subsequently organized a posse to pursue them to Jacksonville, and two suspects were caught at Sanderson. The thieves confessed, and a Lake City judge sentenced each of them to thirty-nine lashes. They suffered their punishment on the public square on November 8, and Ives recalled that he "would not go to see them, but have heard they were badly cut up. I could hear every stripe, about 100 yards off." Six days later the culprits were released from jail and forced to leave town. "Sheriff Mickler and some of our citizens," remembered Ives, "made up enough to pay their expenses to Jacksonville."[22]

Often citizens went to great lengths to capture robbers. In spring 1858 a party of Tampans traveled more than 150 miles over a three-week period in pursuit of two men, Locke and Sheldon. The hunted men were accused of robbing a jewelry store and stealing several horses. The party tracked the fugitives to a hideout on the Suwannee River, captured Locke, and recovered the jewelry. Sheldon had already left with the horses. "The pursuing party [then] divided," according to a contemporary account, "some of them going in pursuit of the other thief, the others starting for this place with Locke." Those proceeding further traced Sheldon to the Sixty Mile Railroad Station near Jasper, where the robber made a determined resistance and was severely wounded. Both prisoners disappeared on their way back to Tampa. "It is whispered . . . by knowing ones," related the account, that they "will *never steal again!*"[23]

Although mail robbery was a federal offense, the U.S. mail carrier was an inviting target. It was common practice to enclose banknotes inside letters, and post offices were subject to burglary just as were other establishments where valuables were kept. Armed gangs also preyed on lone mail-riders and on stagecoaches carrying the mail.

The greatest threat to mail security sometimes proved to be the postal carrier. In 1843, for instance, authorities arrested Morris Everett, the carrier between Alligator (Lake City) and Jacksonville, for mail robbery and forgery. Reportedly, the incident was only one of "a series of crimes of like character of which the individual is suspected."[24] In 1860 mail service irregularities in East Florida led postal authorities to send special agent George Center to investigate. Center followed a number of clues to Micanopy and laid a trap for the mail rider. When nineteen-year-old Deputy Postmaster E. P. Jordan rode out from town for some distance, he was stopped and searched. Center "opened the bags and found that the letters which had been put in for decoys had [had] the monies extracted." Jordan was arrested, and the evidence eventually obtained suggested that "this thing . . . has been carried on for some time."[25]

Robbers occasionally used force to break into post offices. On October 28, 1850, Gov. Thomas Brown issued a proclamation for the arrest of Ozias Thigpen, who had held up the Ocala post office.[26] Ten years later, the Econfina post office was robbed of two gold watches and $100 in cash.[27]

Mail stages, their drivers, and cargo often were at risk when traveling over virtually uninhabited stretches of frontier. One incident occurred in the Pensacola area in 1845. While drinking at Pons's grogshop, two soldiers, S. P. Fletcher and Thomas Carrol, hatched a plot to rob the mail stage after Fletcher informed Carrol that a Spaniard would be carrying $10,000 in gold on the stage arriving that evening. The plan was to "lay in the woods" and ambush the stage at some propitious place. Carrol became frightened, however, and exposed the plot. Fletcher then was arrested on charges of conspiracy to rob the mail.[28] A similar incident was reported in 1828. Martin Hutto and an accomplice attacked Thomas Jones, who was carrying the Tallahassee mail on the road between Alaqua and Pensacola. Pensacola Postmaster William H. Hunt, who also edited the *Pensacola Gazette,* reported that one attacker shot at Jones and the other attempted to stab him with a "large Spanish dirk knife." Miraculously, Jones managed to escape with the mail. Hunt used the incident to remind mail carriers that they should always be well armed and able to protect the mail in case of attack.[29]

Arson

On June 19, 1858, Tampa's *Florida Peninsular* reported that Hance Wyatt's Bradenton home had burned. The editor announced that there was little doubt that Wyatt had been victimized by arsonists. "Suspicion strongly rests upon three brothers, named Oglesby," reported the newspaper, "whose disgraceful conduct compelled their neighbors to advise them to leave the county. These vagabonds . . . have lived upon their villainies for the last two or three years." If, as suspected, the incident was an act of retribution, the editor believed that retaliation should be harsh and swift. "We unhesitatingly suggest," he wrote, "the use of *hemp* in their case."

Because it threatened lives as well as property, arson was by far the most feared property crime. Contemporary observers understood, as historians have asserted, that arson often served as a hidden means of revenge for those powerless to effect open retribution of wrongs. Arson thus was the appropriate remedy for those least powerful; that is, it constituted a hidden method of expressing outrage either against shoddy treatment by "betters" or, on the part of blacks, against the conditions of their enslavement. It was, as Bertram Wyatt-Brown has noted, "a gesture of despair and nihilism."[30]

Besides being a handy method of retribution or revenge, arson also was a convenient method to expunge records and to express disapproval of a "courthouse clique." Whenever courthouses burned, and they often did, incendiaries were suspected. For that matter, only rarely did any fire break out without someone suggesting that it was the work of an incendiary. Slaves often were suspected, but so were recalcitrant whites—especially those who had been shamed or publicly humiliated. Arson thus was a way to "get even." Few methods were as swift, certain, and difficult to detect.

The Criminal Code of 1832 dictated that any person convicted of arson would suffer death.[31] But no Floridian, black or white, was legally executed for the crime. The general assembly in 1847 recognized the problems of obtaining convictions and gave juries far more flexibility by providing graded punishments of $1,000 to $5,000 and six months to five years in jail for those convicted of firing courthouses, jails, or other buildings other than dwelling houses.[32] A number of suspected arsonists were prosecuted, but the nature of the crime made it difficult, if not impossible, to convict arsonists in a court of law. Available court records show that a total of twenty-one Floridians (twelve whites and nine blacks) were prosecuted for arson. Of that total only five (four whites and one black) were convicted.

The difficulty of conviction did not imply a lack of arson. Few Florida communities escaped the crime's effects, beginning in the territory's earliest years. In 1825, for instance, Pensacola Mayor John Jerrison proclaimed that two fires had broken out under suspicious circumstances. "It is of the utmost importance, if evil disposed persons are lurking about this city," he asserted, "that they should be brought to justice."[33] In 1841 authorities again suspected that arsonists were lurking in the city. In February two attempts to fire the city had been detected. "Something must be done, and done immediately to protect our city . . . against the hellish designs of the incendiary," declared a local editor. City authorities organized patrols to counter the threat, but one year later several dwellings on one of Pensacola's important thoroughfares were in ashes. The blaze started in Antoine Collins's hotel and eventually consumed the "whole of Indendena street on both sides."[34]

Of all Florida communities, Jacksonville proved the most combustible. In 1854 its business district, including more than seventy structures, was consumed.[35] The disaster was accidental, but three years later, after it became clear that arsonists were at work in the city, Jacksonville's *Florida News* insisted that this "gang of rascals, who through malice, rebelliousness, or revenge, light the midnight torch . . . not only destroy property but aim at life." Its editor concluded, "There is only one remedy to put a stop to it—and that is a gallows where the hellish devils should be made to swing at rope's end."[36] Local fear of arson already had been heightened for years. In 1852 a vigilance committee cornered Samuel Gibson, an arson suspect who had returned to town after a two-year absence. Attempting to escape, the man fled to the roof of his home and threatened to shoot at the crowd with his revolver. Instead, someone from the crowd fired on him, and he was induced to give himself up. Gibson was thereupon lodged in jail "to await the first means of transportation from the limits of the state."[37]

From 1842 to 1844 Apalachicola was subjected to a veritable plague of arson. The train of events began in April 1842 when a fire broke out on Commerce Street, and incendiaries were believed responsible. Several months later, another disaster was averted when a carefully prepared bundle of fire was discovered on the roof of a house. Fortunately "it would not take," and the city guard was alerted to be on the lookout for "incendiary scoundrels."[38] The scoundrels appeared again in 1844. In June Judge George S. Hawkins's new house went up in flames. "It is presumed," noted the *Apalachicola Commercial Advertiser* on June 22, "that it was set fire by some of the scoundrels who escaped justice at our last court term." Finally, on August 19, 1844, the same journal reported that another "Alarming Fire" consumed six houses. The circumstances left little doubt that the blazes were the "work of some fiendish incendiary."

In 1849 the Gadsden County courthouse went up in flames "on the evening before the commencement of the circuit court." A local man recorded, "No doubt is entertained but that it was the work of an incendiary." Similar suspicions followed the burnings of the Columbia, Jackson, and Monroe County courthouses.[39]

Historians have noted that arson was a risky but effective vehicle of expressing dissatisfaction.[40] Whenever structures burned, slaves accordingly were suspected. In 1849, for example, when fire consumed the Presbyterian church in Quincy, a slave belonging to William Forbes was accused of the crime. A correspondent of a local newspaper reported that the bondsman had torched the church as an act of revenge against his master, "a devoted member of the Church, by whose liberality the edifice had, in great part, been erected."[41]

Whether or not the paucity of indictments and convictions (one of nine) means that Floridians had more effective means than the courts in dealing with slaves accused of arson is difficult to determine. But the case of Rachel, a slave belonging to James Baker of Pensacola, indicated that if slaves were convicted of arson, they could expect to suffer harsh penalties. In 1849 Rachel was indicted in Escambia County for "attempting to set fire to . . . and burn a certain dwelling house of Matilda Jordan." A jury found her guilty, and she was sentenced to "receive 39 lashes, and have her ears nailed to a post for one hour."[42]

The most controversial case involving slave arson was that of Simon, who was accused of firing three Pensacola dwellings in 1853. Once he was suspected, an angry mob apprehended him and extracted a confession. The slave only narrowly escaped lynching. Simon was subsequently tried and convicted, but judgment was suspended and the case was taken up by the Supreme Court of Florida on a writ of error. The slave's counsel contended that Simon's confession was made under duress. The court reversed the judgment and ordered a new trial on the basis that the lower court did not allow the jury to consider whether the confession was voluntary. But Simon never stepped foot in court again. A lynch mob ended his life before he could be retried.[43]

Slave Stealing

On June 22, 1822, Gov. Thomas Bennet of South Carolina issued a proclamation that foretold important implications for Floridians. The governor called for the capture of James T. Williams, who had just escaped authorities in Edgefield District and was one of an extensive and lawless gang of slave stealers "infesting this and the states of Alabama, Tennessee, Georgia, and the Territory of Florida." Bennet indicated that Williams would attempt to join confederates in Georgia and perhaps make his way to Florida.[44] For the next forty years, slave stealing remained a critical concern for Floridians. Until the end of the Civil War, legislators passed laws against it, and residents—to a large extent—ordered their lives around the protection of their slave population. Persons who stole or enticed away slaves either for humanitarian reasons or for personal gain were dealt with severely, either legally or extralegally.

The 1832 criminal code provided that persons convicted of slave stealing or enticing a slave to run away were to be fined up to $1,000, placed for one hour on the pillory, jailed for six months, and branded with the letters "SS," at the discretion of the jury. In 1845, perhaps influenced by the celebrated Jonathan Walker case in Pensacola, in which Walker, an abolitionist, was apprehended attempting to abscond with several slaves, the legislature made slave stealing a capital offense.[45] The crime was perhaps the most difficult of all crimes against property to prosecute because it usually required black testimony to convict whites; and black testimony against whites was inadmissible in Florida courts, as it was in almost all Southern states. Even so, several whites were convicted. The most celebrated and successful effort to prosecute slave stealing occurred in Gadsden County. In 1846 four members of the Holloman gang were hanged in Quincy for the crime.[46] Gov. Thomas Brown saw fit to save two men from the gallows. On April 26, 1852, Brown pardoned George Stahl, "provided that he leave the state of Florida Never to Return." More complicated was the case of Redding Evans, who pleaded guilty in Jefferson County. Evans's conviction carried the maximum sentence, but Brown granted him executive clemency because of "special circumstances of the case." Trial testimony revealed that Evans "stole" Rose, a slave in the temporary custody of a man who was sexually abusing her.[47]

When slaves disappeared, planters often suspected whites, free blacks, or even abolitionists of stealing or enticing them away. For example, in 1839 John Neal offered a $250 reward for the capture of a family of six slaves who escaped from his plantation near Monticello. The absence most dearly felt was that of George, the father and husband of the party, since he "has always had charge of his master's affairs, is rather an intelligent fellow, can read and most probably write." Neal suspected that George "was backed by some white man, who will try to carry the Negroes out of the country."[48]

Runaways from the lower counties of Alabama often made their way to Pensacola. James De Jarnett of Autauga County, Alabama, offered a $1,000 reward in 1838 for Celia and a Yankee merchant named Coolidge whom he accused of stealing her. De Jarnett speculated that Coolidge stole Celia to "answer the place of a wife" and that the two would attempt to disguise themselves and pass under fictitious names. In a similar case, John Bolling of Greenville, Alabama, appealed for the capture of John Raburn and three slaves he stole. In 1838 a planter near Montgomery reported that three of his slaves had been stolen. Virgil, the leader of the party, was a "notorious runaway and a villain. He has always aimed for Pensacola on his runaway trips, and once succeeded in getting to that place."[49]

Free blacks sometimes stole slaves or enticed them into running away. White Floridians deemed the mere presence of free blacks a threat to their slave population; the image of blacks living in freedom, they thought, was too great an inducement to slaves who yearned for a change in their own condition. The Adams-Onis Treaty (1821) granted freedom to free blacks who remained in Florida after the transfer of flags, but it was a freedom circumscribed by statute. Most of the free blacks lived, however, in Pensacola, St. Augustine, and scattered sections of East Florida where special ordinances and a system of "salutary neglect" gave them more rights and privileges than in other locales. Even so, many whites viewed them as social outcasts, and attempts occasionally were made to eject them from the state or territory. If free blacks were convicted of a crime and unable to pay the fine, a statute passed in 1832 provided that they could be sold into either temporary or permanent slavery.[50]

Whites habitually suspected free blacks of either harboring runaways or contributing to the debasement of the master-slave relationship. In 1858, for example, the Duval County Grand Jury asserted that free blacks in Jacksonville "living in the midst of the slave population produced a general laxity and immorality. . . . We are well assured also that they have made combinations and frequently induced insubordination among slaves. This class can not be too strongly under the strict surveillance."[51] More than two decades earlier, the jury's Monroe County counterpart had expressed similar fear. Emancipated slaves flowing into Key West from the British West Indies, its members contended, were perhaps the tools of "fanatics and abolitionists . . . [who were] attempt[ing] by and through the agency of free persons of color, to tamper with and corrupt our slave population."[52]

Fears of slave alienation by free blacks prompted continuing calls for tighter laws. On October 5, 1830, the editor of the *Tallahassee Floridian and Advocate* typically called for closer regulation of economic activities of the capital city's slave and free black population. According to the editor, this would ensure greater "self protection and security . . . at a time when fanaticism, or mistaken philanthropy leads many in the Northern or middle states, to interfere in the condition of a large portion of the population in this section of the Union." In 1852 the Jefferson County Grand Jury noted that the practice of allowing "several negro drivers to attend single teams hauling cotton to market towns is doing much mischief." Runaways were being carried off; in addition, the practice "offered inducements to refractory slaves to leave their masters."[53]

Although rumors continuously circulated of abolitionists absconding with slaves, the reality was otherwise. Accordingly, few successful prosecutions were conducted. In 1852 a Tallahassee newspaper reached into Georgia to find a successful prosecution of an "abolitionist emissary" in Thomasville. To the editor's glee, the culprit was convicted of enticing slaves to run away and was sentenced to four years in the penitentiary.[54] Despite the paucity of abolitionist prosecutions, boats loading cotton and bringing in supplies in Middle Florida ports on Apalachee Bay were always closely monitored. Especially targeted were vessels either arriving from or departing to Northern ports. Concerned citizens felt that these vessels might either be used to spirit runaways to freedom or contain crew members with abolitionist tendencies. One letter published in 1840 claimed that abolitionists commonly entered Florida ports under the guise of commerce to spread abolitionist tracts among free blacks and other blacks with whom they came into contact. "They are bribed to the work, and furnished with incendiary tracts, artfully contrived for the furtherance of their hellish purposes," its author asserted. "These are read and expatiated upon in secret assemblages of slaves."[55]

Free blacks serving as crew members on Northern commercial vessels often shipped into Florida. Once in port they could not help but come into contact with slaves. Even if they did not intend to facilitate escapes, casual acquaintances with slaves could create circumstances that could lead to this result. In 1849 Ambrose Taylor, a free black from Pennsylvania employed as a cook on board the brig *Ocilla* tied at anchor in St. Marks, found himself involved in a legal battle that threatened to strip him of his own freedom. Just as the boat was about to depart for New York, two runaways were discovered secreted among the cotton. After a thorough examination, both confessed that Taylor had enticed them on board. Wakulla County authorities took Taylor into custody and lodged him in the Leon County jail to await trial. The *Wakulla Times* used Taylor's prosecution to demand a firmer "enforcement of our free Negro laws." Taylor, declared the *Times*, was not really a thief in the true sense of the word, but a "poor simple instrument in the hands of *white* Northern fanatics, whose *black hearts* concoct what they dare not execute." Taylor's guilt or innocence is unknown, but his case provided journalists with the opportunity to rail against the evil designs of abolitionists.[56]

Even when circumstantial evidence existed against whites accused of enticing or stealing, it was difficult to secure convictions because often the only witnesses against them were the slaves themselves. In St. Marks, for example, a runaway detected on board the schooner *William Pettis* confessed that he had been hidden there by two brothers named Jones who promised to take him to New Orleans. On the strength of an affidavit sworn to by the captain of the vessel, the two were lodged in jail, but the grand jury decided not to indict since the slave's testimony was all that was available.[57] A similar case in Newport found four crew members of the brig *Catherine Mary* of Boston being taken into custody on a charge of burglary and disorderly conduct. One of the party, mistaking the cause of their detention, panicked and admitted secreting a runaway on board the ship. After a thorough search, however, the slave was not apprehended.[58]

Complicated rules and procedures regulated the movement of slaves between states. Slave traders always risked detention if they could not prove they were conducting business legally, and whites traveling with gangs of slaves were often suspected of stealing. Law officers vigilantly watched for suspicious characters traveling with slaves, and suspects were sometimes jailed until they could prove they were operating legally. In 1846, for example, authorities in Jackson County committed Dempsey Tidwell and six blacks in his possession to jail. Circumstances surrounding Tidwell's seizure indicated that the slaves had been stolen from nearby plantations in Florida and Georgia. Jackson County Sheriff Sam Stephens published the description of the slaves and asked their owners to come forward, pay charges, and take them away.[59]

On occasion, individuals legally engaged in transporting slaves were detained. On October 5, 1847, an outraged Hamilton County resident published a formal complaint in the *Tallahassee Florida Sentinel*. Joel Redding of Jasper charged that he was wrongly imprisoned in the Leon County jail for slave stealing. He declared the incident "disgraceful, . . . and highly injurious to my character." Leon County authorities had taken Redding into custody when one of the bondsmen he was transporting accused him of stealing slaves.

Even in questionable cases, however, some suspects were cleared. When Morton Davis, an absconding larcenist, was captured after making off with a horse and buggy, he faced a much more serious charge when the slave of a local planter was found in his company. Davis was prosecuted in Jackson County on a charge of larceny and slave stealing. In the tense trial that followed, the jury, after being given a long charge by the judge as to exactly what constituted the capital offense of slave stealing, decided that the slave was not stolen but had merely hitched a ride to freedom. The jury found Davis guilty of larceny only and sentenced him to fifteen lashes.[60]

Among all lawbreakers in antebellum Florida, those who committed crimes against property—larceny, arson, and slave stealing—were the most despised. Judges and juries were reluctant to punish a man severely for breaking a law in defense of himself, his family, or his honor. That was not true of a man guilty of personal greed or the illegal acquisition of another person's property. Those guilty of the wanton destruction of property and those who secretly plotted to subject their fellows to a fiery death were deemed proper subjects for the gallows. The same fate awaited those willing to imperil societal order by stealing slaves. Antebellum Floridians sought stability in their communities and did not tolerate thievery. Those who put the fraudulent acquisition of property above their concern for the safety of their community were dealt with harshly. Punishment was usually swift and severe. The use of stripes and the pillory—punishments fit only for slaves or others without honor—served notice to both the offender and the community that stealing broke both the moral and the legal code.

Eight

Crime against Public Order and Morality

> The laws against gaming are materially defective, and are easily evaded by those who are disposed to violate them. There is no class of offenders who ought to be so strictly watched as this order of men who break in upon the comfort and happiness of families.
>
> —Leon County Grand Jury Presentment (1828)

Throughout the antebellum decades, Florida lawmakers struggled to protect their society against various symptoms of sin and immorality; however, their efforts usually failed to stem the rising tide they feared. Laws enacted to enforce public order and morality reflected, at least in theory, the values of lawmakers and the constituents who elected them. But when it comes to legislative intent, the motives of legislators are exceedingly difficult to ascertain. Careful examination of the penal code offers some insight into societal values, but as Lawrence Friedman has written, too much dependence on statutory provisions can "trap us in a circle. . . . People often say one thing and do another; the laws against morality certainly represent values people think they *ought* to have, but not at all necessarily what they (secretly) think or want."[1]

Both the laws themselves and the degree to which they were enforced are important elements of the story. Court records show patterns of indictments and convictions. They also reflect tremendous variation from county to county. In some counties indictments for these types of crimes were almost nonexistent, while in other counties they tended to dominate the court's criminal affairs. More than any other type of crime, decisions about enforcement, prosecution, and even toleration of these offenses reflected the values of law enforcement officers, community leaders, and the public at large. Each county's experience was unique when it came to the prosecution of these types of crimes. There seemed to be no pattern from county to county. Diversity ruled.

Again, surviving court records offer numerous hints as to what society intended. For example, prosecutions for adultery and fornication (fifty-one) in Alachua County almost equaled prosecutions for assault and battery (fifty-two). In St. Johns (zero), Gadsden (zero), and Leon (thirteen) Counties, prosecutions for these offenses were almost nonexistent. Does this necessarily mean that residents of Alachua County were immoral and the others moral, or that violations of such laws were of common occurrence in Alachua County but unknown in the other counties? Hardly. On the contrary, it indicates that Alachua County's public officials made a conscious decision for rigid enforcement. These decisions reflected the temper of the community, its leaders, and its law enforcement officials.

Leslie A. Thompson, the state's early compiler of laws, organized crimes against public order and morality into several broad categories, including "Crimes against Religion, Chastity, Morality, and Decency"; "Offenses against the Public Peace"; "Offenses against Public Justice"; "Offenses against Trade, Public Highways, and Navigation"; and "Malicious and Fraudulent Mischief." "Offenses Relative to Slaves and Other Persons of Color" extended the regulatory effort beyond the white population. The strictures addressed subjects varying from adultery, fornication, lewdness, and incest, to gambling, carrying arms secretly, and aiding escape from jail.[2]

Crimes against public order and morality usually fall within our category of "victimless crimes," usually moral offenses committed by two or more consenting individuals. Normal methods of prosecution and detection often were thwarted in these cases because the injured party rarely complained or voluntarily came forward with information. Authorities themselves had to detect the crime and bring culprits to justice, a difficult task since much of this criminal activity functioned on an underground level.

The notion of "victimless crimes" would have been unintelligible to many antebellum Floridians, who were highly sensitive to the inherent danger of a moral breakdown within their communities. Thus polite society viewed the offenses as not merely crimes committed between consenting individuals but as symptoms of an acute social sickness that threatened the moral fiber of the entire community. They believed, as expressed by the "social organism" theory, that one diseased part threatened the entire body. There was a tendency in many frontier communities to be more interested in enforcing established norms of behavior than in creating an environment in which individuals determined for themselves what kind of lifestyle was best. As some historians have noted, maintaining public order was more important than respecting the individual rights of the accused.[3] Lawrence Friedman has written that freedom in the antebellum America did "not mean shaping your own way of life. . . . It was not a freedom to contrive a

Leslie A. Thompson was compiler of Florida's legislative statutes and author of *A Manual or Digest of the State Law of the State of Florida* (Tallahassee, 1848). (Courtesy of the Florida Supreme Court, Tallahassee, Florida)

life style; the body and mind still proceeded within narrow but invisible ruts."[4] The modern concept of "live and let live" would have been neither understood nor tolerated, especially in cases of sexual "misconduct." Statutes, accordingly, were carefully crafted to regulate and curtail the activity of what lawmakers believed was a crime-prone, wicked, and disreputable element.

The most commonly prosecuted crimes against morality were adultery and fornication. The precise legal distinction between these offenses is obscure. In modern parlance, adultery usually refers to a married person engaging in sex with someone other than his or her spouse. In the nineteenth-century vernacular, though, the meaning more closely reflected the biblical definition of adultery as any sexual activity outside marriage. The distinction between adultery and fornication is murkier still because culprits often were prosecuted under one or both offenses. The 1832 criminal code provided that, if any "man and woman shall live together in an open state of adultery or fornication," they would be subject to fines of from $500 to $800.[5] Most indictments were straightforward but included few details. That of Clement Moseley in 1861 was typical. That year the Clay County Grand Jury charged him with fornication and adultery, "the said Moseley being a married man and the said Lotty Register being then and there a woman."[6]

The goal of these statutes was not only to prevent sexual misconduct but also to admonish recalcitrant individuals to legalize illicit cohabitation by marrying. The law thus stipulated that "it shall at any time be in the power of the parties to prevent or suspend the prosecution by marriage legally solemnized."[7] In 1828, for example, Alachua County indictments against John Ivy and Elvina Crews were dropped once they proved to the satisfaction of the court that their marriage had been "legally solemnized."[8] Similarly, in 1851 Lewis Sparkman was released from custody "after it appeared to the court that the defendant had intermarried with the female with whom he is charged."[9]

Acts of "open lewdness," which statutes defined as "notorious public indecency tending to debauch the morals of society," also prompted criminal proscription. The exact nature of the crime could be, and probably was, interpreted widely. Sheriffs, grand juries, and judges could have determined a whole host of actions—from prostitution to profanity—as indictable offenses. Those convicted received up to a $100 fine, three months in jail, or thirty-nine lashes, at the discretion of the jury.[10]

Some historians have doubted the commitment of nineteenth-century Americans to the vigorous enforcement of laws dealing with sexual offenses, claiming that these laws were holdovers from America's colonial past.[11] The case in Florida is difficult to determine. What may have been at work is what some historians call the "Victorian Compromise." Essentially this meant tolerating some crimes, particularly sex crimes, as long as they did not get out of hand. The idea was not to decriminalize them or make them legal but to drive them underground, not prosecuting them unless they became "open," "notorious," or "flagrant." Thus a modicum of moral crime violations were tolerated up to a point, as long as they remained underground.[12] Surviving court records do suggest that prosecution was more prevalent at certain times or more common in certain counties than in others. This likely means simply that some local leaders and law enforcement officials were more serious about the prosecution of offenses than were their counterparts elsewhere. In some jurisdictions this type of lawbreaking may have been unnoticed or entirely overlooked; in others, prosecutions were prompted by a grand jury, local authorities, or religious leaders.

It is plausible to assume that most prosecutions of adulterers targeted society's lowest orders. The economic status of fornicators, adulterers, vagrants, and other petty criminals is often difficult to trace because census takers often ignored this transient flotsam and jetsam. Occasionally, however, prosecutors unexpectedly snared members of what on the surface seemed stable families. For example, in the May 1851 term of the Alachua County Circuit Court, Arnold Fussell (age forty-four) and Melinda McKinney were indicted for adultery and fornication. One year earlier the census taker recorded that they occupied farms close to one another. Despite spouses and plenty of children to keep them busy, they found time to break the law. Both were found guilty in the December term of court and fined $100.[13]

Prosecutions were also launched against owners of public establishments that catered to illicit entertainment. The code of 1832 criminalized keeping a "lewd house" (most likely places where prostitution was carried on) or a "disorderly house." The latter offense was often employed against persons who used public establishments to conduct illegal economic activity, including gambling, receiving stolen goods, and trading with slaves. Such practices were deemed to undermine the community's social stability. Those convicted could receive up to a $300 fine or a six-month jail term, at the jury's discretion.[14] If violators committed these offenses in the course of conducting legitimate enterprises, their licenses could be revoked.

Careful enforcement of laws against retailing goods or spirits without a license, receiving stolen goods, keeping a disorderly house, and trading with slaves was aimed at curtailing underground criminal activity and regulating slave behavior. Violators of these laws were considered particularly dangerous because they threatened to undermine the sacrosanct relationship between master and slave. Retailers who traded illegally with slaves for liquor and certain other items risked stiff fines and alternative punishments. In 1838, for instance, Joseph Alton, a Pensacola shopkeeper, was assessed $150 for trading boots and other stolen property with a slave named David and with a man named Charles A. Tweed. The same term, Alton was indicted for keeping a "disorderly, tippling house," where he procured "certain persons . . . black and white, men and women, of evil name and fame, and of disorderly conversation, to frequent and come together" for the purpose of "drinking, tippling, whoring, and misbehaving themselves." Alton's establishment allegedly also was infamous as a place of "swearing [and] quarreling." Like so many other violators of the disorderly house laws, Alton chose to abandon his establishment rather than face prosecution.[15] Town councils also passed ordinances to guard against houses of ill fame and their employees. Typically, Key West in 1829 approved "An Ordinance to Punish Lewd Persons," which subjected to a fine "any female of evil fame . . . supporting and maintaining herself by the unlawful profits of prostitution."[16]

The offense of "indecent exposure" was also proscribed, and numerous prosecutions were pursued. In 1857 John Long and a number of other men were indicted in Jackson County for "open lewdness." Long was charged for having gone "naked and unclothed for a long space of time . . . on a public highway, . . . intending to debauch the morals of society." A jury found him not guilty, but two others who pleaded guilty were fined $5.[17] The previous year Deusin Rochembeau was caught fighting with a "party of marines from the navy yard" who were bathing naked under a bridge near Pensacola Bay. An army officer who broke up the affray later swore that only one of the men, a soldier named McCloskey, "had no drawers on." Nonetheless, four men were convicted for "notorious acts of public indecency" and sentenced to five days in jail.[18]

Floridians also were subject to prosecution for malicious mischief and for disturbing religious worship. By 1832 it was illegal to disrupt "divine worship at a church, chapel, synagogue, or camp-meeting" through "vociferation, noise, [or] selling spirituous liquors." Those convicted could be fined up to $100, receive up to thirty-nine stripes, or be jailed for up to six months.[19] Proceedings often were initiated for this offense. In 1845, for example, Joseph Kinsey and William Stuart were indicted in Jefferson County for disrupting a "Congregation of Methodists" by "willfully and contemptuously . . . talking, cursing, and swearing with a loud voice."[20] A disturbance at one Key West church threw the entire community into an uproar for several weeks. In 1851, according to a report, "outrage upon outrage has been committed in our midst. . . . The sanctuary of God has been on several occasions desecrated—infamous hand-bills have been posted in our streets—the hand of the incendiary has attempted its work, and to finish this catalogue of demonical attempts, the assassin seeks the life of one of the ministers of God." Queried the local editor, "Are there not means of ferreting out these fiends of hell, and bringing them to justice, or is the arm of the law . . . impotent?"[21] The grand jury subsequently indicted eight individuals (six males and two females) for disturbing a religious worship, but only one member of the group, Jeremiah Roberts, was found guilty. He was sentenced to twenty-four hours in jail.[22]

The territory's towns also suffered from malicious mischief. In 1844, for example, four Walton County youths were convicted of this offense after burning down the stocks in front of the county courthouse. They were fined a total of $14, but, because of the instigation of a number of citizens, including Circuit Judge Dillon Jordan, the governor remitted the fine on the condition that they rebuild the stocks.[23] In 1843 Pensacola residents awoke one morning to find "the private parts of a man" painted on the side of a house on Palafox Street. Two men named Shaw and Kallinskin were prosecuted, but the outcome is unknown.[24]

Floridians suffered from a whole host of persons generally guilty of committing offenses of a fraudulent nature. Such men were highly mobile and took advantage of the lack of communication among frontier communities that could have exposed their schemes. Swindlers, fraudulent operators, confidence men, and sharpers of various kinds victimized individuals and communities. Even visitors seemed aware of the problem. "Florida," wrote Bishop Henry Whipple in 1843, "is the tip of the top for rascality and knavery. Nowhere this side of Texas can you find so many rascals who live by their wits." Whipple calculated that half of those who inhabited Florida towns were "ruined spendthrifts," and "too many of the balance" were "rogues and scoundrels."[25]

Swindlers and sharpers often operated alone, but teamwork also proved profitable. In 1850 a Macon newspaper warned Floridians to be on the lookout for a band of three swindlers moving south. One of the three, a man named Jackson, "alias the 'American Deer,' " was a "professional runner" and drew crowds by performing a number of fascinating athletic feats. Jackson had two companions in crime who worked the crowd as he performed: A. M. Maxfield, an "Englishman of small stature and sinister countenance," was the leader of the trio, and J. B. Langston, a "tall, good looking man with large whiskers," was their traveling companion. While Maxfield stationed himself and Jackson inconspicuously in the crowd, Langston auctioned off "*galvanized* gold watches and pencils at prices enormous for genuine articles." Later they used loaded dice to win back all the items auctioned off.[26] Often, however, accomplices were not detected and could offer invaluable assistance. Those who drew crowds by entertaining the public sometimes were assisted by a confederate who roamed through the village ransacking unguarded stores or through the crowd picking pockets. Persons caught in the act could expect harsh, immediate punishment, but those fortunate enough to be imprisoned to await trial often mysteriously escaped in ways that strongly hinted at the aid of accomplices. Such was the case of one Julius Cowles, a magician who plied his trade in several Florida port towns in 1839. Cowles and his assistant, a man named Dickinson, were wanted in Georgia for the murder of a jeweler, but they usually seemed to leave town just before word arrived of their crimes. Cowles finally was jailed in Pensacola, but he escaped with Dickinson's help. The accomplice eventually was apprehended in Alabama, but Cowles disappeared.[27]

Private individuals commonly offered rewards for the arrest of wrongdoers, sometimes supplementing a reward issued by state authorities. The advertisement-like notices publicized the misdeeds of the transient criminal element. The most frequent offenders were swindlers, seducers, confidence men, and absconding debtors—in short, anyone traveling under false pretenses. The headings of private notices left little doubt about the publicized misdeed: "Mark the Scoundrel," "Stop the Rogue," "Look Out for Swindlers," "Look Out for the Scoundrel," "More of the Villain," "Seducer and Poisoner," "Caution to the Public," "An Imposter," "Look Out for the Gentleman," "Be On Your Guard," "The Gay Deceiver," and "A Precious Rascal." Such a proclamation, its issuers believed, was a "public service," a warning to others. In 1858 a Key West man publicized Thomas Norcum as a "Seducer-Poisoner, Hypocrite-Coward-Ingrate." The advertiser wanted to warn "other communities as well as we can of the malignant infectiousness which marks all association with such a double-dyed scoundrel. All papers please copy. Hand him round, until his infamy is as wide as the realm which in common with his outraged fellow man he inhabits, but pollutes by his presence."[28]

Hotels were favorite targets for swindlers and confidence men. Often masquerading as gentleman travelers, they ran up huge debts, perpetrated frauds, and absconded to other towns. In 1843 citizens of St. Marks and Port Leon warned their neighbors in Apalachicola and elsewhere of a "scoundrel" named William Spivey, "a man who left many persons in this section of Florida to suffer from his dishonorable Conduct." Spivey, who claimed to be a minister, left a trail of unpaid debts and was "guilty of other acts and violations which would stamp him as the most accomplished trickster and swindler."[29] Similarly, in 1837 a Tallahassean warned the public against an accomplished swindler who called himself Henry Thorn. Thorn claimed to be a merchant and left a string of unpaid bills in Marianna, Quincy, and Tallahassee.[30]

Many swindlers masqueraded as members of religious sects. The case of William Spivey offers one example. In another instance, Methodist leaders in Savannah notified St. Augustine citizens in 1832 to be on the lookout for Milton Wilson, who came to Savannah "as an agent for the Methodist Society in St. Augustine, for the purpose of collecting money to build a parsonage in that place." It was soon discovered that Wilson had also collected money in St. Marys, Georgia, and had fled to Suwannee Springs in East Florida. Wilson continued his sojourn to South Florida and eventually died of an unknown illness in Key West.[31]

Some disreputable persons obtained property through other forms of deceit. In 1836, for example, James Thompson of Macon, Georgia, warned residents of Tallahassee to be wary of a man "calling himself McGee" who had falsely represented himself as a government agent, "buying horses for the [Second Seminole War] campaign in Florida." Thompson offered $100 for both his mare and the thief.[32] R. S. Hubbard, the owner of Tallahassee's City Hotel, warned citizens in 1843 against J. Melton. "Under false pretenses," according to Hubbard, Melton had procured Hubbard's horse and buggy and had not been seen since.[33]

Sometimes private proclamations sought to unmask the schemes of seducers. In 1848 the editor of the *Pensacola Gazette* exposed his competitor, James A. Baughey of the *Pensacola Democrat,* as a man lately turned "gay deceiver." Baughey allegedly had "absconded from the city . . . taking with him a young woman of respectable family" while leaving a wife and child behind.[34] In 1857 another Pensacola newspaper chronicled the bigamous escapades of Columbus Reddick, a man who married two West Florida women—one in Milton and another in Warrenton—in the space of two months. The father of the wronged woman from Milton had tracked down the couple in Mobile, Alabama, as they were preparing to depart for Montgomery.[35]

Besides adultery and fornication, gambling was the most frequently prosecuted public order and morality crime; but, as with adultery and fornication, prosecution was difficult to sustain. Surviving records show that of 227 indictments for gambling, juries found 69 guilty and 34 not guilty. More than half of all the indictments (124) never reached a verdict. But these numbers are skewed because of Leon County, which led all other counties in gambling prosecutions (139). Elsewhere the experience of prosecution was mixed, reflecting the whims and peculiarities of the county at large and of its law enforcement officers.

Gambling was a constant source of irritation to public officials and lawmakers. When Gov. Robert R. Reid addressed Florida's legislative council in 1841, he noted that the laws "against gaming are severe enough to extinguish the offence and banish the offenders from the territory." And yet, as Reid observed, the evil had gone on "increasing year after year to the detriment of public morality." The governor wondered out loud "if the severity of human laws could effect anything."[36] Having previously served as a district judge, Reid knew that laws had been repeatedly passed against gaming but little progress against the evil had been made. Reid likely knew as well that whenever men congregated, socialized, engaged in sport, or blew off steam, wagering took place under friendly or unfriendly circumstances. But to many, gambling threatened the stability of hearth and home. Perhaps the most outspoken opponent of gambling in the territory was William H. Hunt, editor of the *Pensacola Gazette*. Hunt thought gambling altered a person's mental faculties. Moderate success at gambling fostered the notion that skilled wagerers could make a living without honest work, a concept that sanctioned idleness and warred against moralistic, upright living.[37]

Contemporary observers and historians have noted that gambling, though illegal, was far more popular and tolerated in the antebellum South than in the North. Historians have speculated variously as to the cause, and most have reasoned that gambling was merely a natural pastime in a society whose entire way of life was a gamble. Wagering was an inherent additive to the dangers of travel, Indian massacre, slave uprisings, and business enterprises. Life was perilous, and gambling was part and parcel of life on the southern frontier. It also was evident, though, in more settled regions of the South.[38] According to John Findlay, gambling served a "formalizing" function in "planter society by ritualizing competition and confining aggression in a personal context that still managed to uphold codes of honor and manliness." Findlay asserts that dueling, card playing, and horse racing were "valuable outlets for troublesome passions. Gambling thus became an integral strand in the fabric of southern civilization."[39]

Historians have also recognized the class nature of gambling and have emphasized the tendency of the practice to legitimize a person's rank in society. Timothy Breen and others have found this to be true especially among the Virginia gentry in the eighteenth century.[40] Speculations as to the cause have ranged from the depraved nature of humanity to the thrill and excitement of the contest. Gambling was also a natural result whenever men congregated together in the presence of an ample supply of liquor. Perhaps the most likely conclusion to draw from Florida's experience with gambling jibed with Alexis de Tocqueville's observation that "those who live in the midst of democratic fluctuations have always before their eyes the image of chance; and they end by liking all undertakings in which chance plays a part."[41]

Florida statutes passed in 1822, 1832, 1839, 1846, and 1847 imposed criminal penalties for gambling. The 1839 law, for instance, made it illegal to "keep, have, exercise, or maintain a gambling table, or room, or any house, booth, tent, shelter, or other place for the purpose of gaming . . . to procure, suffer or permit any person or persons to play for money," or any other thing of value, "for the purpose of winning or losing." Those convicted were subject to a fine of between $200 and $2,000 and a jail term of between six months and one year. The 1839 law also offered an inducement to prosecution of gamblers. The district attorney was to be awarded $25 for every successful prosecution, the sum to be added to the bill of costs against the defendants.[42] Whether from a belief that penalties were too severe to secure jury convictions or because lawmakers deemed the crime of gambling less important, punishments for gambling became less stringent as time went on. Laws passed in 1847 and 1852 lowered fines and sanctioned either fine *or* imprisonment, not both.

Vagrancy laws were aimed, in part, at restraining and detecting gamblers. The criminal code provided that "any person wandering or strolling about, able to work or otherwise able to support himself in a respectable way, or leading an idle, immoral or prolifigate [*sic*] course of life, or keeping or exhibiting . . . [gambling] tables or faro banks, or any other gaming tables or bank" was liable to arrest by a justice of the peace, mayor, alderman, or constable. The culprit, thus confined, would be forced to give sufficient security for good behavior and future industry for one year or be punished by a fine of up to $500. Those convicted of vagrancy might also be sold to the highest bidder for a specified period of time or receive thirty-nine stripes, at the discretion of the jury.[43]

Local statutes supplemented territorial and state statutes. In Apalachicola, for example, a city ordinance stipulated that all owners of houses or taverns at which faro, roulette, or other gambling games were played could be fined up to $500 at the discretion of the mayor (half of the fine would go to the informant). Hotel and tavern owners would have their licenses "instantly forfeited" for breaking the ordinance.[44]

Gambling often is a product of urbanization; yet, Florida had few urban centers of any consequence. Some towns, however, did experience seasonal growth spurts that provided gamblers with the necessary numbers and dollars to fuel wagering activities. Port towns such as Key West, Pensacola, Tampa, Jacksonville, and Apalachicola provided such scenes at the end of the year when planters conducted annual business. The population of county seats such as Quincy, Monticello, St. Augustine, Marianna, Madison, and Newnansville also swelled on court days. These occasions naturally attracted gamblers.

Territorial, state, and local statutes were particularly aimed at itinerant professionals. They habitually arrived on the scene, fleeced the young and unsuspecting, and departed as quickly as they came. These "seasonal appendages" plagued many communities. Grand juries, particularly cognizant of this type of activity, often admonished authorities to act. In Tallahassee authorities could usually expect the arrival of gamblers to coincide with the legislature's annual meeting or at year's end when planters came to town to settle their accounts. In 1838 the Leon County Grand Jury remonstrated that gamblers were particularly adept at timing their visits with the conclusion of the season. The frustrated jurors observed that professional gamesters, "after swindling the imprudent and unwary out of large sums of money, depart with their ill-gotten gains only in time to escape the presentment of the Grand Jury of the next term."[45]

In the Gulf port towns of Apalachicola and Pensacola, matters were much the same as at Tallahassee. The Franklin County Grand Jury in 1837 complained of the large number of "professional gamblers who infest their community" and admonished officials and citizens to work together to "rid themselves of this evil."[46] Its Spanish population, large military establishment, and close proximity to Mobile and New Orleans made Pensacola a particularly attractive place of respite for gamblers. When Presbyterian missionary David Preston visited the town in 1829 he attributed the large number of "gambling shops" to the predominance of the Roman Catholic Church, but surviving evidence proves that the Anglo population also enjoyed this pastime.[47] As the grand jury noted in 1839, "Anglo-American gamblers [are] as dexterous in evading the laws as they are in handling cards." Even so, the jurors had indicted more than twenty gamblers during the previous court term.[48] Pensacola authorities ultimately found it impossible to stamp out gambling. Disagreement between the Creole and Anglo populations over the activity exacerbated the problem. When Creoles gained temporary control of the board of aldermen in 1841, it asked the local legislative delegation to "use their best endeavors to procure the passage of a law authorizing the city of Pensacola to License one or more gaming houses."[49]

Gambling offered natural enhancement to sporting contests. Horse racing was popular in Middle Florida from its earliest years. The Tallahassee Jockey Club was organized in 1832, and Thomas Brown's Marion Race Track became the scene of biannual contests. Clubs also formed in Gadsden and Franklin Counties, and newspapers kept readers abreast of the winners, losers, and prize money offered.[50] Most spectators attended these sporting events for the sheer excitement; others viewed the extravaganza as a chance to socialize. But the races also attracted spectators ready to place money on favorites, and, as the years progressed, crowds at the Marion course became less distinguished for their orderly behavior. By 1843 the grand jury was complaining that the track was a "public nuisance, a hot-bed of vice, intemperance, gambling, and profanity, deserving the just censure and loud condemnation of every lover of decency and good order."[51]

The interest of antebellum Floridians in betting extended far beyond the horse track. Residents placed bets on just about everything. Cock and dog fights, though less respectable than horse racing, were popular and offered wagering opportunities.[52] Gambling also occurred at inns and public houses, which offered tenpin and billiards for the amusement of their patrons. Poker and other card games likewise attracted continuing public interest. The rules and even the names of many popular gambling games are obscure, but surviving records offer hints as to what manner or combination of cards, wheels, dice, or checks (chips) was used. John Gillison was indicted in 1845, for example, for procuring people to "come together to play for money at a game called Rondo Coolo" at his Key West residence. Five years later Edward Fox was prosecuted in Monticello for "playing a certain game called 'high die.' "[53] Another popular game was keno, which resembled modern-day bingo. This game was popular among soldiers and blacks at Tampa's military garrison, Fort Brooke.[54]

Aside from poker, Florida's most popular gambling game probably was faro, a sophisticated game that swept through the Old Southwest during the 1830s and 1840s. Though practically unheard of today, it may have been the most widely played gambling game in the United States in the nineteenth century. The dealer (banker) drew cards from a metal box, and players placed bets against the house on cards drawn. The players placed chips on a "layout" embossed with cards. The game was particularly suited to professionals since it required a complicated mixture of paraphernalia, including portable tables with "layouts," a dealing box, checks, and a casekeeper, similar to a counter on a billiard table. A "rolling" version of the game was also played in which a wheel, similar to a roulette wheel, was spun.

Faro was perfectly suited to sophisticated schemes of cheating, and resourcefully designed mechanisms were often built into the apparatus.[55]

Throughout the antebellum decades, authorities were on the lookout for itinerant faro dealers. Though players were prosecuted, the most sought after were those who actually conducted the games. The Jefferson County Grand Jury brought a typical indictment in 1835 against Jefferson Sanders and twelve others for "misdemeanors." The body referred to Sanders as a person of "idle, dissolute, vicious, and depraved habits" who maintained a "gaming table commonly called a Faro table and did procure and permit divers silly and weak-minded persons [to play faro]."[56] Faro's charms also snared the well established and well heeled. Three years before Sanders's trial, prosecutors had proceeded against some of Jefferson County's wealthiest planters.[57]

By the late 1850s the prosecution of faro dealers had become less haphazard and more efficient. Municipal ordinances particularly were more sharply drawn. But prosecutions still often were unsuccessful because they involved the long-term process of affidavits, grand jury investigations, and detailed rules of indictment. Thus authorities often chose to prosecute under the local proscriptions since they provided that offenders could be immediately apprehended, the case investigated, and an appropriate fine assessed. For example, in 1858 Tallahassee authorities, led by the mayor, raided a local haunt where the "laws and authority of the city were being held in defiance. The visit ended in arresting a Faro dealer while in the very act of practicing his profession." The mayor held an examination on the spot, and Ogden Hoffman Whitman was fined $300.[58]

Most counties or towns experienced protracted periods when gambling seemed to overshadow all other illegal activity. In Leon County, indictments for gambling appear in nearly every court term. Numbers of prosecutions in spring 1843 (forty-three indictments) and in 1854 (seventy-five indictments) indicate either that authorities had engaged in a periodic crackdown or that the county was temporarily infested with sharpers. Of the forty-three 1843 indictments, the grand jury found eight for keeping a gaming table, nine for procuring and permitting gaming, twenty-five for gaming, and one for keeping a faro table. As was usually the case, prosecutions met with only limited success. Seven of the indictments resulted in a guilty verdict, netting the state $1,452 in fines. Two were found not guilty, fourteen were placed on the dead docket, and two were dismissed; in four of the cases the prosecutor declined prosecution, and four cases disappeared from the docket.[59] The whereabouts of this illicit activity is unknown, but at the conclusion of the term the jury denounced the Marion racecourse. They also lamented that "gambling to an enormous and unprecedented degree . . . has crept into this community and threatens to sap the very foundation [and] vitiate the tastes . . . and moral . . . principles of our society."[60] Similarly, Alachua County likely experienced a time of trouble in 1853. During the May term of its circuit court, seventeen culprits were prosecuted on various charges: thirteen for "Playing and Betting at Cards" and one each for "Keeping a Gaming Table," "Keeping a Gaming Room," "Playing and Betting at Billiards," and "Gaming." Guilty verdicts were found against nine of the accused, and each was fined $10.[61]

There were numerous reasons for the difficulty of sustaining indictments for gambling. Most witnesses were the accused themselves, and, even if this were not the case, social values, such as they were, would have made it unlikely that friends or acquaintances would testify against their companions. In Hillsborough County the grand jury in 1854 formally indicted thirty-seven individuals for gaming and three for keeping a gaming house. Two days later the solicitor either withdrew or quashed all the indictments. During the same term fifty-one other indictments, most of which differed with the previous list, were all styled "Not a True Bill."[62] Perhaps the grand jury and solicitor reasoned that the indictment process alone was enough of a deterrent.

Wherever gambling took place, cheating followed close behind. The excitement of the moment sometimes prevented losers from realizing it was fraud rather than bad luck that had cost them, but once cheaters absconded the reality often set in. Such was the case of Leon County's Edmund Wester, who found no humiliation in taking out an announcement proclaiming that he had been cheated. In 1831 a Tallahassee newspaper published an announcement by Wester forewarning "all persons from trading for a note of hand given by me to Thomas Gill for 100 dollars worth of cattle." Wester declared that he would not pay the note unless "compelled by Law—as it is a Gambling debt and I was joked out of the same."[63]

The most potentially dangerous aspect of gambling was its tendency to lead to violent (and also alcohol-fueled) conflicts. Events at Pensacola offered corroboration. In 1838 Peter Suchet, who was convicted and fined $25 for "Keeping a Common Gaming House," was also indicted for "Assault with Intent to Kill" after firing a pistol at a patron. The case of Antoine Collins—part-time hotel owner, part-time sheriff, and full-time roughneck—was more typical. Collins was indicted in 1826 for assault and battery. The disagreement stemmed from an argument with a man named

Dealy in a billiard parlor. The atmosphere was boisterous, and one witness remembered that when Collins entered the crowded room, several gentlemen were seated playing cards, "drinking and amusing themselves as well as they could." When Dealy complained of Collins looking over his shoulder, the latter remarked in Spanish that Dealy was having "pretty good luck at Drawing." Dealy, taking offense at both Collins's remarks and his position in the room, charged Collins with being "concerned with the Banker." Collins denied the charge and demanded satisfaction. He then angrily stomped out of the room and waited outside. When Dealy emerged, Collins wrested a cane out of his hand and struck Dealy over the head. Once he regained consciousness, Dealy swore out a complaint. Collins was arrested and required to take out an appearance bond. He eventually was indicted but likely had already left town. In May 1828 the district attorney decided not to pursue the case.[64]

Gambling disputes sometimes resulted in death, as is illustrated by another Pensacola incident. In June 1852 Henry Prior, Adam Thomas, and several other slaves were playing cards late one evening. Thomas accused Prior of cheating and warned others not to continue playing. Prior thereupon stood up, told Thomas not to "meddle with my business," and "then struck [Thomas] down." Testifying at his own trial, Prior swore that he did not realize he had killed Thomas; when told at the time that he had done so he responded, "Oh, he is only drunk." He then picked up Thomas and asked him, "Did I hurt you?" According to a witness, "Adam tried to talk but could not." Standing a full six feet, one and one-half inches tall, Prior possessed a powerful frame. His blow to Thomas's temple proved mortal. He was taken into custody, escaped, and was recaptured. Convicted of manslaughter, Prior was sentenced to stand at the pillory for two hours and receive twenty-five lashes.[65]

Florida statutes prohibited blacks and whites from gambling together. Although these laws were ignored just as often as were other gambling statutes, racial animosities spurred by gambling disagreements were an invitation to violence. Such was the case of a man named Murray, a black scout employed by the U.S. Army during the Second Seminole War. White enlisted men resented Murray's rank and privileges. One evening the scout entered a tent where several men were playing cards. He warned the party not to play with a sergeant named James Edgar, claiming that Edgar had cheated him on several occasions. The sergeant countered that he never gambled with blacks and ordered Murray away. Murray responded that he "*ranked him* and threatened to report him to colonel Whistler." Edgar became enraged and later that night shot Murray in his sleep with a rifle. Edgar was taken to Newnansville and indicted for murder at the superior court, but he jumped bail and was never apprehended.[66]

More than any other type of offense, crimes against public order and morality reflected a diversity of public opinion. There were disagreements over both the laws themselves and their enforcement. Some would have argued (though far less than today) that such laws violated personal liberty. Others would have contended that rigid enforcement was a waste of time. But in the end it is "society" that makes the decision about what crime is and whether or not it should be enforced. Society, of course, refers to the people who make laws, enforce them, and support their mandates, seeing them as vital to the maintenance of a safe, stable environment. In antebellum Florida "society" was people struggling to scratch a living out of the soil, people trying to protect whatever property they had managed to accumulate in their chosen vocations. "Society" was also people trying to preserve some semblance of morality and dignity in a transient, tumultuous, and dangerous frontier setting. In antebellum Florida "society" was not Indians, blacks, criminals, and other elements that laws were directed against. "Society" was lawmaker, not lawbreaker. Women, though not empowered by modern concepts of civil rights, were, at least in some respects, beneficiaries of society's laws.

The ineffectiveness of prosecution might also shed light on societal values. Criminal prosecution of all types in antebellum Florida was notoriously ineffective, but prosecutions for fornication and adultery were the most difficult of all to sustain. Of a total of 237 indictments, only 51 (26 guilty and 25 not guilty) ever reached a verdict. These figures may suggest that indictment was what mattered most. To indict was to expose "notorious" or "open" acts. Unlike prosecutions for assault or theft, the goal was not as much to punish or exact retribution as it was to pronounce such a course of conduct reprehensible and ensure its cessation. In other words, formal indictments may have served as a kind of public censure. Court records fail to detect the degree to which individual citizens or groups of citizens—of their own accord—were involved in enforcing what they believed were the mandates of society. It may have been that the courts and these groups cooperated on these issues. To indict was to identify. If courts did not do the actual job of punishment, they could bring miscreants to the attention of vigilance committees, church groups, or other arbiters of public morals. These matters are highly speculative, and it is difficult to arrive at definitive answers to these questions. What is clear, however, is that each community, village, and county had a definite character of its own, its own set of circumstances, and its own predilections, all of which set it apart from others.

Laws that defined crimes against public order and morality were written to protect society from practices that a majority of Floridians found offensive or threatening to community mores. But this "majority" was amorphous and ever-changing. Public opinion is always difficult to trace, and whether or not these attitudes changed over time is even harder to determine. But when it came to the very laws themselves, their violation, and their enforcement—these are yet other examples of the state's diversity.

Nine

Blacks, Crime, and the Law

> It is manifest that a slave accused here is entitled . . . to all the rights and privileges to which a free white man would be entitled if standing in his situation, at the Bar of Justice.
>
> —Judge Robert R. Reid (1837)

Up to now the focus has been almost exclusively on issues pertaining to crime and white society. But the very presence of blacks affected the makeup of the laws and their enforcement. It now becomes necessary to extend the discussion to blacks, crime, and the law.

Scholars have addressed the issue of blacks and the law in general studies of antebellum slavery.[1] Even though studies of the peculiar institution in Florida have also explored the legal ramifications of slavery, few have actually analyzed slave crime and criminal prosecutions using superior and circuit court records or records from the territorial and state governments.[2] These sources, taken together with newspapers and various secondary sources, can serve to illuminate important aspects of the peculiar institution in antebellum Florida. Historians disagree as to whether the law of slavery was driven from a humanitarian need to protect persons or a pragmatic concern to protect property. Most have agreed that slaves represented an unusual dichotomy as represented in the law.[3] But even as these two conflicting forces struggled for ascendancy, most Southern states, as Daniel Flanigan has noted, "sought to bring slaves *within the law* by granting them the same procedural rights that criminally accused whites enjoyed."[4] Whether procedural fairness was afforded blacks in the antebellum South is another hotly debated issue. Some scholars have argued that Southern courts bent over backwards to ensure procedural fairness to blacks accused of crimes, while others contend that fairness is either nonexistent or overemphasized.[5] This chapter will explore these issues while examining aspects of slave crime, prosecution, and punishment in antebellum Florida. But first it is necessary to examine both the unusual characteristics and the laws of America's southernmost slave state.

The task of generalizing about blacks, crime, and the law is made all the more difficult not only because of the individual circumstances of each case but also because of the extensive regional variations represented in the state. These differences made uniform enforcement of existing statutes almost impossible. It has already been noted that the force behind the increasingly restrictive slave codes was the Middle Florida planting establishment. Daniel Schafer and other scholars have argued that at least in the early decades, holdovers from the Spanish era dominated social and economic life in East Florida and managed to resist many of the restrictive laws regarding miscegenation, manumission, and slave management. But the pressure of restrictive legislation mounted, and so did the immigration of Georgia and South Carolina slaveholders, who insisted on more rigid enforcement of the laws. The result was that by the 1850s, East Florida's demographic changes, along with national events such as the growing influence of sectionalism, eventually affected the political process and contributed to a merging of outlook with the rest of the state.[6]

Florida's criminal slave code originated from "An Act Relating to Crimes and Misdemeanors Committed by Slaves, Free Negroes, and Mulattoes" (1828). With some minor revisions, the code remained in force throughout the entire antebellum period, and all blacks—bond or free—were subject to its proscriptions. Under this code blacks could not buy and sell commodities or liquor, keep firearms, own livestock, assemble publicly, or use insulting language toward a white. Such offenses, if convicted, carried a punishment of up to thirty-nine stripes.[7]

Much evidence of criminal activity of slaves has been lost, since most petty offenses were punished on the spot by masters or overseers and thus never reported or prosecuted in the courts. Another reason for the lack of surviving documentation arose from the fact that the Florida Slave Code of 1828 stipulated that noncapital offenses were to be prosecuted before a justice of the peace. (Only a small number of cases were prosecuted in the superior and circuit courts.) Justices of the peace had the authority to hear testimony, determine guilt or innocence, and assess punishment. Some information from these cases has survived, however, because the masters of slaves convicted in these lower courts had the right to appeal judgments to a superior or circuit court.[8] Assaults committed by blacks against blacks were also adjudicated in civil cases against the offender's owner. These cases were usually tried by a justice of the peace or in a municipal court.[9]

Blacks charged in capital cases were prosecuted in the superior and circuit courts. In addition to the usual capital offenses of murder, rape, and arson, blacks could be hanged after the conviction of several other crimes. The code defined as capital any offense committed against a white deemed not to be in self-defense. Included in this broad description were assault and battery, insurrection, conspiracy to murder, poisoning, or assault with intent to rape a white woman. Blacks could also suffer, at the discretion of the jury, death for robbery and burglary. In lieu of death blacks convicted of these offenses could have their ears nailed to a post for one hour or receive thirty-nine lashes, at the discretion of the court.[10]

The code stipulated that the "same rules and regulations shall be observed as are now observed in the trial of free persons." Thus in Florida's antebellum years slaves accused of capital crimes received essentially the same procedural safeguards as whites. Equal justice was denied, however, for a number of reasons: whites and blacks were prosecuted under different criminal codes; blacks could not serve on juries; and black testimony against whites was excluded. Florida's slave code, modeled after those of other slave states, stipulated that black testimony was admissible only in cases where blacks were a party to the cause, "and in no other case whatsoever."[11] This stipulation ruled out entirely the possibility that black testimony could ever be used for or against a white person. Given these defects, harsh though they were, blacks accused of capital offenses and tried in the superior and circuit courts in Florida could expect to be prosecuted in the much the same manner as whites. Indeed, judges, members of the bar, and newspaper editors often insisted that nothing less could be tolerated. Florida Supreme Court Justice Charles H. DuPont expressed this idea in 1860 when he wrote the following in his opinion in an appeal of a slave accused of rape: "It is true that the unfortunate individual who stands charged with the commission of the offense is one of an inferior caste—a slave. But it is the crowning glory of our 'peculiar institutions,' that whenever life is involved, the slave stands upon as safe ground as the master. The same tribunals of justice are open to each—the same form of proceedings—the same safeguards that are extended to one are fully and freely awarded to the other."[12]

Florida law provided that if a master was either unwilling or unable to provide legal counsel for his slave, the court appointed one. Court cases reveal that slaves were represented by some of the most talented members of the legal profession in Florida.[13] Attorneys voluntarily defended blacks either from a sense of civic responsibility or because they felt that blacks were wrongly accused. Enterprising lawyers likely sought out these cases, if for no other reason than to showcase their talents in crowded courtrooms. (Capital cases were always well attended.) Whites might not like it if skilled attorneys got slaves acquitted, but they could not help being impressed with their skill.

Punishment of blacks was on the average much harsher than for whites.

Charles H. DuPont served on the Florida Supreme Court from 1854 to 1868. (Courtesy of the Florida Supreme Court, Tallahassee, Florida)

The most common mode of punishment against blacks was lashing. Though barbarous punishments such as nailing ears to posts, cropping the ears, or branding could have been imposed, court records reveal that they rarely were. It must also be remembered that corporal punishment (lashes and stripes) was commonly inflicted on white thieves or adulterers. Two catch-all provisions of the 1828 code broadened the power to punish. Under section sixty-one juries could impose up to one hundred stripes on blacks convicted of misdemeanors or violation of other laws in the code. Finally, section thirty-seven of the code stipulated that in cases where blacks were convicted of a felony not punished by death, the court was empowered to inflict "such other corporal punishment as [it] shall think fit."[14]

An important factor that affected not only the construction but also the administration of Florida's slave codes was the state's condition as a frontier. The state possessed vast unsettled tracts where runaways could hide out for long periods of time, and this was an important determinant of Floridians' attitudes toward the judicial prosecution of slaves. The fear that slaves might run away and conspire with the Indians to form isolated settlements was a legacy from the Spanish era in Florida. There was, of course, a long history of Indian and black collaboration,[15] and the experiences of the Second Seminole War (1835–42) rekindled these fears in a way that brought general alarm to all regions in Florida.[16] There were always enough instances of runaways committing crimes on the frontier to intensify this apprehension.

Whenever murder was committed on deserted roads or trails, runaway slaves were suspected. In 1834 James Roundtree, a native of Lowndes County, Georgia, was killed near the Georgia line while hauling supplies from St. Marks to his farm in Georgia. Runaways were suspected, and a posse scoured the area and found Roundtree's wagon and groceries near the vacant hideout of two runaways, Crittenden and Joe. A proclamation for the arrest of the two offered a sizable reward, and both slaves were captured, jointly tried, and convicted for murder. They were both hanged.[17] In the midst of the Second Seminole War, the body of Captain Gilliland of Alachua County was found on the St. Augustine Road about thirty miles west of Newnansville. The killing resembled an Indian outrage. But soon two runaways named John and Tom were apprehended, and they confessed to the murder. Judge Robert Reid was summoned from St. Augustine, and in a special session of court both were convicted and hanged.[18]

Runaways who banded together in inaccessible areas of Florida's frontier could escape detection for weeks or even months at a time. If discovered, they often desperately defended themselves, even to the death. In May 1839, for example, a desperate encounter took place when a group of whites unexpectedly stumbled upon a runaway hideout in swamps twelve miles north of Apalachicola. Shots were exchanged, and Caesar, the leader of the gang, killed a man named Herring, but was wounded himself. A local newspaper reported that Caesar was owned by a man in Columbus and employed in Apalachicola. He was "well known" in that city as a "desperate outlaw." When the group returned to Apalachicola, the sheriff organized a posse and followed in hot pursuit.[19]

The identity of two other slaves was soon established. Caesar and a slave named Richard had both been employed on a steamboat and made their escape somewhere on the lower Apalachicola River a year before.[20] Another of the runaways was Hunter, who had escaped from John D. Parish's plantation on Lake Miccosukee in Jefferson County about a month before. Hunter was employed in Apalachicola at the same time Caesar and Richard were there.[21] The slaves fled west, and Caesar and Hunter were finally captured near Pensacola about a month after the encounter with the whites. By early July they were in irons awaiting trial in Apalachicola. Authorities suspected that the runaways were responsible for a number of other crimes in West Florida, and one local newspaper speculated that they were in close collaboration with the Creek Indians and in some way "connect[ed] with free negroes . . . and unprincipled whites" who had "furnish[ed] them with powder, arms, and such information as has enabled them to elude their pursuers."[22]

Both slaves escaped from the Apalachicola jail in August while awaiting trial. Caesar was soon recaptured, but whether or not Hunter was ever retaken is unknown. Both slaves were indicted in the December 1839 term of the Franklin County Court, but Caesar alone was convicted. After an unsuccessful appeal, he was hanged.[23]

Another surprise encounter occurred in 1860 when a hunting party scouring the banks of the St. Marys River discovered three blacks skinning a cow. Shots were exchanged; one black was killed, another was wounded, and a third was taken prisoner. A jury of inquest identified the dead man as a runaway from a local plantation who had been at large for at least eighteen months. A local newspaper recommended a more thorough policing of the thinly settled region near the Georgia-Florida boundary.[24] A number of inaccessible frontier regions, particularly in East and South Florida, offered runaways safe havens until the outbreak of the Civil War.

One Southern white justification for black enslavement was that bondsmen possessed an infantile notion of right and wrong. Without constant supervision, the argument went, blacks would fall prey to childlike instincts, commit crimes, and likely do harm to themselves and others. The remarks of judges, grand juries, and newspaper editors confirm the popularity of this notion.

Whites often attributed slave crime to loose management or neglectful supervision—a circumstance that resulted in disorder, which in turn loosened restraints, undermined the natural relationship between master and slave, and thereby created a situation that led to crime. Constant supervision by responsible whites was necessary to ensure stability and order in the slave community. Without it, the argument went, blacks would resort to dissipation and lawbreaking.

Close surveillance of its slave and free black population was one of the most difficult tasks of every Florida village community. State law and local ordinances outlined the duties of watches, patrols, and militia. If contemporary complaints by citizens, editors, and grand juries are to be taken seriously, however, these groups rarely functioned efficiently. The law empowered patrols to police locales against the late-night ministrations of blacks, yet in most counties these patrols were often neglected. Local magistrates and justices of the peace enforced laws regulating patrols, but public apathy made their task difficult. The Jackson County Grand Jury, for example, excoriated the magistrates for neglecting their duty. In 1829 the Gadsden County Grand Jury found the "Patrole [*sic*] Law [a] shadow without substance, and answers none of the purposes it pretends *to sustain*." The Leon County panel found evidence in 1853 of the "entire neglect of the patrol duty in this county." On the eve of the Civil War, matters were much the same.[25] Unless the community was in the midst of crisis, authorities found it difficult to ensure that patrols functioned properly. As one recent study has noted, in most Southern communities "patrols operated sporadically. . . . A patrol was like a group of deputy sheriffs on call. When the community felt the need for its services, the patrol could respond quickly."[26]

Community leaders particularly were concerned about movement within the slave quarter, from plantation to plantation, or from residence to residence in towns. Such activities provided opportunities either for fun and frolic, pilfering property, trading stolen goods for liquor, or frequenting haunts where tippling or gambling was allowed. These activities were deemed especially dangerous because they provided opportunity for blacks, poor whites, and others to congregate without careful supervision. Free blacks and poor whites were always suspected of instigating these illicit practices. Extensive efforts to discipline these elements met with only limited success, primarily because black testimony against whites was inadmissible in the courts. Whites who were accused of committing crimes alongside blacks could always use the color of their skin to escape prosecution. Conviction was possible only if other whites were willing to testify.

The failure of the law to deal adequately with irresponsible or indulgent masters constituted a crucial problem. A Pensacolan observed as early as

1825 that a recently passed law dealing with illegal trade between slaves and whites was defective because it assigned punishments to slaves when they "should be inflicted on their masters."[27] Subsequent statutes corrected this deficiency, but masters seldom were prosecuted for allowing their slaves to trade illegally. Some no doubt found it in their own interest to allow it to go unpunished. Most villages and towns had certain unregulated sections where whites and blacks might congregate, and there underground criminal activity flourished. In Marianna, for instance, the Jackson County Grand Jury proclaimed the "shanties" belonging to Dr. Horace Ely and another white miscreant on either side of the Chipola River Bridge a "public nuisance." The structures provided shelter for a "regular system of trading between negroes and white men [where] Negroes are often seen drunk, and frequently caught with whiskey." Yet the grand jury did not indict the white offenders. These "vile reptiles who poison and pollute our society" go free because "negroes can not be a witness in a court of justice in our state against a white man. Therefore the wretch who vends the article escapes justice." Ely's own slaves were often involved in lawbreaking, with at least two participating in serious crimes.[28]

Other towns possessed late-night haunts that catered to the amusement of slaves and free blacks. In 1827 Pensacola was rife with "negro gambling houses and tippling shops [which] resulted in manifold disorders to the interruption of the peace of the city." Urban tumults also resulted from "Balls and [unauthorized] Assemblies of the Negro slaves." As in the case of Marianna's Horace Ely, grand juries often publicly denounced those they were unable to indict under the law. In Gadsden County, for example, Elizabeth Miller's house in Quincy was "usually crowded with Negroes to the great annoyance of persons living or walking in that neighborhood." In Madison and Jefferson Counties matters were much the same. The grand jury complained that "tippling shops" were "dependant . . . on trade with slaves" and amounted to a kind of "licensed receptacle for stolen produce." The jury insisted that new regulations be written that would guarantee not only the "rights of the master" but also the "morality of the slave, and the security of the country."[29]

Both masters and slaves often disregarded laws that forbade the latter from carrying on economic transactions in their own interests. Prosecutions for this crime were rare, and violations were probably handled outside a court of law. Even so, planters who continually flouted the law might find themselves under indictment for "permitting a slave to hire his own time." For instance, in Putnam County former governor William D. Moseley and circuit court Judge Benjamin A. Putnam were indicted four times for this offense in 1857 and 1858. While Moseley and Putnam probably viewed these indictments as a nuisance, the actions proved that even rich and powerful slaveholders could not violate the law with impunity.[30] Yet authorities felt little enthusiasm for enforcing these laws if local citizens felt it in their interests not to obey them. In 1858, for example, the Duval County Grand Jury presented against the "growing evil" of slaves being permitted to hire their own time. "Our laws strictly forbid it," they declared. At the heart of the problem was the growing number of free blacks in Jacksonville. Free blacks, the jurors warned, "are generally vicious . . . and have made combinations and frequently induce insubordination among slaves. This class can not be too strongly under strict surveillance."[31]

The presence of free blacks in Florida's port towns caused confusion by making it difficult to discriminate between free blacks and slaves. This offered an added incentive for slaves to function as if free. Thus port towns almost always found themselves plagued with illegal economic activity carried on either secretly or openly by slaves. The common council of Key West, for example, proclaimed in 1849 that slaves were "permitted to trade horses, cattle, mules, and other articles as if free."[32] In some port towns, slaves commonly lived apart from their masters while employed in town. Numerous city ordinances made this illegal, but violations were common. In Apalachicola, according to the Franklin County Grand Jury, slaves were allowed to rent houses and pay masters an agreed-upon sum. Invariably, when in town slaves neglected their labor. "The quarters of the slave too often becomes the resort of the profligate [*sic*] and abandoned of his own color," the jurors complained in 1837. Eventually "the slave resorts to larceny, to housebreaking, and other trespasses on the property of others, to make up his wages—it is being with him a paramount object, to continue his abandoned course." Subsequently Apalachicola ordinances addressed slave management, but their effectiveness can only be speculated upon.[33]

In Florida's upper-tier black-belt counties of Jackson, Gadsden, Leon, and Jefferson, circumstances were similar to the experiences of Florida's port communities. Daily living conditions differed slightly, but the same problems of lackadaisical and slipshod surveillance plagued these areas as well. Masters were either neglectful or indulgent. Tallahassee, which served not only as territorial and state capital but also as a commercial center for cotton planters in the region, was the scene of much illegal commercial activity among slaves and whites. In the fall of 1830, a local editor complained that planters failed to provide slaves with passes to come to town and sell articles. Thus runaways "find access to the kitchens in Town and are enabled to obtain subsistence and elude detection." The city police could do little until people took the responsibility of policing their own premises.[34]

In 1853 the Leon County Grand Jury again deplored the neglectful management of slaves, "resulting in theft and general insubordination." Grand juries in adjoining counties east and west of Leon also complained of loose management of slaves. In 1851 the Jefferson County body charged that slaves were not only left alone on plantations but were also allowed to haul cotton to market alone in wagons, thus subjecting neighborhoods to petty thefts and crimes. In 1837 the Gadsden County Grand Jury denounced the custom of trading on the Sabbath, especially since the slave population used the "Sabbath [as] a day of amusement, dissipation, and debauchery." The slaves use the "opportunity to pilfer from their masters and others those articles which are readily exchanged for spirituous liquors."[35]

Florida law, to a limited degree, also sought to regulate the relationship between master and slave. The 1828 slave code made it illegal for masters, overseers, or others to inflict "cruel and unusual punishment" on slaves.[36] Masters and overseers were sometimes indicted, but even worse, when suspected or convicted of this offense they were socially ostracized. They might also be subjected to extralegal punishment by community leaders. Neglect, though less indictable, was equally reprehensible, and grand juries publicly denounced masters who failed to provide adequately for the maintenance of their bondsmen. In 1852, for example, the Jefferson County Grand Jury found several instances of owners who neglected to provide their slaves with adequate food and clothing. The next session of court found matters unchanged. This state of affairs, they lamented, provided "our enemies abroad their most powerful weapons for assailing our institutions . . . our whole country receives that odium which is only justly merited by a few." A negligent or cruel master injured not only himself but also his "country" and "his neighbor." Such miscreants, "should be dealt with by the laws which our legislators have wisely and humanely intended as a barrier against oppression."[37]

Indictments for cruelty to a slave were difficult to sustain since both law and custom fully recognized a master's right to use the lash when he felt it necessary. But there were limits to such discipline. If they went too far, masters or overseers risked the public shame of an indictment for cruelty to a slave. Perhaps the most widely publicized case of this description occurred in Pensacola when Peter Williamson of Jackson County was prosecuted for beating Katy, his slave. Williamson acquired Katy while transacting business in Pensacola. As the papers were being drawn up, Katy ran away with her children. Williamson soon found Katy, whipped her, tied a chain around her neck, secured her to the axle of his wagon, and hauled her through the streets of Pensacola until a number of outraged citizens intervened. Williamson was hauled before a magistrate, and the slave was provided with medical attention. An examining physician found a large cut on Katy's head and several bruises on her body. Several witness testified to Williamson's brutal treatment. One witness testified that Williamson roared while inflicting blows that "he showed her he was her master and could reduce her." Williamson was bailed for $1,000 and indicted for cruelty to a slave.[38] He defended himself on the basis of the "bad character" of the slave, the "slight nature of the injury inflicted," his own intoxication, and his respectable character. The jury rejected this paltry defense, found him guilty, and fined him $100. Indignant, Judge Henry Brackenridge, as he sentenced Williamson, denounced his cruelty. Brackenridge only wished that it was within his power to place the unfortunate slave "in the hands of another master."[39]

Though always available as a last resort, the law was seldom used as a corrective against cruel masters. Why was the enforcement of laws to protect slaves less than vigorous? Why were the laws regulating slavery only loosely administered? Of course, much of Florida was a frontier and suffered from the typical difficulties of law enforcement in such regions. But the primary cause was that the vast majority of Florida communities were rural and agricultural. A rural society, where personal relationships counted for much, undermined the efficient, impersonal administration of justice. Personal autonomy of masters over their slaves was sacrosanct. Intervention from the state or community violated this precept, and thus there was little motivation for rigorous enforcement of the law. Such a practice would have interfered with the master's relationship with his slaves. Officers of the law were reluctant to intervene unless public safety was clearly at risk or if they were admonished into doing so by their superiors or an outraged community. Florida's experiences jibe with Eugene Genovese's contention that the "slaveholders did not intend to enforce the severe legislation strictly and considered it a device to be reserved for periods of disquiet and especially for periods of insurrectionary scares. In practice this easy attitude confirmed the direct power of the master."[40] The unwritten ethic of masters disciplining their own slave property without any intervention from the outside usually overrode statutory provisions. Sheriffs and constables, already overworked, had other responsibilities that prevented them from attending to these matters. Pay was so low that most had to take other jobs. In addition, sheriffs, as elected public officials, were often unwilling to challenge or prosecute masters who violated ordinances. Also, deficiencies in surveillance arose because patrols were haphazard and not efficiently organized.

Another reason for the less-than-stringent enforcement of the laws regulating slavery was that it is likely that the code's provisions were viewed by the majority of whites as too harsh. Canter Brown, who has studied the legislative history of the slave code in Florida, has contended that the 1828 slave code was enacted out of an overreaction to friction between Seminoles and whites in East Florida in 1827. The consummate fear that the Seminoles and their black allies in East Florida threatened the existence of plantation slavery itself caused these harsh legislative enactments—enactments for which there was only doubtful support among the majority of Florida whites. Legislative efforts, Brown contends, arose principally from "planters' immediate fears of slave revolt and black and Indian insurrection." Even though race relations were influenced by events occurring outside the territory, it was the impact of local politics, and the territory's frontier experience, that shaped statutory law. "Laws enacted in such a climate stepped far beyond the bounds of community consensus and, once the particular emergency passed, they often commanded so little respect as to be unenforceable."[41] The danger of runaway slaves working in unison with Indians was a reality throughout the antebellum period, and this inspired harsh laws to protect against the possibility of renewed frontier outbreaks. The problem was that when these alarms subsided, these harsh, restrictive enactments were still on the books. Yet the disposition of lawmen to enforce them and of the slaveholders to follow them had subsided.

Easier targets of restrictive legislation were free blacks. In 1841, newly appointed governor Robert R. Reid used his experience both as a judge and as a resident in war-torn East Florida to suggest that the legislative council move to further circumscribe the movement of free blacks. The law as it stood did not adequately "provide for the punishment of those who may aid and concert with the Indian enemy." Free blacks were the most difficult to monitor, and thus Reid recommended that they be "placed under the guardianship of respectable white persons." The legislative council responded by enacting the first in a series of laws of this nature.[42]

Daniel Flanigan has noted that whether the "slave was to be treated primarily as person or as chattel depended on the nature of the crime he committed and the jurisdiction in which he resided." He has also found that Southern "courts were in many respects astonishingly considerate of slaves' procedural rights in major criminal cases."[43] This was also the case in Florida. The surviving evidence of slave prosecutions in Florida indicates that masters, judges, and members of the bar shared a commitment to afford blacks the same procedural safeguards as whites. These feelings no doubt sprang from both paternalism and self-interest. Yet in an emotionally charged atmosphere, court officials had difficulty imparting legal niceties on angry citizens when evidence against slaves seemed cut and dried. Even so, most judicial officers seemed particularly conscious of the fact that slaves were especially vulnerable to the whims of whites. Judges, attorneys, and other concerned citizens, especially after 1830, grew increasingly aware that the "North was watching." They realized that flagrant miscarriages of justice would be isolated and magnified by the Northern press and abolitionist agitators as proof of the South's inhumane system of slavery; and defenders of the institution were never willing to admit that the institution was inhumane. Moreover, most understood that allowing blacks many of the same procedural safeguards as whites did not undermine the institution. On the contrary, these safeguards strengthened it.

An example of Florida jurists' high regard for due process and procedural fairness in the prosecution of slaves is demonstrated by the case of Ben, a slave accused of killing his overseer. In 1828 one proud Floridian used Ben's prosecution to proclaim that "our statutory provisions on the subject of slave felons, are highly creditable to the good feeling and humanity of our legislators." The commentator noted that "in all respects they have the same mode of trial with white felons; indictment by the Grand Jury, and fair and open trial by a jury of twelve householders before the Judge of the Superior Court of the Territory." If the master failed to provide adequate representation for his slave, Florida law directed that the court provide the slave legal counsel, and gave his attorney the right to "challenge twenty jurors peremptorily." The commentator noted that Ben's owner, Dr. Isaac Mitchell, "employed as good counsel as our bar affords, and in all other respects afforded the prisoner every aid in his power, without manifesting any disposition to impede the regular course of the law. Indeed, throughout, the Doctor's deportment was that of a gentleman, humane master, and good citizen."[44]

It took almost two years for Ben to be convicted and hanged. In October 1827 the Leon County Grand Jury indicted Ben, and upon his arraignment he pleaded not guilty. Ben was thereupon tried, convicted, and sentenced to be hanged. His attorneys made a motion to arrest judgment, challenging an Indian's testimony to the grand jury. A mistrial was granted, and in the next term Ben was indicted again and tried. Once more his attorneys vigorously argued his case, but they lost. Ben was convicted and hanged on May 23, 1828. A local newspaper merely repeated the impressions of a large segment of the Tallahassee community when it noted that Ben was "ably, though unsuccessfully defended, his counsel fighting every inch of ground."[45]

Given the dynamics of the Southern slave society, crimes of violence committed by slaves against whites demanded swift and harsh retribution. Of all the crimes for which blacks were prosecuted, the most potentially threatening to the rights of the accused was rape. The prosecution of this crime was perhaps the most difficult to bring to a legal conclusion. Surviving court minutes, however, show that the majority of cases prosecuted in Florida reached a verdict. Of the eight slaves prosecuted for rape (four) or assault with intent to rape (four), six (three and three) were convicted, one was acquitted, and one did not reach a verdict. And yet, public outrage against this offense was often so great that strong circumstantial evidence, or emotional accusations by the victim, combined with a weak commitment of law officers to protect the accused, might result in the summary execution of the culprit. Such was the case of Dick, a slave indicted and convicted in the Leon County Superior Court in 1840. Dick was lynched while his case was being considered on a writ of error by the territorial court of appeals.[46]

Yet Dick's case was not typical. For example, in 1859, Stepney, a slave, was indicted in Santa Rosa County for the rape of Mary L. Carrol. Stepney was granted a change of venue to Escambia County, and he was acquitted.[47] In 1847, Charles, a slave indicted in Hamilton County for assault with intent to commit rape on Zilphia Pennington, escaped the gallows on a technicality. The 1828 slave code required that prosecutions could not go forward unless it could be proved that the victim was a white woman. Charles's counsel, J. Wayles Baker and Samuel Carmack, maintained throughout the trial that Pennington was of mixed blood. After Charles's conviction, they appealed the case on writ of error to the Florida Supreme Court, which overturned Charles's conviction.[48]

The case of Isaac, charged with an attempted rape in Santa Rosa County but tried in Escambia County, demonstrates that if slaves were convicted on less than substantial evidence, they stood a reasonable chance of executive clemency. Charged, indicted, and convicted of assaulting Mrs. Lena Webster at her Milton plantation, Isaac escaped the gallows because Mrs. Webster admitted she could not swear that it was Isaac who had assaulted her. Footprints outside the plantation house did not match Isaac's shoes. Immediate interrogation of Isaac failed to link him with the crime. In addition, a number of men from the area testified to Isaac's good character. This was enough to convince Gov. Richard K. Call that the slave was a fair subject for executive clemency, stating, "Doubts may reasonably be entertained of the identity of the person by whom this most atrocious crime was committed."[49]

The successful prosecution of Monday, a runaway who in 1829 was accused of raping Sarah Cason, the wife of an Alachua County planter, suggests that even in the most heinous cases resort to summary execution was not automatic. According to one account, the outrage was "marked with the most brutal barbarity, and produced a general excitement as soon as it was known." After a brief period at large, Monday was apprehended by a posse, severely wounded by buckshot, and committed to jail. He was indicted and tried at Newnansville. The court assigned Charles Downing as defense counsel, but his efforts were unsuccessful. A jury found Monday guilty, and he was hanged.[50]

It is tempting to conclude that rapes of white women were committed by blacks as a way of striking out against masters. Florida's experience mirrors the findings of Daniel Flanigan, who has noted that resistance was not necessarily a factor in most rape cases. Few cases of rape were "committed against members of a master's family." His study found that "most of the victims were lower class white women. In many of these cases there were hints of previous sexual relationships or at least flirtations with either blacks or even with the accused."[51] It reasonably follows, then—and this was the case in Florida—that if a slave was to be convicted on a charge of rape, much depended on the social class of the female victim.[52] If the accused was a woman of dubious reputation, conviction might be difficult.

One instance of the latter occurred in 1859, when Susan Leonard of Marianna swore out an affidavit that she had been raped by Cato, "a one-eyed negro slave." Cato was immediately taken into custody, charged, and eventually indicted by the Jackson County Grand Jury for the crime. Cato's defense team, led by John Milton (who within a matter of months would occupy the governor's chair), constructed a defense around the contention that Leonard's accusations should be rejected on the grounds of her "bad Character as a prostitute." Moreover, Cato's counsel obtained a change of venue on the grounds that his client's case had been "generally canvased in the county and that persons have busily engaged in prejudicing the public mind against him," demanding that Cato "be hung." Cato's counsel also underscored the fact that a change of venue was necessary on the grounds that prejudice existed against his master, Dr. Horace Ely, who was accused of conducting numerous illegal activities in the county. Cato's counsel pleaded that these matters should be carefully considered, since the defendant was entitled to a fair trial "as if he was free man . . . by the laws of the land." After carefully considering the plea, Judge Jesse J. Finley ordered

Cato transported to Calhoun County for trial. Cato was convicted, but on appeal the supreme court granted a mistrial. At a subsequent trial, Cato was acquitted. The jury was influenced by several factors. First, Cato's identity as the rapist was clearly in doubt. In addition, Cato's counsel successfully questioned the character of Susan Leonard, whom they accused of "keeping a house for the purpose of making money by taking men in."[53]

When all is said and done, these cases offer up many tantalizing questions but few answers. How frequent were biracial sexual contacts? How fearful were whites of the so-called "black rapist"? Were the few instances of sexual assault made out of some sort of retaliation for white abuses of a similar nature? The answers to these questions are probably impossible to tease out of surviving records. Moreover, the individual peculiarities of each case and the human emotions involved make it altogether impossible to form much of an appraisal. Furthermore, it is likely they were almost as unclear at the time as they are today. In his study of slave crime in Virginia, Philip Schwarz offers a reasonable assessment of the value of these records. "[They] offer," he writes, "a good indicator of sexual attacks and as a rough index, and an index only, of the number of such incidents."[54] The same assessment can be reasonably made for antebellum Florida. Yet what emerges above all else from these cases is that when charged with sexual assault, slaves could reasonably expect to receive a trial under the normal arrangements of the law. Local circumstances were the most important determinant concerning whether the normal legal process would or would not prevail.

Violence stalked free blacks and slaves at many different levels. There were many instances in which slaves committed murder. Whites also killed slaves. Florida law provided that if a white killed a slave in the act of insurrection, this was justifiable homicide. One of the most visible symbols of slaves' oppression was owners or overseers, so they were the most common target of slave wrath. There were numerous examples of slaves killing their owners or overseers. In 1840 in Jefferson County, for example, Simon killed his master, Richard Cole, by beating him to the ground and then throwing him into a creek. He was convicted and hanged. Two other slaves were also indicted, but they were found not guilty. In a cruel irony the court ordered Caroline Cole, the widow of the deceased, to pay William Dilworth $50 for the defense of her slaves, as the law directed.[55] In another case involving the murder of a master, William Pearce of Madison County was killed when his slave Hall drew an ax that he had concealed and "split [his head] in twain, . . . scattering the brains in every direction." Hall fled but soon gave himself up. He was eventually hanged.[56]

One of the most shocking cases of slaves murdering an overseer occurred in 1860 when M. D. Griffin was murdered by a gang of slaves on J. B. Watts's Madison County plantation. Griffin was struck down from behind with an ax. His body was placed in a wheelbarrow, tied in a sheet, attached to an anvil, and then sunk in twenty feet of water. As many as eleven slaves were originally charged in the crime. After a lengthy trial, six were convicted: three were hanged and three were pardoned.[57]

Female slaves were also prosecuted for committing violence on whites. In 1849, Martha, the slave property of Leon County planter Charles Bannerman, was charged with the murder of her overseer, Christopher Bryant. Bannerman employed a skilled defense attorney, who was able to prove to the jury's satisfaction that the death occurred from accidental causes. An acquittal was granted once it was determined that Martha threw up a "hoe she had in her hand, to ward off the whip with which [the overseer] was chastising her."[58] Phoebe, a slave, also owed her life to a skilled legal defense. When she was accused of attempting to poison a man named Landon, to whom she was leased, her master, Clarissa Anderson, employed Benjamin A. Putnam to represent her in the Duval County Superior Court. Mrs. Anderson did not attend the trial but received daily reports of the proceedings. The day after the not-guilty verdict was delivered, Putnam wrote Mrs. Anderson that Phoebe "made a very narrow escape; . . . the evidence against her was substantial."[59]

Slaves were also put on trial for killing fellow bondsmen. In 1842 Bryan was put on trial in Jackson County for killing Toney, a fellow slave, while they and ten other runaways were hiding out. Testimony at the trial revealed that the killing occurred during an altercation between Bryan and Toney. In the course of the disagreement, Bryan pointed a gun at Toney, who grabbed the muzzle, begging Bryan not to shoot. A witness testified that Bryan wrested the gun free and shot Toney through the head.[60] In another argument among bondsmen, in Jefferson County, Ben, a slave, stabbed his cousin Tom "in a scuffle." When Tom expired, Ben fled but was soon captured. Ben's owner employed Richard K. Call and two other skilled attorneys to defend the slave. They succeeded in having the charge reduced to manslaughter. Ben was convicted and sentenced to receive thirty-nine lashes.[61]

In 1853, Ned, a slave of L. A. Thompson, killed Lewis, the property of William Burroughs, in an argument while the two walked together on a trail north of Tallahassee. Ned swore that he was only defending himself from Lewis's attack. Ned, indicted for murder, was convicted of manslaughter and sentenced to receive thirty lashes and three months in jail. The presiding judge recommended Ned's case to the governor as a subject for

Benjamin A. Putnam was a prominent East Florida attorney and served as judge of the Eastern Judicial Circuit from 1857 to 1865. (Courtesy of the Florida State Archives, Tallahassee, Florida)

executive clemency. Gov. James Broome partially compiled by remitting his jail term.[62] In a similar case it took three trials to convict Lewis, who killed a fellow slave in Leon County. The killing occurred on Christmas Day in 1856, but Lewis was not successfully convicted of manslaughter until October 1860. He received fifty lashes for his crime.[63]

Florida law allowed masters whose slaves were killed wrongfully to sue the killer, or the owner of the killer, to recover the damages. For example, when Tom, a slave, shot Harry, also a slave, in a hunting accident in Escambia County in 1821, the killing ended up as a financial dispute between owners. When Tom's owner refused to reimburse Harry's owner, Sarah McNeil sued Henry Wilson for $600, the estimated value of the slave.[64] The results of this action are unknown.

Whites who committed violence against slaves could be criminally prosecuted under the crimes of assault and battery, manslaughter, and murder. White violence against blacks was common. Yet much of the violence committed against blacks indicates significant routine contact between blacks and whites in circumstances that did not come within the usual framework of the master-slave relationship. In 1831, for example, Lt. William H. Baker, an army officer attached to the naval yard in Pensacola, accidentally shot and killed Maria, a young female slave belonging to another officer. Maria's death occurred as the two were teasing one another in the company of a large biracial gathering. Baker was indicted and prosecuted. Extensive testimony indicated that Maria was shot by accident. According to one witness, "neither party was angry, they were playing together . . . blagarding [*sic*] each other." Another witness claimed the defendant "was in the habit of playing roughly with his pistols." Finally the jury found Baker not guilty of manslaughter.[65]

Overseers were usually criminally prosecuted if they killed slaves. Nathaniel Sanders, an overseer in Madison County, was prosecuted in 1850 for beating to death Charles, a slave under his care. Sanders fled to nearby Patterson Hammock, and Deputy Sheriff Joseph Morris wrote Gov. Thomas Brown of the incident and complained that Sanders "can not be brought to justice." Brown issued a proclamation for his arrest. The culprit was taken up, indicted for murder, and put on trial, but a jury found him not guilty.[66] When Guilford Dawkins whipped to death Jane, a slave under his care, he was indicted for murder in the Jefferson County Superior Court. Dawkins was jailed but broke custody before he could be tried.[67] In 1853 New Yorker George Thompson, an overseer employed at a St. Johns River plantation, was apprehended after shooting a slave in his custody. Thompson was indicted for murder in the Orange County Circuit Court, and a jury found him guilty of manslaughter, fining him $300.[68]

Whites also served jail time for killing slaves. In 1856 Nassau County man Henry Williams was indicted for murdering a slave named John with "sticks, switches, and clubs." The charge was reduced to manslaughter, but a jury found Williams guilty and sentenced him to eight months in jail.[69] In Leon County in 1843, another man named Williams killed a slave while acting as an overseer. A jury of inquest determined that the slave died from "severe punishment" and concluded that there did not appear to be any "provocation or extenuating circumstances." John Williams was convicted of manslaughter and sentenced to thirty days in jail.[70]

Surviving records of prosecutions and trials indicate that the wanton killing of blacks was taken seriously by Florida law enforcement officers. Besides the previously mentioned Dawkins of Jefferson County, other killers demonstrated by their flight that they were not willing to risk their lives to the judgment of a jury. In 1829, for example, Gov. William P. DuVal authorized a $200 reward for the capture of Edward Robinson, accused of murdering Claiborne, a slave in Gadsden County.[71] Several others fled rather than risk prosecution. In 1844 in Wakulla County, Patrick Matthews fled after killing Charles, a slave.[72] In Jackson County two whites, J. D. Dickson and John Durden, fled after killing slaves.[73]

At least one white Floridian was executed for taking the life of a black man. The details of the case are obscure, but in 1857 Ferdinand McCaskill stabbed a "negro" at Wolsey, near Pensacola. Two and a half years later, McCaskill was executed for the crime.[74]

At least twenty-eight black males were executed under judicial process in antebellum Florida, a number roughly similar to the total for whites. Most slaves executed were convicted of murder (twenty-five), but they were also hanged for rape (two) and assault with intent to kill (one). Two black females also suffered the severest penalty of the law, one for infanticide and one for murder. In the majority of cases, slaves charged with felonies were indicted, prosecuted, and punished following the normal processes of law. Nevertheless, there were instances in which slaves were lynched during their apprehension or prosecution. Though not the norm, lynching was always a possibility in emotional cases or when officers of the law were either unwilling or unable to protect the accused. Lynching might also result when circumstantial evidence was strong, definitive evidence was weak, or acquittal came on a technicality. (These matters will be explored more fully in chapter 13.) On the whole, however, the Florida experience demonstrated that justice was usually served even when the above conditions existed.

The laws regulating Florida's black population were specifically designed to legislate black inferiority. The goal was not simply to carefully regulate white and black contacts but rather to rule them out completely—except as they applied to the relationship between master and slave. But these regulations had only limited success. If local testimony, grand jury reports, court cases, and newspaper accounts are any evidence at all, most efforts at keeping whites, free blacks, and slaves from associating with one another failed. Loose management of the slave population, the failure to administer patrols effectively, and the overall laxity of law enforcement with regard to the slave population were constant themes.

As with all aspects of the institution of slavery, experiences in prosecution reflected the contrasting and competing forces of humanity versus interest, compassion versus ambivalence, and paternalism versus power. Present in most circumstances were human motives of greed, meanness, and hate, but also sympathy, concern, and compassion. Florida's treatment of slaves in its criminal justice system mirrored conflicting values and impulses inherent in the slave system itself.

Measured against the modern concepts of constitutional protection and civil rights, slaves and free blacks were not treated fairly by Florida's criminal justice system. Blacks did not serve on juries, and black testimony was inadmissible against a white person. Many blacks were punished unjustly because of these deficiencies. Yet given these handicaps, blacks were, in most capital cases, given the same legal protection as that afforded whites. But blacks were subject to the same inequities and prejudices suffered by others accused of crime. The heinousness of the offense, the social status of the offender, the victim, and the master—these factors might unfairly affect the prosecution of a case. As in modern instances, justice might not be served because of any number of circumstances, either in the apprehension of the accused or during the trial itself. Yet whether from paternalistic instincts or from motives of self-interest, blacks were represented by some of the best lawyers in the state, who took their defense very seriously. Given the social demands that the institution of slavery be upheld and protected—and given the perils inherent in such a system—the justice afforded blacks in Florida courts was about as good as could be expected and probably superior to that provided for decades after the Civil War.

Ten

Florida's Antebellum Lawmen

> It has been but a few months since [Escambia County Sheriff Francis] Maura received his commission and entered on his official duties, and it is with gratification we bore witness to the efficiency with which his services have been performed. All business that has been confided to him has been dispatched with promptitude and fidelity. His gentlemanly bearing and mode of action during the transaction of official business often brings to a successful and happy issue what, under different circumstances would have resulted in failure or disaster. As a peace officer [he is] vigilant, active, fearless, and indefatigable. . . . Even the cheerless darkness of night—trackless forests and swamps, bayous and marshes are no barriers to his determined energies—nor do superior natural powers with pistol and Bowie knife wielding cause him to shrink from arresting the robber or seizing the assassin; in short nothing impedes the progress of his duties.
>
> —*Pensacola Gazette,* March 5, 1853

Though such public commendations were rare, a majority of Florida lawmen also would have deserved these accolades. Sheriff Maura's dangerous occupation offered few rewards other than the personal satisfaction of serving the public. Pay was minimal, responsibility was great, and public support was often lacking. Despite these obstacles, federal marshals, county sheriffs, their deputies, and a whole host of lesser officials such as city marshals, constables, and jailers struggled to maintain law and order in antebellum Florida. Yet most, like Maura, only served one or two years before quitting.

Florida's law enforcement scheme functioned under what was essentially a two-tiered system. Representing federal authority in the territory and state were U.S. marshals, who carried presidential appointments and served at the behest of the federal courts. In the territorial period marshals were appointed for each judicial district and functioned primarily under the direction of the federal judge. Marshals were present at the meeting of each superior court and wielded considerable influence. They worked alongside sheriffs, who functioned at the county level.

During the early territorial period, conflicting legislation often brought confusion to Florida's law enforcement system. The congressional act creating the territory made marshals subject to whatever "regulations and penalties as the Legislative Council shall impose while acting under and in virtue of the Territorial laws."[1] In 1824 a territorial act liberated sheriffs from the marshal's control and gave them complete authority over their county's criminal affairs. Moreover, it stipulated that sheriffs "shall have custody of all prisoners hereafter confined by marshals."[2] This law brought immediate protests from some federal marshals, who insisted not only that the legislative council lacked authority to reduce a federal official's jurisdiction, but, more importantly, that dual federal and territorial authority in this case was unworkable.[3] Two years later Congress finally clarified the situation, decreeing that, as the executive officers of the superior courts, U.S. marshals would "execute all process of the superior courts" arising under the laws of the United States or the territory.[4] This essentially relegated sheriffs to the role of a marshal's deputy. But this was the case only if marshals chose to deputize county sheriffs. As Gov. William P. DuVal explained the situation to Pres. Andrew Jackson in 1831, "By our local laws allmost [*sic*] all the important duties, which are in the States assigned to Sheriffs—are given to the united States Marshals."[5] There the matter stood until Florida became a state.

Florida's territorial inhabitants looked to marshals rather than to sheriffs for their law enforcement needs. In 1840, for example, a number of distressed citizens from Garey's Ferry in Duval County appealed to U.S. Marshal Joseph Sanchez to appoint a deputy from their community, claiming that the "lives of private citizens were placed in jeopardy for the want of proper civil officers."[6] As the territorial population grew and needs arose, marshals frequently appointed deputies to enforce the law or fulfil other duties in many of the territory's outlying areas.

The decision to rely more heavily on the marshal in law enforcement was probably the only workable alternative. Superior courts had both federal and territorial jurisdiction, and any attempt to divide executive authority between marshal and sheriff would have been confusing and costly. Sheriffs, especially in these early years, would not have had the means at their disposal for adequate law enforcement. The habit of deputizing sheriffs as assistant marshals continued throughout the antebellum period.

Marshals served as a kind of chief financial-administrative officer of their respective judicial districts, and as such they were in charge of collecting

William P. DuVal was governor of the Florida Territory from 1822 to 1834. (Courtesy of the Florida State Archives, Tallahassee, Florida)

and dispersing monies. Judges relied on marshals and, later, sheriffs to assist them with the court's or their own financial needs when riding circuit. Also, when the territorial or state treasury was not "in funds," judges looked to marshals and sheriffs to provide them with money to operate. In 1846, for example, when Judge Thomas Douglas applied to the state treasurer for partial payment of his salary to defray his expenses in riding circuit, the comptroller informed him that the treasury was empty and directed him to apply to a sheriff of the region to cash his salary warrant. Douglas thus requested the St. Johns County sheriff to oblige, claiming that "it will perhaps save you a trip to Tallahassee."[7]

It was also the marshal's responsibility to arrange for locations to hold court. In 1840, for example, Jesse Carter of Newnansville offered to sell Marshal Joseph Sanchez a structure he had built in Newnansville to serve as a courthouse. Carter's offering price was $1,000, but he added that "for further compensation" he would build additional rooms for the judge, marshal, and clerk.[8]

After statehood (1845), marshals' criminal responsibilities were reduced to enforcing federal laws, and they almost faded from view. The old judicial district structure was abolished, and the Northern and Southern District courts of Florida were created. Attached to these two courts, marshals' activities were strictly confined to enforcing the mandates of the federal courts. They maintained federal property and prisoners, oversaw census taking, and assisted federal collectors at the various ports of entry.[9] After 1845, newly created state circuit courts prosecuted all criminal cases except for those involving violations of federal law, and thus sheriffs assumed the marshal's role as the primary law enforcement officer in the state.

According to an 1845 statute, sheriffs were the "executive officer of the circuit court in their respective counties." In addition to other, less specific, duties, sheriffs apprehended criminals, served arrest and search warrants, summoned jurors and witnesses, maintained prisoners in the county jail, supervised jailers and constables, collected fines, transported prisoners to and from court, executed punishments, and generally maintained law and order in each county. Sheriffs served two-year elective terms. They were required to post a bond of $2,000 to $20,000, as set by the solicitor and the circuit judge. They were also burdened with other responsibilities not connected to law enforcement, such as opening and closing court, collecting taxes, supervising elections, seizing and selling property under court order, and holding runaway slaves.[10]

Lawrence Friedman has noted that the early nineteenth century experienced a movement toward greater professionalism among law enforcement officials.[11] This trend was extremely slow to take hold in Florida, and it probably was not even apparent until late in the nineteenth century. Florida lawmen were almost entirely "nonprofessionals." They conducted their duties and responsibilities without much training and supplemented their income through additional work. Requirements for the job were mainly reliability, honesty, good character, and a willingness to take on dangerous tasks. Most sheriffs were also engaged in farming, and a surprising number

Joseph Sanchez served as marshal for the Eastern Judicial District from 1837 to 1842 and as sheriff of St. Johns County from 1845 to 1847. (Courtesy of the St. Augustine Historical Society)

owned slaves. Of the 160 sheriffs who served from 1845 to 1861, 70 owned slaves.[12] If slave ownership is a measure of wealth, then a good many sheriffs were quite well off. Of course, wealth or well-established credit would have been necessary to post the required bond of the office. Some sheriffs were also tradesmen. Leon County Sheriff Haley Blocker (1851–57) was a surveyor and operated a livery stable in Tallahassee. Sheriff Thomas Land of Calhoun County (1852–55) was a shoemaker.[13] Clinton Thigpen, who served as Franklin County sheriff throughout most of the 1850s, was a butcher by trade.[14] The absence of a salary likely discouraged a number of good men from serving as sheriff.

Even federal marshals had to seek other employment to supplement their income. The $200 annual salary and fees for services were simply insufficient for most men. Marshals were often frustrated by federal regulations precluding some outside occupations. In 1838, no doubt reacting to charges that his administration was politicizing the federal bureaucracy, Pres. Martin Van Buren directed that all presidential appointees divest themselves of any connection to newspapers. This edict seemed unfair to Marshal Peter Gautier, who threatened to resign if he was forced to sell his interest in the *St. Joseph Times*. "It is due to myself to inform you," he asserted to Secretary of State John Forsyth in 1838, "that the emoluments [of this office] are insufficient, unconnected with any other business, to meet the ordinary expenses of a family man. I must rely upon something beside the Marshalship for support—and can see no good reason why an interdict should be pronounced against my profession as an Editor." Gautier's situation was extremely critical for him because of Florida's impending admission to the Union. "If I am compelled to meet the wishes of the President," he added, "I may find myself without office & . . . my present establishment gone."[15]

Until 1829, when the office became elective, territorial governors appointed sheriffs. As elected officials, sheriffs were accountable to the public; but they were also subjected to the whims of local politics. Antebellum Florida, like the rest of the nation, was caught up in the movement of Jacksonian Democracy—a movement that proclaimed that the people themselves should govern. Such a mentality not only discouraged long-term service, it even promoted "rotation" in office as a guard against the establishment of an entrenched civil bureaucracy unanswerable to the people. The movement discouraged professionalism in Florida's law enforcement ranks. But it was not only the notion of Jacksonian Democracy that discouraged professionalism; it was also the realities of poor education, low literacy rates, and poor pay in the office.

Campaigning every two years was not only a nuisance, it could also be hazardous to a person's health. Such was the case for N. A. McLeod of Marion County, who died during a hotly contested election. During the course of his campaign for reelection in 1858, McLeod succumbed after suffering for more than twelve hours "all the horrors of *delirium tremens*" brought on by an excess of "strong drink" during the campaign.[16]

Ascertaining just what type of person served as sheriff is difficult. The office's political nature favored some and excluded others. Administrative skills obviously were necessary. Most surviving evidence points to a rapidly changing force, with few sheriffs serving more than one term. Out of the 160 sheriffs who served from 1845 to 1861, only 43, roughly 27 percent, served more than one two-year term. Holding the distinction as the state's longest-serving sheriff was Nassau County's Alexander J. Braddock, who held office from statehood to secession. Besides Nassau County, Leon and Gadsden Counties, each with three sheriffs (1845–61), seem to have had the most stability in the office. In Madison County, Thomas Anderson and John Patterson traded the office back and forth five consecutive terms from 1849 to 1859. Continuity must have been difficult in Alachua, Duval, Hamilton, St. Johns, and especially Escambia Counties. From 1845 through 1861 the first four counties had seven sheriffs, while Escambia had nine. The county with the most instability in the sheriff's office must have been Sumter, which averaged one sheriff per year from its founding in 1853 to the outbreak of the Civil War.[17]

With rewards so limited, many men likely gravitated to the sheriff's office after failing in other enterprises. Such seems to have been the case for Levi Bell, an immigrant to Quincy from South Carolina. Noting that Bell had borrowed money from a number of Gadsden Countians, a local resident inquired of another South Carolinian in 1837, desiring to find out just "what kind of a man Mr. Levi Bell was thought to be when in your place. . . . He is hear [*sic*] in this place at this time and if a stranger should see him he would think him to be a man worth thousands." Yet he seemed unwilling to pay his debts. In the short time since his arrival in Quincy and his election as Gadsden County sheriff, Bell had failed in a number of enterprises, including the hotel business, the grocery and dry goods business, carpentry, and gambling.[18]

Sheriffs frequently found themselves swamped with heavy responsibilities but with little means to execute them. They consulted vaguely written laws outlining their duties, following them as best they could. Some relied on instructions from predecessors, while others looked to state prosecutors for assistance. Manuals containing samples of writs, forms, and legal jargon translated from Latin to plain English provided some relief.[19] Correspondence from recently elected sheriffs offers hints of both high turnover rates and chaotic administrative situations. Newly elected Holmes County Sheriff David Brownell's predicament was typical. He informed State Comptroller Theodore Brevard in 1860 that he had no official seal of office because the previous sheriff had lost it before departing for Texas. Brownell enclosed lists of witnesses and fines without the proper forms. Finally, he concluded his correspondence with the plea, "P.S. if I have made eny [*sic*] mistakes pleas [*sic*] let me know as I am a new hand."[20] Orange County Sheriff J. C. Stewart had contacted Brevard in a similar vein the previous year. Stewart was overburdened with prisoners and behind in his tax collection duties. At that very moment he was en route to the Ocala jail with a prisoner. "I hope you will have patients [*sic*] with me," he concluded. "I know you would if you knowed [*sic*] all that I have had to do, and knew that it was not neglect on my part."[21]

Both marshals and sheriffs received fees for their services and filed account schedules for every prisoner prosecuted in every term of court.[22] Indeed, this was the only remuneration sheriffs were entitled to. From time to time Florida legislatures provided fee schedules for all its judicial and law enforcement officials. In 1834 the legislative council authorized the following fees for marshals and sheriffs:

> Executing a peace or search warrant, one dollar.
> Committing prisoner to jail, one dollar.
> Releasing prisoner, twenty-five cents.
> Removing prisoner, per mile, ten cents.
> Serving and returning Writ of Habeas Corpus, one dollar.
> Taking and approving every bond, fifty cents.
> Calling jury in each suit, twenty-five cents.
> For whipping a person by sentence of court, two dollars.

The law also provided reimbursement for executing writs and for keeping slaves and livestock seized under court order. Lawmen were also allowed a percentage of monies collected under an execution or attachment. Their duties necessitated considerable travel, and they were authorized four cents per mile to and from the courthouse. The act also provided fees for justices of the peace, constables, jailers, district attorneys, witnesses, and jurors.[23]

The fee system confounded those with little education or few administrative skills. Account schedules had to be filled out carefully, certified by a judge, and forwarded to the territorial auditor or state comptroller for reimbursement. Neglectful record keeping caused many individuals to lose out on fees they rightfully deserved or left them responsible for costs in transporting or maintaining criminals. Some of the most unfortunate left office with their accounts hopelessly in arrears, and a number of men were compelled to resign.

The challenges of the fee system changed little from the territorial period to the statehood period. The only difference was that the state comptroller, rather than the territorial auditor, guarded the state's resources—often in ways that some lawmen found arbitrary and unfair. The result was that reimbursement for emergency services was not always forthcoming. In 1831, for example, Leon County Sheriff Romeo Lewis was disappointed to learn that compensation for the jailer he hired would have to come out of his own funds. "The sheriff is by law the jailor," wrote territorial auditor Leslie Thompson. "If he chooses to delegate part of his duties to a deputy, he cannot have an equitable claim upon the Territory."[24] This particular problem was later rectified when the legislature created the position of jailer.

Marshals, sheriffs, and their deputies also had to keep track of ever-changing rules governing the collection and disbursement of monies. Among the problems were those caused by the lack of a stable currency. In 1833, for example, territorial treasurer Charles Austin directed, "In consequence of the great number of uncurrent Bank Notes now in circulation in this territory . . . No Bank Notes will be received but such as are current at the time the payment is made into the treasury."[25] Indeed, the late 1830s were the most financially unstable period in the antebellum era, and public officials were not immune to the same kind of frustration that private citizens experienced. Marshal Charles Evans of the Western District explained his intolerable situation in a letter of resignation to Pres. John Tyler in 1841. The Panic of 1837 had thrown territorial finances into chaos, and federal monies were not forthcoming. Evans insisted that he could not continue to provide for criminals out of his own funds in the hope of future reimbursement. "I have not hesitated what course it was most prudent for me to persue [*sic*]," he wrote.[26] Evans's predecessor, Peter Gautier, had faced a similar dilemma in 1838 when he arrived in Pensacola for his first court session without government funds to pay court expenses. Gautier had no choice but to borrow money on his own credit and then give jurors and others the choice of accepting the type of currency offered. Fortunately, no one declined.[27]

A few decades later lawmen had more means at their disposal, but the fee system continued to create hardships. As one sheriff explained in 1857, the state had earned such a poor reputation of properly compensating its lawmen that few good men were willing to serve. "I can assure you," Duval County Sheriff Benjamin Frisbee explained to Comptroller Brevard, "that it is not easy to get a constable—'*because the State don't pay*'—that it is more trouble to collect these little items than it is worth."[28] Emergency situations often demanded deputizing special guards or assistants. Florida's frontier status dictated that prisoners had to be transported back and forth from jail to court over relatively uninhabited regions. Most counties lacked jails in these early years, and a law passed in 1828 authorized magistrates to order that offenders be transported to other counties for confinement. With such long distances involved, sheriffs had to hire additional guards, and other substantial costs were incurred. All special services and expenses had to be carefully recorded, certified by a judge, and presented for payment.[29]

As with reimbursement, pay for extra hands was uncertain, and officials might be left responsible. Accordingly, a lawman had to weigh every expense incurred in the line of duty with the possibility that he might not be reimbursed, and sheriffs, jailers, and county clerks naturally considered decisions not to pay legitimate costs as arbitrary and unfair. When denied proper reimbursement, most lawmen had no qualms about expressing their displeasure to public officials. Such was the case of Marion County Clerk James Johnson, who in 1857 demanded compensation for county jailer Robert Bulloch. The comptroller had denied payment because of an administrative oversight by the previous sheriff, whereupon Johnson replied in a blistering fashion. He demanded to know why Bulloch's replacement, a man named Harris, was paid for the same services, and then leveled charges against the comptroller. "I have proposed to offer Mr. Bulloch's accounts precisely as Mr. Harris' and still you say 'you can not audit the account,' " he declared. "Now Sir, why you can allow this favoritism, I do not know, nor do I care—but I do say it is despicable in a public officer. I have but little more to say [but your] favoritism shall be showed in its true colors in every paper printed in the State of Florida."[30]

Because of poor record keeping, faulty administrative procedures, or outright negligence, some accounts took years to settle. For some law enforcement and related officials, the only hope was to petition the legislature for relief. Five years elapsed before Jackson County physician Charles Hentz was paid for services performed at a coroner's inquest. The general assembly's Committee of Claims finally granted Hentz $25 even though "nothing was done . . . professionally; the corpse being in a too putrid state for examination."[31] The legislative council in 1833 similarly compensated Joseph Wachob for "certain services rendered to this Territory in arresting and apprehending certain criminals charged with a violation of the criminal laws." The services had been performed two years earlier.[32]

Occasionally even a court order to perform service could not ensure proper compensation. Columbia County Sheriff Arthur Wright experienced such difficulties even though Circuit Judge William Forward specifically ordered him in 1855 to hire a number of extra guards to watch the county jail. "You have several prisoners in jail for capital offenses," Forward directed, "and it having been made to appear they are desperate men with outside accomplices and will if possible break jail, and learning from you as well as the citizens generally that the jail is insecure without [a] guard, you are hereby authorized to employ a suitable guard." When he submitted his accounts to the state for payment, Wright enclosed his correspondence with Forward and Solicitor James Baker, explained the specific services performed, and provided detailed affidavits from each guard. The total claim stood at $217.50.[33] Whether the men ever were paid is unrecorded.

Beyond the administrative and ministerial burdens of the office, sheriffs faced immediate concerns as settlers chose to resist legal sanction in a forcible manner. In 1827, for example, an Escambia County magistrate ordered Sheriff R. L. Cotton to arrest Isaac Cobb, accused of harboring runaway slaves. Cotton found Cobb reclining under a peach tree, shook hands with him, and informed him that he was his prisoner. Cobb thereupon drew a pistol and swore that he would never be brought in "except in strings." Cotton confronted Cobb on two subsequent occasions, but each time he "ran off and would not be taken."[34]

Cobb's case was typical. Lawbreakers regularly simply refused to be taken, and unless their apprehension was deemed important enough to compel civilians to support the sheriff in a decisive way, apprehension of determined, well-armed fugitives was practically impossible. Even though a lawbreaker could be expected to resist arrest with violence, a surprising number of sheriffs persisted. In the process many were threatened and injured, and some lost their lives. One instance of this occurred in 1851 when Escambia County Constable Thomas Green suffered a severe beating when he tried to arrest Elvin Taylor, accused of shooting a hog. As Green took Taylor into custody, Charles Brightly came to the rescue and "did beat, wound, and ill-treat" Green and did "rescue and put at large [Taylor], to the great hindrance of justice and the Evil Example of all others." Brightly and similar malefactors were dutifully indicted and prosecuted for their crimes, but surviving court records show that of the twenty-six Floridians prosecuted for aiding a prisoner to escape and obstructing legal process, only two were found guilty. The vast majority of these cases (twenty-one) never reached a verdict; most perpetrators no doubt absconded with those they had liberated. Such a dismal record hardly served to deter others from violently resisting judicial process. As for Brightly, he was found not guilty.[35]

Many lawmen understood that even detaining one who perpetrated violence against a peace officer was uncertain at best. A second Escambia County incident illustrates the point. On March 29, 1829, Constable Foster Chapman was seriously wounded when he tried to serve a warrant on William Mimms. According to Chapman, he leaned through the window of a house and told Mimms he had a warrant for his arrest. Mimms replied, "[I] shall not be taken." When the constable answered that he must do his duty, Mimms escaped out the back door. Chapman gave chase until he found himself face to face with Mimms, who brandished a stick and ordered Chapman to stand back. Chapman answered "Don't be a fool" and came closer. Mimms drew a gun, shot Chapman, and ran off. He later was taken into custody long enough to be indicted for assault with intent to kill. Instead of paying for his crime, though, Mimms jumped bail and was never captured.[36]

Assisting lawmen also could be dangerous. In April 1859 Washington County's John Joyner was stabbed to death when he came to the aid of a deputy sheriff named Taylor. The killing occurred as Enoch Johns, his son, and a large number of others were attending court at Vernon. The younger Johns began abusing the deputy, a fight broke out, and Johns stabbed the deputy in the back. Drawing his own knife, the father entered the melee, and John Joyner caught him around the waist. Johns ordered Joyner to let him go, Joyner refused, and Johns stabbed Joyner, severing the femoral artery. Washington County Sheriff G. F. Gainor took immediate control and summoned a posse, which apprehended both father and son. Deputy Taylor's condition was not reported.[37]

Numerous lawmen were killed in the line of duty. Sheriff Lewis Williams was fatally wounded in a swamp near Marianna in 1844 while trying to arrest William Watson of the notorious Avant gang. Watson, wounded in the shoulder, managed to escape, changed his name to Black, and joined his father in East Florida, remaining there undetected for four years.[38] His true identity would probably never have been discovered had he not shot another sheriff—this time Alachua County's William Gibbons. The fatal confrontation occurred at an inn in Newnansville during a poker game. At some point in the game, Watson accused Gibbons of cheating, the lawman called for his pistols, and the two men adjourned to the piazza. Shots rang out, and Gibbons was found dead with a bullet wound through his side. Subsequently, Watson's father, who also had been in the game, admitted that Black was actually his son. A Newnansville posse joined two other parties already looking for Watson and his father, who had also fled. (The pair had subsequently committed a number of robberies and murders in Camden County, Georgia.) Finally, Watson was arrested, and he was positively identified by the gunshot wound on his shoulder. An Alachua County grand jury indicted Watson for murder, but he was granted a change of venue to Duval County. Several months later, however, for some unknown reason, the district attorney dropped the case.[39] Watson's fate remains unknown.

Even though they were inadequately compensated and seldom provided with sufficient means to get the job done, sheriffs and other lawmen faced criticism for any perceived wrongdoing. Some were rebuked for failing to keep updated lists of qualified jurors. Others were blamed when a prisoner escaped.[40] Yet, as the case of a Jasper town marshal illustrates, they were also abused if they "acted too precipitately." According to "P," a correspondent of a local newspaper, the marshal was at fault in the killing of a "highly esteemed" settler of Hamilton County named J. C. McBain. The row ensued when McBain, heavily intoxicated, violated a town ordinance. The marshal arrested McBain, a friend interfered, and a fight ensued. The marshal drew a hunting knife and stabbed McBain in the heart. "P" admitted that the marshal was "justified measurably in defending himself" but insisted that "there can be no doubt . . . that there was no necessity for the deed." Either the Jasper lawman anticipated the public outcry or he decided to find a less dangerous profession, for on the next day he "decamped for parts unknown."[41]

A sheriff sometimes received only casual assistance or support from the people, and the position was often a thankless job. Not only were the duties dangerous, but he could be held criminally liable for mistakes committed in their execution, either by criminal intent or by negligence. Florida lawmakers understood the potential for abuses by law enforcement officers and were determined to strictly regulate their behavior. The law imposed harsh punishments for negligence or malpractice and provided that, if any law officer refused to receive a prisoner or voluntarily permitted him to escape, he could be fined up to $10,000 and be imprisoned up to five years. Conviction for willfully falsifying public documents could result in a fine of up to $1,000, thirty-nine stripes, or twelve months in jail. Sheriffs also hired jailers whose behavior was strictly regulated. As early as 1832 the legislative council provided that if any jailer induced a prisoner to "give evidence against some other person" or subjected prisoners to "willful inhumanity and oppression," he would be subject to a fine of up to $300 or up to thirty-nine stripes.[42] These sanctions, though employed against lawmen only in extreme circumstances, were available if necessary.

Citizens and the press usually were prepared to act if a lawman exceeded his authority. In 1828, for example, Pensacola's mayor, in the absence of evidence, arbitrarily directed the city constable to whip a man accused of a number of unsolved crimes, including highway robbery. Two whippings had occurred before editor William H. Hunt of the *Pensacola Gazette,* ever vigilant against the wrongdoing of public officials, made the whipping the subject of a lengthy editorial. Entitled "Lynch's Law," the essay declared,

"If our Magistrates & Officers are permitted to judge without trial & to punish without following the forms of the law; we shall soon be at the mercy of every petty, tyrannical despot, who may be clothed with a little brief authority." Hunt held the mayor mainly responsible for the outrage and demanded an investigation.[43]

Sheriffs were sometimes prosecuted if they refused to carry out an assigned duty. For example, the Jefferson County Grand Jury in 1845 indicted Sheriff George Taylor for refusing to execute a warrant for the arrest of Solomon Tanner, a well-known roughneck. Adam Winick's complaint had charged that the culprit had beaten him over the head with a stick and stolen his mule. After a magistrate ordered Taylor to arrest Tanner, the sheriff refused, preferring legal sanction rather than facing Tanner alone.[44]

Occasionally, some even sought to hold lawmen responsible for the prosecution costs of escaped prisoners. Efforts were undertaken in 1860 to sue Holmes County Sheriff David J. Brownell for $170. The money represented the amount of an uncollected fine and costs from a prisoner who escaped just as the jury was delivering the verdict. Brownell maintained throughout that he was "not to blame in the least in regard to the matter." Upon further examination, Solicitor William Barnes concurred. "I hardly think, as the absconding prisoner departed the court without leave and before the verdict was rendered," Barnes observed to the comptroller, "that the sheriff can be made liable upon his bond for escape." In Barnes's opinion the prisoner's sureties were responsible.[45] One can only speculate as to Brownell's culpability had the prisoner escaped after the verdict had been rendered.

Trying, convicting, and housing lawbreakers in accordance with the U.S. Constitution was expensive. Lawmakers expected the criminal justice system, through collection of fines and court costs, to pay for itself. It never did, and only rarely were lawmakers willing to fund the system adequately. The public was also to blame. Few would have supported increasing taxation for such a purpose. "The pathetic point," as Philip Jordan has written, "is that the American people never wanted law and order badly enough to support any pay for effective law enforcement."[46] The lack of commitment weighed most heavily on the local law enforcement official, and insufficient compensation, combined with inadequate financial support, drove many good men out of the field. Indeed, given the circumstances, it is remarkable that there were men willing to risk their lives or their honor to serve. Even so, many did—and Florida benefited from their service.

Eleven

Catching Criminals on the Antebellum Frontier

It never entered the head, probably of M. Daguerre, when perfecting the process of causing the sun beams to play the limner, that his beautiful application of science would become a resource for the suppression of crime. Such, however, is the fact; and now the French police, when any suspicious person or known criminal is arrested, cause him to be daguerreotyped, and his likeness is appended to the register; so that if, after he is set at liberty, he shall again be implicated in any offence, his likeness being exhibited to the various police agents, the detection becomes more easy. The rogues, however, have found this out and now, when subjected to the process of daguerreotyping, make such hideous grimaces as entirely to alter the usual expression of their countenance.

—*Tallahassee Florida Sentinel,* January 14, 1842

Unfortunately, few Florida lawmen used such modern methods of criminal detection as the daguerreotype. They relied, instead, primarily on the contributions of frontier settlers working in concert with an undermanned police force. If not firsthand or by word of mouth, they learned of crime through proclamations issued either by state executives or by private individuals. The proclamations sometimes were published in Florida newspapers, and handbills also were circulated.

A shortage of professional law enforcement officers, Florida's status as a frontier society, and poor transportation demanded that citizens play an active role in capturing fugitives. In 1831, for example, the legislative council authorized Florida lawmen to form special citizens' groups to chase fleeing felons into the territory's vast uninhabited sections. Florida's "posse law" empowered "any marshal, sheriff, or constable serving any criminal process to summon a sufficient number of men to assist in arresting or safe keeping any person who refuses to be taken, or who is likely to make his escape." Any person who failed to answer the call might be fined $10.[1]

Although regular army personnel could not always be relied upon, civil authorities often requested their aid in the capture of fleeing felons. Military assistance to the civil authority was more forthcoming in the territorial period, largely because of an absence of a clash between state and federal jurisdiction. Regular army commanders were far more likely to assist federally appointed governors, judges, or U.S. marshals than state officials in the apprehension of criminals. Relations between civil and military officials sometimes was less than cordial, but the following cases demonstrate that civil and military could work together. Maj. James Glassell, commander of the Key West garrison, dispatched a detachment of regulars to assist Deputy U.S. Marshal P. B. Prior in arresting Fluendo Caldez, a Spaniard accused of murdering a man at Charlotte Harbor. The men captured Caldez, and in 1831 a Monroe County grand jury indicted him for murder.[2] If they had a personal stake in the outcome, however, military personnel could be all too eager to assist in capturing fleeing felons. In 1850, for example, Jose Epperfino was convicted of murdering a soldier at a Tampa oysterhouse. Only a few days before he was scheduled to hang, Epperfino escaped; he was captured by a military posse and brought back dead to Tampa.[3]

The capture of dangerous criminals was a major concern for state executives, and, as mentioned earlier, proclamations provided a useful means for initiating the process of capturing criminals. Gubernatorial proclamations publicized lawbreakers' misdeeds and offered financial incentives for their capture. The legislative council in 1828 additionally empowered governors to offer rewards of up to $200 for the apprehension of dangerous malefactors.[4]

An ordinary gubernatorial proclamation included four important parts. First there was the reward, usually $200. Next came a short account of the misdeed. Always included were a physical description of the felon, information regarding his personal habits, and some speculation as to where he might flee. Finally, the name of the official party issuing the proclamation—whether governor, sheriff, or jailer—was listed at the bottom. From time to time, each administration established rules and procedures regulating proclamation issuance and reward collection. In 1831, James D. Westcott, Gov. William P. DuVal's secretary, corresponded with Webbville's P. W. Bower regarding the arrest of Jessee Montford, accused of murdering a Jackson County man. Westcott specified that a certified copy of the coroner's inquest and an affidavit of Montford's flight would be sufficient for issuance of a proclamation. The governor cannot, he warned, "act on loose . . . or exported representations of individuals." Westcott continued, "Please do the Governor the justice to correct misrepresentations afloat on these subjects." An administrative oversight could—and in Montford's case,

$200 REWARD.

PROCLAMATION BY THE GOVERNOR.

WHEREAS, it has been represented to me that Washington Dudley was recently murdered at St. Marks, in the county of Wakulla, by one JOHN FREDERICK, and that one JOHN MILLER was present aiding and abetting in said murder; and whereas, the said Frederick and Miller are fugitives from justice.

Now, therefore, I, WILLIAM D. MOSELEY, Governor of the State of Florida, by virtue of the authority in me vested by the laws of said State, do hereby offer the above reward of two hundred dollars for the apprehension of said Frederick and Miller, and their delivery to the sheriff of Wakulla county—or one hundred for the apprehension or delivery of either of them.

Mem.—John Frederick is a Canadian by birth, is about 34 years old, five feet seven inches high, has dark eyes, dark hair and a dark complexion, and when spoken to has a downcast look.

John Miller is a Norwegian by birth, is about 35 years old, five feet ten or twelve inches high, has light eyes, light hair and a fair complexion, and speaks English very broken.

They are supposed to have made their escape in a small boat.

[SEAL] IN WITNESS WHEREOF, I have hereunto set my hand and caused the great seal of the state to be affixed, this the 18th day of May, A. D., 1849.

WM. D. MOSELEY, Governor.

Attest: A. E. MAXWELL, Secretary of State.

☞ Sentinel and Apalachicola Advertiser copy 4t.
May 19, 1849. 20—4w

Gubernatorial proclamations similar to the above were published in Florida newspapers throughout the antebellum era. (*Tallahassee Floridian and Journal,* May 19, 1849; *Apalachicola Commercial Advertiser,* May 26, 1846) did—allow precious time to elapse. "The governor," added Westcott to Bower, "has informed me that he has distinct recollection of receiving some letter on the subject from some person, perhaps the coroner, but if he did it [has], in the confusion, occasioned by the sickness of himself and family, been mislaid." The executive also lacked a physical description of Montford for the proclamation.[5]

Hillsborough County Sheriff Edward F. Kendrick allowed killer Ely Stephens a two-week head start on law officers in 1854 by forgetting to include copies of an inquest and other supporting documents in a letter to Gov. James E. Broome. By the time Kendrick learned of his negligence, Stephens had already fled the state. "I can not officially issue a proclamation, prior to the finding of a Grand Jury," Broome explained to Sheriff Kendrick, "as I would have nothing to base a proclamation upon, should the party be arrested beyond the limits of the state."[6]

Sheriffs, jailers, and coroners usually informed state executives of absconding felons. Typically, in 1851 Gadsden County Sheriff J. B. Love wrote Gov. Thomas Brown that Thomas Boatright, confined and awaiting trial on a charge of slave stealing, had broken out of the Quincy jail. Love supplied appropriate details, including that he had shot Boatright in the hand while attempting to "arrest him, leaving only the thumb and the forefinger on the right hand." Boatright still managed to escape, and Brown issued an arrest proclamation.[7] The previous year, county coroner James Gilchrist had informed Brown that James Riggins had murdered John White, a Chattahoochee man. Gilchrist insisted that the murder was of "such a character as justifies the highest reward the law authorizes" and added that he thought Riggins was still lurking about Chattahoochee. Again, the governor acted.[8]

Victims' friends and relatives also supplied executives with important information. Thomas Broxson wrote Governor Broome in 1856 from Anderson's Mill in Holmes County that his son's murderer, Elijah Whatley, was at large. The accused had been taken into custody, but after four hours he had broken free while Broxson and other guards were attending the dead man. The father asked the governor to add to the $500 reward that he had personally offered. Broxson speculated that Whatley might be found in the Pensacola and Mobile area.[9]

A fugitive's facial features were usually the most prominent item on a proclamation. All of the following were fugitives sought in Florida. Authorities described James Huguenin as having a "down look." Simeon King, it was said, "in talking shows his teeth very plainly which are much decayed . . . and has a rather guilty look." Daniel O'Neil had a "heavy countenance" and "very penetrating grey eyes." Jessee Goodman possessed "sharp black eyes." A "feminine voice and a rather down, sly look" characterized James Ellison. William and Charmack Selph presented "down cast countenances." William Adams had both a "florid complexion" and a "downcast, vicious look."[10]

Personality traits, personal habits, and manners of speech further identified fleeing felons. John Bembry, a notice warned, might be found "drinking and frolicking whenever he can get liquor." James Riggins was "addicted to drinking," and James Huguenin was "inclined to intoxication." Leonard Dozier's arrest proclamation stated that his "manners are pleasing when sober, but very boisterous when drunk." James Hall, a "vagabond" who killed William T. Holmes of Hamilton County, was "quick spoken and cunning as a fox." John Barkwell of Hawkinsville, Georgia, offered a private reward for Jordan Godwin, who stole his horse. The thief was "low, chunky made, somewhat stooped or humped shouldered, . . . can't look a person in the face steadily, has a peculiar grin or small scar on upper lip, fond of drink and petty gambling."[11]

Scars and other bodily features helped to identify absconding felons. The French killer Henry Jourardin had a "slouching carriage." William Passmore, charged with the murder of William Raffenburg in Ochessee, had a "white swelling in his right leg, which is much smaller than the other." King Gill, Passmore's accomplice, had "partial loss of two fingers." Owen Fountain carried "several old scars about the head." James Hall was "remarkably hump shouldered" and roamed about with his "head thrown back." Bryant Meridith, who committed murder in Jackson County, was "rather hard of hearing."[12]

Proclamations might list accomplices and traveling companions of killers. Mississippi Gov. Albert Brown speculated that a planter named Benjamin Wood, who had killed his overseer, would be accompanied by his slave, Thomas. The jailer at Columbus, Georgia, offered a $600 reward in 1839 for five escaped gang members. Their recognized leader, a man named Thurston, was a small, slender man with long black hair. He was "generally known as the 'bank robber.' " Authorities warned *St. Joseph Times* subscribers that Thurston would probably "dress in women's clothes and pass for the wife" of one of the others.[13]

Sometimes wives of fugitives accompanied their escaping husbands, as was the case with accused slave stealer B. J. Thompson. Before the fugitive was safely lodged in the Leon County jail in 1859, he had been at large for about ten months after fleeing Mississippi. When the sheriff and a large posse in that state's Lauderdale County had surrounded his house,

Thompson jumped from the back porch using his wife as a shield. She was shot in three places, but they had continued their flight.[14]

Floridians who captured dangerous felons expected to be paid, but they had to prove that they had acted on the governor's proclamation. The man who captured John Ellison, accused in the murder of Benjamin Schwerin, faced such a technical requirement. Secretary of State F. L. Villepigue informed the local solicitor that payment could only be made if it could be proven that Ellison "was apprehended by virtue of said proclamation." Insisted Villepigue, "Let your clerk make out his account against the state under a proper affidavit that he did so apprehend him."[15]

During the territorial period matters were not quite so complicated. When accused murderer George Harris escaped from the Leon County jail in 1830, for example, Governor DuVal issued an arrest proclamation. Daniel Macon captured Harris and personally delivered him to the governor. The executive took charge of Harris himself and directed the territorial auditor to pay the reward.[16] On the other hand, William Blount, "at great risk of life," turned over the notorious gang leader James Avant to the U.S. marshal in 1844. Nonetheless, because of an administrative error, Blount still had to petition the general assembly for payment.[17]

Private contributions offered additional incentives for the apprehension of dangerous killers. The $2,500 reward that "respectable gentlemen" of Madison offered for the capture of William Tooke's murderer was probably the most important factor leading to his arrest. Thomas Drew, the killer, covered himself with turpentine and grease to prevent the dogs from following his trail. For a time he eluded the sheriff and his posse, but two bounty hunters stayed on his trail. They tracked Drew for approximately seventy miles before taking him in a swamp north of Quitman, Georgia. Drew's captors seized him as he was "sitting down apparently asleep, grasping in one hand his double-barreled gun and in the other a colt repeater." He also had a pair of steel-barreled rifle pistols, two knives, a supply of ammunition, and provisions to last a week.[18]

In Florida's semitropical wilderness, fleeing felons could easily escape detection, but they also faced the natural frontier dangers. The following case represents one of the great unsolved mysteries in antebellum Florida's criminal history. On December 20, 1846, a heavily decomposed body was found in a Columbia County swamp. The headless corpse was "mostly eaten up by hogs, wolves, and buzzards," and a gun lay beside it. Authorities identified the body as that of Dr. John C. Clyde, a physician wanted for the murder of Augustus Noyes, a fellow tenant at a Lake City boardinghouse. Earlier, Noyes had found the doctor in possession of personal items belonging to the other guests and ordered him to leave. Reportedly Clyde's "character was generally considered to be infamous, and [he] was constantly boasting that he had killed a man in Middle Florida."[19] The circumstances surrounding Noyes's death proved that Clyde was capable of cold, calculated murder. "On the evening of the murder," noted a report, "Clyde, after having taken tea with Mr. Noyes, rose from the table . . . went out on the back piazza . . . and, without any words of an angry nature having passed, shot Noyes through the open door as he rose from the table, lodging nine buckshot in his abdomen." An angry mob of citizens pursued Clyde in the woods, but he evaded capture until his body was found. Yet authorities were apprehensive about closing the book on the resourceful villain. Some speculated that the corpse might turn out to be Noyes's. The killer, rumors suggested, might have obtained Noyes's body, beheaded it, dressed it in his own clothes, and exposed it to prevent pursuit.[20] Positive identification of the body remained unsubstantiated, but Clyde was never heard from again.

Arranging for the capture and return of felons fleeing from one state to another was a gubernatorial duty. Article IV of the U.S. Constitution, the "comity clause," requires that most fugitives be returned to the state from which they had fled. Extradition—or, more precisely, rendition—was a vital ingredient of what was considered comity or a courteous code of behavior. In short, it constituted "the informal and voluntary recognition by courts of one jurisdiction of the laws and judicial decisions of another." Comity among the states was further encouraged in 1793 when Congress required all states to cooperate in the apprehension of fugitives. Florida's legislative council in 1835 made it the "duty of governors to issue proclamations for fugitives from other states on demand."[21]

Executives from other states continually pressured Florida governors to aid in the arrest of absconding felons. In 1844 the governor of Louisiana informed Gov. Richard Keith Call that eight slaves had stolen a ship at the mouth of the Mississippi River. The fugitives were captured near St. Augustine, and Call ordered authorities there to turn them over to Capt. William Taylor, the Louisiana governor's authorized agent.[22]

Fugitives from other states regularly were returned for prosecution, sometimes at the urgent behest of local residents. When a Darlington, South Carolina, man visiting Jacksonville in 1846 identified William Powell as a man wanted for stealing a slave and a stallion from his home state, a Duval Countian asserted to Gov. William D. Moseley "that I believe it to be the desire of the people generally of this county to get clear of this man whose character seems to be very notorious." Moseley agreed and issued an order for Powell's release to a South Carolina agent.[23]

Local citizens occasionally took an even more active role in the process. A Georgia man accused of murder, Henry Rogers, sought refuge in Tallahassee during 1826. Only two days passed before authorities in the territorial capital received the Georgia executive's proclamation describing the fugitive and his offense. Rogers managed to leave town, but within a few hours "five parties of men commenced a hot pursuit—on foot and on horseback." They captured him in Gadsden County and brought him back to Tallahassee. After a hearing, Judge Augustus Woodward ordered that Rogers "stand committed and await the disposition of the Governor of Florida and Georgia." Governor DuVal thereupon arranged for the U.S. marshal to transport the fugitive to the proper Georgia authority.[24]

Perhaps the most interesting fugitive to visit Florida was Julius W. Cowles, an accomplished villain and master of disguise. In February 1839 the *St. Joseph Times* announced that citizens would have the "pleasure of witnessing the truly wonderful performances of Mr. J. W. Cowles, the magician, [juggler], and ventriloquist . . . this evening." As an encore, the notice added, Cowles "will perform his celebrated and astonishing gun trick, in which he will allow any person to bring his own gun, powder and ball, and load it in the presence of the company, and then fire at him. [He] will catch the ball in his hand or on the point of a sword, with other tricks that will surprise the audience—*let us all go and see him!*"[25] Cowles and his assistant, Dickinson, also performed before astonished crowds in Jacksonville, St. Augustine, Key West, and Apalachicola. But he always managed to leave town just before the incoming mail that named him as the murderer of Icabod Isaacs, a jeweler from Jones County, Georgia.

Cowles's luck almost ran out in Pensacola on February 15 when someone noticed a Savannah newspaper account describing the murder of a jeweler in that city by a ventriloquist named Cowles. Once confronted, Cowles argued that "there were a good many J. W. Cowleses in the United States" and then vanished. About that time the brig *Caspian* arrived at the port, and its captain remarked that Cowles had been his passenger from Charleston to Key West and St. Joseph. The man and his assistant had a large amount of "jewelry which they offered for sale and exhibited at different places." Georgia Gov. George Gilmer's description of a five-foot, seven-inch, "very trim built, well made" man who was "very active and upright in his walk" fit Cowles perfectly. Town authorities promptly called a meeting on the public square, and a reward of $200 was offered. The town subsequently was searched, and Cowles was found concealed in the forecastle of a vessel lying at anchor. The town magistrate committed the fugitive to jail to await the demand of Georgia's governor, but Cowles escaped with his assistant's help before the proper documents arrived. "Alas the bird has flown," lamented the town's editor. Cowles never was apprehended, but Dickinson was taken in Alabama.[26]

Complex rules regulated the extradition of fugitives, and extensive legal documentation and interstate cooperation were required. Sometimes, however, suspects were shanghaied or kidnapped, although such action did not always please Floridians. Future governor John Milton of Jackson County informed Gov. Thomas Brown in 1849 that a man named Jones, "with force of arms and without having or pretending to have any legal authority seized upon and took off [four area citizens] to Georgia" and lodged them in the Decatur County jail. Three of the men, suspected of cattle stealing, were eventually discharged for lack of evidence, and the fourth "broke jail and returned to this state." Jackson County citizens, Milton declared, regarded Jones's conduct and that of the others as a "great outrage upon personal liberty." Milton enclosed a Jackson County circuit court indictment against Jones and offered his services in the matter.[27] Nothing is known of any resulting action.

Individuals who thought they had been wrongly accused routinely appealed to the governor for protection. P. B. Woolen of Leon County was indicted in 1853 for assault with intent to kill in Thomas County, Georgia. He escaped to Florida and wrote Gov. James Broome that he was "ready to stand trial—if I can have *justice,* but I am . . . certain that in Thomasville, I can get no sort of justice." Woolen continued, "Give me a trial in my own state—I demand it—and am ready to give myself up any time. Now Sir, I claim your protection." He added that the Thomas County judge was strongly prejudiced against him. "To be carried to Thomasville would be equivalent to condemnation unheard," he concluded. "I demand a trial in my own state . . . I can not suffer myself to be taken to Thomasville. . . . If necessary, I must resist—for me to do it is equivalent to death—give me a trial in my own *state* and I will abide by the consequences."[28]

Florida governors often requested executives from other states to turn fugitives over for prosecution. Bennett L. Caro was charged in 1848 with assault with intent to kill in Franklin County. He escaped and Gov. William Moseley asked the Louisiana governor to arrest Caro and hand him over. The process usually involved designation of an appointed agent to receive the fugitive into custody. Gov. Richard Keith Call, for instance, in 1844 appointed Eben Dorr of Pensacola to go to Mobile, Alabama, and take charge of George Lang. Escambia County authorities had charged Lang with larceny. The same year, Gov. John Branch received word that George Thomas, lodged in a North Carolina jail, was the same man indicted for murder in Leon County four years earlier. Branch requested the North Carolina governor to see that Thomas was turned over to John Manning and William Hooks.[29]

Slaves who committed crimes might be spirited out of the state by their masters to prevent prosecution. A Putnam County lawman asked Governor Broome in 1855 to provide for the return of Edenborough, a slave accused of stealing from a Palatka citizen named Wickwire. The slave's owner, explained the lawman, "carried him to Charleston to save him from the law. Mr. Wickwire went there last week and had him arrested, but they will not deliver him up, without your Excellency's requisition." Broome complied and appointed Wickwire agent to claim the fugitive.[30]

Even when a criminal could be brought back to Florida for trial, the witnesses necessary for a successful prosecution could not be compelled to attend. When accused murderer John Henderson broke out of the Escambia County jail in 1845, he escaped to New Orleans. For five months the fugitive went unnoticed until he was identified by two Pensacola men. On the strength of their affidavits, Henderson was taken into custody, and arrangements were soon under way to return him to Pensacola. Governor Moseley promptly approved an extradition request, but Henderson could not be prosecuted. Vital witnesses remained out of the state, and it was impossible to find a true bill of indictment against him. Judge George Macrea had no choice but to release him because "witnesses now reside outside the State of Florida and . . . their attendance can not therefore be compelled to appear by this court."[31]

Sometimes interstate fugitives voluntarily turned themselves in. Such was the case of Dr. Simon Taylor, a Columbia, South Carolina, resident who in 1840 was accused of murdering a Leon County man named Hugh Rose. When he had learned of Taylor's wish to give himself up, Gov. Thomas Brown appointed a special agent to take charge of Taylor's return to Tallahassee. A trial commenced immediately, and Taylor employed some of the best legal counsel in the state and proved to the jury's satisfaction that he had been compelled to shoot Rose in self-defense. A Tallahassee editor speculated that Taylor's ten-year absence was the deciding factor in the verdict. "Had the case been concluded here [in 1840]," he wrote, "the prisoner would have been hung, as a matter of course."[32]

Extradition did not always go so smoothly. Two cases—one involving bank swindling and the other relating to slaves—illustrate the problem of Northern and foreign governments refusing to extradite absconding felons. The incidents—each taking place about the time Florida was admitted to the Union—intensified already-existing sectional distrust. The first involved alleged frauds committed by a New Yorker, James Graham, whom the Leon County Grand Jury had indicted in 1844 for conspiracy and misdemeanor (embezzlement) in connection with his actions as president of the Bank of Florida. His flight had left Tallahassee depositors holding mountains of worthless paper.[33]

Governor Call used every means available to have him returned, including demands upon the governor of New York. That state's executive refused to surrender him, citing technical deficiencies with the indictment and the fact that the crime did not involve treason or felony. Call was indignant at the refusal. He did not understand why the indictment he sent could not remove even the "most fastidious objections to its authenticity." Moreover, he insisted, the "Act of Congress does not make the 'enormity of crime' a matter to be decided by Executive authority."[34] Call's logic was sound, but he and other Florida authorities were unsuccessful in bringing Graham to justice.

The second incident began in early September 1843 when seven slaves ran away from a plantation near St. Augustine. After stealing a boat they made their way to Key Biscayne, where they murdered a settler and thereafter escaped to the Bahamas. Extensive efforts were made to have the runaways returned. U.S. Marshal Joseph Browne traveled to Nassau and presented British Gov. Francis Cockburn with bills of indictment issued by the grand jury of the Monroe and Dade County Superior Court. His efforts were to no avail, and the bondsmen were not returned.[35]

Florida's frontier status hampered measures to apprehend offenders and made it easy for criminals to escape detection. Poor transportation and communication facilities also conspired to thwart their capture. Lacking a strong, centralized state police force, Floridians resorted to a variety of official and unofficial persons to apprehend criminal elements in the antebellum decades. The criminal justice system was extremely haphazard, and its glaring defects would not be fully rectified until late in the nineteenth century. For the time being, whatever success the system enjoyed was attributable mainly to the resourcefulness of Florida's overburdened lawmen.

Twelve

Jails and Escapes

> Persons charged with the most heinous offenses are necessarily discharged upon recognizance, a bond in such cases being the only security for the appearance of the accused. And even this is optional with the culprit, if he refuses it and offers to deliver himself up. The officer having no place sufficient for his safe custody is compelled to permit him to go at large.
>
> —Leon County Grand Jury (1838)

Florida, state and territory, generally was poor and boasted few of the public amenities common in more well-to-do areas. Among the facilities it often lacked were suitable places to confine criminals. Apalachicola, for example, had no jail in 1837. While the Franklin County Grand Jury could congratulate the community upon the fact that the "vices and outrages which mark a frontier population are fast receding from our view," its members still noted, "much remains to be done." Several offenders had committed serious crimes and were likely to be released before their crimes could be investigated. The jury recommended that the county take immediate steps to erect a jail. Two years later another grand jury again was compelled to note the deficiency. There was "great difficulty in enforcing the laws or preserving public order" without an adequate jail. And, for the time being, there the matter stood.[1]

Most thoughtful Floridians recognized that jails were indispensable to the proper enforcement of the law, but the problems related to incarcerating criminals were similar to catching them. The most obvious was the lack of funding. Most counties simply lacked the resources to build and adequately maintain jails. Funds were slow in coming, and their allocation depended largely on the administrative ability of local officials. In most counties expenditures of this kind simply were not a high priority. Under such circumstances, operating jails, like apprehending criminals, necessitated large-scale cooperation of local citizenry in keeping them secure, and, in times of emergency, local citizens were expected to assist jailers as guards. But few counties possessed jails strong enough to hold lawbreakers for any length of time. Antebellum Florida's jails answered few of the purposes of modern-day penal institutions. They served mainly as temporary places of incarceration for dangerous criminals awaiting trial, prisoners serving short sentences (rarely longer than a few months), and runaway slaves. When it came to rehabilitation and retribution, Florida's antebellum jails fulfilled none of the former and little of the latter function. The state's other pressing financial needs left few funds for long-term incarceration. The construction of a penitentiary and the imposition of long sentences as part of a well-thought-out plan for the rehabilitation of criminals was a luxury that few Floridians would have thought the state could afford, and thus a penitentiary was not constructed until well into the century. Accordingly, long- or short-term incarceration—an important ingredient in any well-functioning criminal justice system—was simply not possible.

The problem of incarcerating criminals began in the territory's earliest days. When American authorities first came to Pensacola in 1822, they lamented the lack of an adequate jail. District Attorney William F. Steele informed Secretary of State John Quincy Adams that the dilapidated structure the Spaniards used was totally inadequate. "The Calobozo or public Gaol of Pensacola," he observed, "is wholly unfitted for the confinement of offenders." A "stronger edifice" would be necessary for the accommodation of the increasing criminal class.[2] Newly appointed U.S. Marshal William F. Sebree was more specific. There was no adequate jail in Pensacola or anywhere else in West Florida. Holding prisoners for trial without an adequate jail "may become a very precarious matter," he asserted. The "Calobozo" the Spanish had constructed was crumbling and could not be repaired.[3]

Escambia County's first assembled grand jury recognized that a jail was critical to the community's security. The absence of a jail encouraged violation of the laws, especially since Pensacola, "located on the extremity of the continent . . . [was] most liable to be made the harbour of Fugitives who here resort to commit crimes with impunity."[4] As late as 1840 Escambia County's needs still were not fully answered. Territorial delegate Charles Downing took up the issue with a congressional committee, explaining that Pensacola's precarious geographical location demanded immediate congressional attention. Pensacola was both a seaport and very close to the Alabama and Georgia borders, and thus it was often the destination of a "mixed, lawless, and desperate floating population." At that time there was "no jail to hold a prisoner, or a house to try him in."[5]

If any locality had cause to request a federal appropriation to build a jail, it was Key West. Situated at the extreme southernmost point of the United States, this island town became a temporary stop-off for persons Judge James Webb referred to as a "heterogenous mass, congregated from various parts the world." Appealing to Washington for financial assistance, Webb explained that these disorderly folk were "unacquainted with the operation of our laws." They had "for several years . . . been living in a state of licentious freedom."[6] Other Key West officials likewise pleaded for assistance. The Monroe County Grand Jury, for instance, informed Congress that a federal appropriation to build a jail was "necessary for our safety and the lives of prisoners." The jurors observed that Key West's population was composed primarily of "mariners employed in the wrecking business" and that their "habits [and] mode of life . . . when upon shore, are . . . well known." The communication reminded the national legislature that "the strong arm of the law is too often required to preserve order among them and punish the guilty." The present makeshift jail, they contended, was totally insufficient. Despite the obvious need for federal funding to adequately maintain a jail in Key West, the island community's needs remained unfulfilled.[7]

As late as 1841 the Key West jail remained insufficient. "Key West," claimed Judge William Marvin at this time, "is particularly exposed to the aggressions of imported villains. It is a kind of '*Half Way House*' for travellers upon the high seas. Here they stop, refresh themselves, and not infrequently commit crimes against the laws." Marvin asked congressional delegate David Levy (Yulee) to appeal to federal authorities for assistance because the territorial treasury was bankrupt, adding that U.S. law could not be enforced without an adequate jail. "Revolts, Mutinies, Stealing from wrecks, assaults and batteries, and murders upon the high seas," he explained, "are of no infrequent occurrences in this court."[8]

All communities possessed disorderly elements that had to be restrained, and most residents understood that jails were an indispensable vehicle for effective enforcement of the law. The Leon County Grand Jury, for example, concluded that threat of incarceration was the only way to restrain some unruly transgressors from disorder and crime. "They have no character nor property to lose, and they can only be effected by a loss of personal liberty," the jurors noted.[9] The members of the Madison County Grand Jury similarly noted that laws could not be executed without a jail. Such a condition, this report stated, "affords to the evil disposed and common disturbers of the peace, the unrestricted indulgence of every riotous and disorderly feeling." The absence of a jail was a "great draw-back and hindrance to the faithful and speedy administration of criminal justice." Until 1855, county prisoners had to be confined in jails of adjacent counties.[10]

During times of Indian troubles the shortage of jails became even more acute. In Duval County in 1840, criminals were either "permitted to go at large, or officers [were] compelled to muster a large force to guard prisoners." The only other alternative was to carry them forty miles along a road "endangered by lurking Indians" to St. Augustine for confinement.[11] Likewise, in Alachua County the added strains of the Second Seminole War hampered adequate administration of the law. Military authorities took over the jail in 1841 and turned it into a storehouse. Lawmen were forced to convey prisoners to St. Augustine for confinement, returning them at each session of the court, at great cost and hazard.[12]

If short-term incarceration was a problem, long-term confinement was next to an impossibility. Jail sentences clearly were important deterrents to lawbreaking, yet most counties possessed no facilities adequate for long-term confinement until late in the antebellum period. Such jails as did exist served mainly as temporary holding places for dangerous criminals while they awaited trial. Florida had no penitentiary, and in most cases a fine or corporal punishment was the most common form of punishment for lawbreakers. In many cases this meant merely administering a flogging and sending the culprit on his way. Many recognized the insufficiency of those punishments as opposed to confinement. Editor William H. Hunt, for one, asserted that punishing horse thieves with a whipping and a fine was "worse than lame. . . . Horse thieves are almost always from amongst the poor classes of men; a fine therefore is merely nominal." Fines could not be collected, and whipping was no deterrent either. "Anyone despicable enough to steal," declared Hunt, "would stand fifty lashes without changing countenance, to such men the disgrace is nothing and the chance of acquiring a good horse, is well worth the risk of a flogging."[13] Extended periods behind bars were the only remedies for such rogues, he believed. The Gadsden County Grand Jury came to the same conclusion. "It is a fact which is proved by the observation of everyone," the panel stated, "that the dread of the deprivation of personal liberty, and disgrace consequent upon it, is a much greater preventative of crime than a fine, however severe. . . . The most peaceable and best regulated communities in our country have the strongest and most secure prisons."[14]

The sudden destruction of the Leon County jail by fire in 1836 brought to light the impossibility of proper law enforcement without such a facility. "Convicts are suffered to escape with a nominal punishment and the proceedings of the trial and conviction become a mere mockery of public justice," the local grand jury noted one and a half years later. Admitting prisoners to bail was also problematic. Persons charged with serious offenses often refused bail, knowing full well that the county had no way to confine them. The officer "is compelled to permit him to go at large," the jurors declared. "If he is confident of being acquitted of the charge he will appear at court, if he considers his case doubtful, he has only to keep out of the way of the officer until the term of court has passed," declared the grand jurors.[15]

The circumstances in Monroe County were similar. Key West's exposed position in the Caribbean, its transient population, and its lack of an adequate jail all combined to make proper administration of justice impossible. In 1837 the Monroe County Grand Jury presented that the jail was unusable. The marshal improvised by committing some prisoners to a private house and hiring special guards at great public expense. A few of the more dangerous criminals were sent to St. Augustine and Middle Florida for confinement, but many of the others had been set free. "The want of a secure and suitable jail," they complained, "had allowed criminals to refuse to obey the mandates of the magistrate's tribunal." The situation was so bad that prisoners were thus allowed to refuse either to be held in custody or to find bail—"a tacit acknowledgement that petty offenses . . . may be committed without fear of punishment."[16]

The situation in Leon and Monroe Counties was not novel. Most counties suffered from the same difficulties if they lacked adequate jails for prisoners. In 1848 the Escambia County Grand Jury declared that their lockup was an "engine of discipline," without which "it is impossible for the best system of laws, however enforced or respected, to be effective." Therefore, the jail's dilapidated condition was "calculated to hinder the continued existence of good order in the community." Likewise, the grand jury in newly formed Wakulla County noted in 1847 that "the want of a jail in this county is much felt, and the jury believes the erection of one would greatly aid in the prevention of crime, by increasing the certainty of punishment." As late as 1861 Clay County lacked an adequate jail of its own. "We ought to have a good jail, a full execution of the law can not be had without so necessary a building," complained the grand jury.[17]

As the Second Seminole War wound down in the early 1840s, the pace of settlement in peninsular Florida quickened and the lack of adequate facilities to hold dangerous lawbreakers soon became apparent. In 1847 the Marion County sheriff had to transport criminals "a great distance of many miles to other prisons." Plans to construct a jail in Ocala began immediately.[18] Elsewhere in the region, county authorities moved more slowly. The Hillsborough County Commission called for sealed proposals for the construction of a jail only in 1850. Even then the proposed facility was humble at best. The specifications called for a structure "twenty-one by fifteen feet, enclosed with Pickets sufficiently strong to prevent encroachments from without."[19]

Responsibility for jail construction fell on the county authorities. The county probate judge served ex officio as chairman of the county commission, which assumed the responsibility of receiving bids, supervising construction, and maintaining jails. Grand jury reports serve as the best source of information about jail conditions and construction. Their biennial pronouncements goaded county commissioners to action. In Jefferson County, for example, the jury in 1845 announced that the present jail structure was insufficient and urged the "building [of] a safe jail at once." A few days later the county commissioners formed a committee to select a site, furnish a plan, and estimate the probable cost. A plan was submitted and published in the local newspaper, and several bids were received. The committee awarded the contract to John Stevens, whose bid of $3,800 was the lowest submitted. The builder filed his bonds in the courthouse, and construction began immediately. Within a month the jury reported that a new "efficient and safe receptacle for the vicious and violent" was under construction. The project took slightly more than a year to complete. Stevens reported to the board in April 1848 that the jail was ready, and after examining the structure the board certified that the builder had completed it to the specifications of the contract. The commissioners then ordered Sheriff James Tucker to take custody, "possession, and charge of the . . . jail as the law provides."[20]

In Duval County, jail building progressed in much the same way. In 1835 the county jail burned, but not until 1840 were efforts made to build another one. The county commissioners appointed subscription committees from magistrate districts in Black Creek, Mandarin, and Jacksonville to raise money. A building committee was appointed to superintend construction and receive money from the county treasury as the county judge ordered. But conflicts soon arose over the jail's location. Some wanted it to be placed where it could be monitored. This, adherents claimed, was necessary because there were no plans for the jailer to reside nearby. Others sought to locate the edifice in an isolated place where it would not disturb the peace or devalue property. The grand jury insisted that it should not be built in the most pleasant spot in town but "where the clanking of chains and the imprecations of criminals can not be heard." Construction eventually proceeded at the more desirable location. Despite numerous complaints the location remained unchanged, and the jail began receiving prisoners in 1842.[21]

Negative community reactions to the location of new jails was a fact of life with which many local governing bodies had to live. The Apalachicola city council in 1839 received a plan and specifications for the construction of a "city prison." The committee on improvements approved the plan and asked the county commissioners to have the committee on contracts authorize the building of a jail. The site was selected, but there were objections. The lot was too costly and too narrow. The jail would be "so hemmed in and confined as to be unfit." But most of all, a jail located on the proposed site would depress property values and stunt the growth and prosperity of the city.[22]

Jails may not have been popular in central locations, but structures located in remote, relatively inaccessible parts of towns facilitated escapes. In Key West Sheriff Edwin Page and his jailer decided in 1845 that keeping prisoners at a house situated in a "thickly inhabited quarter of the city [was] more economical and safe." Appealing to the general assembly for extra funds, the men explained that escapes were likely from the regular jail because it was both insufficient and remote from inhabited parts of the town. Such a large number of prisoners had accumulated that Page and the jailer had decided to abandon the regular jail and move as many prisoners as they could to the U.S. military garrison. Others were locked up in a house near the middle of town.[23]

Once a jail had been constructed, lack of funding for the confinement and maintenance of prisoners often left marshals, sheriffs, jailers, constables, and their assistants with major problems. The public wanted dangerous criminals locked up, but often little provision existed for their confinement. The problem was particularly acute in Florida's earliest days as a territory. A situation in 1823 is illustrative. That year an Escambia County jury convicted two men of mayhem, fined them $200 each, and sentenced them to two years in jail. Because there was no jail, Judge Brackenridge ordered Col. George Brooke, the commander of the military garrison, to "keep them in the same manner as convicts for offenses in the army are kept until public buildings in this place can be prepared for their reception." Whether or not the military authorities complied with the judge's "order" was unrecorded.[24]

Pensacola's situation improved a little in 1824 when a makeshift jail was put in the courthouse basement. According to one observer, it was "much preferable to the Old Calobozo." Still, it was the only jail in the whole district of West Florida, and U.S. Marshal William Sebree complained that he had many prisoners but no means to provide for them. "Expenses of this kind," he claimed, "will not be paid by the United States." Consequently, he was forced to let several prisoners go. Congress had made no provision for their maintenance. "The only alternative left me," Sebree argued, "is either to support the prisoners, which I am not able to do, or to turn them out, or confine them without food, to perish in prison. Humanity dictates that they shall be turned out, and reason teaches that offenders against the laws of the country must go unpunished until the government will provide some means for sustaining prosecutions, and the safe custody of the accused." As a last resort, Sebree attempted to have someone from the community support the prisoners, "but not one would do it, upon the faith of the Territory."

Marshal Sebree searched for a solution to the dilemma, though without much success. He asked Judge Brackenridge for instructions, but all the judge was willing to do was blame the legislative council. He insisted that the United States could not be expected to pay all county and territorial expenses. "It has not been done elsewhere," the judge declared, "and it is not probable that it ever will be done—It [is] therefore the duty of the territory to levy a tax for this purpose." As to Sebree's responsibilities, Brackenridge at least believed that the marshal was not required to support them out of his personal funds. "All that can be expected of you," he told Sebree, "is to keep them as safely and as consistent with the feelings of humanity [as you can]. Rather than suffer them to perish of hunger; you will be justifiable in turning them out of prison." Brackenridge explained that under the present circumstances, "you would be perfectly justifiable in pursuing any course which would not be oppressive or cruel."[25]

The deplorable situation in Pensacola continued. In 1827 Sebree again was confronted with the same dilemma. That summer he took into custody two dangerous men—John Pate, accused of robbery, and William Frye, charged with stabbing his wife. Eleven days after Pate's arrest, his attorney appealed to the county judge for the prisoner's relief. Under the circumstances of his confinement, Pate was "under fair prospects of perishing of hunger." He had not eaten since his arrest. The judge ordered Sebree to either release Pate or provide for him out of his own funds. Responding that he had no public or private funds at his disposal, Sebree released Pate. Frye's confinement was considered so critical to the community's safety that a town meeting at the courthouse resolved that application be made to the Pensacola Board of Aldermen for a special appropriation. A committee of citizens appeared before the board seeking funds, but the requests were rejected and Frye was released.[26]

The situation appeared to be out of control. One outraged citizen expressed the sentiments of many when he blamed the legislative council.

The "privilege" of legislation "has been extended to Florida for five years, and we are *Without a Dollar* in the treasury to *sustain a murderer in prison until he can be tried*." Editor Hunt expressed his outrage through satire. In a column entitled "Important to Murderers &c!" he declared that "all vagabonds, thieves, counterfeiters, and other criminals to whom these presents may come, will see" by the situation in Pensacola "that there is at last a place where they can with impunity perpetrate their crimes." Hunt also hinted that "while laws can not be enforced," citizens might impose "*Lynch's Law*."[27]

The lack of both federal and territorial legislative direction caused much of this confusion. Congress had not specifically earmarked funds for the purpose of confining criminals, and the legislative council also had failed to act. Until this oversight was corrected, criminals were not and could not be adequately housed to await trial.

If funds to provide for the maintenance of prisoners was slow in coming, jail conditions throughout the antebellum era also were deplorable. Grand juries provided oversight, as they were required to examine the county jail. They reported to the county commissioners on healthiness, the need for repairs, overcrowding, food, how prisoners were confined, and the relative security of jails. Their presentments usually depicted dirty, damp, unhealthy, and "leaky" conditions.

Once again, Key West offers an example. The jail in Key West was exceedingly unhealthy. According to one description, it was "but a small box" thrown up in 1827 for the "confinement of disorderly sailors." In 1828 the grand jury complained that seven prisoners had been confined there since the last court term. "During the summer the heat of the room was nearly insufferable," so much so that their lives were endangered. Within a year one prisoner had died and two were seriously ill "for want of air and exercise."[28] The structure was not only unhealthy, it was insecure. "A man of ordinary strength if placed within its walls could extricate himself at his own pleasure." In 1833 a new jail was constructed, but the next year the jury found that the mortar holding the stone walls together was "mostly sand, and good for nothing." The walls could be easily torn down. In short, the jail was useless.[29]

By 1841 matters had not much improved. That year, it was said, the "flimsiness of its materials and construction render it entirely insecure and its weakness is laughed at and despised by the wicked and deplored by the good." The structure was so insecure that authorities were forced to hire a twenty-four-hour guard to watch the prisoners.[30] Eight years afterward gratings were out of the windows and the cell doors were broken. Nor was the structure secure from the outside. "It has come to our knowledge," grand jurors reported, "that spirits and implements for breaking out have been passed through the gratings to the prisoners by which one has already escaped." The jury recommended placing a twelve-foot-high stone wall around the jail, "capped with pickets or Iron (or broken glass) to prevent effectively any communication with the inmates except by the proper authorities." Twelve months later the situation was uncorrected. No wall had been erected, and "liquor" and "other articles" were still passing through jail windows.[31]

In most parts of Florida jail conditions were inadequate for the safe confinement of prisoners. The Ocala jail in 1857 was "exceedingly dirty, and need[ed] a thorough cleaning."[32] In 1838, rooms in Fort Marion used to confine prisoners were found to be "damp, unsafe, and unhealthy," although "provisions furnished the prisoners [were] wholesome and in abundance."[33] By 1858 the Apalachicola jail had degenerated to the extent that one outraged citizen castigated the county commissioners and sheriff for wanton neglect. The prisoners in "our Bastille," charged "Howard" in a letter to the local newspaper, "have no beds, pallets or covering. . . . Several are *calaboosed* [without] even a *bundle of straw* to lie upon or a coal of a fire to warm their benumbed bodies! We profess both humanity and Christianity! Where are our county commissioners and sheriff?"[34]

Lack of maintenance obviously was a problem, and grand juries often chided county commissioners for not keeping jails adequately repaired. The Leon County jail in 1845 needed glass in its windows, a banister along the stairway leading to the upper story, and a window in the hall of the second story.[35] Five years later it needed a whitewashing, and holes in the floor needed to be filled up and cemented over. The grand jury also recommended the purchase of cots and beds because prisoners were sleeping on the floor.[36] Conditions were similar in nearby Gadsden County. The Quincy jail in 1853 was "revolting to humanity."[37] St. Augustine's Fort Marion, according to the St. Johns County Grand Jury in 1851, was an "unfit receptacle for any one entitled to the rights of humanity, being damp, unwholesome, and in every respect incapable of affording comfort or even security." Such a jail was unbefitting the "humanity and the character of a Christian Community."[38]

The state of medical science in antebellum America, however primitive, fully recognized health hazards for prisoners confined in close, dark, damp, cold, or ovenlike jails. Even though jail security was a constant concern, local authorities made constant appeals for jails with proper ventilation. Jackson County grand jurors in 1858 presented that windows in the Marianna jail needed to be "enlarged . . . to admit sufficient pure air." But the problem persisted. Three years later the "jail [was] wholly unfit for the confinement of any human being." The grand jury predicted that, unless the matter was corrected, all the inmates would die of disease.[39] One unfortunate Jackson County inmate was John Ammons, condemned to death but waiting for an appeal. His pathetic situation pointed up the fact that long-term confinement could break even the healthiest of men. Ammons languished in the Marianna jail for more than a year. Finally, a number of citizens wrote Gov. Madison Starke Perry on his behalf. "Once a robust man," they explained, "Ammons had been reduced to a skeleton."[40] Nevertheless, Ammons was hanged.

Given such unhealthy jail conditions, physicians often petitioned governors for the release of prisoners, claiming that jails threatened life if not limb. Two doctors asked Gov. William Moseley in 1849 to release convicted murderer Thomas Holton from the Leon County jail. They claimed that the prisoner's horrible physical condition was made worse by the "bad atmosphere of the jail." Moseley remitted Holton's twelve-month sentence but required him to take out a $100 "personal good behavior bond."[41] Moseley also released at least two other prisoners for health reasons. Physicians taking care of Leonidus McNeal in Duval County had predicted death for their patient from lack of "pure air." Isaac Kent, confined in the Gadsden County jail, was released on similar grounds. Kent's doctors convinced the governor that further confinement would make him "an invalid for life."[42]

Personal safety, particularly in the case of female prisoners, could constitute a health concern. Moseley, for instance, spared a woman the rigors of a jail sentence when in 1846 he pardoned Elizabeth Conner, a poor Apalachicola woman jailed for selling "spirituous liquor" to a slave. The certain humiliation and hardship in store for any female serving a sixty-day sentence was more than the governor would allow. Accordingly, Conner was pardoned "by reason of her *sex*."[43]

Appeals in the interest of endangered prisoners sometimes came from seemingly strange quarters. On December 9, 1856, future Confederate general Joseph Finegan wrote Gov. James Broome on behalf of Henry Williams, convicted of killing one of Finegan's slaves. "The negro . . . was a favorite slave of mine," Finegan acknowledged. Yet Williams's "health has already suffered from long confinement and his life may be seriously endangered."[44]

Some prisoners were so worn down by their confinement that they lacked the energy to escape. An 1840 Apalachicola newspaper story recounted the aborted escape of two prisoners from the Franklin County jail the evening before. The men were easily recaptured because they "were so debilitated by their long confinement that they were unable to elude or outstrip their pursuers." The journal used the incident to insist that jailers make the jail more secure and enclose the lot so that the prisoners would have the opportunity to take exercise in the warm summer months.[45]

Inevitably, some prisoners succumbed to unhealthy jail conditions. George Beaty, confined in the Duval County jail for the murder of Henry Hawkins, died from a fever in 1857. According to A. J. Baldwin, a physician who supervised his care, Beaty became ill and his life was so threatened that the jailer removed him to a house nearby. That, claimed the physician, "was the only chance of saving his life." Nevertheless, Beaty died a few days later.[46]

Jail overcrowding exacerbated unhealthy conditions. Again, the Marianna jail offers a case in point. For most of the antebellum period, Jackson County, except for Pensacola, had the only secure jail west of the Apalachicola River. At any given time prisoners from Washington, Holmes, Calhoun, Franklin, Walton, and Santa Rosa Counties could be found there. Holding prisoners from faraway counties placed added strain on county funds and officers and led to extreme overcrowding. The grand jury complained in 1859 that, out of the nine men being held in their jail, six were from other counties. Thus "the lives of these prisoners are endangered from necessarily crowding them together in small rooms." They demanded that the general assembly force "each county to sustain the inconvenience and expense of keeping [its own] prisoners."[47]

Additional uses to which jails were put added to overcrowding problems. In 1845 the Leon County Grand Jury protested against the "great evil practice of using the jail as a common 'lockup' for slaves, taken for executions." The panel's members estimated that more than a hundred "slaves of all ages and both sexes . . . promiscuously jumbled together into small confined cells" inhabited the jail at one time. This circumstance was "calculated to engender disease among themselves" and among other prisoners.[48] Later county juries complained that the jail served unintended uses. Aside from providing for prisoners, it was used as a horse and mule lot, a receptacle for lunatics, and a powder magazine. During the Civil War the Confederates commandeered it for use as a guardhouse. The grand jury protested, but to no avail.[49]

All Florida counties faced crises that endangered the safe confinement of prisoners. Extra guards might be hired, but more often judges ordered sheriffs to transport dangerous prisoners to jails in other districts. Until the 1840s those accused or convicted in Franklin County were transported up the Apalachicola River to Quincy, in Gadsden County, although its jail's reputation for holding prisoners was less than reassuring. Escapes were common. In fact, within one year at least five accused felons brought to the Quincy jail from other counties escaped.[50] The 1850 Gadsden County Grand Jury found its jail "dilapidated and insecure" from overuse and a lack of maintenance, and the jurors recommended that the county commissioners build a new one as soon as possible. Throughout the 1850s it remained a useless eyesore. The situation had come full circle, and Gadsden County prisoners had to be confined elsewhere.[51] As late as 1861, Judge J. Wayles Baker directed that a prisoner be taken to Leon County, pointing out that the jail in Quincy was "insecure and not in a condition for the safe and comfortable keeping of prisoners."[52]

Even if criminals were unfortunate enough to be locked up during Florida's antebellum period, experience proved that few jails could hold those determined to escape. For the most desperate of lawbreakers, special measures were necessary, but they were not always implemented. Escapes were common. Some of the most desperate saw escape as their only hope. Condemned killer David Rogers, for example, writing his uncle in South Carolina from a Leon County jail cell, maintained that he had "no justice done me in this county." Rogers concluded that his only hope was to escape. "I think there are a few friends of mine who intend to rescue me if it is in their power," he optimistically predicted. Still, Rogers admitted that he was at "quite at a loss how to make my escape." Nonetheless, he sought "shipping somewhere on the Coast of Florida." Tampa Bay, Apalachicola, and Pensacola were alternatives. His hope was to "leave the United States entirely" for either Cuba or Texas. Rogers now thought of his relations. "Again, I ask you, tell them all Farewell for me. I shall never see them again. If nothing turns up for my relief, I shall be in eternity long before this reaches you." His escape never materialized, however. Rogers hanged only days later.[53]

During the antebellum decades, a number of brothers or father-son combinations committed violent crimes and became fugitives. Such lawbreakers obviously were tied by close blood relationships, and they took advantage of natural bonds not usually found among other criminals. In October 1854 Governor Brown ordered the arrest of William and Charmack Selph, escaped from the Hernando County jail while waiting trial for the murder of Thomas Stanfield.[54] Both Selphs, along with two other brothers, had migrated to South Florida from Hamilton County, where Charmack had served as constable. Authorities chased the fugitives around the state for four months, finally capturing them in Eufala, Alabama, where they were about to board a steamboat. The men made a full confession, and authorities lodged them in the Leon County jail. But few jails could hold such resourceful men. Within a month the Selphs had somehow managed to remove their irons, pick the lock of their jail cell, and force open the front door. A heavy rain, according to a local newspaper, "obliterated all traces of their escape and the course of their flight, and up to this hour nothing has been heard of them. . . . They will most probably not be a third time captured as they are strangers to the people in this region."[55] The editor was right. The Selphs were never heard from again.

In 1859 Florida newspapers documented the exciting exploits of another clan—the Jernigans—who committed murder and escaped. The Jernigans were among the first settlers in Orange County. Aaron Jernigan was a former state legislator, militia captain, and cattleman. But the Jernigans were also well known in Florida for their violent tendencies, and they were often involved in bloody clashes with their neighbors. At one such encounter, Aaron Jernigan and his three sons—Louis, Moss, and Aaron Jr.—killed a man named William Wright in a "general fight" at the Orlando post office. The Jernigans turned themselves in, and the Orange County Grand Jury unexpectedly indicted them. Judge Benjamin Putnam ordered the prisoners lodged in the Marion County jail and directed the sheriff to hire a special guard for the trip.[56] The four broke free on April 22, their thirteenth day of custody. The father was later recaptured. About a year later an Ocala newspaper reported that the elder Jernigan "again became weary of confinement . . . and very unceremoniously left." As the jailer brought dinner to the prisoner, Jernigan "made a hard struggle" and succeeded in taking the jailer's gun. Once free, the fugitive mounted a nearby horse and "made his escape before anyone could respond to [the] call for help." Even though there appeared to be no question of a struggle, some suspected that others had colluded in Jernigan's departure. Conspiracy or not, Jernigan was never recaptured.[57]

The notorious Ellison brothers (John, Moses, and James), confined for the murder of Benjamin Schwerin, escaped from the Madison County jail in 1859 as the jailer carried them their supper. At the given signal two brothers caught the jailer by the arms and throat. This allowed the third brother and another man to bolt through the open jail door. The Ellisons held the jailer for at least three minutes until he struggled free and gave an alarm. The fugitives had obviously planned their escape with someone on the outside, for only minutes after the escape a horse was found grazing near the jail, its saddlebags containing clothes, weapons, and provisions. But in their haste the horse was left behind. Local authorities formed a posse, and within minutes "a party of pursuers with dogs, were on the trail."

A reward totaling $700 was offered, and eventually the brothers were captured.[58]

Thomas Horan, a condemned killer, broke out of the Leon County jail only a few days before he was to be executed. Horan loosened his chains just before mealtime and then overpowered the jailer when he opened the cell door. Horan then began crying "Murder!" Mistaking Horan's voice for the jailer's, the man stationed below unlocked the door at the top of the stairs. Horan floored the guard and, finding the front door locked, rushed into one of the side rooms and sprang through a window. The guard quickly recovered and shot Horan in the arm, but the wound did not prevent him from making his escape. Although authorities speculated that Horan would make for Apalachee Bay, an acquaintance spotted him heading east through Monticello, well armed and on horseback. But the fugitive was at large only a few days. Deputy Marshal K. M. Moore, at the head of a posse, captured Horan at a public house about five miles east of Monticello and brought him back to Tallahassee. Horan eventually met his death on the gallows.[59]

Escapes from Florida jails demonstrated both the resourcefulness of prisoners and the shameful lack of security. Occasionally prisoners were able to acquire tools to effect their escape. Some, like the previously mentioned Julius Cowles, used duplicate keys. James Simonds, a native of Hartford, Connecticut, and commander of the schooner *Lydia,* was confined in the Monroe County jail waiting to be tried on indictments of larceny, piracy, and murder. Indicted in December 1834, Simonds was charged with whipping to death one of his crew members, a man named Price. Though special precautions were taken to secure him for trial, a local newspaper reported three months after his initial confinement that he escaped by "means of false keys." He was never recaptured.[60]

Accomplices sometimes aided and abetted escapes. When John Branch, charged with committing murder in Thomas County, Georgia, broke out of the Pensacola jail in 1846, authorities suspected that he had benefited from the aid of a confederate. Branch and a horse thief from Santa Rosa County used an auger to cut away the facing of the door where the lock was attached. The breakout was especially embarrassing to Pensacola authorities. A local newspaper reported that the escape represented "the labor of several hours and produced considerable noise—but what difference does that make, no one lives in or near the jail, and there is no city Police to guard it." The journal reported that this was the second time within a month that a murderer had escaped from the jail. "It is high time that county authorities take some steps to secure prisoners. As things now are it is a mere mockery to commit felons to prison."[61] Voicing similar frustration in 1860, the *Madison Messenger* reported, "Our jail is again disgraced." The journal suspected white accomplices in the escape of six slaves charged with the murder of M. D. Griffin. The prisoners were chained to the wall, but they used the wire handle of a water bucket to "wrench the locks to pieces. Thus freed, they tore up two planks from the floor, . . . scratched a hole under the wall, pried the rock from the foundation of the building," and fled.[62]

Perhaps the most "leaky" of all the jails in Middle Florida was the Jefferson County jail in Monticello. Most of the criminals confined there for capital offenses escaped. In 1834, typically, the Jefferson County Grand Jury lamented that four accused murderers had broken free and escaped.[63] Two years later, Leonard Dozier, a man accused of Thomas Redding's murder, also escaped.[64] Hugh Duncan, confined for stabbing Wildman Hines, tunneled his way through the floor. Alek, a slave accused of arson, absconded at the same time.[65]

The case of James Huguenin, jailed temporarily in Monticello, demonstrates the difficulties of incarcerating dangerous killers who were determined to escape. Charged with murder in Tallahassee, Huguenin was brought before Judge Thomas Randall in 1838 on a writ of habeas corpus. Finding the Leon County jail unfit, the judge ordered the marshal to transport Huguenin to the Jefferson County jail and "commanded the sheriff to hire a competent and sufficient guard of good and trustworthy men." Samuel Barrington was sworn in as "gaoler" and put in charge of the guards. Huguenin remained in jail for approximately two months, but on April 1, 1837, according to a bill of indictment charging Barrington with malfeasance, he was "allowed to escape."[66] Huguenin soon was captured, and Deputy Marshal Samuel Duval and a number of others guarded him for twenty days until the jail in Gadsden County was secured. Duval turned Huguenin over to authorities in Quincy on May 4, but on July 29 he again escaped, never to be recaptured. Like his counterpart in Jefferson County, Gadsden County jailer John Withers was prosecuted successfully "for neglect of his duties" and ordered to pay a fine of $37.50.[67]

Escape artists confounded countless Florida lawmen. Besides mail robber Martin Hutto and killer Julius Cowles, whose exploits have already been noted, Matthew C. Eubanks was probably the state's most notorious escape artist. Eubanks, a professional criminal and master of disguise, was wanted in Cahaba, Alabama, for horse stealing and other crimes. Alabama officials offered a reward in 1847 and recounted his movements over the last several months. Eubanks was arrested at Tampa Bay, and authorities transported him to Montgomery, Alabama, where he was wanted on a forgery charge. Eubanks broke free again. In an advertisement describing his escape and offering a reward, Alabama officials speculated that he would "make his way towards East Florida." Afflicted with tuberculosis, Eubanks constantly "complain[s] of his breast and [has] a cough that causes hoarseness. . . . His health is such as to induce him to make his way to a more Southern Circuit."[68]

Eubanks's journeys were far from over. As predicted, in May 1848 he turned up in St. Augustine and was captured. Sheriff Michael Usina lodged him in the Fort Marion jail, but the jailer failed to search Eubanks, and the prisoner smuggled in a box of matches. Using chips of wood from his bunk, Eubanks set fire to the door. Emerging from the room, he used the same means to "open the wicket gate of the Fort by burning off the lock."[69] Although he was retaken, his ingenious talents for escape continued to perplex the minds of state and federal officials alike. On June 1, 1848, Circuit Judge Isaac Bronson wrote Sen. David L. Yulee that "there is some doubt whether he can be punished in the state courts [for escape] as the site of the fort [is] under the jurisdiction of the United States."[70] Despite such doubts, James Rogers, alias Matthew Eubanks, was convicted of "Burning and Breaking the jail" in the St. Johns Circuit Court and sentenced to pay a $1,000 fine and stand one hour on the pillory.[71]

The 1855 Duval County Grand Jury might have been speaking of all of Florida's jails when it declared that "past experience [has] fully shown that no prisoner can be detained within its walls against his will." The report continued, "The startling fact exists that no prisoners charged with high offenses and lodged in this jail have yet been detained sufficiently long to undergo a trial. They either through their own exertions or by the assistance of friends and accomplices from without, invariably break jail before the time of holding court." Conditions were worsened by the "perfect ease with which [the jail] can be approached at any time by night or by day."[72] Prisoners took advantage of poorly constructed and inadequately maintained jails. Jailers and guards were poorly paid and seldom supported in their work. Manpower was lacking, as was monetary support. Inmates found numerous opportunities to escape. They found it relatively easy to communicate with the outside, and they often obtained instruments or even physical assistance from those without. It may not be too far off the mark to conclude that in some cases, particularly with regard to petty criminals, as long as the culprits escaped from the district in which they were confined and were not likely to return, the matter was dropped. Once free, they would be the worry of citizens of another district. But above all, escapes from Florida's antebellum jails demonstrated not only the will of its prisoners but also the lack of will of Florida's citizens and authorities to hold criminals behind bars.

The system of incarcerating lawbreakers was crippled from both the lack of adequate funding and the administrative ineptitude of jail officials. Not only was taxation inadequate, but those responsible for providing relief to jailers failed to provide adequate assistance. Clear lines of responsibility were not defined. Often the legislative council, the general assembly, or Congress failed to appropriate money. Especially in the territorial period, the exact source for funds for these purposes was uncertain. Localities blamed territorial or state legislatures, which in turn evaded their responsibilities. Territorial and state officials insisted that, since many of the lawbreakers broke federal law, the U.S. government was responsible. But federal appropriations were slow and inadequate. As a result, jailers were often appointed or elected, given the keys to the jail, and expected to confine and provide for prisoners under trying circumstances. If the situation got bad enough, a local body of concerned citizens might raise money, although such remedial action was rare.

Properly constructed and maintained jails served as an indispensable ingredient in the criminal justice system. But not only did jails fail to ensure long-term confinement for convicted felons, they also failed in their most critical role of holding accused lawbreakers for trial. As was demonstrated time and again, criminals accused of either serious or lesser crimes could not be dealt with properly. The most dangerous offenders sometimes had to be transported hundreds of miles, and those charged with less serious crimes often refused bail and were set free on their own recognizance. The vast majority of counties simply lacked the funds or the initiative to provide for the housing of lawbreakers. Inadequate incarceration facilities made it less likely that the state's dependence on corporal punishment (lashing)—especially for petty offenses—would be lessened.

Once the state finally began providing for the maintenance of prisoners, uncertain funding again proved a stumbling block. The thirty-seven and a half cents a day provided for prisoners was not forwarded unless accounts had been certified by a judge and sent to the auditor or comptroller for payment. Even then payment was not certain. As noted, jailers could only hope that expenses would be paid. The time lag between submission of accounts and actual payment was prejudicial to the system and worked extreme hardships on jailers as well as other law officers. Funds were grossly inadequate, but jailers and other lawmen made the best of the means at their disposal.

Thirteen

Outlaw Gangs, Lynch Mobs, and Regulators

Policing the Antebellum Frontier

> What is our Constitution—what are volumes of statutes worth, if life, liberty, and property are thus placed at the mercy of a *mob?* Under such a state of things, no man's life is safe—to be *suspected* is death; to be *unpopular* may be ruin. . . . Lynch law is only to be tolerated in a new settlement where no courts of justice are established—then necessity makes law, but, in counties where Judicial Tribunals are established its exercise is certainly indefensible.
>
> —*Apalachicola Commercial Advertiser,* May 9, 1846

The most feared among all who broke the law were violent thieves who organized themselves into gangs. It was easy for banditti to operate in the sparsely settled, poorly policed sections of Florida's frontier. Passing back and forth across the Georgia and Alabama state lines, many gangs used Florida as a sanctuary. Bands of robbers, slave stealers, and desperadoes made life on isolated family farms dangerous. These types of criminals were the most difficult to prosecute under the normal sanctions of the law. At times it appeared as though Florida's criminal justice system was entirely unable to protect Floridians from the threat of lawless gangs. If captured, members of gangs were often punished by extralegal means.[1]

Lynching, though usually depicted as a postbellum phenomenon, occurred frequently in antebellum Florida. The practice was employed by Floridians who felt threatened either by lawless gangs or by persons disposed to tamper with the state's slave population. Floridians did not live in constant fear of servile insurrection, but there were periods when scares of this kind were widespread.[2]

The dangers of the frontier, concern over slave insurrections, the growing abolitionist agitation in the North—all were additional factors in unleashing fear that might trigger extralegal punishment. Frightened people responding not only to these various threats but also to a myriad of complex local conditions—often in contradictory ways—heightened tension among political factions, and this contributed to even greater potential for a breakdown in the normal judicial process. Events often demonstrated that public opinion was divided over these issues. As relations between the North and the South degenerated, debate over the handling of the state's most difficult criminal justice questions took on added volatility. Though resort to extrajudicial punishment was not the norm in antebellum Florida, it did occur when local conditions were ripe, tarnishing what was an otherwise laudable history of prosecuting criminals under the normal sanctions of the law. This chapter examines antebellum Florida's experience with extrajudicial punishment in the context of the local circumstances in which it occurred. Vigilance committees and lynch mobs left Florida a grisly heritage—a heritage that post–Civil War Floridians drew from to make that era the most violent in its history.[3]

Though important regional differences must be taken into consideration, fear of black uprisings was widespread among white Floridians. In East Florida the experience of slaves taking advantage of Indian hostilities to run away and join the fighting against their white masters was not soon forgotten. Also of significant concern were "Murrellites"—whites who plotted black insurrections for the purpose of stealing and looting. In 1835 the discovery in Mississippi of a planned insurrection of white slave stealers, led by a man named John A. Murrell, riveted the attention of Floridians as well as other Southerners. Newspapers reported accounts of a wide-ranging underground network—the Mystic Clan of the Confederacy—with accomplices scattered throughout the South poised to begin the rebellion at the agreed-upon date. The scare eventually proved a hoax, but newspapers exaggerated accounts, rumor fed rumor, and fantasy fed fact. One Florida editor declared in September 1835 that "the 25th of December next would have been the time for the general massacre of the whites throughout the great portion of the Southern Country, had it not been for the timely discovery."[4] "Murrellite" became the code word for Southerners' and Floridians' greatest fears and apprehensions—an insurrection of slaves instigated and directed by unscrupulous whites.

The Murrellite scare roughly coincided with growing abolitionist ferment in the North, and that fall two "impostors"—one in Jackson County and the other in the St. Augustine area—were detained and questioned. Finally, both suspected Murrellites were expelled from their respective communities by vigilance committees.[5] Even though Florida judges deplored the tendency of outraged citizens to employ what Judge Robert Reid called "Vicksburg Justice"—a reference to the well-publicized summary execution of gamblers in Vicksburg, Mississippi, in 1835—lynching on suspicion of inciting slaves to rebel did occur. One of the Murrellite scare's victims was a Dr. Cotton of Madison; this ringleader of a suspected slave rebellion, along with a black accomplice, was lynched by the "Livingston Committee."[6] Not all community members agreed with these methods, however. In fact, the Murrellite scare spurred vigorous debate over the proper way to deal with such suspicious characters.

The growing fear of abolitionist designs on the part of those in the North played heavily on Floridians' minds. They saw little difference between those they considered misguided fanatics seeking to free slaves on humanitarian grounds and those who used force or persuasion to steal slaves for resale elsewhere. Whether these intruders acted from misguided or evil motives, the results were the same—both threatened to upset the "natural" relationship of master and slave, a relationship that most white Floridians thought necessary for the stability of their society.

Closely connected to Floridians' fear of Murrellites and abolitionists was the dread of gangs engaged in stealing slaves. Slave stealing was the most widely feared gang activity. Stealing slaves on Florida's open, unpoliced frontier and running them back and forth across state lines for illegal sale was threatening enough to public order, but the greater fear was that the slaves might actually join the gangs themselves. Many suspected that the outlaws offered sanctuary to runaways and that some secret form of communication existed between gang members and slaves.

One of the most critical challenges to law and order that antebellum Floridians ever faced occurred in the decade after statehood. During these years, gangs of outlaws terrorized the region on both banks of the Apalachicola River. They hid in inaccessible swamps and bayous and emerged to prey on travelers, planters, and mail riders. Gangs also operated along the St. Johns River and west to the region between Ocala and Lake City. Using swamps and hammocks as hiding places, they targeted travelers moving through uninhabited regions on their way to Madison, Jasper, Lake City, and Jacksonville. How Floridians dealt with, punished, and confronted gangs in these years had significant implications for the future.

The criminals operated unchecked until local law enforcement officials and community leaders organized effective means to capture them. For one or two lawmen to confront well-armed and well-fortified desperadoes alone was impossible, so they had no choice but to summon and organize bands of local citizens to assist them. Once militia-type organizations were called to action, the danger always existed that they might exceed their original purpose or rise again of their own volition.

If the fear of Murrellites kept Floridians on edge, incidents like the following demonstrated that vigilante organizations remained constantly on the alert and could be summoned to action at a moment's notice. On August 13, 1846, Florida's capital was "in the midst of a great excitement." The driver of the mail stage, a man named Jesse Fish, had been shot near Quincy. "All our people are out today after [the killer], with a pack of bloodhounds. . . . These dogs are very ferocious," a local man wrote. "If they can get to him, I would not give a straw for his life—they will tear him limb from limb." Gov. William Moseley had also joined the chase.[7]

At the time of Fish's slaying, Gadsden County authorities had a number of men in custody on suspicion of mail robbery and slave stealing. Their confessions uncovered a "regular band of villains extend[ing] from Florida to Texas, estimated by some to number more than three hundred." A Tallahassee newspaper asserted, "[Not] since the existence of Murrel's gang of robbers and murderers, has the country been cursed with a worse one than the present." A number of stolen slaves had been recovered, from whom even more information on the gang was obtained, and a citizen force had helped round up the suspects. The same journal commended the "vigilance, activity, and public spirit [of the] people of that country in searching out and arresting these offenders." Such conduct deserved the "thanks not only of every Floridian, but of the whole Southern Country."[8]

The man the posse had sought was Samuel Holloman, the leader of a gang of slave stealers and robbers that had operated in the Gadsden County area for several months. Holloman, it was soon learned, killed Fish because he feared his victim would expose the gang. Several of the clan, including Holloman and Alvin Flowers, his brother-in-law, were mail stage drivers. After hearing of the arrest of other gang members, Flowers departed on the mail stage on July 10 and succeeded in robbing the mail somewhere between Marianna and Geneva, Alabama. Upon reaching New Orleans, he was apprehended and returned for trial.[9]

Fish's murder occurred just as Flowers was being returned to Quincy. Several others also were in custody, and local citizens petitioned Judge Thomas Baltzell to hold a special term of court to try the outlaws. They cited a number of important reasons for the irregular move—especially the probability of a "popular outbreak, and the summary punishment of the offenders; which spirit is suppressed under the hope of a speedy trial by the proper constituted authorities of the land."[10] Sensing the inherent danger of inaction, Baltzell acquiesced and a trial began immediately.

According to the testimony of a young boy named William Carruthers, Holloman and two accomplices ambushed Fish about a mile from Quincy.

Thomas Baltzell served as judge of the Middle Judicial Circuit from 1845 to 1850. (Courtesy of the Florida Supreme Court)

The accomplices fled after the shooting and were never apprehended, but Holloman was taken immediately into custody. The disclosures were sufficient to convict Holloman of murder. In related trials, Holloman, Flowers, and two others convicted of slave stealing were sentenced to hang. Testimony also revealed that members of the gang had participated in similar activities in Alabama and Georgia.[11]

If Judge Baltzell had not acted so precipitously, evidence strongly suggests that the gang members would not have survived long enough to be tried. The public wrath against them was so great as to command punishment by extralegal means. Judge Baltzell's controversial move probably forestalled a mass lynching. "The result of these trials," announced the editor of the *Tallahassee Floridian*, "gives renewed assurance that the laws, when properly administered are sufficient for the . . . protection of both life and property."[12] Such self-gratifying rhetoric might seem overdone, yet few such violators ever received legalistic treatment. The case was unusual. Gang members who fell into the hands of citizen posses were usually questioned and, if determined to be guilty, lynched on the spot.

Only a year earlier the area directly west of the Apalachicola River had been victimized by the notorious Avant gang. According to one account, James Avant was "a monster in human form," a man whose life for "years had been marked by crimes of the deepest dye." Avant first came to Florida after shooting an Alabama magistrate. Having committed murders in Pensacola and Marianna, Avant fled to the nearby swamps and assembled a "band of outlaws" that "perpetrated murder and robbery upon all who fell in his way." Soon travel in the region became so dangerous that search parties were organized, and Avant and a number of others were captured in swamps north of Apalachicola. The culprits were returned to Marianna, and on June 20, 1845, their leader was hanged, as one source noted, "without form of trial." The lynching party also threatened "four gentlemen of the blackleg order . . . that if they were found in the place after the lapse of ten hours they should suffer the same fate."[13]

The editor of the *Pensacola Gazette* differed in principle with the Jackson Countians' version of lynch law. Still, he recognized that the "peace and well-being of the community demanded that such a villain [as Avant] should meet with retribution for his outrages." No adequate jails existed for holding the prisoner, and even if there were, few believed that Avant would remain incarcerated long enough for a trial to take place. Moreover, "Lynch's Code" was necessary because there were yet others "of the same desperate character in the swamps about the county, and an example, which the slow process of the law could not afford, was necessary to strike them with terror."[14] The next year another Jackson County outrage suggested that the gang, despite the seizure of its leader, was still active. Some suspected that the unsolved murder of Edward Pittman was an act of cold, calculated revenge against a man who had played a prominent role in Avant's lynching. "Without knowing the fact," a Tallahassee editor insisted, "we can not entertain a doubt that the lamented Pittman fell a victim to resentment of these scoundrels, for some public spirited effort to uphold the laws. Others may be already marked as victims, and may be sacrificed if energetic and prompt action is not had." He suggested that "these scoundrels have some kind of organization—a compact for offense and defence and mutual support and succor."[15]

Such a well-armed and fortified set of criminals represented a formidable threat, and special quasi-legal methods would be necessary to bring them to justice. The citizens themselves, the Tallahassee editor demanded, "must organize and furnish men and means to assist the officers of the law in bringing offenders to punishment. The country should be scoured, and all suspicious persons arrested. Every vagabond and idler—every man who can show no honest means of gaining a livelihood, is a proper subject of suspicion." He attributed the sudden outbreak of gang activity to the recent immigration of thieves and robbers from Alabama, "whence they were driven by a terror of the penitentiary system." Not until Floridians constructed a similar prison system for themselves would they be free of such outrages. Florida's lawmakers had failed in their important duty of protecting society from such outrages. Instead of providing for adequate means to enforce the law, they had wasted the state's time and treasure on "idle and senseless discussions about party humbugs." Only a state penitentiary would be able to "vindicate the laws [and] strike terror in evil doers."[16] But not until after the Civil War would Florida have a penitentiary system. Until then, the modes of punishment for larcenists included fines, short sentences in county jails, and, most commonly, stripes, branding, or the pillory. For aggravated cases, especially those perpetrated by gangs, Floridians continued to apprehend, confine, and punish offenders in the only way possible. Limited funds and means caused them to use the summary code of Judge Lynch.

On January 6, 1846, a Tallahassee storekeeper recorded in his diary that there was "excitement in Jefferson County. A man . . . was hanged by convention."[17] The lynch mob's victim was Stephen Yeomans, a man who headed a band of outlaws accused of stealing slaves, changing their names, and running them into Alabama and Georgia for resale. Yeomans's depredations had begun during the Second Seminole War, when, as members of the Burney gang, he and others had disguised themselves as Indians and murdered, stolen from, and terrorized populations in Jefferson and Leon Counties in Florida and in several south Georgia counties. David and William Burney directed the gang until they fled the state after murdering Jefferson County lawman Joseph Manning in 1843. Governors from both states issued proclamations for their arrest. By then Yeomans had gained a leadership role in the gang. His depredations in Jefferson County were so threatening that on November 19 county leaders organized a vigilance committee and selected prominent planter William Bailey to chair the organization. The body published a description of Yeomans' deeds, speculated on his whereabouts, and raised a $500 reward for his capture.[18]

Yeomans was indicted for his crimes, but the private reward most likely led to his capture. Wanted for similar crimes in Thomas, Lowndes, and Baker Counties in Georgia, Yeomans was arrested in Baker County and released. Close behind were three men who immediately apprehended him and took him back to Jefferson County. During the trip, Yeomans confessed and implicated a number of confederates. Once word reached the surrounding community that Yeomans was in Monticello, the vigilance committee interrogated Yeomans and a number of other witnesses. At the end of the proceedings, a formal vote was taken: the members voted to hang Yeomans by a sixty-seven to twenty-three vote. (A simple majority was all that was necessary.) The usual justifications were cited: the insecurity of jails and the certainty that a band of accomplices would forcibly set him free. Moreover, the prospects of conviction in a normal court of law, where rules of testimony must be closely adhered to, were remote.[19]

Area newspapers were silent on the Yeomans affair—that is, until a confederate, a man named Jackson Jewel, was executed in the same manner three months later. Both Apalachicola's *Commercial Advertiser* and Tallahassee's *Florida Sentinel* roundly condemned the practice that had become all too common over the past year. Both journals fully recognized the guilt of Yeomans and Jewel. Still, they deplored the extralegal means of punishment. The *Commercial Advertiser* was especially displeased to see such activities "in two of our oldest and most populated counties, where the tribunals of justice are regularly established and officers of justice fully installed. . . . We are told," the newspaper continued, "how respectable the crowd—how dispassionate and orderly the proceedings. Such attempts of extenuation, are offensive to good taste and reason and an insult to . . . the law abiding portion of our citizens."[20] The *Florida Sentinel* agreed: "Yeomans & Jewel, hardened villains though they were, had just as clear a right to a trial by jury before an impartial tribunal, as the best one of those who consigned them to an unlawful death." Both men, insisted the editor, had a "much dearer right than that of property"—the right of a fair trial as "guaranteed . . . by the Constitution and Laws."[21]

The grand juries of Leon County and neighboring Thomas County, Georgia, also publicly denounced the lynching. "A number of individuals," the Thomas County panel declared, "on both sides of the line between Georgia and Florida have banded themselves together and styled themselves 'Regulators.' This association has taken the laws of the two states into its own hands—constituted itself a Court—had individuals arrested—heard testimony irregularly—condemned them to death and summarily executed its own decrees." Despite their judge's admonition to ferret out those responsible and indict them for murder, the jury stopped short of anything more than verbal condemnation. To that end they appealed to the "heads of this company, as intelligent, sensible men to reflect on the evil tendency of their conduct, and the danger to which they expose themselves."[22] But many who felt at risk in Jefferson County were not persuaded by such abstract principles. Ruthless men threatened the delicate equilibrium of society by stealing slave property. Those who sought to enrich themselves and risked the safety of the community, they reasoned, must be punished in the quickest and surest way possible.

During the next few years vigilance committee organizations, increasingly styled "regulators," were formed in the plantation-belt counties of Madison, Columbia, Duval, and Alachua to answer the invisible yet real threat of gangs. Outspoken against such societies was the *St. Augustine News*, but a number of letters to its editor defended the necessity for such organizations.[23] The issue became so controversial that some even tried to make approval or disapproval of vigilantes an issue in the 1848 gubernatorial race. The election pitted a Democrat, William Bailey (prominent in the Jefferson County lynching), against Thomas Brown, the Whig nominee. The Whigs "have endeavored to injure [your uncle] on the regulation business," Bailey's sister informed her son, "and I expect, it has had some influence with the people."[24]

But Bailey's supporters openly lauded their man's leadership role in the Jefferson County vigilance committee. In doing so, they represented him as the friend of order and stability and the enemy of outlaw gangs. Years earlier the Whigs had been charged with being soft on slavery. Now they were accused of favoring outlaws over regulators. A spoof letter to the *Jacksonville News* demonstrated the tactic: "Murrellite," a supporter of Brown, represented his candidate as a "good-hearted, humane, law-abiding man, who would always give us a fair trial, and all chances for a run; and besides, if we should be caught and convicted, we could get some of our influential Whig friends to intercede for us and get us pardoned. . . . We have all determined to go Whig this time, and make a desperate effort to keep up our clan; for we know if we fail and [Bailey] is elected, we are ruined."[25] For some Democrats, opposition to extralegal measures against gangs translated to support for Murrellites.

Though Bailey was defeated, it cannot be determined whether his affiliation with the regulators cost him the election, but it is safe to say it was a major issue in the campaign. Moreover, the issue of how to deal with gangs continued to be a factor in upcoming political struggles of the 1850s.

In the remaining years of the 1840s, gangs in upper East Florida murdered, stole, and looted in the name of personal gain. In 1846 the passengers of the mail stage were robbed near Black Creek. Another brutal robbery led a Jacksonville newspaper to complain about the bold and high-handed band of "fearless outlaw wretches" in the area. Only a few months later a group of "fiendish assassins" shot Alachua County planter Cornelius Rain, robbed his house of $4,000, and fled.[26]

The region's most feared outlaw that year was John B. Hardin, a larcenist, burglar, and horse and slave stealer. Hardin, also a bigamist, had no scruples about using runaway slaves in his misadventures. Temporarily jailed in Jacksonville, he escaped and continued his career of crime for three more years west across the panhandle. Usually working alone but sometimes forming a gang, Hardin ranged far into Mississippi and Alabama. The *Jacksonville News* labeled him "undoubtedly the most enterprising, and daring villain now in the Southern Country." Hardin's career came to an abrupt end, however, at the hands of a Santa Rosa County lynch mob. In 1851 Hardin eloped with the wife of a Milton planter, robbed and killed another man, and stole a slave who later assisted him in further crimes. A "delegation" from Milton arrested the outlaw and the slave in Alabama and brought them back to Milton. Fully satisfied as to their guilt, the mob hanged both men. Later, they were buried in the same grave.[27]

By the 1850s, as sectional tensions continued to mount, well-organized vigilance committees dedicated to rooting out all armed bands suspected of lawbreaking continued to operate. In August 1855, near the Okefenokee Swamp, one such "Band of Regulators" attacked and routed what a newspaper referred to as a "band of scoundrels who have regularly organized themselves for the purpose of stealing negroes and passing counterfeit money." The gang had plagued the counties along the Georgia-Florida border. An impressive amount of money, jewelry, and other valuables was recovered. Runaway slaves had also participated in the gang's activities.[28] Gangs of slave stealers also prowled thinly settled areas of West Florida. In 1857 a newspaper reported that seven slaves employed on the Alabama-Pensacola Railroad were either kidnapped or lured away by a band of outlaws. "It is believed," the journal reported, "that an organized band of these rascals are at work between the Suwannee and Pensacola."[29]

The advent of railroad travel was a further boon to outlaw activity. In 1859 a train was robbed as it passed through Patterson Hammock, near

Madison. According to a correspondent, the area had "always heretofore been a retreat for rascals." A posse was summoned, the baggage was recovered, and the thieves were "regulated with the law that regulates such crimes in this country."[30]

In the Tampa Bay area, the aftermath of the Third Seminole War contributed in early 1858 to the emergence of regulating bands.[31] The immediate demobilization of the volunteers left the region swarming with men. They had been mustered out of service without pay, and some were disposed to stealing and committing other crimes. With civil authorities simply unable to meet the challenge, conditions were ripe for the formation of an extrajudicial organization. A clarion call for action came from the Hillsborough County Grand Jury itself. In the spring term of the circuit court the body presented that the "universal and fearful increase of crime . . . is truly alarming to our conservative population. High crimes, immorality, and vice, stalk boldly through our county bidding our criminal laws defiance . . . and our only hope is that the prudent, wise, and good, will combine for mutual protection."[32] Tampa's *Florida Peninsular* was soon speaking of a "secret sworn band." The first public acknowledgment of the activities of the regulators came on May 1, when the journal announced the capture and summary execution of John A. Sheldon and a man named Locke. The two had stolen horses and jewelry and absconded to a hideout on the Suwannee River. The paper also reported that John Haywood was found hanging from a tree near the racetrack. A jury of inquest determined that the man "was hung by some person or persons unknown."[33] The "success" of the above episodes no doubt encouraged the continuance, expansion, and intensification of the area's regulator movement. Though regulators' activities are difficult to trace with any degree of certainty, evidence suggests that they branched out beyond Hillsborough to Polk and Hernando Counties.

Some citizens spoke out against the excesses of the regulators, but they were either treated with contempt, or, one suspects, even threatened with physical abuse. The case of James T. Magbee, a prominent yet controversial attorney and political leader, is illustrative. Magbee began denouncing the regulators, claiming that his oath to the Constitution as an attorney prevented him from sanctioning their actions. On June 12 the *Florida Peninsular* countered that Magbee was pandering to public opinion "intended for effect outside this county. It is a deliberate falsehood, for it is a fact well-known to our citizens that here, he approves of the acts of the so-called 'secret-band.' " Another Magbee opponent, "Veritas," a correspondent to Newport's *Wakulla Times*, remarked that Magbee "cannot point out *one* single instance, wherein he has had any opposition with the so-called 'secret sworn band.' On the contrary . . . on many and all occasions, [he] spoke of them as the securers of the peace."[34]

The subsequent activities of the regulators in the Tampa Bay area are all but impossible to chronicle with any degree of certainty because newspapers offered conflicting accounts. This pattern began on June 24 when S. T. Bowen, claiming to be a resident of Tampa, wrote a letter to the editor of the *Savannah Republican,* informing him that an "Executive Committee" had hanged four men in the city. "The outrage," claimed Bowen, was politically motivated since all four were leading members of the American or Know-Nothing Party. Bowen asserted that he was making these facts known to the *Republican* because, "as a law-abiding citizen of this city, I feel it to be my duty to state certain facts to the world." The *Florida Peninsular* refused to recognize the truth, Bowen lamented. "Our little paper here, and in fact every paper in this portion of the State, is either in league or fear of their vigilance and tyranny." Bowen begged the editor of the *Republican* to make an "appeal to the General Government for protection or at least demand an investigation."[35] The *Republican* stood by Bowen's account, and several other newspapers copied the letter and commented on its veracity.[36] The *Florida Peninsular* remained silent on the affair, but on July 10 Tallahassee's *Floridian and Journal* pronounced the account a "hoax." A party of men visiting the capital convinced the editor that neither S. T. Bowen nor the four men named as hanged in his letter lived in Tampa. Although the truth or fiction of the story will perhaps never be known, reminiscences tend to corroborate the mass lynching. More than thirty years later, Capt. W. B. Watson, an elderly resident of Jacksonville, told a newspaper reporter that regulators were active in 1858, when he was mustered out of his military service at Tampa Bay. He was anxious to return home, and as soon as he could he "lit out for Enterprise." On his way out of town, he "passed close by the bodies of three men swinging stark by their necks near the roadside."[37]

Many Floridians wondered why extrajudicial activity had become so widespread in the 1850s. In a charge to the Monroe and Dade County Grand Jury, Judge William Marvin noted that sheriffs and officers of the court had been negligent in bringing criminals to justice.[38] In 1858, "Locomotive" wrote the *Florida Peninsular* that vigilance committee activity had increased because the courts blindly adhered to "Old English laws and forms of pleading," which prevented juries from getting at the truth. While judges and lawyers haggled over what evidence was permissible, guilty men were "turned loose on society to steal, gamble, rob, murder, or do some other crime when their dishonesty or guilt was as plain as the noon day sun. . . . But let these same jurors hear the evidence without any charge from the court or pleading of Lawyers, and I will bet my red shirt they will not err in their decision once in fifty times." "Locomotive" argued that if trial rules were changed, the guilty would be justly punished, not released on technicalities. Dishonest lawyers were also at fault. "The saying that 'tis better to clear ten murderers than to punish one innocent man' has done much damage to communities by being handled and perverted by dishonest Lawyers to clear the guilty." Let lawyers contend for the truth instead of technicalities, the argument went, and "you will not find a Regulating Company in Florida one year after the change."[39] Instead of encouraging justice, claimed "Locomotive," lawyers thwarted it.

The editor of Tallahassee's *Floridian and Journal* agreed. He attributed the rise in "Regulating Clubs" to the "lameness of our laws," which permit "notorious characters . . . to go at large" and commit crime after crime. "It is this acknowledged inefficiency of the punishing power, that induces our citizens to take the law into their own hands."[40] For many, extralegal bodies such as regulators who functioned secretly and out of public view became indispensable to counter what Floridians feared most—the secret designs of gangs or abolitionist groups. They were not restricted to judicial rules regarding testimony of blacks, children, or females. When an emergency arose they could be formed quickly and summoned to action. Most commentators recognized certain inherent dangers but insisted that abolitionist agents who plotted secretly had to be countered. It was better to be ready for the worst than to be thrust into a situation unprepared. "It is a calamity," advised the *St. Augustine Examiner,* "to any community, to be influenced and governed by *regulators,* yet people must have protection to their person and property. If government and law fail in that protection, a community is thrown back upon its own right arm, in which case, it seldom fails, that might becomes right. Justice is recognized as blind but regulators always see."[41] The new emergency demanded unusual and, if needed, extralegal action.

The threat from gangs and abolitionists caused the formation of vigilante organizations that could respond quickly to emergencies. In the early 1850s these groups had, for the most part, effectively stamped out the threat from gangs, but the constant fear of outside interference with the slave population kept them intact and on the alert. By the end of the decade, similarly constituted regulator bands—organized more along political lines—roamed East Florida. The experience gained in going after secretly organized criminal gangs was put to use uncovering abolitionist plots.

With the advent of the Republican Party—a party most Floridians considered the tool of Northern abolitionists—these groups expanded their operations. As secession issues and the abolitionist movement seized the thinking of state leaders, vigilance committees—organized as much for political motives as for public safety—moved to discipline recalcitrant elements who questioned local politics. They operated outside the normal control and supervision of regularly constituted authorities and extended their activities far beyond simple law enforcement. As the election of 1860 approached and the arguments over the wisdom of secession raged, regulating activity, which began as a means of destroying or expelling an uncontrollable lawless element, was converted to political purposes. John Brown's raid and the presidential candidacy of Abraham Lincoln—a man committed to halting the extension of slavery in the Western territories—were represented by Florida's editorial community as the beginning of a Northern plot to subjugate or even drench the state with the blood of servile insurrection. The South and Florida, many became convinced, were under siege. Regulating activity in the Tampa Bay area and in the upper East Florida counties of Alachua, Marion, Columbia, and Duval, as well as similar political violence in West Florida known as the "Calhoun County War," demonstrated that regulators had turned from policing Florida's frontier to enforcing political solidarity in the face of national developments.[42]

Clement Eaton has noted that the lynching of blacks was more likely whenever there was "fear of servile insurrection or the brutal murder of a master or overseer by a slave."[43] Both of these conditions existed in the two years before Florida seceded from the Union. During these years at least six masters and overseers were murdered by bondsmen. Sensational newspaper coverage ensured that in such an emotionally charged atmosphere, criminal activity was often interpreted within the context of ongoing political controversies with the North. Abolitionist scares, instigated by a flurry of virulent press agitation, intensified, and blacks accused of committing violence against whites often did not get a fair trial. Florida's laudable heritage of according blacks the same procedural protection as whites was all but forgotten. A number of whites remained committed to maintaining high judicial standards, but to many it seemed as though race war loomed imminent—to them their lives and property were at stake. In such an atmosphere little else mattered. In the years preceding Florida's secession from the Union, the state descended into an orgy of black lynching.

On April 13, 1858, for example, "one of the boldest acts ever perpetrated by the followers of Judge Lynch" was committed in Nassau County. While a jury deliberated the fate of a slave accused in the murder of a white man, the regulators marched into court, seized the man, and hanged him.[44] In December 1860 an Alachua County vigilance committee passed sentence on a group of blacks charged with concocting a plan to murder their master and his family. A few days later they were hanged at Waldo. In a familiar theme of justification, the vigilance committee declared that some mysterious outside influence was controlling and directing a new and, until now, unheard-of spate of black crimes. Fernandina's *East Floridian* joined others in regretting that "the infamous white scoundrels, who have doubtless hired these poor creatures, can not he hung up at the same time and place."[45]

In October 1860 a white-black conspiracy was suspected in the murder of Albert Clarke in Hernando County. Clarke was shot in his carriage while on a return trip from Brooksville. Neighbors suspected that his new wife and a stepson named James Boyd had murdered him. A lynch mob extracted a confession from Clarke's slave, Hemp, who confessed that he was promised $200 by the mother and the son to commit the murder. Hemp was executed in front of the courthouse. The two white conspirators were taken into custody, but their fate is unknown.[46]

On January 21, 1860, in nearby Tampa a local newspaper defended a lynch mob that hanged a slave named Adam who had recently been convicted of murder in the circuit court but was awaiting news of an appeal filed by his attorneys. In an unrelated case, a white man named Buckley had been convicted that same session of court and sent to the gallows in December 1859 as his sentence directed. Thereupon the mob had stormed the jail, removed Adam, and hanged him from the same scaffold. In defending his community from an attack by the *Jacksonville Republican,* the editor of the *Florida Peninsular* reminded his readers that the *Republican* was the only journal in Florida that supported Stephen Douglas for the presidency. Moreover, the outrage was excusable because not one attempt had been made to obtain a writ of error for a "penniless white man but for quibble or an informality, a slave worth $1,500 could have another chance for his life by the 'law's delay.' " No doubt this was also the logic used by the leaders of the lynch mob.

When in February 1860 Dr. W. J. Keitt, the brother of the famous South Carolina fire-eater Lawrence M. Keitt, was found dead on his Marion County plantation, a gang of his slaves was suspected and immediately lodged in jail. A local newspaper reported that "a committee of twelve freeholders appointed by a large meeting of citizens" determined that Lewis, one of the slaves, was responsible and "executed" him. Further investigation resulted in two more executions, one banishment, and three more slaves receiving between twenty-five and fifty stripes a day for ten days.[47] The

Cedar Keys Telegraph was convinced that the fact that Keitt's brother was one of the South's most distinguished secessionists was more than a mere coincidence. "This is no doubt the beginning of the incendiary influence which has commenced its hellish work in our midst. No doubt but that this atrocity was instigated by some JOHN BROWNITE, any number of whom are secretly working in our midst."[48]

Similar outrages occurred in upper East Florida. In Jacksonville a crowd of "respectable citizens" arrested seven blacks they suspected of murdering a man near Mandarin. All seven were found guilty: three were hanged, and four were given a total of 310 lashes.[49] Increasingly, the message was that the normal mechanisms of law enforcement and the courts were unable to handle these new challenges.

In November 1860 a mob in Fernandina kidnapped nine free blacks from two Northern ships lying at anchor just off Cumberland Island. The town's *East Floridian* denounced the act and attributed it to some sort of retaliation for the election of Lincoln. "The great Cause of Southern Rights," the editor proclaimed, "might have progressed steadily and grandly forward, without the occurrence of any act calculated to bring disgrace or odium upon the movement. No wrong can be repaired by the commission of a similar wrong. If our Northern brethren see fit to deprive us of our property, that fact is not sufficient reason to Southern men to commit violations of the laws."[50] The *East Floridian*'s stand was courageous when measured against the fact that many believed public safety required drastic extralegal action in the face of abolitionists' designs. An irrational fear gripped many in Florida who were disposed to believe what they read in the newspapers—that abolitionists, John Brownites, and their ilk were preparing to descend into Florida and wrap the state in an orgy of rapine and rebellion.

During the last three months of 1860, vigilance committees were formed in all the major settlements of East Florida. These movements were no doubt strengthened by rumors of insurrectionary scares in Madison and Columbia Counties.[51] Announcing the creation of a vigilance committee, the *Micanopy Peninsular Gazette* noted in September that "it will be seen that our people are taking steps in the right direction in preparing to meet any emergency that may be precipitated upon us by the insurrectionary plottings of those Abolitionist fiends who are infesting many portions of the South." The committee clearly would not be hampered by the normal restraints of the law. "From what we heard at the meeting," claimed the editor, "we would advise those incendiary scoundrels to keep away from this section unless they wish to leave the world by summary process."[52]

In Fernandina a vigilance committee was formed, bylaws were prepared, and leaders were selected. The names of former governor James E. Broome, Joseph Finegan, and W. H. Babcock, who were to serve as officers, demonstrated that the group was no outlaw band of ruffians.[53] St. Augustine moved in the same direction. There the leaders' names were not made public because, the *St. Augustine Examiner* explained, "their labors in ferreting out and detecting the villainy of abolitionist measures, should any visit us and attempt to put in practice any of their unhallowed schemes, might prove more effectual." The organization expressly declared that its most important task was to "keep a strict watch upon the movements of strangers and our slave population." According to the paper, those guilty of fomenting insurrection should "be hung up high and dry as examples to deter others, and not cut loose upon other states to continue their villainy." Their motto, proclaimed the *Examiner,* "is justice to all—justice to an abolitionist, in our humble opinion means hemp and short shrift in all cases."[54]

In Jacksonville a vigilance committee was formed to intimidate all who did not wholeheartedly favor secession. Northerners were specifically singled out for scrutiny. Calvin Robinson, a Massachusetts man who set up a merchandising operation in Jacksonville in 1857, remembered some years later that he had no enemies until the beginning of the "excitement of secession." John Brown's raid, the breakup of the Democratic Convention in Charleston, and the Republican candidacy of Abraham Lincoln in 1860 instigated a hysteria he likened to a "reign of terror." The vigilance committee made it "almost suicidal" for a "northern man to utter openly his love for the Union." In fact, remembered Robinson, it was "dangerous to talk 'Union talk' with anybody."[55]

One of the most active and well-organized groups of regulators was formed in Columbia County. But the band was also active in other upper East Florida counties. Beyond enforcing community solidarity and rounding up those suspected of criminal activity, they monitored people suspected of opposing the South's right of secession. Recent immigrants from the North fell under close scrutiny. Dissenters—especially those who spoke out against regulators' activities—risked brutal retaliation. For example, on July 28, 1860, Dr. William Hollingsworth of Starke, riding on the Florida Railroad, "expressed his disapprobation of the conduct of certain persons, calling themselves the Regulators." The next day the group attacked his house. Ably defending themselves, Hollingsworth and his thirteen-year-old son killed the leader of the band, later identified as a man named Dowling, and mortally wounded several others while suffering only slight injuries themselves. The attacks on Hollingsworth continued. The regulators twice "waylaid him," and he received several anonymous letters threatening his life. The day before the attack on his house he received a letter informing him he was a doomed man.[56]

But the extended persecution of Hollingsworth troubled a number of citizens. In some circles Hollingsworth had achieved a kind of hero status. His "conduct," reported one newspaper, was "generally applauded by the community." In a letter to the editor, "A Citizen of Florida" noted that these regulating bands had gotten out of hand. The affair was "disgraceful to a civilized community." Hollingsworth had courted disaster in speaking out against the methods of the illegal band. Had he died, the correspondent noted, he would have been considered a martyr in the cause of justice. The present "reign of terror" called "loudly for Executive interference."[57] Yet the Columbia County regulators expanded and extended their activities in the months to come. Increasingly, their activities took on more political significance.

On September 8, Washington Ives recorded in his diary that "William Hollingsworth, the 'Hero of Starke,' was in town all day today." That evening the Union Party held a meeting and nominated candidates for the upcoming election. By now community leaders who opposed the ministrations of the regulators were prepared to adopt the same measures to confront them. Ives recorded that after dinner the "Anti-Regulators held a meeting around the pond."[58]

Young Ives chronicled regulator violence in Columbia County that summer and fall. A month previous to the Hollingsworth attack, the regulators had whipped a Lake City man named Button George. On May 22 they administered a severe beating to Peter Pent, a cabinetmaker. Another man named Keene was also beaten. On September 21 the courthouse burned, and the regulators were suspected. One week later Ives recorded that "there was much excitement all day. . . . The Regulators held a large meeting in front of General Smith's office, Colonel Wynne made a long speech to them. Dr. Day read the Constitution and bylaws. Then Jack Smiley made a political speech." A month later the regulators hanged a man named Tindale in Newnansville (a week earlier a jury in Gainesville had found the man not guilty of murder). In December 1860 the regulators focused their attacks on an opponent named Samuel Wester. On December 7 they beat him "almost to death." Four days later, the antiregulators held a meeting at Wester's house, obtained the names of the perpetrators, and turned all their information over to a justice of the peace. Eighteen days later, Wester's house was burned. More than sixty people watched the blaze consume his dwelling, but, according to Ives, "not more than twenty did anything to arrest the flames." About two weeks later, Wester turned up missing. "Everybody," recorded Ives, "supposes that the Regulators have got him." And yet the violence continued. In January 1861 regulators shot and killed a man named William Roberts at his home in Lake City.[59]

That regulator bands carried out such wide-ranging activities suggests a breakdown of law and order. It was the regulators themselves who were responsible for much of the criminal disorder they were created to eradicate. Florida's criminal justice system—already overburdened—was on the verge of collapse. It even seems as though parts of the state had slipped into a state of anarchy. Extralegal bands that had operated against robbers and slave stealers rose again to thwart perceived threats to community order, but this time the secrecy and anonymity of membership afforded regulators freedom from discipline or control by the regularly constituted authorities.

Most lynch mobs in antebellum Florida—whether they arose spontaneously in answer to an immediate emergency or were the by-product of a well-organized vigilance committee—acted against black-related offenses. Most victims of lynching were either members of gangs suspected of stealing or harboring slave property or those suspected of instigating a slave rebellion. Such wrongdoers acted secretly, hidden from the view of the community. Theirs were crimes of suspicion or conspiracy, thus rendering them immune to the regular provisions of the law. Despite the admonitions of judges, politicians, and many newspaper editors, leaders of vigilance committees took pride in their activities, usually operated in the open, provided the culprits with some semblance of a trial, and considered their motives patriotic and noble. The majority of members felt that they acted in the best interests of their communities.

At the core of such activity was the firm belief that abolitionists, "Black Republicans," and others poised to reap the benefits of evildoing had to be uncovered and driven out. The resort to lynch law sprang from spontaneous or long-standing fear. There was growing apprehension that the evil designs of abolitionists had to be countered. If the regularly constituted authorities were either ill-equipped or unwilling to ensure the stability of Florida's slave population, then special measures had to be adopted.

In the period prior to 1855, vigilance committees were formed to control gang activity because the regularly constituted authority was deemed insufficient. Of primary importance was the fear that criminal gangs were either stealing slaves or using stolen slave property in the perpetration of crimes. Once the threat of gangs was virtually wiped out, the skeletal framework of these organizations remained. Increasingly, in the later years these organizations came to be used not only to monitor the slave population but to enforce political solidarity.

The experiences of Floridians with lynch mobs, regulators, and vigilance committees in the last two years before Florida seceded from the Union left a bloody legacy that would haunt the state for the remaining years of the nineteenth century. During the Civil War (1861–65), extralegal bands terrorized the inhabitants of the St. Johns River area who attempted either to remain neutral or to assist Union forces in their attempt to reestablish federal control of the area. Persons were killed and property was destroyed.[60] But what followed was even more devastating. Florida's most violent era—Reconstruction (1865–77)—ushered in a period of social and racial conflict never before witnessed in the state's history. Many of those who joined the Klan and committed racial or political violence for the purpose of nullifying the changes that the Civil War had wrought drew from their experiences in clandestine operations before the Civil War.[61]

Fourteen

Our Violent Past
A Heritage of Honor and Frontier

Some of the findings of this study of crime and punishment in antebellum Florida mirror those of other scholars engaged in similar investigations of Southern states. Yet the state's isolation and extreme frontier conditions made it unique. Even a cursory examination of indictments in Florida's antebellum court minutes reveals a number of trends.

First, indictments for crimes against person were far more frequent than those for crimes against property. There was little variation of this trend throughout the state, whether plantation belt or port. For example, records available in Florida's black-belt counties of Jackson, Gadsden, Leon, Jefferson, and Madison show that indictments for violent crimes outpaced crimes against property by a total of 911 to 239.[1] In the counties containing the Florida port towns of Key West, Tampa, and Pensacola, the results were the same. Surviving records show that indictments for violent crimes outnumbered those for property crimes by a total of 543 to 213.[2] For the state as a whole, prosecutions for crimes against person constituted 1,871, or roughly 40 percent of the total (4,648), while crimes against property constituted 582, or roughly 12 percent. Finally, assault and battery was the most frequently prosecuted crime in antebellum Florida. With over 1,253 cases prosecuted, it constituted almost 27 percent of the total criminal prosecutions in the state, far outpacing larceny with only 439.

And yet these numbers do not explain *why* Florida was so violent. Both contemporary observers and historians have speculated variously as to the cause: the ever-present specter of slavery, the Scotch-Irish ethnicity of many of the whites, overindulgence in alcohol, and even the weather—both separately and together—played a role. But the primary causes for Florida's violent past were the ethic of honor and the dangers of the frontier.

A second aspect of the story was that punishment for people convicted of property crimes was more severe than it was for those found guilty of violent crimes, excluding murder. Those convicted of crimes against person usually could expect fines, sometimes as low as one cent. Even though perpetrators of personal violence could be assessed fines of up to $1,000, they rarely were. Moreover, only manslaughter and murder carried the possibility of corporal punishment. Florida law precluded stripes for whites found guilty of assault and battery.

Usually jail time or, more frequently, stripes were in store for those who stole. The reason for the difference was that stealing property violated antebellum Southerners' cherished honor code. Like its neighboring Southern states, Florida had a rural, agricultural society that placed a premium on personal integrity, which included a strong sense of economic morality. Honesty, truthfulness, and a determination not to acquire money or goods under false pretenses were traits not only desired but demanded. Stealing or pilfering property was a violation of that trust. People convicted of crimes against property received the law's and society's sternest punishment—punishment designed as retribution for the crime and to shame the culprit in the eyes of the community.

In contrast, offenders charged with crimes against person experienced no bar to respectability in the community. On the contrary, the opposite was sometimes true. Florida's courts were full of substantial citizens who felt it their duty to defend themselves, their family, their property, or their honor against any threat, real or imagined. Not that Floridians habitually broke the law without compunction—far from it. Yet when given the clear choice of observing the law or defending their honor, they usually defended their honor. Such lawbreakers were treated with dignity and respect. Juries were reluctant to convict a man of a crime against person if they believed that the offender had acted under provocation—and provocation was loosely defined. Moreover, a large percentage of those convicted of assault and battery were assessed fines of less than a dollar. Juries were forgiving, judges were forbearing, and citizens were permissive.

Another striking feature of the state's criminal prosecutions in the antebellum era involved the criminal prosecution of those charged with crimes against public order and morality. The frequency of prosecutions, of course, demonstrates that Florida's antebellum leadership was determined to monitor activities thought at the time to be immoral, practices that Floridians found offensive or threatening to community mores. Sanctions of this sort were more numerous, but so were the individual prosecutions. Prosecutions of whites for crimes against public order and morality accounted for 2,185, or roughly 48 percent of the total of 4,552. This large percentage, however, would be reduced if carrying arms secretly, and riot, affray, and mayhem (a total of 685)—offenses more associated with violent crimes—were recognized as crimes against person. Patterns of punishment for those found guilty of crimes against public order and morality were similar to those found guilty of property crimes. Stripes and the pillory were appropriate punishments for those who, by their dishonorable conduct, forfeited their right to be treated with respect.

Another relevant issue with regard to crime and punishment in antebellum Florida has to do with the efficiency of the prosecution of criminals. One striking feature along this line is the large percentage of indictments that never reached a verdict (2,611 of 4,648, or roughly 56 percent). Instead of guilty (28 percent) or not guilty (15 percent) verdicts, prosecutions were often concluded with the words "dismissed" or "*nolle prosequi,*" and many of the cases simply disappeared from the docket. A number of features conspired to thwart successful prosecutions of criminals. Included among these were the scarcity of secure jails, which made efficiently managed bail procedures almost impossible; the unsettled nature of the Florida frontier, which facilitated escapes; and the difficulty of securing witnesses and compelling them to testify against the accused, especially if several months had elapsed since the crime was committed. Given these difficulties, it is perhaps remarkable that verdicts were reached in as many cases as they were.

When it came to blacks, slave and free, a number of themes were also apparent. Florida's slave code provided that blacks were tried under a different set of criminal statutes. But a large number of blacks accused of crimes never entered the courtroom. Slave owners themselves punished minor violations, but for slaves accused of serious offenses such as murder, rape, or arson a surprising degree of procedural fairness was afforded. Convicted blacks were almost always subjected to corporal punishment no matter what the offense.

In capturing, confining, transporting, trying, and punishing criminals, officers of the law were hampered by inadequate funding. To a degree unparalleled in the modern era, Florida lawmen were aided, sometimes overzealously, by a cooperative citizenry. In many instances, law enforcement was a community effort. Despite the physical barriers of Florida's harsh geography, lawmen often succeeded.

The enforcement and administration of the law was largely determined by Florida's frontier status. But what made the issue of the frontier even more critical was the presence of Indians, runaway slaves, outlaw gangs, and, by the 1850s, the growing fear—more imagined than real—that fanatics inspired by radical political fervor in the North were targeting Florida's peculiar institution. By the late 1850s, Florida's system of law enforcement, like all its other institutions, was swept up in the rising tide of sectional politics.

This book has sought to shed light on the lives of the ordinary citizens involved in Florida's criminal justice system. Criminal, constable, sheriff, justice of the peace, judge, jury, and citizens—their collective history makes up a vital part of the social history of Florida in the forty years before the Civil War. For each individual tried and found guilty or prosecuted and found innocent, for each lawbreaker who served time or managed to escape, for each lawyer, juror, or judge who succeeded, failed, or ignored his duty—for each of them—what mattered most was his individual life and circumstances. At least in part, these chapters have told their story.

Appendix 1

Legal and Extralegal Executions

I. Legal Hangings

A. Whites

Name	Place	Date	Comments
Benjamin Donica[1]	Pensacola	June 20, 1827	Murdered his commanding officer, Major Donoho
Edward Sinclair[2]	St. Augustine	Aug. 28, 1828	Murdered John Stafford
Andrew Crail[3]	Pensacola	Mar. 30, 1829	Murdered Ann Walker
Norman Sherwood[4]	Key West	Dec. 10, 1830	Murdered John Wilson
David S. Rogers[5]	Tallahassee	July 27, 1832	Murdered John Farmer
Robert Breen[6]	Pensacola	Dec. 20, 1833	Murdered Peter Alba
[?] Waters[7]	Tallahassee	[1835?]	Murder, no details
Ad Kinson[8]	Tallahassee	[1835–36?]	Murdered his wife
Samuel Wright[9]	St. Augustine	July 10, 1837	Murdered Robert Bassacre
Thomas Horan[10]	Tallahassee	[Feb.?] 1842	Murdered James Ramsey
Chandler Hastings[11]	Newnansville	June 1, 1842	Murdered Philip Rhorback
James Greer[12]	Newnansville	June 1, 1842	Murdered his wife
George Everhart[13]	Tallahassee	June 16, 1843	Murdered his wife
Samuel Holloman[14]	Quincy	Oct. 3, 1846	Murdered Jesse Fish
Thomas Smith, Almon Flowers, and John Black[15]	Quincy	Oct. 9, 1846	Slave stealing
Josiah Jacobs[16]	Newport	[June?] 1852	Murdered Darling Cherry
James Burns[17]	Washington County	July 9, 1852	Murdered Joshua Alston
George M. Buckley[18]	Tampa	Dec. 16, 1859	Murdered George Goodwin
[Two sailors?][19]	Key West	[1860?]	Murdered Capt. Morantes (mutiny)

James O'Connor[20]	Apalachicola	June 29, 1860	Murdered his wife
Ferdinand McCaskill[21]	Pensacola	Oct. 12, 1861	Convicted of murdering George Young (a black?)
John Ammons[22]	Holmes County	June 12, 1861	Murdered Samuel McQuagg

B. Blacks

Name	Place	Date	Comments
Monday[23]	Alachua County	[Dec.?] 1830	Raped Sarah Cason
Ben[24]	Tallahassee	May 23, 1828	Murdered his overseer, Mr. Kent
Joe and Crittenden[25]	Tallahassee	Dec. 15, 1834	Both convicted of murdering James Roundtree
Jane[26]	Tallahassee	[1835?]	Infanticide
Tom and John[27]	Newnansville	Aug. 14, 1837	Murdered L. Gilliland
Henry[28]	Pensacola	Dec. 28, 1838	Murdered his master, Dr. Parker
Wilkes[29]	Pensacola	May 25, 1839	Murdered [?] Vaughn
Adam[30]	Pensacola	June 14, 1839	Murdered his master, John Sunday
Caeser (alias Sam Jones or Hunter)[31]	Apalachicola	[1840–41?]	Murdered Robert Herrin
Will[32]	Euchee Anna	May 21, 1841	Murdered Mrs. Nancy Senterfeit
Anthony[33]	Tallahassee	Nov. 24, 1843	"Felony"
Cella[34]	Jacksonville	Sept. 22, 1848	Murdered her master, Jacob Bryant
Simon[35]	Monticello	Dec. 15, 1848	Murdered his master, Richard Cole
Arnold[36]	Calhoun County	[Fall?] 1850	Murdered Elizabeth Burgess
Abraham[37]	Columbia County	June 11, 1852	No details
Joe[38]	Calhoun County	[1853?]	Murder
Hall[39]	Madison	[1856?]	Murdered his master, William Pearce
Bill Jones, a slave[40]	Milton	Dec. 12, 1856	Rape
Simon[41]	Gainesville	[1857]	Assault with intent to kill white man
Three slaves[42]	Madison	[May?] 1860	Murdered their overseer, Mathew Griffin
Ned[43]	Liberty County	Apr. 6, 1860	Murdered Duncan A. McPhail

Appendix 1: Legal and Extralegal Executions

II. Extralegal Hangings (Lynchings)

A. Whites

Name	Place	Date
Dr. [?] Cotton[44]	Madison County	[Nov.?] 1835
James Avant[45]	Marianna	June 20, 1845
Stephen Yeomans[46]	Monticello	Jan. 2, 1846
Jackson Jewel[47]	Monticello	[Apr.?] 1846
John B. Hardin[48]	Milton	[May?] 1851
John A. Locke and [?] Sheldon[49]	Somewhere between Tampa and Jasper	[Apr.?] 1858
John Haywood[50]	Tampa	[Apr.?] 1858
John J. Early, D'Witt Lucian, Jerome Baker, and J. Alfonso Crockett[51]	Tampa	[May–June?] 1858
Unnamed gang of thieves[52]	Madison County	[Jan.?] 1859

B. Blacks

Name	Place	Date
Dick[53]	Tallahassee	[May?] 1840
Unnamed black[54]	Milton	[May?] 1851
Simon[55]	Pensacola	[June?] 1853
Jack or Such[56]	Nassau County	Apr. 13, 1858
Adam[57]	Tampa	[Jan.?] 1860
Lewis, Israel, and Allen[58]	Marion County	[Apr.] 1860
Hemp [Hampton?][59]	Brooksville	[Oct.?] 1860
Unspecified number of blacks[60]	Waldo	[Dec.?] 1860
Ephraim, Wesley, and Ed[61]	Jacksonville	Apr. 26, 1861

Appendix 2

County Seats and Superior/Circuit Courts

The following list enumerates Florida's antebellum counties and county seats, along with the date of the first meeting of their superior or circuit court. The sites for holding court often varied from year to year, especially during Florida's territorial years. In 1824 the legislative council created three judicial districts—Western, Middle, and Eastern. It stipulated that superior courts would be held in Jackson, Walton, and Escambia Counties in the Western District. In the Eastern District two counties held superior courts: one at Jacksonville for settlers in Duval and Nassau Counties; and one at St. Augustine for settlers in St. Johns, Mosquito, Alachua, and Monroe Counties.[1]

The creation of county courts was a prerequisite to the implementation of the circuit court. In 1824 the council also directed that these courts be organized in Mosquito, Nassau, Alachua, Leon, Gadsden, Walton, and Jackson Counties.[2] It was further specified that the three county judges in each county appoint "three discreet and impartial persons, two of whom shall be chosen from opposite extremes, and the third from the centre of said counties, as nearly as may be, whose duty it shall be, under the commission of said courts to examine and select the most convenient and eligible situation for the permanent seat of justice." The agreed-upon location was to "henceforth constitute the seat of justice of said counties respectively until otherwise provided by law."[3] In most cases these hastily selected county seats proved controversial, and petitioners often requested that they be changed. In response, subsequent councils and, after 1845, legislatures ordered local elections to select county seats agreeable to the majority of settlers. As a result, several counties had a number of different county seats. As the case of Calhoun and Hernando Counties demonstrates, it often occurred that county seats moved whenever sufficient numbers of voters became disgruntled enough to petition for a change. Even when the legislators mandated elections for that purpose, the results were sometimes challenged, lost, or unrecorded. Thus the county seats of Lafayette, New River, Suwannee, and Taylor Counties are not known. Exactly when they held their first superior or circuit court also is difficult to determine, since counties did not automatically hold these courts once they were created. Lost court records make the issue even less certain. If a county lacked adequate population or facilities, provision was often made for its settlers to attend court in an adjacent county. Court minutes, newspapers, legislative acts, period maps, and other sources provide clues.

Appendix 2: County Seats and Superior/Circuit Courts

County	County Seat	First Superior or Circuit Court
Alachua[4]	Newnansville	1828
Brevard[5]	Susanna (Ft. Pierce)	1855
Calhoun	St. Joseph, Iola, Abe Springs Bluff, Blountstown[6]	1838
Clay	Middleburg	1859
Columbia[7]	Lancaster, Alligator (Lake City)[8]	1833
Dade[9]	Indian Key, Miami[10]	1836
Duval	Jacksonville	1824
Escambia	Pensacola	1822
Franklin[11]	Apalachicola, St. Joseph, Apalachicola	1832
Gadsden[12]	Quincy	1827
Hamilton[13]	Wallburg, Jasper[14]	1830
Hernando[15]	DeSoto, Bayport, Pierceville, Brooksville[16]	1845
Hillsborough[17]	Tampa	1845
Holmes	Hewitts Bluff[18]	1849
Jackson[19]	Marianna	1824
Jefferson[20]	Monticello	1828
Lafayette	House of Aziel Jones[21]	1856
Leon	Tallahassee	1824
Levy[22]	Waccasassa	1850
Liberty	Ricoes Bluff (Bristol)	1855
Madison[23]	Madison	1840
Manatee	Manatee (Bradenton)	1858
Marion[24]	Ocala	1848
Monroe[25]	Key West	1828
Nassau	Nassau Court House[26]	1830
New River	Store of William Roberts[27]	1858
Orange[28]	Mellonville (Sanford), Orlando[29]	1847
Putnam	Palatka	1849
St. Johns	St. Augustine	1822
Santa Rosa[30]	Milton	1842
Sumter	Adamsville, Sumterville[31]	1853
Suwannee	House of William Hines[32]	1858
Taylor	House of David Bryant[33]	1856
Volusia	Enterprise[34]	1854
Wakulla[35]	Newport	1843
Walton[36]	Alaqua, Eucheeanna	1830
Washington[37]	Roaches Bluff[38]	1833

Appendix 3

Law and Judicial Officers

I. Territorial Court Officials, 1821–1845

A. Western Judicial District

Judges

Eligius Fromentin	1821–22
Henry Marie Brackenridge	1822–32
John A. Cameron	1834–38
Dillon Jordan	1838

District Attorneys

Alexander Anderson	1821
Tipton Harrison	1822
William F. Steele	1823–25
Albert J. Claggett	1825
Benjamin Wright	1825–31
George Walker	1831–40
James T. Archer	1840
John L. Wilson	1841 (declined)
Walker Anderson	1841–45

Marshals

James G. Forbes	1822
William Sebree	1823–27
Henry Wilson	1827–28
Adam Gordon	1828–29
James W. Exum	1829–38
Peter W. Gautier	1838
George Willis	1838–39
Charles Evans	1839–41
Ebenezer Dorr	1841–45

B. Apalachicola Judicial District

Judges

Richard C. Allen	1838–41
Samuel W. Carmack	1841–45

District Attorneys

William Brockenbrough	1838–42
George S. Hawkins	1842–45

Marshals

Peter W. Gautier	1838–41
Robert Myers	1841–42
Hezekiah Hawley	1842–43
Robert Myers	1843–45

C. Middle Judicial District

Judges

William Blair	1824
Augustus B. Woodward	1824–27
Thomas Randall	1827–40
Alfred Balch	1840–41
Samuel Douglas	1841–45

District Attorneys

Benjamin Wright	1824–25
Adam Gordon	1825–27
Willian Allison McRea	1827–28
James G. Ringold	1828–31
James A. Dunlap	1831 (died before serving)
John K. Campbell	1831–33
George K. Walker	1833–34
James D. Westcott	1834–37
Charles S. Sibley	1837–40
Vinton Butler	1840 (never served)
Isham Searcy	1840 (declined)
Charles S. Sibley	1841–45

Marshals

John M. Hanson	1824–27
Alexander Adair	1827–31
Thomas E. Randolph	1831–37
Samuel H. Duval	1837–40
Leigh Read	1840–41
Minor Walker	1841
John G. Camp	1841–45

D. Eastern Judicial District

Judges

William P. Duval	1821–22
Joseph L. Smith	1822–32
Robert R. Reid	1832–40
Isaac Bronson	1840–45

District Attorneys

John G. Bird	1821
Greenbury Gaither	1821–22
Alexander Hamilton	1822–23
Edgar Macon	1823–26
Thomas Douglas	1826–45

Marshals

James Forbes	1821 (for East and West Florida)
Waters Smith	1823–31
Samuel Blair	1831–37
Joseph S. Sanchez	1837–42
John Beard	1842–45

E. Southern Judicial District

Judges

James Webb	1828–39
William Marvin	1839–45

District Attorneys

William Allison McRea	1828–29
John G. Stowers	1829 (never served)
Edward Chandler	1830–34
Adam Gordon	1834–35
William Marvin	1835–39
Charles Walker	1839–40
L. Windsor Smith	1840–42
George Macrea	1842–45

Marshals

Henry Wilson	1828–29
John Dean	1829–30
Lackland Stone	1830–32
Thomas Easton	1832–36
Charles Welles	1836–40
Joseph Browne	1840–45

II. State Court Officials, 1845–1861

A. Western Circuit

Judges

George S. Hawkins	1845–53
Jesse J. Finley	1855–60
Allan H. Bush	1860–65

Solicitors

John Caraway Smith	1845–49
James Landrum	1849–52
James McClellan	1853
James Landrum	1853–57
W. D. Barnes	1857–61

B. Middle Circuit

Judges

Thomas Baltzell	1845–50
J. Wayles Baker	1851–67

Solicitors

Thomas Jefferson Hair	1845–49
Samuel B. Stephens	1849–53
William S. Dilworth	1853
Samuel B. Stephens	1853–65

C. Eastern Circuit

Judges

Isaac Bronson	1845 (declined)
Thomas Douglas	1845–53
William A. Forward	1853–57
Benjamin Putnam	1857–65

Solicitors

Felix G. Livingston	1845–49
John P. Sanderson	1849–53
S. St. George Rogers	1853
James Baker	1853–56
James B. Dawkins	1856–59
Lewis J. Fleming	1859–65

D. Southern Circuit

Judges

William Marvin	1845 (declined)
Samuel Carmack	1845 (declined)
George W. Macrea	1846–48
Joseph B. Lancaster	1848–53
Thomas F. King	1853–65

Solicitors

R. F. Brantly	1845 (resigned)
Thomas F. King	1846–49
Ossian B. Hart	1849–53
James Gettis	1853

Hardy D. Kendrick	1853–57
Henry L. Mitchell	1857–65

E. Suwannee Circuit

Judge

James Baker	1859–61

Solicitor

Samuel McLin	1859–61

III. Antebellum Sheriffs

The following is a partial list of Florida's antebellum sheriffs. During Florida's early years as a territory, governors appointed sheriffs with the advice and consent of the legislative council. In 1829 the office was made elective, and the first elections were held in 1830. Sheriffs elected from that time until 1845 are the hardest to document. Until the "Roster of State and County Officials," which picks up sheriffs in 1845, only scattered and incomplete records in the Florida State Archives, newspapers, and a few other sources provide any information as to who was elected. Sheriffs served two-year terms. In case of vacancies, governors filled the position until elections could be held.

Alachua County (1824, Newnansville)

Simeon Dell	1827–[?]
John B. Tiner	1832–[?]
Thomas Barron	1840–41
John McNeill	1842–43
Issac Blanton	1844–45
Thomas Ellis	1845–47
William Gibbons	1847–48
Thomas Ellis	1848
A. E. Geiger	1848–49
Charles L. Wilson	1849–55
George B. Ellis	1855–57
S. W. Burnett	1857–65

Brevard (previously St. Lucie) County (1855, Susanna, Ft. Pierce)

J. A. Armour	1855–57
W. B. Davis	1857–63

Calhoun County (1838, St. Joseph, Iola, Abe Springs Bluff, Blountstown)

Gerry Pattason	1832–[?] (Fayette County)
Francis A. Ross	[1839?]
Thomas Green	1840–42
Alexander McAlpine	1843–43
Isaac Jackson	1845–47
Ellis Branch	1847–51

Thomas J. Land	1852–55
James B. Stone	1855–59
James Stanfield	1859–61
Clay County (1858, Middleburg)	
E. J. Daniels	1859–63
Columbia County (1832, Alligator, Lake City)	
N. M. Moody	1840–42
John W. Love	1843
Charles Fitchett	1844
Thomas B. Fitzpatrick	1845–49
Asa A. Stewart	1849
Arthur J. T. Wright	1849–53
Reuben Hogans	1854
Thomas Mickler	1855–61
Dade County (1836, Indian Key, Miami)	
Lemuel Otis	[1840?]
Joseph Bethel	[1844?]
Edwin Quimby	1846–47
Duval County (1822, Jacksonville)	
Daniel C. Hart	1826–34
A. J. Phillips	1833–34
A. J. Phillips	[1841?]
Jacob Gulterson	1842–44
Harrison B. Blanchard	1844–45
Thomas Ledwith	1845–47
William G. Saunders	1847
Thomas Ledwith	1849
John G. Smith	1849–51
George H. Smith	1851–53
Uriah Bowden	1853–59
Paul B. Canova	1859–61
Escambia County (1822, Pensacola)	
Charles Mifflin	1827–28
Henry Wilson	1828–[?]
Adam Gordon	1828 (resigned)
Florencio Commyns	[1829?]
Peter Woodbine	[1840?]
Ebenezer Dorr	1842–46
Mortimer Bright	1846
Angus Nicholson	1846–47
Antoine J. Collins	1847–51
Francis de la Rua	1851–52
Francis Maura	1852–54

Joseph Crosby	1854–57
William M. R. Jordan	1858–59
Daniel Williams	1859–65

Franklin County (1832, Apalachicola, St. Joseph)

N. Baker	1832–[?]
Henry Williams	1842
Charles Shepard	1843–44
John Lucas	1845–49
Benjamin Lucas	1849–51
Clinton Thigpen	1851–59
Henry K. Simmons	1859–63

Gadsden County (1823, Quincy)

Robert Forbes	1827–[?]
Roderick Shaw	1840–43
William H. McMillan	1844
Benjamin C. West	1845–49
Samuel B. Love	1849–55
James M. Smith	1855–63

Hamilton County (1827, Wallburg, Jasper)

Shaddrack Sutton	1828–[?]
John G. Smith	1840–45
Milton Bryans	1846
Josiah Baisden	1846–47
John G. Smith	1847–49
William J. J. Duncan	1849–51
James N. Hendry	1853–57
Larkin B. McTyier	1857–59
Alexander Bell	1859–65

Hernando (previously Benton) County (1843, DeSoto, Bayport, Pierceville, Brooksville)

James B. Bates	1845–47
N. M. Moody	1847–50
Charles J. McMinn	1853–60

Hillsborough County (1834, Ft. Brooke, Tampa)

[William Ellis Junior?]	[1834?]
R. V. Buffum	1839–43
David Boney	1844
John Parker	1845–47
John J. Hooker	1847–49
Benjamin J. Hagler	1849–53
Edward T. Kendrick	1853–55

Henry Parker	1855–58
William S. Spencer	1858–65
Holmes County (1848, Hewitts Bluff, Cerro Gordo)	
James E. Turner	1848–49
Ethelred Hewett	1849–51
Robert R. Golden	1851–55
John A. Vaughan	1855–57
Daniel J. Brownell	1857–65
Jackson County (1822, Marianna)	
William S. Mooring	1826–[?]
Samuel Stephens	1840–47
John Myrick	1847–49
Samuel Stephens	1849–51
James Griffen	1851–59
Henry O. Bassett	1859–62
Jefferson County (1827, Monticello)	
Asa Townsend	1827–29
Solomon E. Mathers	1830
William R. Taylor	1842–45
Smith Simpkins	1845–47
James R. Tucker	1847–51
Daniel T. Lingo	1851–53
Joel Walker	1853–55
William H. Andrews	1855–57
B. W. Edwards	1857–59
William H. Ellis	1859–61
Lafayette County (1856)	
William Edwards	1857–59
G. W. Lyons	1859–60
James J. Ward	1860–65
Leon County (1824, Tallahassee)	
William Cameron	1825
Romeo Lewis	1827–[?]
James Barry	1842–45
Alfred A. Fisher	1845–51
Haley T. Blocker	1851–57
Richard Saunders	1857–67
Levy County (1845, Wacassasa)	
William D. Andrews	1845–47
Robert Waterson	1847

E. Allan Weeks	1848–49
Robert W. Randall	1850–53
Robert Waterson	1854–55
Joseph F. Prevatt	1855–63
Liberty County (1855, Ricoes Bluff)	
Seaborn Johnson	1857–59
Joseph Shepard	1859–62
Madison County (1827, Madison)	
William Dowling	1828–[?]
James Wallace	[1834?]
Sherrod Edwards	1840–42
William Bridges	1842–44
Elisha Summerlin	1844–45
Thomas Langford	1845–47
Adoniram Vann	1847–49
Thomas M. Anderson	1849–51
John H. Patterson	1851–53
Thomas M. Anderson	1853–55
John H. Patterson	1855–57
Thomas M. Anderson	1857–59
E. W. Vann	1859–61
Manatee County (1855, Manatee)	
W. H. Whitaker	1856–57
J. D. Green	1858–59
J. W. Whidden	1860–61
Marion County (1844, Fort King, Ocala)	
William Strifel	1844
Edmund D. Howse	1845–51
Simeon Helvenston	1851–55
N. A. McLeod	1855–57
Simeon Helvenston	1857–59
Daniel Cappleman	1859–64
Monroe County (1824, Key West)	
Lemuel Otis	1829
Benjamin A. Vun	1841
Samuel T. Vail	1842
B. K. Kerr	1842–44
Edwin Page	1844
John Coslin	1845–47
James V. Ogden	1847–49
Robert Clark	1849–55

William Lowe	1855–58
Edgar A. Coste	1858–61

Mosquito (1824) and St. Lucie County (1844, New Smyrna, Enterprise)

James Pellicer	1827–[?]
John C. Houston	1840–45
Mills O. Burnham	1846–47
F. M. K. Morrison	1847–49
C. L. Brayton	1850–51
Francis Daston	[1855?]

Nassau County (1824, Nassau Court House)

Harman Holliman	1827–[?]
Lewis Bailey	[1828?]
James Lord	1842–44
John Jones	1844–45
Alexander J. Braddock	1845–63

New River County (1859)

Roland Thomas	1859–61

Orange County (1845, Mellonville, Orlando)

William H. Williams	1845–47
John Simpson	1846–51
Elijah Watson	1851–55
J. C. Stewart	1855–61

Putnam County (1849, Palatka)

R. T. Boyd	1850–53
Nathan Norton	1853–54
J. B. Brown	1854–57
Howel A. Baisden	1857–[60?]

St. Johns County (1822, St. Augustine)

James Hanham	1821–[?]
Squire Streeter	1827–28
Daniel G. Gardiner	1828
James Keogh	1840–42
George Acosta	1842–44
Francis Ferriera	1844–45
Joseph S. Sanchez	1845–47
James M. Gould	1847–48
Michael Usina	1848
Rafael B. Canova	1849–53
Jacob Mickler	1854
James A. Mickler	1855

Paul Sabate	1855–57
Alberto D. Rogero	1857–61

Santa Rosa County (1842, Milton)

Thomas Mitchell	1842–44
Thomas V. Mims	1844–45
William W. Harrison	1845–49
James R. Mims	1849–51
Isiah Cobb	1851–55
James C. McArthur	1855–59
Isiah Cobb	1860–61

Sumter County (1853, Adamsville, Sumterville)

U. Z. Wood	1853
E. H. Crow	1853–55
George R. Mobley	1855–56
W. L. Story	1857
John W. Matchett	1857–59
William G. Parker	1860
William M. Christian	1860–61

Taylor County (1856)

S. R. White	1857
John Sherrod	1858–59
Edward Jordan	1859–65

Volusia County (1854, Enterprise)

H. E. Osteen	1855
Elijah Watson	1855–57
Thomas Y. Brooke	1857–59
James C. Marsh	1860–61

Wakulla County (1843, Newport)

E. Madden	1843
R. H. Alexander	1844
Abijah Hall	1845–53
N. G. W. Walker	1853–55
R. H. Alexander	1855
Robert M. Spencer	1855–61

Walton County (1824, Alaqua, Euchee Anna)

Michael Vaughn	1827–[?]
Alexander McKenzie	[1830?]
Alexander Campbell	1840–42
Giles Bowers	1842–44
William W. McCallum	1844–45
Enos Evans	1846–47

Anthony H. Brownell	1847–49
William W. McCallum	1850–53
Alexander C. Monroe	1853–55
John C. Campbell	1855–60

Washington County (1825, Roaches Bluff)

Mortimer Bright	1826–27
John W. Bush	1827–30
William Hall	[1830?]
Stephens Daniel	1840–42
John W. Cook	1842–44
Stephen J. Roche	1844–45
John W. Cook	1845–47
John R. Miller	1847–49
Levi F. Miller	1849–51
John A. Tabor	1851–55
John B. Pearsons	1855–57
George F. Gainor	1857–61

Sources

RG 151, Office of the Secretary of State, ser. 259, Lists of Territorial, State, and County Officers, 1827–1923, 1960, and ser. 1284, State and County Directories, 1845–61, FSAr; *Acts of the Legislative Council* (1822–45); *Acts of the General Assembly* (1846–61); Clarence E. Carter, ed., *The Territorial Papers of the United States,* vols. 22–26 (Washington, D.C.: U.S. Government Printing Office, 1956–62); "Roster of State and County Officers Commissioned by the Governor of Florida, 1845–1868," Jacksonville: Florida Historical Records Survey, Works Progress Administration, February 1941; *The Florida Sheriff: Yearbook of the Florida Sheriffs Association* (1958): 23–88; Kermit L. Hall and Eric W. Rise, *From Local Courts to National Tribunals: Federal District Courts of Florida, 1821–1991* (Brooklyn: Carlson Publishing Co., 1991).

Appendix 4

Prosecution Tables by County

Alachua (Columbia, Hillsborough, and Levy) County
1828-1835, 1838-1843, *1840-1849, 1850-1857

CRIMES AGAINST PERSON	Number	Guilty	Not Guilty	No Verdict
Murder/Manslaughter	18	6	5	7
Accessory to Murder	0	0	0	0
Assault and Battery	52	11	2	39
Assault with Intent to Kill	26	14	2	10
Rape	3	1	1	1
Robbery	4	1	2	1
Assault with Intent to Rape	1	1	0	0
False Imprisonment	5	0	0	5
Felony (unspecified)	0	0	0	0
Aiding and Assisting a Felony	0	0	0	0
Extortion	0	0	0	0
Piracy	0	0	0	0
Mutiny	0	0	0	0
Total	109	34	12	63
CRIMES AGAINST PROPERTY				
Horse Stealing	5	1	1	3
Cattle Stealing	0	0	0	0
Larceny	28	3	9	16
Burglary	0	0	0	0
Forgery	0	0	0	0
Arson	0	0	0	0
Slave Stealing	4	0	1	3
Counterfeiting	0	0	0	0
Stealing from Vessel in Distress	0	0	0	0
Fraudulently Marking Cattle	2	1	0	1
Total	39	5	11	23

*1840-1842 duplicate earlier book—only new years are 1847-1849

Appendix 4: Prosecution Tables by County

CRIMES AGAINST MORALITY/ PUBLIC ORDER	Number	Guilty	Not Guilty	No Verdict
Adultery and Fornication	51	8	3	40
Aiding a Prisoner to Escape	0	0	0	0
Allowing Negro to Carry Gun	0	0	0	0
Assisting a Slave to Escape	0	0	0	0
Being Concerned in a Duel	6	1	0	5
Bestiality	0	0	0	0
Bigamy	0	0	0	0
Breaking Jail (Escape)	0	0	0	0
Bribery	0	0	0	0
Buggery	0	0	0	0
Buying Soldier's Clothing	0	0	0	0
Carrying Arms Secretly	20	13	4	3
Cheating	0	0	0	0
Concealing the Birth of a Child	0	0	0	0
Conspiracy to Obtain Money by a Trick with Cards	0	0	0	0
Cruelty to a Slave	0	0	0	0
Disturbing Religious Worship	3	0	0	3
Employing Slaves on the Sabbath	0	0	0	0
Enticing a Soldier to Desert	1	0	1	0
Enticing Slave to Run Away	1	0	0	1
Fornication with a Colored Female	0	0	0	0
Fraudulent Voting	0	0	0	0
Gambling, Gaming, Betting	21	11	3	7
Giving Ticket to Slave of Another	0	0	0	0
Harboring Felons	1	0	0	1
Incest	0	0	0	0
Keeping a Gaming Table	0	0	0	0
Keeping a Gaming, Disorderly House	8	0	2	6
Keeping Billiard Table/Ten Pin Alley without a License	5	2	0	3
Leaving Slaves on Plantation without a White	0	0	0	0
Libel	0	0	0	0
Malfeasance of Public Official	0	0	0	0
Malicious Mischief (Wickedness)	0	0	0	0
Maliciously Killing Animals	2	0	1	1
Maliciously Pulling Down a Fence	0	0	0	0
Marrying a Colored Female	0	0	0	0
Misdemeanor (unspecified)	0	0	0	0
Notorious Public Indecency	0	0	0	0
Nuisance (Disturbing the Peace)	2	0	0	2
Obstructing a Public Road	0	0	0	0
Obstructing Legal Process	6	0	0	6

	Number	Guilty	Not Guilty	No Verdict
Obtaining Goods under False Pretenses	0	0	0	0
Open Lewdness	0	0	0	0
Performing a Marriage for White Man and Colored Female	0	0	0	0
Perjury	0	0	0	0
Permitting a Slave to Hire His Own Time	0	0	0	0
Permitting a Slave to Trade as Free	0	0	0	0
Practicing Medicine without a License	0	0	0	0
Receiving Stolen Goods	1	1	0	0
Retailing Liquors to a Slave	0	0	0	0
Retailing on the Sabbath	12	10	0	2
Retailing without a License	8	3	0	5
Riot, Affray, Mayhem	29	8	5	16
Selling Intoxicating Liquors to Military	0	0	0	0
Selling Liquor to Indians	3	0	2	1
Selling Liquor without a License	28	7	12	9
Selling Unwholesome Provisions	0	0	0	0
Shipping Cattle from County without Inspection	0	0	0	0
Sodomy	0	0	0	0
Trading with a Slave	8	2	2	4
Trespass	0	0	0	0
Trespassing on School Lands	0	0	0	0
Vagrancy	0	0	0	0
Violating Auction Laws	0	0	0	0
Total	216	66	35	115
SUBTOTAL	364	105	58	201

CRIMES COMMITTED BY SLAVES AND FREE BLACKS

CRIMES AGAINST PERSON

	Number	Guilty	Not Guilty	No Verdict
Murder	0	0	0	0
Assault and Battery	0	0	0	0
Rape	1	1	0	0
Assault with Intent to Rape	0	0	0	0
Assault with Intent to Kill	2	1	0	1
Consulting and Advising to Kill	1	1	0	0
Felony (unspecified)	0	0	0	0
Attempt to Poison	0	0	0	0
Revolt	0	0	0	0
Total	4	3	0	1

CRIMES AGAINST PROPERTY	Number	Guilty	Not Guilty	No Verdict
Larceny	0	0	0	0
Burglary	0	0	0	0
Arson	0	0	0	0
Horse Stealing	0	0	0	0
Total	0	0	0	0
CRIMES AGAINST MORALITY/PUBLIC ORDER				
Forging Free Papers	0	0	0	0
Enticing a Slave to Run Away	0	0	0	0
Receiving Stolen Goods	0	0	0	0
Maliciously Killing Animals	0	0	0	0
Maliciously Wounding Animals	0	0	0	0
Buggery	0	0	0	0
Migration of Free Persons of Color into the Territory	0	0	0	0
Total	0	0	0	0
SUBTOTAL	4	3	0	1
GRAND TOTAL	368	108	58	202

PERCENTAGES OF TOTAL PROSECUTIONS BY CATEGORY

Crimes against Person	30.71%
Crimes against Property	10.60%
Crimes against Morality/Public Order	58.70%
Cases with Guilty Verdict	29.35%
Cases with Not Guilty Verdict	15.76%
Cases with No Verdict	54.89%

Clay County
1859-1861

CRIMES AGAINST PERSON				
Murder/Manslaughter	1	0	0	1
Accessory to Murder	0	0	0	0
Assault and Battery	7	7	0	0
Assault with Intent to Kill	2	2	0	0
Rape	0	0	0	0
Robbery	0	0	0	0
Assault with Intent to Rape	0	0	0	0
False Imprisonment	0	0	0	0
Felony (unspecified)	0	0	0	0

	Number	Guilty	Not Guilty	No Verdict
Aiding and Assisting a Felony	0	0	0	0
Extortion	0	0	0	0
Piracy	0	0	0	0
Mutiny	0	0	0	0
Total	10	9	0	1

CRIMES AGAINST PROPERTY

	Number	Guilty	Not Guilty	No Verdict
Horse Stealing	0	0	0	0
Cattle Stealing	0	0	0	0
Larceny	0	0	0	0
Burglary	0	0	0	0
Forgery	0	0	0	0
Arson	0	0	0	0
Slave Stealing	0	0	0	0
Counterfeiting	0	0	0	0
Stealing from Vessel in Distress	0	0	0	0
Fraudulently Marking Cattle	0	0	0	0
Total	0	0	0	0

CRIMES AGAINST MORALITY/PUBLIC ORDER

	Number	Guilty	Not Guilty	No Verdict
Adultery and Fornication	1	0	0	1
Aiding a Prisoner to Escape	0	0	0	0
Allowing Negro to Carry Gun	0	0	0	0
Assisting a Slave to Escape	0	0	0	0
Being Concerned in a Duel	0	0	0	0
Bestiality	0	0	0	0
Bigamy	0	0	0	0
Breaking Jail (Escape)	0	0	0	0
Bribery	0	0	0	0
Buggery	0	0	0	0
Buying Soldier's Clothing	0	0	0	0
Carrying Arms Secretly	3	0	1	2
Cheating	0	0	0	0
Concealing the Birth of a Child	0	0	0	0
Conspiracy to Obtain Money by a Trick with Cards	0	0	0	0
Cruelty to a Slave	0	0	0	0
Disturbing Religious Worship	0	0	0	0
Employing Slaves on the Sabbath	0	0	0	0
Enticing a Soldier to Desert	0	0	0	0
Enticing Slave to Run Away	0	0	0	0

Appendix 4: Prosecution Tables by County

	Number	Guilty	Not Guilty	No Verdict
Fornication with a Colored Female	0	0	0	0
Fraudulent Voting	0	0	0	0
Gambling, Gaming, Betting	0	0	0	0
Giving Ticket to Slave of Another	0	0	0	0
Harboring Felons	0	0	0	0
Incest	0	0	0	0
Keeping a Gaming Table	0	0	0	0
Keeping a Gaming, Disorderly House	0	0	0	0
Keeping Billiard Table/Ten Pin Alley without a License	0	0	0	0
Leaving Slaves on Plantation without a White	0	0	0	0
Libel	0	0	0	0
Malfeasance of Public Official	0	0	0	0
Malicious Mischief (Wickedness)	0	0	0	0
Maliciously Killing Animals	2	0	0	2
Maliciously Pulling Down a Fence	2	0	0	2
Marrying a Colored Female	2	0	0	2
Misdemeanor (unspecified)	0	0	0	0
Notorious Public Indecency	0	0	0	0
Nuisance (Disturbing the Peace)	0	0	0	0
Obstructing a Public Road	0	0	0	0
Obstructing Legal Process	0	0	0	0
Obtaining Goods under False Pretenses	0	0	0	0
Open Lewdness	0	0	0	0
Performing a Marriage for White Man and Colored Female	0	0	0	0
Perjury	0	0	0	0
Permitting a Slave to Hire His Own Time	0	0	0	0
Permitting a Slave to Trade as Free	0	0	0	0
Practicing Medicine without a License	0	0	0	0
Receiving Stolen Goods	0	0	0	0
Retailing Liquors to a Slave	1	0	1	0
Retailing on the Sabbath	0	0	0	0
Retailing without a License	0	0	0	0
Riot, Affray, Mayhem	0	0	0	0
Selling Intoxicating Liquors to Military	0	0	0	0
Selling Liquor to Indians	0	0	0	0
Selling Liquor without a License	0	0	0	0
Selling Unwholesome Provisions	0	0	0	0
Shipping Cattle from County without Inspection	0	0	0	0
Sodomy	0	0	0	0
Trading with a Slave	1	0	1	0

	Number	Guilty	Not Guilty	No Verdict
Trespass	0	0	0	0
Trespassing on School Lands	0	0	0	0
Vagrancy	0	0	0	0
Violating Auction Laws	0	0	0	0
Total	12	0	3	9
SUBTOTAL	22	9	3	10

CRIMES COMMITTED BY SLAVES AND FREE BLACKS

CRIMES AGAINST PERSON

	Number	Guilty	Not Guilty	No Verdict
Murder	0	0	0	0
Assault and Battery	0	0	0	0
Rape	0	0	0	0
Assault with Intent to Rape	0	0	0	0
Assault with Intent to Kill	0	0	0	0
Consulting and Advising to Kill	0	0	0	0
Felony (unspecified)	0	0	0	0
Attempt to Poison	0	0	0	0
Revolt	0	0	0	0
Total	0	0	0	0

CRIMES AGAINST PROPERTY

	Number	Guilty	Not Guilty	No Verdict
Larceny	0	0	0	0
Burglary	0	0	0	0
Arson	0	0	0	0
Horse Stealing	0	0	0	0
Total	0	0	0	0

CRIMES AGAINST MORALITY/PUBLIC ORDER

	Number	Guilty	Not Guilty	No Verdict
Forging Free Papers	0	0	0	0
Enticing a Slave to Run Away	0	0	0	0
Receiving Stolen Goods	0	0	0	0
Maliciously Killing Animals	0	0	0	0
Maliciously Wounding Animals	0	0	0	0
Buggery	0	0	0	0
Migration of Free Persons of Color into the Territory	0	0	0	0
Total	0	0	0	0
SUBTOTAL	0	0	0	0
GRAND TOTAL	22	9	3	10

Appendix 4: Prosecution Tables by County

PERCENTAGES OF TOTAL PROSECUTIONS BY CATEGORY

Crimes against Person	44.45%
Crimes against Property	0.00%
Crimes against Morality/Public Order	54.55%
Cases with Guilty Verdict	40.91%
Cases with Not Guilty Verdict	13.64%
Cases with No Verdict	45.45%

Escambia County
1822-1833, 1833-1838, 1838-1842, 1842-1845, 1846-1854, 1855-1866

CRIMES AGAINST PERSON	Number	Guilty	Not Guilty	No Verdict
Murder/Manslaughter	32	7	5	20
Accessory to Murder	0	0	0	0
Assault and Battery	231	101	25	105
Assault with Intent to Kill	39	16	7	16
Rape	1	0	0	1
Robbery	2	1	1	0
Assault with Intent to Rape	1	1	0	0
False Imprisonment	2	0	2	0
Felony (unspecified)	0	0	0	0
Aiding and Assisting a Felony	0	0	0	0
Extortion	4	0	4	0
Piracy	1	0	1	0
Mutiny	0	0	0	0
Total	313	126	45	142

CRIMES AGAINST PROPERTY	Number	Guilty	Not Guilty	No Verdict
Horse Stealing	1	0	0	1
Cattle Stealing	0	0	0	0
Larceny	87	21	33	33
Burglary	3	1	0	2
Forgery	3	1	1	1
Arson	5	4	0	1
Slave Stealing	8	2	2	4
Counterfeiting	2	0	0	2
Stealing from Vessel in Distress	0	0	0	0
Fraudulently Marking Cattle	0	0	0	0
Total	109	29	36	44

CRIMES AGAINST MORALITY/ PUBLIC ORDER	Number	Guilty	Not Guilty	No Verdict
Adultery and Fornication	50	5	13	32
Aiding a Prisoner to Escape	0	0	0	0
Allowing Negro to Carry Gun	0	0	0	0
Assisting a Slave to Escape	2	1	0	1
Being Concerned in a Duel	0	0	0	0
Bestiality	0	0	0	0
Bigamy	3	1	0	2
Breaking Jail (Escape)	2	0	0	2
Bribery	0	0	0	0
Buggery	0	0	0	0
Buying Soldier's Clothing	1	0	0	1
Carrying Arms Secretly	29	15	8	6
Cheating	0	0	0	0
Concealing the Birth of a Child	0	0	0	0
Conspiracy to Obtain Money by a Trick with Cards	0	0	0	0
Cruelty to a Slave	1	1	0	0
Disturbing Religious Worship	0	0	0	0
Employing Slaves on the Sabbath	0	0	0	0
Enticing a Soldier to Desert	0	0	0	0
Enticing Slave to Run Away	0	0	0	0
Fornication with a Colored Female	0	0	0	0
Fraudulent Voting	3	0	3	0
Gambling, Gaming, Betting	24	3	7	14
Giving Ticket to Slave of Another	0	0	0	0
Harboring Felons	0	0	0	0
Incest	0	0	0	0
Keeping a Gaming Table	2	1	0	1
Keeping a Gaming, Disorderly House	23	13	4	6
Keeping Billiard Table/Ten Pin Alley without a License	0	0	0	0
Leaving Slaves on Plantation without a White	0	0	0	0
Libel	7	2	0	5
Malfeasance of Public Official	1	0	1	0
Malicious Mischief (Wickedness)	4	1	2	1
Maliciously Killing Animals	0	0	0	0
Maliciously Pulling Down a Fence	0	0	0	0
Marrying a Colored Female	0	0	0	0
Misdemeanor (unspecified)	9	2	2	5
Notorious Public Indecency	4	0	0	4
Nuisance (Disturbing the Peace)	0	0	0	0
Obstructing a Public Road	0	0	0	0

Appendix 4: Prosecution Tables by County

	Number	Guilty	Not Guilty	No Verdict
Obstructing Legal Process	0	0	0	0
Obtaining Goods under False Pretenses	2	0	0	2
Open Lewdness	0	0	0	0
Performing a Marriage for White Man and Colored Female	0	0	0	0
Perjury	0	0	0	0
Permitting a Slave to Hire His Own Time	0	0	0	0
Permitting a Slave to Trade as Free	0	0	0	0
Practicing Medicine without a License	0	0	0	0
Receiving Stolen Goods	7	1	1	5
Retailing Liquors to a Slave	17	10	2	5
Retailing on the Sabbath	1	0	0	1
Retailing without a License	10	2	0	8
Riot, Affray, Mayhem	50	9	4	37
Selling Intoxicating Liquors to Military	0	0	0	0
Selling Liquor to Indians	0	0	0	0
Selling Liquor without a License	34	7	24	3
Selling Unwholesome Provisions	0	0	0	0
Shipping Cattle from County w/out Inspection	0	0	0	0
Sodomy	2	1	0	1
Trading with a Slave	4	3	1	0
Trespass	0	0	0	0
Trespassing on School Lands	0	0	0	0
Vagrancy	0	0	0	0
Violating Auction Laws	0	0	0	0
Total	292	78	72	142
SUBTOTAL	714	233	153	328

CRIMES COMMITTED BY SLAVES AND FREE BLACKS

CRIMES AGAINST PERSON

	Number	Guilty	Not Guilty	No Verdict
Murder	4	4	0	0
Assault and Battery	3	1	0	2
Rape	1	0	1	0
Assault with Intent to Rape	2	2	0	0
Assault with Intent to Kill	0	0	0	0
Consulting and Advising to Kill	0	0	0	0
Felony (unspecified)	0	0	0	0
Attempt to Poison	0	0	0	0
Revolt	0	0	0	0
Total	10	7	1	2

CRIMES AGAINST PROPERTY	Number	Guilty	Not Guilty	No Verdict
Larceny	14	6	2	6
Burglary	0	0	0	0
Arson	3	1	0	2
Horse Stealing	0	0	0	0
Total	17	7	2	8
CRIMES AGAINST MORALITY/PUBLIC ORDER				
Forging Free Papers	1	0	0	1
Enticing a Slave to Run Away	0	0	0	0
Receiving Stolen Goods	2	0	1	1
Maliciously Killing Animals	0	0	0	0
Maliciously Wounding Animals	0	0	0	0
Buggery	1	1	0	0
Migration of Free Persons of Color into the Territory	0	0	0	0
Total	4	1	1	2
SUBTOTAL	31	15	4	12
GRAND TOTAL	745	248	157	340

PERCENTAGES OF TOTAL PROSECUTIONS BY CATEGORY

Crimes against Person	43.36%
Crimes against Property	16.91%
Crimes against Morality/Public Order	39.73%
Cases with Guilty Verdict	33.29%
Cases with Not Guilty Verdict	21.07%
Cases with No Verdict	45.64%

Gadsden County
1849-1855

CRIMES AGAINST PERSON				
Murder/Manslaughter	1	0	0	1
Accessory to Murder	0	0	0	0
Assault and Battery	50	30	3	17
Assault with Intent to Kill	6	3	0	3
Rape	0	0	0	0
Robbery	0	0	0	0
Assault with Intent to Rape	0	0	0	0
False Imprisonment	0	0	0	0
Felony (unspecified)	0	0	0	0

Appendix 4: Prosecution Tables by County

	Number	Guilty	Not Guilty	No Verdict
Aiding and Assisting a Felony	0	0	0	0
Extortion	0	0	0	0
Piracy	0	0	0	0
Mutiny	0	0	0	0
Total	57	33	3	21
CRIMES AGAINST PROPERTY				
Horse Stealing	0	0	0	0
Cattle Stealing	0	0	0	0
Larceny	9	0	1	8
Burglary	0	0	0	0
Forgery	0	0	0	0
Arson	0	0	0	0
Slave Stealing	1	1	0	0
Counterfeiting	0	0	0	0
Stealing from Vessel in Distress	0	0	0	0
Fraudulently Marking Cattle	0	0	0	0
Total	10	1	1	8
CRIMES AGAINST MORALITY/PUBLIC ORDER				
Adultery and Fornication	0	0	0	0
Aiding a Prisoner to Escape	0	0	0	0
Allowing Negro to Carry Gun	0	0	0	0
Assisting a Slave to Escape	0	0	0	0
Being Concerned in a Duel	0	0	0	0
Bestiality	0	0	0	0
Bigamy	1	0	0	1
Breaking Jail (Escape)	0	0	0	0
Bribery	0	0	0	0
Buggery	0	0	0	0
Buying Soldier's Clothing	0	0	0	0
Carrying Arms Secretly	12	7	0	5
Cheating	0	0	0	0
Concealing the Birth of a Child	0	0	0	0
Conspiracy to Obtain Money by a Trick with Cards	0	0	0	0
Cruelty to a Slave	0	0	0	0
Disturbing Religious Worship	2	0	0	2
Employing Slaves on the Sabbath	0	0	0	0
Enticing a Soldier to Desert	0	0	0	0
Enticing Slave to Run Away	0	0	0	0

	Number	Guilty	Not Guilty	No Verdict
Fornication with a Colored Female	0	0	0	0
Fraudulent Voting	0	0	0	0
Gambling, Gaming, Betting	6	0	0	6
Giving Ticket to Slave of Another	0	0	0	0
Harboring Felons	0	0	0	0
Incest	0	0	0	0
Keeping a Gaming Table	0	0	0	0
Keeping a Gaming, Disorderly House	1	0	1	0
Keeping Billiard Table/Ten Pin Alley without a License	0	0	0	0
Leaving Slaves on Plantation without a White	0	0	0	0
Libel	0	0	0	0
Malfeasance of Public Official	0	0	0	0
Malicious Mischief (Wickedness)	0	0	0	0
Maliciously Killing Animals	0	0	0	0
Maliciously Pulling Down a Fence	0	0	0	0
Marrying a Colored Female	0	0	0	0
Misdemeanor (unspecified)	6	1	0	5
Notorious Public Indecency	0	0	0	0
Nuisance (Disturbing the Peace)	0	0	0	0
Obstructing a Public Road	0	0	0	0
Obstructing Legal Process	2	1	1	0
Obtaining Goods under False Pretenses	0	0	0	0
Open Lewdness	0	0	0	0
Performing a Marriage for White Man and Colored Female	0	0	0	0
Perjury	0	0	0	0
Permitting a Slave to Hire His Own Time	0	0	0	0
Permitting a Slave to Trade as Free	0	0	0	0
Practicing Medicine without a License	1	1	0	0
Receiving Stolen Goods	0	0	0	0
Retailing Liquors to a Slave	0	0	0	0
Retailing on the Sabbath	0	0	0	0
Retailing without a License	0	0	0	0
Riot, Affray, Mayhem	17	0	0	17
Selling Intoxicating Liquors to Military	0	0	0	0
Selling Liquor to Indians	0	0	0	0
Selling Liquor without a License	0	0	0	0
Selling Unwholesome Provisions	0	0	0	0
Shipping Cattle from County without Inspection	0	0	0	0
Sodomy	0	0	0	0
Trading with a Slave	2	0	2	0

	Number	Guilty	Not Guilty	No Verdict
Trespassing on School Lands	0	0	0	0
Vagrancy	0	0	0	0
Violating Auction Laws	0	0	0	0
Total	50	10	4	36
SUBTOTAL	117	44	8	65

CRIMES COMMITTED BY SLAVES AND FREE BLACKS

CRIMES AGAINST PERSON

	Number	Guilty	Not Guilty	No Verdict
Murder	0	0	0	0
Assault and Battery	0	0	0	0
Rape	0	0	0	0
Assault with Intent to Rape	0	0	0	0
Assault with Intent to Kill	0	0	0	0
Consulting and Advising to Kill	0	0	0	0
Felony (unspecified)	0	0	0	0
Attempt to Poison	0	0	0	0
Revolt	0	0	0	0
Total	0	0	0	0

CRIMES AGAINST PROPERTY

	Number	Guilty	Not Guilty	No Verdict
Larceny	0	0	0	0
Burglary	0	0	0	0
Arson	0	0	0	0
Horse Stealing	0	0	0	0
Total	0	0	0	0

CRIMES AGAINST MORALITY/PUBLIC ORDER

	Number	Guilty	Not Guilty	No Verdict
Forging Free Papers	0	0	0	0
Enticing a Slave to Run Away	0	0	0	0
Receiving Stolen Goods	0	0	0	0
Maliciously Killing Animals	0	0	0	0
Maliciously Wounding Animals	0	0	0	0
Buggery	0	0	0	0
Migration of Free Persons of Color into the Territory	0	0	0	0
Total	0	0	0	0
SUBTOTAL	0	0	0	0
GRAND TOTAL	117	44	8	65

Appendix 4: Prosecution Tables by County

PERCENTAGES OF TOTAL PROSECUTIONS BY CATEGORY

Crimes against Person	48.72%
Crimes against Property	8.55%
Crimes against Morality/Public Order	42.74%
Cases with Guilty Verdict	37.61%
Cases with Not Guilty Verdict	6.84%
Cases with No Verdict	55.56%

Hamilton County
1833-1845, 1855-1867

CRIMES AGAINST PERSON	Number	Guilty	Not Guilty	No Verdict
Murder/Manslaughter	4	0	0	4
Accessory to Murder	0	0	0	0
Assault and Battery	50	18	0	32
Assault with Intent to Kill	9	4	0	5
Rape	0	0	0	0
Robbery	0	0	0	0
Assault with Intent to Rape	0	0	0	0
False Imprisonment	3	0	0	3
Felony (unspecified)	0	0	0	0
Aiding and Assisting a Felony	0	0	0	0
Extortion	0	0	0	0
Mutiny	0	0	0	0
Total	66	22	0	44

CRIMES AGAINST PROPERTY	Number	Guilty	Not Guilty	No Verdict
Horse Stealing	0	0	0	0
Cattle Stealing	0	0	0	0
Larceny	19	2	3	14
Burglary	0	0	0	0
Forgery	0	0	0	0
Arson	0	0	0	0
Slave Stealing	0	0	0	0
Counterfeiting	0	0	0	0
Stealing from Vessel in Distress	0	0	0	0
Fraudulently Marking Cattle	1	0	1	0
Total	20	2	4	14

Appendix 4: Prosecution Tables by County

CRIMES AGAINST MORALITY/ PUBLIC ORDER	Number	Guilty	Not Guilty	No Verdict
Adultery and Fornication	9	1	0	8
Aiding a Prisoner to Escape	0	0	0	0
Allowing Negro to Carry Gun	0	0	0	0
Assisting a Slave to Escape	0	0	0	0
Being Concerned in a Duel	0	0	0	0
Bestiality	0	0	0	0
Bigamy	0	0	0	0
Breaking Jail (Escape)	0	0	0	0
Bribery	0	0	0	0
Buggery	0	0	0	0
Buying Soldier's Clothing	0	0	0	0
Carrying Arms Secretly	22	5	1	16
Cheating	1	0	0	1
Concealing the Birth of a Child	0	0	0	0
Conspiracy to Obtain Money by a Trick with Cards	0	0	0	0
Cruelty to a Slave	0	0	0	0
Disturbing Religious Worship	2	0	0	2
Employing Slaves on the Sabbath	0	0	0	0
Enticing a Soldier to Desert	0	0	0	0
Enticing Slave to Run Away	1	1	0	0
Fornication with a Colored Female	0	0	0	0
Fraudulent Voting	0	0	0	0
Gambling, Gaming, Betting	2	0	2	0
Giving Ticket to Slave of Another	0	0	0	0
Harboring Felons	0	0	0	0
Incest	1	0	0	1
Keeping a Gaming Table	0	0	0	0
Keeping a Gaming, Disorderly House	1	0	0	1
Keeping Billiard Table/Ten Pin Alley without a License	0	0	0	0
Leaving Slaves on Plantation without a White	0	0	0	0
Libel	0	0	0	0
Malfeasance of Public Official	0	0	0	0
Malicious Mischief (Wickedness)	10	0	0	10
Maliciously Killing Animals	1	0	0	1
Maliciously Pulling Down a Fence	0	0	0	0
Marrying a Colored Female	0	0	0	0
Misdemeanor (unspecified)	6	1	1	4
Notorious Public Indecency	0	0	0	0
Nuisance (Disturbing the Peace)	4	0	0	4
Obstructing a Public Road	0	0	0	0
Obstructing Legal Process	0	0	0	0

Appendix 4: Prosecution Tables by County

	Number	Guilty	Not Guilty	No Verdict
Obtaining Goods under False Pretenses	0	0	0	0
Open Lewdness	0	0	0	0
Performing a Marriage for White Man and Colored Female	0	0	0	0
Perjury	1	0	0	1
Permitting a Slave to Hire His Own Time	0	0	0	0
Permitting a Slave to Trade as Free	0	0	0	0
Practicing Medicine without a License	0	0	0	0
Receiving Stolen Goods	0	0	0	0
Retailing Liquors to a Slave	5	0	0	5
Retailing on the Sabbath	0	0	0	0
Retailing without a License	0	0	0	0
Riot, Affray, Mayhem	13	4	0	9
Selling Intoxicating Liquors to Military	0	0	0	0
Selling Liquor to Indians	0	0	0	0
Selling Liquor without a License	0	0	0	0
Selling Unwholesome Provisions	0	0	0	0
Shipping Cattle from County without Inspection	2	0	0	2
Sodomy	0	0	0	0
Trading with a Slave	3	0	0	3
Trespass	0	0	0	0
Trespassing on School Lands	0	0	0	0
Vagrancy	0	0	0	0
Violating Auction Laws	0	0	0	0
Total	84	12	4	68
SUBTOTAL	170	36	8	126

CRIMES COMMITTED BY SLAVES AND FREE BLACKS

CRIMES AGAINST PERSON

	Number	Guilty	Not Guilty	No Verdict
Murder	0	0	0	0
Assault and Battery	1	0	0	1
Rape	0	0	0	0
Assault with Intent to Rape	0	0	0	0
Assault with Intent to Kill	0	0	0	0
Consulting and Advising to Kill	0	0	0	0
Felony (unspecified)	0	0	0	0
Attempt to Poison	0	0	0	0
Revolt	0	0	0	0
Total	1	0	0	1

CRIMES AGAINST PROPERTY	Number	Guilty	Not Guilty	No Verdict
Larceny	0	0	0	0
Burglary	0	0	0	0
Arson	0	0	0	0
Horse Stealing	0	0	0	0
Total	0	0	0	0
CRIMES AGAINST MORALITY/PUBLIC ORDER				
Forging Free Papers	0	0	0	0
Enticing a Slave to Run Away	0	0	0	0
Receiving Stolen Goods	0	0	0	0
Maliciously Killing Animals	0	0	0	0
Maliciously Wounding Animals	0	0	0	0
Buggery	0	0	0	0
Migration of Free Persons of Color into the Territory	0	0	0	0
Total	0	0	0	0
SUBTOTAL	1	0	0	1
GRAND TOTAL	171	36	8	127

PERCENTAGES OF TOTAL PROSECUTIONS BY CATEGORY

Crimes against Person	39.18%
Crimes against Property	11.70%
Crimes against Morality/Public Order	49.12%
Cases with Guilty Verdict	21.05%
Cases with Not Guilty Verdict	4.68%
Cases with No Verdict	74.27%

Hillsborough County
1846-1854, 1854-1866

CRIMES AGAINST PERSON				
Murder/Manslaughter	10	3	2	5
Accessory to Murder	0	0	0	0
Assault and Battery	56	21	8	27
Assault with Intent to Kill	11	3	0	8
Rape	1	0	1	0
Robbery	1	0	0	1
Assault with Intent to Rape	0	0	0	0
False Imprisonment	1	0	1	0

	Number	Guilty	Not Guilty	No Verdict
Felony (unspecified)	0	0	0	0
Aiding and Assisting a Felony	0	0	0	0
Extortion	0	0	0	0
Piracy	0	0	0	0
Mutiny	0	0	0	0
Total	80	27	12	41
CRIMES AGAINST PROPERTY				
Horse Stealing	0	0	0	0
Cattle Stealing	0	0	0	0
Larceny	20	4	10	6
Burglary	0	0	0	0
Forgery	1	0	0	1
Arson	0	0	0	0
Slave Stealing	0	0	0	0
Counterfeiting	0	0	0	0
Stealing from Vessel in Distress	0	0	0	0
Fraudulently Marking Cattle	9	0	2	7
Total	30	4	12	14
CRIMES AGAINST MORALITY/PUBLIC ORDER				
Adultery and Fornication	22	2	0	20
Aiding a Prisoner to Escape	2	0	0	2
Allowing Negro to Carry Gun	1	0	0	1
Assisting a Slave to Escape	0	0	0	0
Being Concerned in a Duel	0	0	0	0
Bestiality	0	0	0	0
Bigamy	4	0	1	3
Breaking Jail (Escape)	0	0	0	0
Bribery	0	0	0	0
Buggery	0	0	0	0
Buying Soldier's Clothing	0	0	0	0
Carrying Arms Secretly	13	1	3	9
Cheating	0	0	0	0
Concealing the Birth of a Child	0	0	0	0
Conspiracy to Obtain Money by a Trick with Cards	4	0	0	4
Cruelty to a Slave	1	0	0	1
Disturbing Religious Worship	3	1	0	2
Employing Slaves on the Sabbath	1	0	0	1
Enticing a Soldier to Desert	0	0	0	0
Enticing Slave to Run Away	0	0	0	0

Appendix 4: Prosecution Tables by County

	Number	Guilty	Not Guilty	No Verdict
Fornication with a Colored Female	0	0	0	0
Fraudulent Voting	0	0	0	0
Gambling, Gaming, Betting	3	0	0	3
Giving Ticket to Slave of Another	0	0	0	0
Harboring Felons	0	0	0	0
Incest	0	0	0	0
Keeping a Gaming Table	11	0	0	11
Keeping a Gaming, Disorderly House	8	0	0	8
Keeping Billiard Table/Ten Pin Alley without a License	0	0	0	0
Leaving Slaves on Plantation without a White	0	0	0	0
Libel	1	0	0	1
Malfeasance of Public Official	4	0	2	2
Malicious Mischief (Wickedness)	0	0	0	0
Maliciously Killing Animals	4	2	1	1
Maliciously Pulling Down a Fence	0	0	0	0
Marrying a Colored Female	0	0	0	0
Misdemeanor (unspecified)	0	0	0	0
Notorious Public Indecency	0	0	0	0
Nuisance (Disturbing the Peace)	0	0	0	0
Obstructing a Public Road	0	0	0	0
Obstructing Legal Process	0	0	0	0
Obtaining Goods under False Pretenses	0	0	0	0
Open Lewdness	1	1	0	0
Performing a Marriage for White Man and Colored Female	0	0	0	0
Perjury	2	0	0	2
Permitting a Slave to Hire His Own Time	0	0	0	0
Permitting a Slave to Trade as Free	0	0	0	0
Practicing Medicine without a License	2	1	0	1
Receiving Stolen Goods	0	0	0	0
Retailing Liquors to a Slave	4	2	2	0
Retailing on the Sabbath	2	0	1	1
Retailing without a License	0	0	0	0
Riot, Affray, Mayhem	13	4	4	5
Selling Intoxicating Liquors to Military	0	0	0	0
Selling Liquor to Indians	1	1	0	0
Selling Liquor without a License	27	6	10	11
Selling Unwholesome Provisions	2	0	0	2
Shipping Cattle from County without Inspection	1	0	1	0
Sodomy	0	0	0	0
Trading with a Slave	2	0	0	2
Trespass	0	0	0	0

	Number	Guilty	Not Guilty	No Verdict
Trespassing on School Lands	0	0	0	0
Vagrancy	0	0	0	0
Violating Auction Laws	0	0	0	0
Total	139	21	25	93
SUBTOTAL	249	52	49	148
CRIMES COMMITTED BY SLAVES AND FREE BLACKS				
CRIMES AGAINST PERSON				
Murder	3	2	0	1
Assault and Battery	0	0	0	0
Rape	0	0	0	0
Assault with Intent to Rape	0	0	0	0
Assault with Intent to Kill	0	0	0	0
Consulting and Advising to Kill	0	0	0	0
Felony (unspecified)	0	0	0	0
Attempt to Poison	0	0	0	0
Revolt	0	0	0	0
Total	3	2	0	1
CRIMES AGAINST PROPERTY				
Larceny	0	0	0	0
Burglary	0	0	0	0
Arson	0	0	0	0
Horse Stealing	0	0	0	0
Total	0	0	0	0
CRIMES AGAINST MORALITY/PUBLIC ORDER				
Forging Free Papers	0	0	0	0
Enticing a Slave to Run Away	0	0	0	0
Receiving Stolen Goods	0	0	0	0
Maliciously Killing Animals	0	0	0	0
Maliciously Wounding Animals	0	0	0	0
Buggery	0	0	0	0
Migration of Free Persons of Color into the Territory	0	0	0	0
Total	0	0	0	0
SUBTOTAL	3	2	0	1
GRAND TOTAL	252	54	49	149

Appendix 4: Prosecution Tables by County

PERCENTAGES OF TOTAL PROSECUTIONS BY CATEGORY

Crimes against Person	32.94%
Crimes against Property	11.90%
Crimes against Morality/Public Order	55.16%
Cases with Guilty Verdict	21.43%
Cases with Not Guilty Verdict	19.44%
Cases with No Verdict	59.13%

Jackson County
1851-1857, 1857-1861, 1861-1865

CRIMES AGAINST PERSON	Number	Guilty	Not Guilty	No Verdict
Murder/Manslaughter	19	2	1	16
Accessory to Murder	2	0	2	0
Assault and Battery	53	20	1	32
Assault with Intent to Kill	25	2	1	22
Rape	1	1	0	0
Robbery	0	0	0	0
Assault with Intent to Rape	1	0	0	1
False Imprisonment	1	0	0	1
Felony (unspecified)	0	0	0	0
Aiding and Assisting a Felony	0	0	0	0
Extortion	0	0	0	0
Piracy	0	0	0	0
Mutiny	0	0	0	0
Total	102	25	5	72

CRIMES AGAINST PROPERTY	Number	Guilty	Not Guilty	No Verdict
Horse Stealing	0	0	0	0
Cattle Stealing	0	0	0	0
Larceny	41	7	10	24
Burglary	0	0	0	0
Forgery	1	1	0	0
Arson	0	0	0	0
Slave Stealing	1	0	1	0
Counterfeiting	0	0	0	0
Stealing from Vessel in Distress	0	0	0	0
Fraudulently Marking Cattle	1	0	1	0
Total	44	8	12	24

CRIMES AGAINST MORALITY/ PUBLIC ORDER	Number	Guilty	Not Guilty	No Verdict
Adultery and Fornication	30	1	1	28
Aiding a Prisoner to Escape	2	0	0	2
Allowing Negro to Carry Gun	0	0	0	0
Assisting a Slave to Escape	0	0	0	0
Being Concerned in a Duel	0	0	0	0
Bestiality	0	0	0	0
Bigamy	3	0	0	3
Breaking Jail (Escape)	0	0	0	0
Bribery	0	0	0	0
Buggery	0	0	0	0
Buying Soldier's Clothing	0	0	0	0
Carrying Arms Secretly	42	9	3	30
Cheating	0	0	0	0
Concealing the Birth of a Child	0	0	0	0
Conspiracy to Obtain Money by a Trick with Cards	0	0	0	0
Cruelty to a Slave	0	0	0	0
Disturbing Religious Worship	8	0	2	6
Employing Slaves on the Sabbath	0	0	0	0
Enticing a Soldier to Desert	0	0	0	0
Enticing Slave to Run Away	0	0	0	0
Fornication with a Colored Female	0	0	0	0
Fraudulent Voting	6	0	2	4
Gambling, Gaming, Betting	9	1	0	8
Giving Ticket to Slave of Another	0	0	0	0
Harboring Felons	0	0	0	0
Incest	0	0	0	0
Keeping a Gaming Table	2	0	0	2
Keeping a Gaming, Disorderly House	0	0	0	0
Keeping Billiard Table/Ten Pin Alley without a License	0	0	0	0
Leaving Slaves on Plantation without a White	1	0	0	1
Libel	0	0	0	0
Malfeasance of Public Official	0	0	0	0
Malicious Mischief (Wickedness)	4	0	1	3
Maliciously Killing Animals	0	0	0	0
Maliciously Pulling Down a Fence	0	0	0	0
Marrying a Colored Female	0	0	0	0
Misdemeanor (unspecified)	0	0	0	0
Notorious Public Indecency	0	0	0	0
Nuisance (Disturbing the Peace)	0	0	0	0
Obstructing a Public Road	0	0	0	0
Obstructing Legal Process	1	0	0	1

	Number	Guilty	Not Guilty	No Verdict
Obtaining Goods under False Pretenses	5	0	4	1
Open Lewdness	4	2	2	0
Performing a Marriage for White Man and Colored Female	0	0	0	0
Perjury	0	0	0	0
Permitting a Slave to Hire His Own Time	0	0	0	0
Permitting a Slave to Trade as Free	0	0	0	0
Practicing Medicine without a License	0	0	0	0
Receiving Stolen Goods	0	0	0	0
Retailing Liquors to a Slave	25	3	4	18
Retailing on the Sabbath	3	2	0	1
Retailing without a License	0	0	0	0
Riot, Affray, Mayhem	17	2	6	9
Selling Intoxicating Liquors to Military	0	0	0	0
Selling Liquor to Indians	0	0	0	0
Selling Liquor without a License	8	0	4	4
Selling Unwholesome Provisions	0	0	0	0
Shipping Cattle from County without Inspection	0	0	0	0
Sodomy	0	0	0	0
Trading with a Slave	19	4	5	10
Trespass	0	0	0	0
Trespassing on School Lands	0	0	0	0
Vagrancy	0	0	0	0
Violating Auction Laws	0	0	0	0
Total	189	24	34	131
SUBTOTAL	335	57	51	227

CRIMES COMMITTED BY SLAVES AND FREE BLACKS

CRIMES AGAINST PERSON

	Number	Guilty	Not Guilty	No Verdict
Murder	4	2	2	0
Assault and Battery	0	0	0	0
Rape	1	1	0	0
Assault with Intent to Rape	0	0	0	0
Assault with Intent to Kill	1	0	0	1
Consulting and Advising to Kill	0	0	0	0
Felony (unspecified)	0	0	0	0
Attempt to Poison	0	0	0	0
Revolt	0	0	0	0
Total	6	3	2	1

CRIMES AGAINST PROPERTY	Number	Guilty	Not Guilty	No Verdict
Larceny	2	0	0	2
Burglary	0	0	0	0
Arson	2	0	1	1
Horse Stealing	0	0	0	0
Total	4	0	1	3

CRIMES AGAINST MORALITY/PUBLIC ORDER				
Forging Free Papers	0	0	0	0
Enticing a Slave to Run Away	0	0	0	0
Receiving Stolen Goods	0	0	0	0
Maliciously Killing Animals	0	0	0	0
Maliciously Wounding Animals	0	0	0	0
Buggery	0	0	0	0
Migration of Free Persons of Color into the Territory	0	0	0	0
Total	0	0	0	0
SUBTOTAL	10	3	3	4
GRAND TOTAL	345	60	54	231

PERCENTAGES OF TOTAL PROSECUTIONS BY CATEGORY

Crimes against Person	31.30%
Crimes against Property	13.91%
Crimes against Morality/Public Order	54.78%
Cases with Guilty Verdict	17.39%
Cases with Not Guilty Verdict	15.65%
Cases with No Verdict	66.96%

Jefferson County
1828-1841, 1846-1854, 1854-1861

CRIMES AGAINST PERSON				
Murder/Manslaughter	13	2	1	10
Accessory to Murder	0	0	0	0
Assault and Battery	191	65	20	106
Assault with Intent to Kill	17	6	0	11
Rape	0	0	0	0
Robbery	0	0	0	0
Assault with Intent to Rape	0	0	0	0
False Imprisonment	15	6	0	9
Felony (unspecified)	0	0	0	0

	Number	Guilty	Not Guilty	No Verdict
Aiding and Assisting a Felony	0	0	0	0
Extortion	0	0	0	0
Piracy	0	0	0	0
Mutiny	0	0	0	0
Total	236	79	21	136
CRIMES AGAINST PROPERTY				
Horse Stealing	4	0	0	4
Cattle Stealing	0	0	0	0
Larceny	45	4	3	38
Burglary	0	0	0	0
Forgery	5	0	5	0
Arson	0	0	0	0
Slave Stealing	7	1	0	6
Counterfeiting	0	0	0	0
Stealing from Vessel in Distress	0	0	0	0
Fraudulently Marking Cattle	2	0	1	1
Total	63	5	9	49
CRIMES AGAINST MORALITY/PUBLIC ORDER				
Adultery and Fornication	15	0	4	11
Aiding a Prisoner to Escape	0	0	0	0
Allowing Negro to Carry Gun	0	0	0	0
Assisting a Slave to Escape	0	0	0	0
Being Concerned in a Duel	0	0	0	0
Bestiality	0	0	0	0
Bigamy	0	0	0	0
Breaking Jail (Escape)	0	0	0	0
Bribery	0	0	0	0
Buggery	0	0	0	0
Buying Soldier's Clothing	0	0	0	0
Carrying Arms Secretly	22	7	5	10
Cheating	1	0	0	1
Concealing the Birth of a Child	0	0	0	0
Conspiracy to Obtain Money by a Trick with Cards	0	0	0	0
Cruelty to a Slave	1	0	0	1
Disturbing Religious Worship	3	1	0	2
Employing Slaves on the Sabbath	0	0	0	0
Enticing a Soldier to Desert	0	0	0	0
Enticing Slave to Run Away	3	0	2	1

	Number	Guilty	Not Guilty	No Verdict
Fornication with a Colored Female	0	0	0	0
Fraudulent Voting	0	0	0	0
Gambling, Gaming, Betting	15	4	1	10
Giving Ticket to Slave of Another	0	0	0	0
Harboring Felons	0	0	0	0
Incest	0	0	0	0
Keeping a Gaming Table	0	0	0	0
Keeping a Gaming, Disorderly House	11	1	4	6
Keeping Billiard Table/Ten Pin Alley without a License	0	0	0	0
Leaving Slaves on Plantation without a White	0	0	0	0
Libel	3	2	0	1
Malfeasance of Public Official	0	0	0	0
Malicious Mischief (Wickedness)	2	1	1	0
Maliciously Killing Animals	1	0	0	1
Maliciously Pulling Down a Fence	0	0	0	0
Marrying a Colored Female	0	0	0	0
Misdemeanor (unspecified)	28	4	3	21
Notorious Public Indecency	0	0	0	0
Nuisance (Disturbing the Peace)	0	0	0	0
Obstructing a Public Road	0	0	0	0
Obstructing Legal Process	0	0	0	0
Obtaining Goods under False Pretenses	0	0	0	0
Open Lewdness	0	0	0	0
Performing a Marriage for White Man and Colored Female	0	0	0	0
Perjury	0	0	0	0
Permitting a Slave to Hire His Own Time	0	0	0	0
Permitting a Slave to Trade as Free	0	0	0	0
Practicing Medicine without a License	0	0	0	0
Receiving Stolen Goods	6	0	0	6
Retailing Liquors to a Slave	12	0	4	8
Retailing on the Sabbath	0	0	0	0
Retailing without a License	0	0	0	0
Riot, Affray, Mayhem	36	15	4	17
Selling Intoxicating Liquors to Military	0	0	0	0
Selling Liquor to Indians	0	0	0	0
Selling Liquor without a License	3	0	0	3
Selling Unwholesome Provisions	0	0	0	0
Shipping Cattle from County without Inspection	0	0	0	0
Sodomy	0	0	0	0
Trading with a Slave	5	0	1	4

Appendix 4: Prosecution Tables by County

	Number	Guilty	Not Guilty	No Verdict
Trespass	1	1	0	0
Trespassing on School Lands	0	0	0	0
Vagrancy	0	0	0	0
Violating Auction Laws	0	0	0	0
Total	168	36	29	103
SUBTOTAL	467	120	59	288
CRIMES COMMITTED BY SLAVES AND FREE BLACKS				
CRIMES AGAINST PERSON				
Murder	5	2	1	2
Assault and Battery	0	0	0	0
Rape	0	0	0	0
Assault with Intent to Rape	2	1	0	1
Assault with Intent to Kill	0	0	0	0
Consulting and Advising to Kill	0	0	0	0
Felony (unspecified)	0	0	0	0
Attempt to Poison	1	0	0	1
Revolt	0	0	0	0
Total	8	3	1	4
CRIMES AGAINST PROPERTY				
Larceny	0	0	0	0
Burglary	0	0	0	0
Arson	3	0	1	2
Horse Stealing	0	0	0	0
Total	3	0	1	2
CRIMES AGAINST MORALITY/PUBLIC ORDER				
Forging Free Papers	0	0	0	0
Enticing a Slave to Run Away	0	0	0	0
Receiving Stolen Goods	0	0	0	0
Maliciously Killing Animals	0	0	0	0
Maliciously Wounding Animals	0	0	0	0
Buggery	0	0	0	0
Migration of Free Persons of Color into the Territory	0	0	0	0
Total	0	0	0	0
SUBTOTAL	11	3	2	6
GRAND TOTAL	478	123	61	294

Appendix 4: Prosecution Tables by County

PERCENTAGES OF TOTAL PROSECUTIONS BY CATEGORY

Crimes against Person	51.05%
Crimes against Property	13.81%
Crimes against Morality/Public Order	35.15%
Cases with Guilty Verdict	25.73%
Cases with Not Guilty Verdict	12.76%
Cases with No Verdict	61.51%

Leon County
1826-1833, 1841-1843, 1843-1847, 1847-1855, 1855-1869

CRIMES AGAINST PERSON	Number	Guilty	Not Guilty	No Verdict
Murder/Manslaughter	17	11	3	3
Accessory to Murder	0	0	0	0
Assault and Battery	288	90	33	165
Assault with Intent to Kill	51	15	8	28
Rape	0	0	0	0
Robbery	0	0	0	0
Assault with Intent to Rape	1	0	0	1
False Imprisonment	1	0	0	1
Felony (unspecified)	26	2	5	19
Aiding and Assisting a Felony	1	0	1	0
Extortion	14	0	3	11
Piracy	0	0	0	0
Mutiny	0	0	0	0
Total	399	118	53	228

CRIMES AGAINST PROPERTY	Number	Guilty	Not Guilty	No Verdict
Horse Stealing	2	1	0	1
Cattle Stealing	3	0	0	3
Larceny	70	12	11	47
Burglary	0	0	0	0
Forgery	9	4	0	5
Arson	5	0	4	1
Slave Stealing	3	1	0	2
Counterfeiting	1	0	0	1
Stealing from Vessel in Distress	0	0	0	0
Fraudulently Marking Cattle	5	0	0	5
Total	98	18	15	65

Appendix 4: Prosecution Tables by County

CRIMES AGAINST MORALITY/ PUBLIC ORDER	Number	Guilty	Not Guilty	No Verdict
Adultery and Fornication	13	0	0	13
Aiding a Prisoner to Escape	2	0	1	1
Allowing Negro to Carry Gun	0	0	0	0
Assisting a Slave to Escape	0	0	0	0
Being Concerned in a Duel	10	1	3	6
Bestiality	0	0	0	0
Bigamy	0	0	0	0
Breaking Jail (Escape)	0	0	0	0
Bribery	0	0	0	0
Buggery	0	0	0	0
Buying Soldier's Clothing	0	0	0	0
Carrying Arms Secretly	71	18	4	49
Cheating	2	0	0	2
Concealing the Birth of a Child	0	0	0	0
Conspiracy to Obtain Money by a Trick with Cards	0	0	0	0
Cruelty to a Slave	0	0	0	0
Disturbing Religious Worship	7	2	0	5
Employing Slaves on the Sabbath	0	0	0	0
Enticing a Soldier to Desert	0	0	0	0
Enticing Slave to Run Away	9	5	1	3
Fornication with a Colored Female	0	0	0	0
Fraudulent Voting	0	0	0	0
Gambling, Gaming, Betting	139	50	20	69
Giving Ticket to Slave of Another	0	0	0	0
Harboring Felons	0	0	0	0
Incest	0	0	0	0
Keeping a Gaming Table	24	4	0	20
Keeping a Gaming, Disorderly House	18	4	2	12
Keeping Billiard Table/Ten Pin Alley without a License	4	2	0	2
Leaving Slaves on Plantation without a White	0	0	0	0
Libel	6	1	1	4
Malfeasance of Public Official	0	0	0	0
Malicious Mischief (Wickedness)	0	0	0	0
Maliciously Killing Animals	6	4	0	2
Maliciously Pulling Down a Fence	2	2	0	0
Marrying a Colored Female	0	0	0	0
Misdemeanor (unspecified)	65	7	15	43
Notorious Public Indecency	0	0	0	0
Nuisance (Disturbing the Peace)	5	1	0	4
Obstructing a Public Road	5	1	0	4

	Number	Guilty	Not Guilty	No Verdict
Obstructing Legal Process	3	1	0	2
Obtaining Goods under False Pretenses	0	0	0	0
Open Lewdness	0	0	0	0
Performing a Marriage for White Man and Colored Female	0	0	0	0
Perjury	0	0	0	0
Permitting a Slave to Hire His Own Time	0	0	0	0
Permitting a Slave to Trade as Free	0	0	0	0
Practicing Medicine without a License	1	0	1	0
Receiving Stolen Goods	3	0	0	3
Retailing Liquors to a Slave	28	4	5	19
Retailing on the Sabbath	0	0	0	0
Retailing without a License	2	1	0	1
Riot, Affray, Mayhem	83	20	11	52
Selling Intoxicating Liquors to Military	0	0	0	0
Selling Liquor to Indians	0	0	0	0
Selling Liquor without a License	38	16	4	18
Selling Unwholesome Provisions	0	0	0	0
Shipping Cattle from County without Inspection	0	0	0	0
Sodomy	0	0	0	0
Trading with a Slave	19	1	3	15
Trespass	0	0	0	0
Trespassing on School Lands	0	0	0	0
Vagrancy	0	0	0	0
Violating Auction Laws	0	0	0	0
Total	565	145	71	349
SUBTOTAL	1062	281	139	642

CRIMES COMMITTED BY SLAVES AND FREE BLACKS

CRIMES AGAINST PERSON

	Number	Guilty	Not Guilty	No Verdict
Murder	9	6	2	1
Assault and Battery	1	0	0	1
Rape	0	0	0	0
Assault with Intent to Rape	0	0	0	0
Assault with Intent to Kill	0	0	0	0
Consulting and Advising to Kill	0	0	0	0
Felony (unspecified)	1	0	0	1
Attempt to Poison	0	0	0	0
Revolt	0	0	0	0
Total	11	6	2	3

CRIMES AGAINST PROPERTY	Number	Guilty	Not Guilty	No Verdict
Larceny	0	0	0	0
Burglary	4	0	2	2
Arson	1	0	0	1
Horse Stealing	1	0	0	1
Total	6	0	2	4

CRIMES AGAINST MORALITY/PUBLIC ORDER				
Forging Free Papers	0	0	0	0
Enticing a Slave to Run Away	0	0	0	0
Receiving Stolen Goods	0	0	0	0
Maliciously Killing Animals	0	0	0	0
Maliciously Wounding Animals	0	0	0	0
Buggery	0	0	0	0
Migration of Free Persons of Color into the Territory	0	0	0	0
Total	0	0	0	0
SUBTOTAL	17	6	4	7
GRAND TOTAL	1079	287	143	649

PERCENTAGES OF TOTAL PROSECUTIONS BY CATEGORY

Crimes against Person	38.00%
Crimes against Property	9.64%
Crimes against Morality/Public Order	52.36%
Cases with Guilty Verdict	26.60%
Cases with Not Guilty Verdict	13.25%
Cases with No Verdict	60.15%

Madison County 1846-1854

CRIMES AGAINST PERSON				
Murder/Manslaughter	7	2	2	3
Accessory to Murder	0	0	0	0
Assault and Battery	65	31	7	27
Assault with Intent to Kill	13	4	0	9
Rape	4	0	0	4
Robbery	0	0	0	0
Assault with Intent to Rape	0	0	0	0
False Imprisonment	0	0	0	0
Felony (unspecified)	2	0	1	1

	Number	Guilty	Not Guilty	No Verdict
Aiding and Assisting a Felony	0	0	0	0
Extortion	0	0	0	0
Piracy	0	0	0	0
Mutiny	0	0	0	0
Total	91	37	10	44

CRIMES AGAINST PROPERTY

	Number	Guilty	Not Guilty	No Verdict
Horse Stealing	0	0	0	0
Cattle Stealing	0	0	0	0
Larceny	11	0	4	7
Burglary	0	0	0	0
Forgery	0	0	0	0
Arson	0	0	0	0
Slave Stealing	0	0	0	0
Counterfeiting	0	0	0	0
Stealing from Vessel in Distress	0	0	0	0
Fraudulently Marking Cattle	0	0	0	0
Total	11	0	4	7

CRIMES AGAINST MORALITY/PUBLIC ORDER

	Number	Guilty	Not Guilty	No Verdict
Adultery and Fornication	5	0	0	5
Aiding a Prisoner to Escape	0	0	0	0
Allowing Negro to Carry Gun	0	0	0	0
Assisting a Slave to Escape	0	0	0	0
Being Concerned in a Duel	0	0	0	0
Bestiality	1	0	1	0
Bigamy	0	0	0	0
Breaking Jail (Escape)	0	0	0	0
Bribery	0	0	0	0
Buggery	0	0	0	0
Buying Soldier's Clothing	0	0	0	0
Carrying Arms Secretly	22	12	1	9
Cheating	0	0	0	0
Concealing the Birth of a Child	0	0	0	0
Conspiracy to Obtain Money by a Trick with Cards	0	0	0	0
Cruelty to a Slave	2	1	0	1
Disturbing Religious Worship	3	2	0	1
Employing Slaves on the Sabbath	0	0	0	0
Enticing a Soldier to Desert	0	0	0	0
Enticing Slave to Run Away	0	0	0	0

	Number	Guilty	Not Guilty	No Verdict
Fornication with a Colored Female	0	0	0	0
Fraudulent Voting	0	0	0	0
Gambling, Gaming, Betting	0	0	0	0
Giving Ticket to Slave of Another	0	0	0	0
Harboring Felons	0	0	0	0
Incest	0	0	0	0
Keeping a Gaming Table	0	0	0	0
Keeping a Gaming, Disorderly House	0	0	0	0
Keening Billiard Table/Ten Pin Alley without a License	0	0	0	0
Leaving Slaves on Plantation without a White	0	0	0	0
Libel	0	0	0	0
Malfeasance of Public Official	0	0	0	0
Malicious Mischief (Wickedness)	2	0	0	2
Maliciously Killing Animals	0	0	0	0
Maliciously Pulling Down a Fence	0	0	0	0
Marrying a Colored Female	0	0	0	0
Misdemeanor (unspecified)	1	0	0	1
Notorious Public Indecency	0	0	0	0
Nuisance (Disturbing the Peace)	3	2	0	1
Obstructing a Public Road	0	0	0	0
Obstructing Legal Process	0	0	0	0
Obtaining Goods under False Pretenses	0	0	0	0
Open Lewdness	0	0	0	0
Performing a Marriage for White Man and Colored Female	0	0	0	0
Perjury	0	0	0	0
Permitting a Slave to Hire His Own Time	0	0	0	0
Permitting a Slave to Trade as Free	0	0	0	0
Practicing Medicine without a License	0	0	0	0
Receiving Stolen Goods	0	0	0	0
Retailing Liquors to a Slave	7	0	5	2
Retailing on the Sabbath	0	0	0	0
Retailing without a License	0	0	0	0
Riot, Affray, Mayhem	17	9	1	7
Selling Intoxicating Liquors to Military	0	0	0	0
Selling Liquor to Indians	0	0	0	0
Selling Liquor without a License	1	0	1	0
Selling Unwholesome Provisions	1	0	0	1
Shipping Cattle from County without Inspection	0	0	0	0
Sodomy	0	0	0	0
Trading with a Slave	1	0	0	1

	Number	Guilty	Not Guilty	No Verdict
Trespass	0	0	0	0
Trespassing on School Lands	0	0	0	0
Vagrancy	0	0	0	0
Violating Auction Laws	0	0	0	0
Total	66	26	9	31
SUBTOTAL	168	631	23	82
CRIMES COMMITTED BY SLAVES AND FREE BLACKS				
CRIMES AGAINST PERSON				
Murder	0	0	0	0
Assault and Battery	0	0	0	0
Rape	1	1	0	0
Assault with Intent to Rape	0	0	0	0
Assault with Intent to Kill	1	0	0	1
Consulting and Advising to Kill	0	0	0	0
Felony (unspecified)	0	0	0	0
Attempt to Poison	0	0	0	0
Revolt	0	0	0	0
Total	2	1	0	1
CRIMES AGAINST PROPERTY				
Larceny	0	0	0	0
Burglary	0	0	0	0
Arson	0	0	0	0
Horse Stealing	0	0	0	0
Total	0	0	0	0
CRIMES AGAINST MORALITY/PUBLIC ORDER				
Forging Free Papers	0	0	0	0
Enticing a Slave to Run Away	0	0	0	0
Receiving Stolen Goods	0	0	0	0
Maliciously Killing Animals	0	0	0	0
Maliciously Wounding Animals	0	0	0	0
Buggery	0	0	0	0
Migration of Free Persons of Color into the Territory	0	0	0	0
Total	0	0	0	0
SUBTOTAL	2	1	0	1
GRAND TOTAL	170	64	23	83

Appendix 4: Prosecution Tables by County

PERCENTAGES OF TOTAL PROSECUTIONS BY CATEGORY

Crimes against Person	54.71%
Crimes against Property	6.47%
Crimes against Morality/Public Order	38.82%
Cases with Guilty Verdict	37.65%
Cases with Not Guilty Verdict	13.53%
Cases with No Verdict	48.82%

Marion County
1848-1855 1855-1861

CRIMES AGAINST PERSON	Number	Guilty	Not Guilty	No Verdict
Murder/Manslaughter	18	7	5	6
Accessory to Murder	0	0	0	0
Assault and Battery	35	18	1	16
Assault with Intent to Kill	29	14	6	9
Rape	0	0	0	0
Robbery	0	0	0	0
Assault with Intent to Rape	0	0	0	0
False Imprisonment	0	0	0	0
Felony (unspecified)	0	0	0	0
Aiding and Assisting a Felony				
Extortion	1	0	0	1
Piracy	0	0	0	0
Mutiny	0	0	0	0
Total	83	39	12	32

CRIMES AGAINST PROPERTY				
Horse Stealing	0	0	0	0
Cattle Stealing	0	0	0	0
Larceny	19	1	3	15
Burglary	0	0	0	0
Forgery	0	0	0	0
Arson	2	0	0	2
Slave Stealing	3	0	3	0
Counterfeiting	0	0	0	0
Stealing from Vessel in Distress	0	0	0	0
Fraudulently Marking Cattle	7	0	2	5
Total	31	1	8	22

Appendix 4: Prosecution Tables by County

CRIMES AGAINST MORALITY/ PUBLIC ORDER	Number	Guilty	Not Guilty	No Verdict
Adultery and Fornication	7	2	2	3
Aiding a Prisoner to Escape	0	0	0	0
Allowing Negro to Carry Gun	0	0	0	0
Assisting a Slave to Escape				
Being Concerned in a Duel	0	0	0	0
Bestiality	0	0	0	0
Bigamy	0	0	0	0
Breaking Jail (Escape)	0	0	0	0
Bribery	1	0	0	1
Buggery	0	0	0	0
Buying Soldier's Clothing	0	0	0	0
Carrying Arms Secretly	27	17	4	6
Cheating	0	0	0	0
Concealing the Birth of a Child	0	0	0	0
Conspiracy to Obtain Money by a Trick with Cards	0	0	0	0
Cruelty to a Slave	4	0	1	3
Disturbing Religious Worship	1	0	1	0
Employing Slaves on the Sabbath	2	2	0	0
Enticing a Soldier to Desert	0	0	0	0
Enticing Slave to Run Away	6	4	2	0
Fornication with a Colored Female	0	0	0	0
Fraudulent Voting	0	0	0	0
Gambling, Gaming, Betting	4	0	1	3
Giving Ticket to Slave of Another	0	0	0	0
Harboring Felons	0	0	0	0
Incest	0	0	0	0
Keeping a Gaming Table	2	1	0	1
Keeping a Gaming, Disorderly House	0	0	0	0
Keeping Billiard Table/Ten Pin Alley without a License	0	0	0	0
Leaving Slaves on Plantation without a White	4	1	0	3
Libel	0	0	0	0
Malfeasance of Public Official	2	0	1	1
Malicious Mischief (Wickedness)	1	0	0	1
Maliciously Killing Animals	4	2	0	2
Maliciously Pulling Down a Fence	0	0	0	0
Marrying a Colored Female	0	0	0	0
Misdemeanor (unspecified)	0	0	0	0
Notorious Public Indecency	0	0	0	0
Nuisance (Disturbing the Peace)	0	0	0	0
Obstructing a Public Road	0	0	0	0
Obstructing Legal Process	1	0	0	1

	Number	Guilty	Not Guilty	No Verdict
Obtaining Goods under False Pretenses	0	0	0	0
Open Lewdness	0	0	0	0
Performing a Marriage for White Man and Colored Female	0	0	0	0
Perjury	6	0	1	5
Permitting a Slave to Hire His Own Time	0	0	0	0
Permitting a Slave to Trade as Free	2	2	0	0
Practicing Medicine without a License	3	2	0	1
Receiving Stolen Goods	2	2	0	0
Retailing Liquors to a Slave	1	1	0	0
Retailing on the Sabbath	4	0	0	4
Retailing without a License	1	0	0	1
Riot, Affray, Mayhem	10	8	0	2
Selling Intoxicating Liquors to Military	0	0	0	0
Selling Liquor to Indians	0	0	0	0
Selling Liquor without a License	12	10	0	2
Selling Unwholesome Provisions	0	0	0	0
Shipping Cattle from County without Inspection	0	0	0	0
Sodomy	0	0	0	0
Trading with a Slave	2	0	0	2
Trespass	0	0	0	0
Trespassing on School Lands	2	2	0	0
Vagrancy	0	0	0	0
Violating Auction Laws	1	1	0	0
Total	112	57	13	42
SUBTOTAL	226	97	33	96

CRIMES COMMITTED BY SLAVES AND FREE BLACKS

CRIMES AGAINST PERSON

	Number	Guilty	Not Guilty	No Verdict
Murder	2	1	1	0
Assault and Battery	2	0	1	1
Rape	0	0	0	0
Assault with Intent to Rape	0	0	0	0
Assault with Intent to Kill	0	0	0	0
Consulting and Advising to Kill	0	0	0	0
Felony (unspecified)	0	0	0	0
Attempt to Poison	0	0	0	0
Revolt	0	0	0	0
Total	4	1	2	1

CRIMES AGAINST PROPERTY	Number	Guilty	Not Guilty	No Verdict
Larceny	0	0	0	0
Burglary	0	0	0	0
Arson	0	0	0	0
Horse Stealing	0	0	0	0
Total	0	0	0	0

CRIMES AGAINST MORALITY/PUBLIC ORDER				
Forging Free Papers	0	0	0	0
Enticing a Slave to Run Away	0	0	0	0
Receiving Stolen Goods	0	0	0	0
Maliciously Killing Animals	4	0	3	1
Maliciously Wounding Animals	0	0	0	0
Buggery	0	0	0	0
Migration of Free Persons of Color into the Territory	0	0	0	0
Total	4	0	3	1
SUBTOTAL	8	1	5	2
GRAND TOTAL	234	98	38	98

PERCENTAGES OF TOTAL PROSECUTIONS BY CATEGORY

Crimes against Person	37.18%
Crimes against Property	13.25%
Crimes against Morality/Public Order	49.57%
Cases with Guilty Verdict	41.88%
Cases with Not Guilty Verdict	16.24%
Cases with No Verdict	41.88%

Monroe County
1828-1830, 1830-1840, 1840-1853

CRIMES AGAINST PERSON				
Murder/Manslaughter	14	2	2	10
Accessory to Murder	0	0	0	0
Assault and Battery	90	27	12	51
Assault with Intent to Kill	16	3	3	10
Rape	0	0	0	0
Robbery	0	0	0	0
Assault with Intent to Rape	2	0	0	2
False Imprisonment	0	0	0	0
Felony (unspecified)	0	0	0	0

Appendix 4: Prosecution Tables by County

	Number	Guilty	Not Guilty	No Verdict
Aiding and Assisting a Felony	0	0	0	0
Extortion	0	0	0	0
Piracy	0	0	0	0
Mutiny	13	3	8	2
Total	135	35	25	75

CRIMES AGAINST PROPERTY

	Number	Guilty	Not Guilty	No Verdict
Horse Stealing	0	0	0	0
Cattle Stealing	0	0	0	0
Larceny	38	7	9	22
Burglary	9	0	2	7
Forgery	1	0	1	0
Arson	0	0	0	0
Slave Stealing	0	0	0	0
Counterfeiting	0	0	0	0
Stealing from Vessel in Distress	8	2	4	2
Fraudulently Marking Cattle	0	0	0	0
Total	56	9	16	31

CRIMES AGAINST MORALITY/PUBLIC ORDER

	Number	Guilty	Not Guilty	No Verdict
Adultery and Fornication	10	4	0	6
Aiding a Prisoner to Escape	6	0	1	5
Allowing Negro to Carry Gun	0	0	0	0
Assisting a Slave to Escape	0	0	0	0
Being Concerned in a Duel	7	2	1	4
Bestiality	0	0	0	0
Bigamy	0	0	0	0
Breaking Jail (Escape)	1	0	0	1
Bribery	0	0	0	0
Buggery	0	0	0	0
Buying Soldier's Clothing	0	0	0	0
Carrying Arms Secretly	9	3	3	3
Cheating	0	0	0	0
Concealing the Birth of a Child	1	0	1	0
Conspiracy to Obtain Money by a Trick with Cards	0	0	0	0
Cruelty to a Slave	3	0	1	2
Disturbing Religious Worship	8	2	1	5
Employing Slaves on the Sabbath	0	0	0	0
Enticing a Soldier to Desert	0	0	0	0
Enticing Slave to Run Away	0	0	0	0

	Number	Guilty	Not Guilty	No Verdict
Fornication with a Colored Female	0	0	0	0
Fraudulent Voting	0	0	0	0
Gambling, Gaming, Betting	4	0	0	4
Giving Ticket to Slave of Another	0	0	0	0
Harboring Felons	1	0	0	1
Incest	0	0	0	0
Keeping a Gaming Table	2	0	1	1
Keeping a Gaming, Disorderly House	15	2	5	8
Keeping Billiard Table/Ten Pin Alley without a License	0	0	0	0
Leaving Slaves on Plantation without a White	0	0	0	0
Libel	0	0	0	0
Malfeasance of Public Official	3	1	0	2
Malicious Mischief (Wickedness)	5	0	0	5
Maliciously Killing Animals	1	0	1	0
Maliciously Pulling Down a Fence	0	0	0	0
Marrying a Colored Female	1	1	0	0
Misdemeanor (unspecified)	0	0	0	0
Notorious Public Indecency	0	0	0	0
Nuisance (Disturbing the Peace)	0	0	0	0
Obstructing a Public Road	0	0	0	0
Obstructing Legal Process	1	0	0	1
Obtaining Goods under False Pretenses	0	0	0	0
Open Lewdness	0	0	0	0
Performing a Marriage for White Man and Colored Female	1	0	0	1
Perjury	0	0	0	0
Permitting a Slave to Hire His Own Time	0	0	0	0
Permitting a Slave to Trade as Free	0	0	0	0
Practicing Medicine without a License	0	0	0	0
Receiving Stolen Goods	7	1	2	4
Retailing Liquors to a Slave	10	7	0	3
Retailing on the Sabbath	0	0	0	0
Retailing without a License	0	0	0	0
Riot, Affray, Mayhem	27	3	11	13
Selling Intoxicating Liquors to Military	1	1	0	0
Selling Liquor to Indians	0	0	0	0
Selling Liquor without a License	8	5	0	3
Selling Unwholesome Provisions	1	0	1	0
Shipping Cattle from County without Inspection	0	0	0	0
Sodomy	0	0	0	0
Trading with a Slave	1	1	0	0
Trespass	0	0	0	0

Appendix 4: Prosecution Tables by County

	Number	Guilty	Not Guilty	No Verdict
Trespassing on School Lands	0	0	0	0
Vagrancy	1	1	0	0
Violating Auction Laws	0	0	0	0
Total	135	34	29	72
SUBTOTAL	326	78	70	178

CRIMES COMMITTED BY SLAVES AND FREE BLACKS

CRIMES AGAINST PERSON

	Number	Guilty	Not Guilty	No Verdict
Murder	0	0	0	0
Assault and Battery	0	0	0	0
Rape	0	0	0	0
Assault with Intent to Rape	0	0	0	0
Assault with Intent to Kill	0	0	0	0
Consulting and Advising to Kill	0	0	0	0
Felony (unspecified)	0	0	0	0
Attempt to Poison	0	0	0	0
Revolt	2	1	0	1
Total	2	1	0	1

CRIMES AGAINST PROPERTY

	Number	Guilty	Not Guilty	No Verdict
Larceny	1	1	0	0
Burglary	0	0	0	0
Arson	0	0	0	0
Horse Stealing	0	0	0	0
Total	1	1	0	0

CRIMES AGAINST MORALITY/PUBLIC ORDER

	Number	Guilty	Not Guilty	No Verdict
Forging Free Papers	0	0	0	0
Enticing a Slave to Run Away	0	0	0	0
Receiving Stolen Goods	0	0	0	0
Maliciously Killing Animals	0	0	0	0
Maliciously Wounding Animals	0	0	0	0
Buggery	1	0	0	1
Migration of Free Persons of Color into the Territory	0	0	0	0
Total	1	0	0	1
SUBTOTAL	4	2	0	2
GRAND TOTAL	330	80	70	180

Appendix 4: Prosecution Tables by County

PERCENTAGES OF TOTAL PROSECUTIONS BY CATEGORY

Crimes against Person	41.52%
Crimes against Property	17.27%
Crimes against Morality/Public Order	41.21%
Cases with Guilty Verdict	24.24%
Cases with Not Guilty Verdict	21.21%
Cases with No Verdict	54.55%

Orange County
1847-1861

CRIMES AGAINST PERSON	Number	Guilty	Not Guilty	No Verdict
Murder/Manslaughter	19	2	1	16
Accessory to Murder	0	0	0	0
Assault and Battery	16	5	0	11
Assault with Intent to Kill	6	2	0	4
Rape	0	0	0	0
Robbery	0	0	0	0
Assault with Intent to Rape	0	0	0	0
False Imprisonment	1	0	0	1
Felony (unspecified)	0	0	0	0
Aiding and Assisting a Felony	0	0	0	0
Extortion	0	0	0	0
Piracy	0	0	0	0
Mutiny	0	0	0	0
Total	42	9	1	32

CRIMES AGAINST PROPERTY				
Horse Stealing	0	0	0	0
Cattle Stealing	0	0	0	0
Larceny	5	2	1	2
Burglary	0	0	0	0
Forgery	0	0	0	0
Arson	0	0	0	0
Slave Stealing	0	0	0	0
Counterfeiting	0	0	0	0
Stealing from Vessel in Distress	0	0	0	0
Fraudulently Marking Cattle	1	0	0	1
Total	6	2	1	3

Appendix 4: Prosecution Tables by County

CRIMES AGAINST MORALITY/ PUBLIC ORDER	Number	Guilty	Not Guilty	No Verdict
Adultery and Fornication	6	0	1	5
Aiding a Prisoner to Escape	0	0	0	0
Allowing Negro to Carry Gun	1	0	0	1
Assisting a Slave to Escape	0	0	0	0
Being Concerned in a Duel	0	0	0	0
Bestiality	0	0	0	0
Bigamy	0	0	0	0
Breaking Jail (Escape)	0	0	0	0
Bribery	0	0	0	0
Buggery	0	0	0	0
Buying Soldier's Clothing	0	0	0	0
Carrying Arms Secretly	7	1	0	6
Cheating	0	0	0	0
Concealing the Birth of a Child	0	0	0	0
Conspiracy to Obtain Money by a Trick with Cards	0	0	0	0
Cruelty to a Slave	0	0	0	0
Disturbing Religious Worship	0	0	0	0
Enticing a Soldier to Desert	0	0	0	0
Employing Slaves on the Sabbath	0	0	0	0
Enticing Slave to Run Away	0	0	0	0
Fornication with a Colored Female	0	0	0	0
Fraudulent Voting	0	0	0	0
Gambling, Gaming, Betting	0	0	0	0
Giving Ticket to Slave of Another	0	0	0	0
Harboring Felons	0	0	0	0
Incest	1	0	0	1
Keeping a Gaming Table	0	0	0	0
Keeping a Gaming, Disorderly	1	0	0	1
Keeping Billiard Table/Ten Pin Alley without a License	0	0	0	0
Leaving Slaves on Plantation without a White	0	0	0	0
Libel	0	0	0	0
Malfeasance of Public Official	0	0	0	0
Malicious Mischief (Wickedness)	0	0	0	0
Maliciously Killing Animals	1	0	0	1
Maliciously Pulling Down a Fence	0	0	0	0
Marrying a Colored Female	0	0	0	0
Misdemeanor (unspecified)	0	0	0	0
Notorious Public Indecency	0	0	0	0
Nuisance (Disturbing the Peace)	0	0	0	0
Obstructing a Public Road	0	0	0	0

	Number	Guilty	Not Guilty	No Verdict
Obstructing Legal Process	0	0	0	0
Obtaining Goods under False Pretenses	0	0	0	0
Open Lewdness	0	0	0	0
Performing a Marriage for White Man and Colored Female	0	0	0	0
Perjury	0	0	0	0
Permitting a Slave to Hire His Own Time	0	0	0	0
Permitting a Slave to Trade as Free	0	0	0	0
Practicing Medicine without a License	0	0	0	0
Receiving Stolen Goods	0	0	0	0
Retailing Liquors to a Slave	0	0	0	0
Retailing on the Sabbath	0	0	0	0
Retailing without a License	0	0	0	0
Riot, Affray, Mayhem	0	0	0	0
Selling Intoxicating Liquors to Military	0	0	0	0
Selling Liquor to Indians	0	0	0	0
Selling Liquor without a License	5	0	2	3
Selling Unwholesome Provisions	0	0	0	0
Shipping Cattle from County without Inspection	0	0	0	0
Sodomy	0	0	0	0
Trading with a Slave	0	0	0	0
Trespass	0	0	0	0
Trespassing on School Lands	0	0	0	0
Vagrancy	0	0	0	0
Violating Auction Laws	0	0	0	0
Total	22	1	3	18
SUBTOTAL	70	12	5	53

CRIMES COMMITTED BY SLAVES AND FREE BLACKS

CRIMES AGAINST PERSON

	Number	Guilty	Not Guilty	No Verdict
Murder	0	0	0	0
Assault and Battery	0	0	0	0
Rape	0	0	0	0
Assault with Intent to Rape	0	0	0	0
Assault with Intent to Kill	0	0	0	0
Consulting and Advising to Kill	0	0	0	0
Felony (unspecified)	0	0	0	0
Attempt to Poison	0	0	0	0
Revolt	0	0	0	0
Total	0	0	0	0

CRIMES AGAINST PROPERTY	Number	Guilty	Not Guilty	No Verdict
Larceny	0	0	0	0
Burglary	0	0	0	0
Arson	0	0	0	0
Horse Stealing	0	0	0	0
Total	0	0	0	0
CRIMES AGAINST MORALITY/PUBLIC ORDER				
Forging Free Papers	0	0	0	0
Enticing a Slave to Run Away	0	0	0	0
Receiving Stolen Goods	0	0	0	0
Maliciously Killing Animals	0	0	0	0
Maliciously Wounding Animals	0	0	0	0
Buggery	0	0	0	0
Migration of Free Persons of Color into the Territory	0	0	0	0
Total	0	0	0	0
SUBTOTAL	0	0	0	0
GRAND TOTAL	70	12	5	53

PERCENTAGES OF TOTAL PROSECUTIONS BY CATEGORY

Category	Percentage
Crimes against Person	60.00%
Crimes against Property	8.57%
Crimes against Morality/Public Order	31.43%
Cases with Guilty Verdict	17.14%
Cases with Not Guilty Verdict	7.14%
Cases with No Verdict	75.71%

Putnam County
1850-1859, 1860-1887 (reviewed through 1861)

CRIMES AGAINST PERSON	Number	Guilty	Not Guilty	No Verdict
Murder/Manslaughter	2	1	1	0
Accessory to Murder	0	0	0	0
Assault and Battery	37	18	2	17
Assault with Intent to Kill	16	5	1	10
Rape	0	0	0	0
Robbery	2	0	0	2
Assault with Intent to Rape	0	0	0	0
False Imprisonment	0	0	0	0
Felony (unspecified)	0	0	0	0
Aiding and Assisting a Felony	0	0	0	0

	Number	Guilty	Not Guilty	No Verdict
Extortion	0	0	0	0
Piracy	0	0	0	0
Mutiny	0	0	0	0
Total	57	24	4	29
CRIMES AGAINST PROPERTY				
Horse Stealing	0	0	0	0
Cattle Stealing	0	0	0	0
Larceny	18	3	1	14
Burglary	0	0	0	0
Forgery	1	0	0	1
Arson	0	0	0	0
Slave Stealing	0	0	0	0
Counterfeiting	1	0	0	1
Stealing from Vessel in Distress	0	0	0	0
Fraudulently Marking Cattle	0	0	0	0
Total	20	3	1	16
CRIMES AGAINST MORALITY/PUBLIC ORDER				
Adultery and Fornication	18	3	1	14
Aiding a Prisoner to Escape	0	0	0	0
Allowing Negro to Carry Gun	0	0	0	0
Assisting a Slave to Escape	0	0	0	0
Being Concerned in a Duel	0	0	0	0
Bestiality	0	0	0	0
Bigamy	0	0	0	0
Breaking Jail (Escape)	0	0	0	0
Bribery	0	0	0	0
Buggery	0	0	0	0
Buying Soldier's Clothing	0	0	0	0
Carrying Arms Secretly	22	12	1	9
Cheating	0	0	0	0
Concealing the Birth of a Child	0	0	0	0
Conspiracy to Obtain Money by a Trick with Cards	0	0	0	0
Cruelty to a Slave	0	0	0	0
Disturbing Religious Worship	2	2	0	0
Employing Slaves on the Sabbath	0	0	0	0
Enticing a Soldier to Desert	0	0	0	0
Enticing Slave to Run Away	0	0	0	0
Fornication with a Colored Female	1	0	0	1

Appendix 4: Prosecution Tables by County

	Number	Guilty	Not Guilty	No Verdict
Fraudulent Voting	0	0	0	0
Gambling, Gaming, Betting	0	0	0	0
Giving Ticket to Slave of Another	1	0	0	1
Harboring Felons	0	0	0	0
Incest	0	0	0	0
Keeping a Gaming Table	0	0	0	0
Keeping a Gaming, Disorderly House	4	2	0	2
Keeping Billiard Table/Ten Pin Alley without a License	0	0	0	0
Leaving Slaves on Plantation without a White	0	0	0	0
Libel	0	0	0	0
Malfeasance of Public Official	0	0	0	0
Malicious Mischief (Wickedness)	0	0	0	0
Maliciously Killing Animals	4	2	0	2
Maliciously Pulling Down a Fence	0	0	0	0
Marrying a Colored Female	0	0	0	0
Misdemeanor (unspecified)	0	0	0	0
Notorious Public Indecency	0	0	0	0
Nuisance (Disturbing the Peace)	0	0	0	0
Obstructing a Public Road	0	0	0	0
Obstructing Legal Process	0	0	0	0
Obtaining Goods under False Pretenses	0	0	0	0
Open Lewdness	0	0	0	0
Performing a Marriage for White Man and Colored Female	0	0	0	0
Perjury	0	0	0	0
Permitting a Slave to Hire His Own Time	4	0	0	4
Permitting a Slave to Trade as Free	2	2	0	0
Practicing Medicine without a License	0	0	0	0
Receiving Stolen Goods	0	0	0	0
Retailing Liquors to a Slave	0	0	0	0
Retailing on the Sabbath	0	0	0	0
Retailing without a License	0	0	0	0
Riot, Affray, Mayhem	25	7	10	8
Selling Intoxicating Liquors to Military	0	0	0	0
Selling Liquor to Indians	0	0	0	0
Selling Liquor without a License	9	3	1	5
Selling Unwholesome Provisions	0	0	0	0
Shipping Cattle from County without Inspection	0	0	0	0
Sodomy	0	0	0	0
Trading with a Slave	4	1	1	2
Trespass	0	0	0	0

	Number	Guilty	Not Guilty	No Verdict
Trespassing on School Lands	0	0	0	0
Vagrancy	0	0	0	0
Violating Auction Laws	0	0	0	0
Total	96	34	14	48
SUBTOTAL	173	61	19	93

CRIMES COMMITTED BY SLAVES AND FREE BLACKS

CRIMES AGAINST PERSON

	Number	Guilty	Not Guilty	No Verdict
Murder	0	0	0	0
Assault and Battery	1	1	0	0
Rape	0	0	0	0
Assault with Intent to Rape	0	0	0	0
Assault with Intent to Kill	0	0	0	0
Consulting and Advising to Kill	0	0	0	0
Felony (unspecified)	0	0	0	0
Attempt to Poison	0	0	0	0
Revolt	0	0	0	0
Total	1	1	0	0

CRIMES AGAINST PROPERTY

	Number	Guilty	Not Guilty	No Verdict
Larceny	0	0	0	0
Burglary	1	1	0	0
Arson	0	0	0	0
Horse Stealing	0	0	0	0
Total	1	1	0	0

CRIMES AGAINST MORALITY/PUBLIC ORDER

	Number	Guilty	Not Guilty	No Verdict
Forging Free Papers	0	0	0	0
Enticing a Slave to Run Away	0	0	0	0
Receiving Stolen Goods	0	0	0	0
Maliciously Killing Animals	0	0	0	0
Maliciously Wounding Animals	0	0	0	0
Buggery	0	0	0	0
Migration of Free Persons of Color into the Territory	0	0	0	0
Total	0	0	0	0
SUBTOTAL	2	2	0	0
GRAND TOTAL	175	63	19	93

Appendix 4: Prosecution Tables by County

PERCENTAGES OF TOTAL PROSECUTIONS BY CATEGORY

Crimes against Person	33.14%
Crimes against Property	12.00%
Crimes against Morality/Public Order	54.86%
Cases with Guilty Verdict	36.00%
Cases with Not Guilty Verdict	10.86%
Cases with No Verdict	53.14%

St. Johns County
1846-1874 (reviewed to 1861)

CRIMES AGAINST PERSON	Number	Guilty	Not Guilty	No Verdict
Murder/Manslaughter	4	1	3	0
Accessory to Murder	0	0	0	0
Assault and Battery	24	13	3	8
Assault With Intent to Kill	9	3	1	5
Rape	0	0	0	0
Robbery	0	0	0	0
Assault With Intent to Rape	0	0	0	0
False Imprisonment	0	0	0	0
Felony (unspecified)	0	0	0	0
Aiding and Assisting a Felony	0	0	0	0
Extortion	0	0	0	0
Piracy	0	0	0	0
Mutiny	0	0	0	0
Total	37	17	7	13
CRIMES AGAINST PROPERTY				
Horse Stealing	0	0	0	0
Cattle Stealing	0	0	0	0
Larceny	13	2	5	6
Burglary	0	0	0	0
Forgery	0	0	0	0
Arson	0	0	0	0
Slave Stealing	0	0	0	0
Counterfeiting	0	0	0	0
Stealing from Vessel in Distress	0	0	0	0
Fraudulently Marking Cattle	0	0	0	0
Total	13	2	5	6
CRIMES AGAINST MORALITY/PUBLIC ORDER				
Adultery and Fornication	0	0	0	0
Aiding a Prisoner to Escape	0	0	0	0

Appendix 4: Prosecution Tables by County

	Number	Guilty	Not Guilty	No Verdict
Allowing Negro to Carry Gun	0	0	0	0
Assisting a Slave to Escape	0	0	0	0
Being Concerned in a Duel	0	0	0	0
Bestiality	0	0	0	0
Bigamy	0	0	0	0
Breaking Jail (Escape)	1	1	0	0
Bribery	0	0	0	0
Buggery	0	0	0	0
Buying Soldier's Clothing	0	0	0	0
Carrying Arms Secretly	20	10	1	9
Cheating	0	0	0	0
Concealing the Birth of a Child	0	0	0	0
Conspiracy to Obtain Money by a Trick with Cards	0	0	0	0
Cruelty to a Slave	0	0	0	0
Disturbing Religious Worship	0	0	0	0
Employing Slaves on the Sabbath	0	0	0	0
Enticing a Soldier to Desert	0	0	0	0
Enticing Slave to Run Away	0	0	0	0
Fornication with a Colored Female	0	0	0	0
Fraudulent Voting	0	0	0	0
Gambling, Gaming, Betting	0	0	0	0
Giving Ticket to Slave of Another	0	0	0	0
Harboring Felons	0	0	0	0
Incest	0	0	0	0
Keeping a Gaming Table	0	0	0	0
Keeping a Gaming, Disorderly House	1	1	0	0
Keeping Billiard Table/Ten Pin Alley without a License	0	0	0	0
Leaving Slaves on Plantation without a White	0	0	0	0
Libel	0	0	0	0
Malfeasance of Public Official	0	0	0	0
Malicious Mischief (Wickedness)	0	0	0	0
Maliciously Killing Animals	3	2	1	0
Maliciously Pulling Down a Fence	0	0	0	0
Marrying a Colored Female	0	0	0	0
Misdemeanor (unspecified)	0	0	0	0
Notorious Public Indecency	0	0	0	0
Nuisance (Disturbing the Peace)	0	0	0	0
Obstructing a Public Road	0	0	0	0
Obstructing Legal Process	0	0	0	0
Obtaining Goods under False Pretenses	0	0	0	0

	Number	Guilty	Not Guilty	No Verdict
Open Lewdness	0	0	0	0
Performing a Marriage for White Man and Colored Female	0	0	0	0
Perjury	0	0	0	0
Permitting a Slave to Hire His Own Time	0	0	0	0
Permitting a Slave to Trade as Free	0	0	0	0
Practicing Medicine without a License	0	0	0	0
Receiving Stolen Goods	1	0	0	1
Retailing Liquors to a Slave	0	0	0	0
Retailing on the Sabbath	0	0	0	0
Retailing without a License	0	0	0	0
Riot, Affray, Mayhem	7	1	0	6
Selling Intoxicating Liquors to Military	0	0	0	0
Selling Liquor to Indians	0	0	0	0
Selling Liquor without a License	2	1	1	0
Selling Unwholesome Provisions	0	0	0	0
Shipping Cattle from County without Inspection	0	0	0	0
Sodomy	0	0	0	0
Trading with a Slave	4	3	0	1
Trespass	0	0	0	0
Trespassing on School Lands	0	0	0	0
Vagrancy	0	0	0	0
Violating Auction Laws	0	0	0	0
Total	39	19	3	17
SUBTOTAL	89	38	15	36

CRIMES COMMITTED BY SLAVES AND FREE BLACKS

CRIMES AGAINST PERSON

	Number	Guilty	Not Guilty	No Verdict
Murder	0	0	0	0
Assault and Battery	1	1	0	0
Rape	0	0	0	0
Assault with Intent to Rape	0	0	0	0
Assault with Intent to Kill	1	0	1	0
Consulting and Advising to Kill	0	0	0	0
Felony (unspecified)	0	0	0	0
Attempt to Poison	0	0	0	0
Revolt	0	0	0	0
Total	2	1	1	0

CRIMES AGAINST PROPERTY	Number	Guilty	Not Guilty	No Verdict
Larceny	0	0	0	0
Burglary	0	0	0	0
Arson	0	0	0	0
Horse Stealing	0	0	0	0
Total	0	0	0	0
CRIMES AGAINST MORALITY/PUBLIC ORDER				
Forging Free Papers	0	0	0	0
Enticing a Slave to Run Away	0	0	0	0
Receiving Stolen Goods	0	0	0	0
Maliciously Killing Animals	0	0	0	0
Maliciously Wounding Animals	1	0	0	1
Buggery	0	0	0	0
Migration of Free Persons of Color into the Territory	0	0	0	0
Total	1	0	0	1
SUBTOTAL	3	1	1	1
GRAND TOTAL	92	39	16	37

PERCENTAGES OF TOTAL PROSECUTIONS BY CATEGORY

Crimes against Person	42.39%
Crimes against Property	14.13%
Crimes against Morality/Public Order	43.38%
Cases with Guilty Verdict	42.39%
Cases with Not Guilty Verdict	17.39%
Cases with No Verdict	40.22%

Aggregate

CRIMES AGAINST PERSON	Number	Guilty	Not Guilty	No Verdict
Murder/Manslaughter	179	46	31	102
Accessory to Murder	2	0	2	0
Assault and Battery	1,245	475	117	653
Assault with Intent to Kill	275	96	29	150
Rape	10	2	2	6
Robbery	9	2	3	4
Assault with Intent to Rape	6	2	0	4
False Imprisonment	29	6	3	20
Felony (unspecified)	28	2	6	20

Appendix 4: Prosecution Tables by County

	Number	Guilty	Not Guilty	No Verdict
Aiding and Assisting a Felony	1	0	1	0
Extortion	19	0	7	12
Piracy	1	0	1	0
Mutiny	13	3	8	2
Total	1,817	634	210	973

CRIMES AGAINST PROPERTY

	Number	Guilty	Not Guilty	No Verdict
Horse Stealing	12	2	1	9
Cattle Stealing	3	0	0	3
Larceny	423	68	103	252
Burglary	12	1	2	9
Forgery	21	6	7	8
Arson	12	4	4	4
Slave Stealing	27	5	7	15
Counterfeiting	4	0	0	4
Stealing from Vessel in Distress	8	2	4	2
Fraudulently Marking Cattle	28	1	7	20
Total	550	89	135	326

CRIMES AGAINST MORALITY/PUBLIC ORDER

	Number	Guilty	Not Guilty	No Verdict
Adultery and Fornication	237	26	25	186
Aiding a Prisoner to Escape	12	0	2	10
Allowing Negro to Carry Gun	2	0	0	2
Assisting a Slave to Escape	2	1	0	1
Being Concerned in a Duel	23	4	4	15
Bestiality	1	0	1	0
Bigamy	11	1	1	9
Breaking Jail (Escape)	4	1	0	3
Bribery	1	0	0	1
Buggery	0	0	0	0
Buying Soldier's Clothing	1	0	0	1
Carrying Arms Secretly	341	130	39	172
Cheating	4	0	0	4
Concealing the Birth of a Child	1	0	1	0
Conspiracy to Obtain Money by a Trick with Cards	4	0	0	4
Cruelty to a Slave	12	2	2	8
Disturbing Religious Worship	42	10	4	28
Employing Slaves on the Sabbath	3	2	0	1
Enticing a Soldier to Desert	1	0	1	0
Enticing Slave to Run Away	20	10	5	5

	Number	Guilty	Not Guilty	No Verdict
Fornication with a Colored Female	1	0	0	1
Fraudulent Voting	9	0	5	4
Gambling, Gaming, Betting	227	69	34	124
Giving Ticket to Slave of Another	1	0	0	1
Harboring Felons	2	0	0	2
Incest	2	0	0	2
Keeping a Gaming Table	43	6	1	36
Keeping a Gaming, Disorderly House	91	23	18	50
Keeping Billiard Table/Ten Pin Alley without a License	9	4	0	5
Leaving Slaves on Plantation without a White	5	1	0	4
Libel	17	5	1	11
Malfeasance of Public Official	10	1	4	5
Malicious Mischief (Wickedness)	28	2	4	22
Maliciously Killing Animals	29	12	4	13
Maliciously Pulling Down a Fence	4	2	0	2
Marrying a Colored Female	3	1	0	2
Misdemeanor (unspecified)	115	15	21	79
Notorious Public Indecency	4	0	0	4
Nuisance (Disturbing the Peace)	14	3	0	11
Obstructing a Public Road	5	1	0	4
Obstructing Legal Process	14	2	1	11
Obtaining Goods under False Pretenses	7	0	4	3
Open Lewdness	5	3	2	0
Performing a Marriage for White Man and Colored Female	1	0	0	1
Perjury	9	0	1	8
Permitting a Slave to Hire His Own Time	4	0	0	4
Permitting a Slave to Trade as Free	4	4	0	0
Practicing Medicine without a License	7	4	1	2
Receiving Stolen Goods	27	5	3	19
Retailing Liquors to a Slave	110	27	23	60
Retailing on the Sabbath	22	12	1	9
Retailing without a License	21	6	0	15
Riot, Affray, Mayhem	344	90	56	198
Selling Intoxicating Liquors to Military	1	1	0	0
Selling Liquor to Indians	4	1	2	1
Selling Liquor without a License	175	55	59	61
Selling Unwholesome Provisions	4	0	1	3
Shipping Cattle from County without Inspection	3	0	1	2
Sodomy	2	1	0	1
Trading with a Slave	75	15	16	44

Appendix 4: Prosecution Tables by County

	Number	Guilty	Not Guilty	No Verdict
Trespass	1	1	0	0
Trespassing on School Lands	2	2	0	0
Vagrancy	1	1	0	0
Violating Auction Laws	1	1	0	0
Total	2,185	563	348	1,274
SUBTOTAL	4,552	1,286	693	2,573
CRIMES COMMITTED BY SLAVES AND FREE BLACKS				
CRIMES AGAINST PERSON				
Murder	27	17	6	4
Assault and Battery	9	3	1	5
Rape	4	3	1	0
Assault with Intent to Rape	4	3	0	1
Assault with Intent to Kill	5	1	1	3
Consulting and Advising to Kill	1	1	0	0
Felony (unspecified)	1	0	0	1
Attempt to Poison	1	0	0	1
Revolt	2	1	0	1
Total	54	29	9	16
CRIMES AGAINST PROPERTY				
Larceny	16	6	2	8
Burglary	5	1	2	2
Arson	9	1	2	6
Horse Stealing	2	1	0	1
Total	32	9	6	17
CRIMES AGAINST MORALITY/PUBLIC ORDER				
Forging Free Papers	1	0	0	1
Enticing a Slave to Run Away	0	0	0	0
Receiving Stolen Goods	2	0	1	1
Maliciously Killing Animals	4	0	3	1
Maliciously Wounding Animals	1	0	0	1
Buggery	2	1	0	1
Migration of Free Persons of Color into the Territory	0	0	0	0
Total	10	1	4	5
SUBTOTAL	96	39	19	38
GRAND TOTAL	4,648	1,325	712	2,611

PERCENTAGES OF TOTAL PROSECUTIONS BY CATEGORY

Crimes against Person	40.25%
Crimes against Property	12.52%
Crimes against Morality/Public Order	47.22%
Cases with Guilty Verdict	28.51%
Cases with Not Guilty Verdict	15.32%
Cases with No Verdict	56.17%

Notes

Abbreviations

FHSL	Florida Historical Society, University of South Florida
FSAr	Florida State Archives, Tallahassee, Florida
GJP	Grand Jury Presentment
MSL	Manning Strozier Library, Florida State University
NA	National Archives, Washington
NAEP	National Archives, East Point, Georgia
PKYL	P. K. Yonge Library, University of Florida
PL	Pace Library, University of West Florida
RG	Record Group
SAHS	St. Augustine Historical Society
SLF	State Library of Florida, Special Collections, Tallahassee, Florida
USC	South Caroliniana Library, University of South Carolina
USMA	U.S. Military Academy Library, West Point, New York

Preface

1. Catherine Clinton tells her readers in the preface of her work on the role of women in the Old South that her "study includes the seven seaboard states of the plantation South (excluding Florida)." See *The Plantation Mistress: Woman's World in the Old South* (New York: Pantheon Books, 1982), p. xiii. Edward L. Ayers, though making his assertion while analyzing the nineteenth-century Southern penitentiary, writes Florida off as "virtually empty throughout the antebellum era." See *Vengeance and Justice: Crime and Punishment in the Nineteenth-Century American South* (New York: Oxford University Press, 1984), p. 35.

2. Among these are Lawrence M. Friedman, *Crime and Punishment in American History* (New York: Basic Books, 1993), and appropriate sections of idem, *A History of American Law* (New York: Simon and Schuster, 1985); Kermit L. Hall, *The Magic Mirror: Law in American History* (New York: Oxford University Press, 1989); Samuel Walker, *Popular Justice: A History of American Criminal Justice* (New York: Oxford University Press, 1980); David R. Johnson, *American Law Enforcement: A History* (Arlington Heights, Ill.: Forum Press, 1981); David J. Bodenhamer, *Fair Trial: Rights of the Accused in American History* (New York: Oxford University Press, 1992); and Philip D. Jordan, *Frontier Law and Order: Ten Essays* (Lincoln: University of Nebraska Press, 1970). On the South, the following have proven useful: Ayers, *Vengeance and Justice;* Charles S. Sydnor, "The Southerner and the Laws," *Journal of Southern History* 6 (February 1940): 3–23; David J. Bodenhamer and James W. Ely Jr., eds., *Ambivalent Legacy: A Legal History of the South* (Jackson: University of Mississippi Press, 1984); and Michael S. Hindus, *Prison and Plantation: Crime, Justice, and Authority in*

Massachusetts and South Carolina, 1767–1878 (Chapel Hill: University of North Carolina Press, 1980). Less methodological but far more readable are Jack Kenny Williams, *Vogues in Villainy: Crime and Retribution in Antebellum South Carolina* (Columbia: University of South Carolina Press, 1959); idem, "Crime and Punishment in Alabama, 1819–1840," *Alabama Review* 6 (January 1953): 14–30; Waddy W. Moore, "Some Aspects of Crime and Punishment on the Arkansas Frontier," *Arkansas Historical Quarterly* 23 (Spring 1964): 50–64; David J. Bodenhamer, "Law and Lawlessness in the Deep South: The Situation in Georgia 1830–1860," in *From the Old South to the New: Essays on the Transitional South,* ed. Walter J. Fraser and Winifred Moore (Westport, Conn.: Greenwood Press, 1981), pp. 109–19; idem, "The Efficiency of Criminal Justice in the Antebellum South," *Criminal Justice History* 3 (1983): 81–95; idem, "Criminal Justice" and "Criminal Law," in *Encyclopedia of Southern Culture,* ed. Charles Reagan Wilson and William Ferris (Chapel Hill: University of North Carolina Press, 1989), pp. 804–6; Robert M. Ireland, "Law and Disorder in Nineteenth-Century Kentucky," *Vanderbilt Law Review* 32 (January 1979): 281–300; idem, "Homicide in Nineteenth-Century Kentucky," *Register of the Kentucky Historical Society* 81 (Spring 1983): 134–53; Bertram Wyatt-Brown, "Community, Class, and Snopesian Crime: Local Justice in the Old South," in *Class, Conflict, and Consensus: Antebellum Southern Community Studies,* ed. Orville Vernon Burton and Robert C. McMath Jr. (Westport, Conn.: Greenwood Press, 1982), pp. 173–206; and Guion Griffis Johnson, *Antebellum North Carolina: A Social History* (Chapel Hill: University of North Carolina Press, 1937), pp. 644–82.

3. On the social characteristics of antebellum Texas and its connection to Florida see William Ransom Hogan, *The Republic of Texas: A Social and Economic History* (Norman: University of Oklahoma Press, 1946); James M. Denham, "New Orleans, Maritime Commerce, and the Texas War for Independence, 1836," *Southwestern Historical Quarterly* 97 (January 1994): 511–34; and idem, " 'The Peerless Wind Cloud': Thomas Jefferson Green and the Tallahassee-Texas Land Company," *East Texas Historical Journal* 29 (Fall 1991): 3–14.

Chapter 1

1. Judge Webb to the Secretary of the Treasury, April 9, 1829, in Clarence E. Carter, ed., *Territorial Papers of the United States,* 26 vols. (Washington, D.C.: U.S. Government Printing Office, 1934–62), 24:183–84.

2. For population figures see Donald B. Dodd and Wynelle S. Dodd, *Historical Statistics of the South, 1790–1970* (Tuscaloosa: University of Alabama Press, 1973), pp. 14–16. See also Roland Harper, "Antebellum Census Enumerations in Florida," *Florida Historical Quarterly* 6 (July 1927): 42–52; and J. E. Dovell, *Florida: Historic, Dramatic, Contemporary* (New York: Lewis Historical Publishing Co., 1952), pp. 401–2.

3. Joan Cashin, *A Family Venture: Men and Women on the Southern Frontier* (New York: Oxford University Press, 1991); John Solomon Otto, *Southern Frontiers, 1607–1860: The Agricultural Evolution of the Colonial and Antebellum South* (Westport, Conn.: Greenwood Press, 1989); Canter Brown Jr., *Florida's Peace River Frontier* (Orlando: University of Central Florida Press, 1991).

4. Lawrence M. Friedman, *Crime and Punishment in American History* (New York: Basic Books, 1993), p. 6.

5. Ibid., pp. 12–13.

6. Samuel Walker, *Popular Justice: A History of American Criminal Justice* (New York: Oxford University Press, 1980), p. 21; Edward L. Ayers, *Vengeance and Justice: Crime and Punishment in the Nineteenth-Century American South* (New York: Oxford University Press, 1984), pp. 106–7; Friedman, *Crime and Punishment,* pp. 25–26; Peter C. Hoffer and William B. Scott, eds., *Criminal Proceedings in Colonial Virginia: [Records of] Fines, Examinations of Criminals, Trials of Slaves etc. from March 1710 [1711] to [1754] Richmond County* (Athens: University of Georgia Press, 1984), p. xx.

7. Charge of Henry M. Brackenridge to the Jackson County Grand Jury, December 1831, in Carter, *Territorial Papers,* 24:612–13.

8. An Act Providing for the Adoption of the Common Statutes of England and for Repealing Certain Laws and Ordinances," *Acts and Resolutions of the Legislative Council,* 1823, pp. 136–37.

9. Charge of Henry M. Brackenridge to the Jackson County Grand Jury, December 1831, in Carter, *Territorial Papers,* 24:612–13, n. 6.

10. "Census Returns," *Tallahassee Floridian and Journal,* September 8, 1855.

11. Kermit L. Hall, *The Politics of Justice: Lower Federal Judicial Selection and the Second Party System, 1829–61* (Lincoln: University of Nebraska Press, 1979), pp. 15–17, 23–24, 38–43.

12. Frank L. Owsley, *Plain Folk in the Old South* (Baton Rouge: Louisiana State University Press, 1949); Wilber J. Cash, *The Mind of the South* (New York: Knopf, 1941); Grady McWhiney, *Cracker Culture: Celtic Ways in the Old South* (Tuscaloosa: University of Alabama Press, 1988). See also J. Wayne Flynt, *Dixie's Forgotten People: The South's Poor Whites* (Bloomington: Indiana University Press, 1979); I. A. Newby, *Plain Folk in the New South: Social Change and Persistence, 1880–1915* (Baton Rouge: Louisiana State University Press, 1989); and James M. Denham, "The Florida Crackers before the Civil War as Seen through Travelers' Accounts," *Florida Historical Quarterly* 72 (April 1994): 453–68.

13. Jane Landers, "Black Society in Spanish St. Augustine, 1784–1821" (Ph.D. diss., University of Florida, 1988); Canter Brown Jr., "Race Relations in Territorial Florida, 1821–1845," *Florida Historical Quarterly* 73 (January 1995): 287–307; Susan R. Parker, "Men without God or King: Rural Settlers of East Florida, 1784–1790," *Florida Historical Quarterly* 69 (October 1990): 135–55; Daniel L. Schafer, " 'A Class of People Neither Freemen Nor Slaves': From Spanish to American Race Relations in Florida, 1821–1861," *Journal of Social History* 26 (Spring 1993): 587–609. Lee Warner has highlighted the regional differences of slavery as well as its legal constraints through three generations of one family of free blacks, the Proctors. See *Free Men in the Age of Servitude: Three Generations of a Black Family* (Lexington: University of Kentucky Press, 1992).

14. For an excellent overview of the development of the Middle Florida slave system see Clifton Paisley, *The Red Hills of Florida, 1528–1865* (Tuscaloosa: University of Alabama Press, 1989), pp. 107–214; and Julia Floyd Smith, *Slavery and Plantation Growth in Antebellum Florida, 1821–1860* (Gainesville: University of Florida Press, 1973). In an excellent series of articles, Larry E. Rivers has sketched out the slave system in a number of Middle Florida counties. See "Slavery in Microcosm: Leon County, Florida, 1824–1860," *Journal of Negro History* 46 (February 1981): 235–45; "Dignity and Importance: Slavery in Jefferson County, Florida, 1827–1860," *Florida*

Historical Quarterly 61 (April 1983): 404–30; and "Slavery and the Political Economy of Gadsden County, Florida, 1823–1861," *Florida Historical Quarterly* 70 (July 1991): 1–19.

Chapter 2

1. *St. Augustine Florida Herald,* June 20, 1833; Lester B. Shippee, ed., *Bishop Whipple's Southern Diary, 1843–1844* (Minneapolis: University of Minnesota Press, 1937), pp. 26–27.
2. *Pensacola Gazette,* May 2, 1828.
3. Ibid., September 23, 1828.
4. Ibid., November 12, 1842.
5. Ibid., March 8, 1834.
6. W. J. Rorabaugh, *The Alcoholic Republic: An American Tradition* (New York: Oxford University Press, 1979). The problem was particularly acute in the South. See Ian R. Tyrrell, "Drink and Temperance in the Antebellum South: An Overview and Interpretation," *Journal of Southern History* 48 (November 1982): 485–510; Grady McWhiney, *Cracker Culture: Celtic Ways in the Old South* (Tuscaloosa: University of Alabama Press, 1988), pp. 90–92, 106–8, 127–31; Daniel R. Hundley, *Social Relations in Our Southern States* (New York: H. B. Price, 1860); and Shippee, *Bishop Whipple's Southern Diary.*
7. Francis de Castelnau, "Essay on Middle Florida, 1837–1838," trans. Arthur Seymour, *Florida Historical Quarterly* 26 (January 1948): 237.
8. *Pensacola Gazette,* November 2, 1827.
9. Some saw local option as a remedy to the evil. See *Tallahassee Floridian and Journal,* January 1, 1853; Jefferson County GJP, April 16, 1853, Jefferson County, Minutes of the Circuit Court, Book A, p. 456; and Madison County GJP, December Term 1852, in *Tallahassee Florida Sentinel,* December 7, 1852, and *Tallahassee Floridian and Journal,* December 4, 1852. Temperance societies also functioned in Florida. See Jack Cardwell Lavin, "The Temperance Movement in Antebellum Florida" (Master's thesis, Florida State University, 1967); and Rebecca Keith, "The Humanitarian Movement in Florida, 1821–1861" (Master's thesis, Florida State University, 1951).
10. *St. Augustine Florida Herald,* January 10, 1833.
11. Escambia County GJP, May 15, 1837, Escambia County, Minutes of the Superior Court, Book 3, p. 138.
12. Charles A. Hentz, "My Autobiography," pp. 159–60, PKYL.
13. Gadsden County, Minutes of the Circuit Court, Book 1, p. 121.
14. *Tallahassee Florida Sentinel,* June 10, 1842.
15. *Pensacola Gazette,* March 10, 1829.
16. Simon Turman to T. W. Brevard, March 5, 1855, State Comptroller Correspondence, RG 350, ser. 554, box 2, folder 1, FSAr.
17. *Pensacola Gazette,* May 7, 1842.
18. Castelnau, "Essay on Middle Florida," p. 237.
19. *Pensacola Gazette,* September 30, 1828.
20. *Apalachicola Gazette,* December 26, 1837.
21. Castelnau, "Essay on Middle Florida," p. 237.

22. For a discussion of the constitutional rights in this respect in this era see Philip D. Jordan, *Frontier Law and Order: Ten Essays* (Lincoln: University of Nebraska Press, 1970), pp. 11–16. Frank Richard Prassel has explored this issue in the context of the West. See *The Western Peace Officer: A Legacy of Law and Order* (Norman: University of Oklahoma Press, 1972), p. 11.

23. *Apalachicola Gazette,* December 16, 1837. Most newspaper editors roundly condemned the practice of carrying concealed weapons. See, for example, *Ocala Conservator,* October 22, 1851.

24. *Tallahassee Florida Sentinel,* November 18, 1842.

25. *St. Augustine News,* February 16, 1839.

26. *Pensacola Gazette,* May 2, 1828.

27. Ibid.

28. *Jacksonville Florida News,* October 11, 1851.

29. Jack Kenny Williams, *Vogues in Villainy: Crime and Retribution in Antebellum South Carolina* (Columbia: University of South Carolina Press, 1959), p. 16; W. J. Cash, *The Mind of the South* (New York: Knopf, 1941); Clement Eaton, *The Growth of the Southern Civilization* (New York: Harper, 1961); Bertram Wyatt-Brown, *Southern Honor: Ethics and Behavior in the Old South* (New York: Oxford University Press, 1982); Dickson D. Bruce Jr., *Violence and Culture in the Antebellum South* (Austin: University of Texas Press, 1979); Edward L. Ayers, *Vengeance and Justice: Crime and Punishment in the Nineteenth-Century American South* (New York: Oxford University Press, 1984).

30. Leon County GJP, April Term 1828, Leon County, Minutes of the Superior Court, Book 1, pp. 66–67.

31. *Pensacola Gazette,* May 2, 1828.

32. On the institution of dueling in the antebellum South see Bertram Wyatt-Brown, *Southern Honor;* Jack Kenny Williams, *Dueling in the Old South: Vignettes in Social History* (College Station: Texas A&M University Press, 1980); Bruce, *Violence and Culture;* Eaton, *Growth of the Southern Civilization;* idem, "The Role of Honor in Southern Society," *Southern Humanities Review* 10 (Supplement 1976): 47–58; and Kenneth S. Greenberg, *Masters and Statesmen: The Political Culture of American Slavery* (Baltimore: Johns Hopkins University Press, 1985). On dueling in Florida see Herbert J. Doherty, "The Code Duello in Florida," *Florida Historical Quarterly* 29 (April 1955): 243–52; James M. Denham, "Dueling in Territorial Middle Florida" (Master's thesis, Florida State University, 1983); and idem, "The Read-Alston Duel and Politics in Territorial Florida," *Florida Historical Quarterly* 68 (April 1990): 427–46.

33. *Tallahassee Florida Sentinel,* May 20, 1842; *Tallahassee Star of Florida,* May 19, 1842.

34. *Tallahassee Florida Sentinel,* May 13, 1842.

35. Leon County, Minutes of the Superior Court, Book 1, pp. 66–67.

36. The escapees were Moses Townsend, Spencer Townsend, William Saffold, and John McDowell. Jefferson County GJP, November 29, 1834, Jefferson County, Minutes of the Superior Court, Book 1, p. 133; *Tallahassee Floridian,* December 6, 1834.

37. Anonymous to the Secretary of State, October 15, 1822, in Clarence E. Carter, ed., *Territorial Papers of the United States,* 26 vols. (Washington, D.C.: U.S. Government Printing Office, 1934–62), 22:545–46.

38. Jefferson County GJP, November Term 1837, Jefferson County, Minutes of the Superior Court, Book 1, p. 232.

39. Madison County GJP in *Tallahassee Florida Sentinel,* December 7, 1852; *Tallahassee Floridian and Journal,* December 4, 1852.

40. *Tallahassee Floridian and Advocate,* June 2, 1831.

41. *St. Augustine News,* May 28, 1841.

42. Ibid.

43. *St. Augustine East Florida Herald,* November 14, 1826.

44. *Pensacola Gazette,* November 20, 1824.

45. The expert was Edward Bulwer-Lytton (1803–73), a member of the British Parliament. See "The Contagiousness of Crime," *Tallahassee Florida Sentinel,* May 28, 1841.

46. *Tallahassee Floridian,* December 11, May 22, 1841.

47. *Mobile (Alabama) Register* quoted in ibid., December 11, 1841.

48. Ibid.

49. *St. Augustine Florida Herald and Southern Democrat,* December 31, 1840.

50. Wyatt-Brown, *Southern Honor,* pp. 27–32; Bruce, *Violence and Culture,* pp. 12–17.

51. Lawrence M. Friedman, *Crime and Punishment in American History* (New York: Basic Books, 1993), p. 56; David J. Bodenhamer, *Fair Trial: Rights of the Accused in American History* (New York: Oxford University Press, 1992), p. 28.

Chapter 3

1. *Tallahassee Florida Sentinel,* December 3, 1841.

2. The Florida legislature, from time to time, allowed judges latitude in altering meeting times and locations. See, for example, *Acts and Resolutions of the General Assembly,* 1850, p. 112; and 1854, p. 65.

3. Orange County, Minutes of the Circuit Court, Book A, pp. 131–32.

4. Kermit L. Hall and Eric W. Rise, *From Local Courts to National Tribunals: Federal District Courts of Florida, 1821–1990* (Brooklyn, N.Y.: Carlson Publishing Co., 1991), p. 5.

5. For a discussion of the territorial courts see ibid., pp. 5–20; Charles D. Farris, "The Courts of Territorial Florida," *Florida Historical Quarterly* 19 (April 1941): 346–67; and J. E. Dovell, *Florida: Historic, Dramatic, Contemporary* (New York: Lewis Historical Publishing Co., 1952), p. 226.

6. "An Act to Regulate the Counties and Establish County Courts in the Territory of Florida," *Acts,* 1824, pp. 247–51.

7. Farris, "The Courts of Territorial Florida," p. 350.

8. *St. Augustine Florida Herald,* November 18, May 5, 1830; Memorial of the Inhabitants of the County of St. Johns to the Governor and the Legislative Council of Florida, November 4, 1824, Territorial Legislative Council, Unicameral, RG 910, ser. 876, box 1, folder 7, FSAr; *St. Augustine Florida Herald,* April 21, 1830.

9. Petition of Citizens of Escambia County to Legislative Council, 1824, Territorial Legislative Council, Unicameral, RG 910, ser. 876, box 1, folder 7, FSAr; Petition to the Governor from the Inhabitants of Gadsden County, November 20, 1824, ibid.

10. Larry D. Ball, *The United States Marshals of New Mexico and Arizona Territories, 1846–1912* (Albuquerque: University of New Mexico Press, 1978), p. 8.

11. Daniel Webster (Secretary of State) to Minor Walker, May 22, 1841, in Clarence E. Carter, ed., *Territorial Papers of the United States,* 26 vols. (Washington, D.C.: U.S. Government Printing Office, 1934–62), 22:314.

12. William P. DuVal to B. Penrose, February 19, 1841, in ibid., 22:172–73.

13. "Loco-foco" is a name for radical Democrats and comes from a type of match popular during the 1830s and 1840s. The term arose during a boisterous Democratic meeting in New York City held in 1835 when conservatives extinguished the lighting at the meeting and the more radical delegates lit loco-foco matches to continue the proceedings. For the comment on Sanchez see *St. Augustine News,* November 6, 1841.

14. William F. Keller, *The Nation's Advocate: Henry Marie Brackenridge and Young America* (Pittsburgh: University of Pittsburgh Press, 1956); Hall and Rise, *From Local Courts to National Tribunals,* pp. 155–56.

15. Hall and Rise, *From Local Courts to National Tribunals,* pp. 155–56, 171, 174.

16. Ibid., pp. 173, 165.

17. Charge of Judge Henry M. Brackenridge to the Jackson County Grand Jury, December Term 1831, in Carter, *Territorial Papers,* 24:619.

18. Kevin E. Kearney, ed., "Autobiography of William Marvin," *Florida Historical Quarterly* 36 (January 1958): 203–5.

19. Memorial to the President by the Inhabitants of East Florida, January 11, 1830, in Carter, *Territorial Papers,* 22:327; Judge Smith to the President, November 18, 1829, ibid., 22:292. For other instances of confrontations between Judge Smith and others see ibid., 23:169–70, 194–95, 344, 373–74, 392–93, 411–12, 437–38, 504, 506–17, 523–24, 599; *St. Augustine East Florida Herald,* January 17, February 7, 1824, March 1, 8, 26, April 30, May 7, 1825, April 21, 1830; *Pensacola Gazette,* March 5, April 9, 30, May 7, 14, 1825; and *Tallahassee Floridian and Advocate,* May 4, 1830. Even years after he left the bench, Judge Smith's volatile temper continued to get the best of him. In 1843, at the age of sixty-three, he was prosecuted in the superior court for fighting Judge Elias Gould, an old adversary. A visitor who witnessed the scene commented that "occasionally now and then, the people are compelled to witness the public fight & see those who ought to be gentlemen descend to the common bully. [I] witnessed a laughable trial today of which one judge (Judge Smith) for having whipped another judge (Judge Gould) and was somewhat surprised to hear such scurrility and vulgarity allowed in court of justice as was used by one of the parties." See Lester B. Shippee, ed., *Bishop Whipple's Southern Diary, 1843–1844* (Minneapolis: University of Minnesota Press, 1937), p. 27.

20. Reid Diary, October 6, 1833, SLF.

21. Henry Brackenridge to Caroline Brackenridge, May 2, 1830, Henry Marie Brackenridge Papers, PL, photocopies from originals in Darlington Memorial Library at the University of Pittsburgh (hereafter cited as Brackenridge Papers, PL).

22. John Cameron to the Secretary of State, January 28, 1836, in Carter, *Territorial Papers,* 25:229–30.

23. Resolution, n.d., Legislative Council, Unicameral, RG 910, ser. 876, box 3, folder 7, FSAr.

24. *Tallahassee Florida Sentinel,* May 20, 1842.

25. *Pensacola Gazette,* April 25, 1840.

26. Joining Judge Samuel Douglas in the Middle District was U.S. Marshal John G. Camp and U.S. Attorney Charles S. Sibley. Selected as governor was Richard K. Call, who by 1840 was increasingly associated with the Whigs.

27. *Tallahassee Floridian,* December 11, 1841.

28. Leon County, Minutes of the Superior Court, Book 3, p. 199.

29. The first judges and solicitors elected by the people of Florida in 1853 were the following: for the Western Circuit, Jesse Finley (judge) and James Landrum (solicitor); for the Middle Circuit, J. Wayles Baker (judge) and Samuel R. Stephens (solicitor); for the Eastern Circuit, William A. Forward (judge) and James Baker (solicitor); and for the Southern Circuit, Thomas King (judge) and Hardy Kendrick (solicitor). *Tallahassee Floridian and Journal,* November 26, 1853.

30. *St. Augustine News,* September 6, 1845.

31. As to Florida's federal courts in the antebellum era see Hall and Rise, *From Local Courts to National Tribunals,* pp. 21–30.

32. *Tallahassee Star of Florida,* August 1, 1845.

33. *Pensacola Gazette,* August 2, 1845.

34. Ibid., November 29, 1845.

35. *Tallahassee Floridian,* November 1, 1845.

36. Petition of the Citizens of Key West to Legislative Assembly of Florida, November 17, 1845, Nineteenth-Century Florida State Legislature, RG 915, ser. 887, box 1, folder 5, FSAr; Resolutions of the Meeting in Hillsborough County Touching the Alternating System, October 12, 1846, ibid., box 3, folder 4.

37. Hillsborough County, Minutes of the Circuit Court, 1846–54, pp. 1–44.

38. Hillsborough County GJP, November 3, 1845, in *Tallahassee Floridian,* December 13, 1845; *Tallahassee Florida Sentinel,* December 16, 1845; Columbia County GJP, May 1846, in *St. Augustine Florida Herald and Southern Democrat,* June 2, 1846. See also public meeting in Chocochattie in Benton County, October 21, 1847, in *Tallahassee Floridian,* November 13, 1847.

39. *Fernandina East Floridian,* January 15, 1860.

Chapter 4

1. Reid Diary, February 27, 1835, SLF.

2. Preston Journal, typescript copy, pp. 29–30, PL; *Pensacola Gazette,* May 26, 1838.

3. *Pensacola Gazette,* September 21, 1844, November 10, 1849; *Jacksonville Florida News,* April 23, 1853.

4. Escambia County, Minutes of the Superior Court, Book 1, pp. 303, 305, 326, 328, 329. For more on the issue of civil versus military prosecution see James M. Denham, " 'Some Prefer the Seminoles': Violence and Disorder among Soldiers and Settlers in the Second Seminole War, 1835–1842," *Florida Historical Quarterly* 70 (July 1991): 38–54.

5. Samuel Keep to Navy Department, February 18, 1827, Samuel Keep to Nathan Keep, May 7, June 5, 18, 1827, Keep Family Papers, PL; accounts of C. C. Yonge, box 3, folder entitled "CC Yonge 1860," Yonge Papers, PKYL.

6. *Tallahassee Florida Sentinel,* March 27, 1849.

7. Ibid., November 19, 1841.

8. *Tallahassee Floridian and Journal,* May 13, 1853.

9. For an excellent discussion of the economic development of the Apalachicola/Chattahoochee River Valley, especially the cotton trade, see Lynn Willoughby, *Fair to Middlin': The Antebellum Cotton Trade of the Apalachicola River Valley* (Tuscaloosa: University of Alabama Press, 1993).

10. D. G. McLeod to David Gillis, January 30, 1853, box 52, folder entitled "Correspondence 1850–1859," McLean Papers, PKYL.

11. *Apalachicola Gazette,* May 4, 1839, May 2, 1846; "Abstract of Fines and Forfeitures in Franklin County Superior Court for December 1841 and March 1842," box 30, Miscellaneous Manuscripts, PKYL. Also on Apalachicola see William W. Rogers, *Outposts on the Gulf: Saint George Island and Apalachicola from Early Exploration to World War II* (Pensacola: University of West Florida Press, 1986); and Harry P. Owens, "Apalachicola before 1861" (Ph.D. diss., Florida State University, 1966).

12. Henry Marie Brackenridge to Caroline Brackenridge, July 27, 1827, Brackenridge Papers, PL. For an excellent discussion of the social and economic development of Middle Florida's plantation belt, which encompassed the region between and bordering the Apalachicola and Suwannee Rivers, see Clifton Paisley, *The Red Hills of Florida, 1528–1865* (Tuscaloosa: University of Alabama Press, 1989).

13. *Tallahassee Florida Sentinel,* May 2, 1848; *Pensacola Gazette,* November 23, 1839; Simon Peter Richardson, *Lights and Shadows of Itinerant Life: An Autobiography* (Nashville: Barbie and Smith, 1901), pp. 75–76.

14. "Accounts of James D. Westcott, United States District Attorney for the Middle District of Florida, Gadsden Superior Court, May and November Term, 1834," Territorial Florida Account Sheets, MSL; Gadsden County GJP, May 8, 1854, Gadsden County Case Files.

15. *Tallahassee Florida Sentinel,* September 15, 1829; Richardson, *Lights and Shadows,* pp. 105–6.

16. *St. Augustine Florida Herald and Southern Democrat,* January 31, 1839; *Tallahassee Floridian,* January 1, 1842.

17. Hector Braden to Mary Nuttal, January 26, 1840, box 2, El Destino Plantation Papers, FHSL.

18. Comte de Castelnau, "Essay on Middle Florida, 1837–1838," trans. Arthur Seymour, *Florida Historical Quarterly* 26 (January 1948): 236; James T. Campbell, "The Charles Hutchinson Letters from Territorial Tallahassee, 1839–1843," *Apalachee* 4 (1950–56): 15.

19. Richardson, *Lights and Shadows,* pp. 105–6; Leon County GJP, November 1828, in Leon County, Minutes of the Superior Court, Book 1, pp. 117–19.

20. Castelnau, "Essay on Middle Florida," pp. 237–38.

21. Jefferson County, Minutes of the Superior Court, Book 1, p. 164.

22. *Tallahassee Southern Journal,* April 21, 1846; *Tallahassee Floridian and Journal,* December 3, 1853, August 28, 1855, December 20, 1851.

23. See Jerrell H. Shofner, *Daniel Ladd: Merchant Prince of Frontier Florida* (Gainesville: University Presses of Florida, 1978).

24. John S. Tappan to Benjamin French, December 13, 1841, Tappan Papers, SLF.

25. *Newport Gazette,* December 15, 1846.

26. *Tallahassee Floridian and Journal,* April 19, 1851; *Tallahassee Florida Sentinel,* April 15, 1851; Ives Journal, March 14, May 19, 1860, SLF.

27. Corinna and Ellen Brown to Mannevillette Brown, December 14, 1839, Anderson Papers, USMA.

28. Lester B. Shippee, ed., *Bishop Whipple's Southern Diary, 1843–1844* (Minneapolis: University of Minnesota Press, 1937), p. 27.

29. Rebecca Phillips, "A Diary of Jessee Talbot Bernard: Newnansville and Tallahassee," *Florida Historical Quarterly* 18 (October 1939): 119; Corinna Aldrich to Mannevillette Brown, January 26, 1840, Anderson Papers, USMA; Ives Journal, pp. 26–27, SLF; Merlin Cox and Charles Hildreth, *History of Gainesville, Florida, 1854–1979* (Gainesville: Alachua County Historical Society, 1981), p. 9.

30. John Mackay to Eliza Mackay, April 9, 1836, box 45, Miscellaneous Manuscripts, PKYL; George R. Fairbanks to Brother, November 5, 1842, Fairbanks Collection, folder 10, MSL; Shippee, *Bishop Whipple's Southern Diary,* pp. 24–25.

31. *St. Augustine Florida Herald,* June 16, 1838.

32. *Tallahassee Star of Florida,* October 17, 1845; St. Johns County, Minutes of the Circuit Court, Book A, pp. 12, 29.

33. Hatheway Diary, December 1, 1845, MSL.

34. *St. Augustine Florida Herald and Southern Democrat,* May 29, 1840.

35. Ibid., May 29, 1840.

36. Shippee, *Bishop Whipple's Southern Diary,* p. 37.

37. *Tallahassee Floridian,* April 18, 1846.

38. *Tallahassee Sentinel,* June 16, 1846; *Tallahassee Floridian,* June 13, 1846.

39. *Tallahassee Floridian,* May 16, 1846.

40. Judge Webb to Delegate White, October 27, 1828, in Clarence E. Carter, ed., *Territorial Papers of the United States,* 26 vols. (Washington, D.C.: U.S. Government Printing Office, 1934–62), 24:112–13; Henry Wilson to the Secretary of State, October 27, 1828, in ibid., 24:93–94.

41. Judge Webb to the Secretary of the Treasury, April 9, 1829, in ibid., 24:183–85.

42. *Key West Enquirer,* June 13, January 3, 1835.

43. *Pensacola Gazette,* May 8, 1852; *Tallahassee Florida Sentinel,* May 11, 1852.

44. Petition of the Citizens of Monroe County to the Legislative Council, 1839, Territorial Legislative Council, Bicameral, RG 910, ser. 877, box 1, folder 3, FSAr.

45. Monroe County also had difficulty obtaining sufficient numbers of jurors. Judge Webb asked that jurors be paid fair compensation for travel and court attendance. See Judge Webb to Delegate White, April 12, 1836, in Carter, *Territorial Papers,* 25:273–74. Many violent offenders had been allowed to escape under territorial laws that provided for transporting offenders to other districts for prosecution. See Memorial to Congress from the Officers of the Superior Court, Southern District, March 16, 1840, in ibid., 26:125–27.

46. Petition of the Citizens of Monroe County to the Legislative Council, 1839, Territorial Legislative Council, Bicameral, RG 910, ser. 877, box 1, folder 3, FSAr.

47. Report of Monroe County Asking a Repeal of the Act Organizing Dade County, 1839, ibid.

48. See Janet Snyder Matthews, *Edge of Wilderness: A Settlement History of Manatee*

River and Sarasota Bay (Tulsa, Okla.: Caprine Press, 1983); and Canter Brown Jr., *Florida's Peace River Frontier* (Orlando: University of Central Florida Press, 1991).

Chapter 5

1. Contemporary definitions of some of these crimes are obscure, but generally assault referred to (but was not confined to) verbal abuse or threats to bodily harm. Assault and battery referred to the willful and malicious verbal and physical attack of one upon another, while affray was usually defined as breaking the peace by fighting, brawling, or rioting in a public place. In most cases two or more persons were prosecuted for this crime. Mayhem (sometimes called malicious wounding) referred to any attempt to maim or dismember an opponent during physical combat, such as gouging out eyes, biting off ears, noses, fingers, and so on. For more on this see Elliot J. Gorn, " 'Gouge and Bite, Pull Hair and Scratch': The Social Significance of Fighting in the Southern Backcountry," *American Historical Review* 90 (February 1985): 18–43; Tom Parramore, "Gouging in Early North Carolina," *North Carolina Journal of Folklore* 22 (May 1974): 55–62; and James I. Robertson, "Fights, Frolics, and Firewater in Frontier Tennessee," *Tennessee Historical Quarterly* 17 (June 1958): 97–111. For a summary of these crimes and their penalties see Leslie A. Thompson, *A Manual or Digest of the Statute Law of the State of Florida, of a General and Public Character, in Force at the End of the Second Session of the General Assembly of the State, on the Sixth Day of January, 1847* (Boston: Charles C. Little and James Brown, 1848), pp. 490, 498.

2. Also included in this total are prosecutions for riot, affray, and mayhem, categorized in this study as crimes against morality and public order.

3. Bodenhamer notes that the efficiency of prosecution tended to depend on the rural or urban setting, of which he found the latter more efficient. See "The Efficiency of Criminal Justice in the Antebellum South," *Criminal Justice History* 3 (1983): 81–95.

4. Alba was murdered by Robert Breen. See *Pensacola Gazette,* September 25, December 4, 1833; *St. Augustine Florida Herald,* October 31, December 26, 1833, February 6, 1834; Affidavits and Trial Proceedings of Robert Breen for Murder, Correspondence of the Territorial Governors, RG 101, ser. 177, box 1, folder 2, FSAr. Read was murdered by Willis Alston. See James M. Denham, "The Read-Alston Duel and Politics in Territorial Florida," *Florida Historical Quarterly* 68 (April 1990): 427–46. McRae was murdered by Charles E. Hawkins. His murder is discussed in the next chapter.

5. For Chenney see *Territory v Daniel Chenney,* 1828, Escambia County Case Files; and Escambia County, Minutes of the Superior Court, Book 1, pp. 390, 395. For Holloman see *Territory v Jessee Holloman,* 1840, Jefferson County Case Files; and Jefferson County, Minutes of the Superior Court, Book 1, p. 498. For Jacobs see *Tallahassee Florida Sentinel,* August 19, 1851, May 11, June 22, 1852; J. Robertson to George Jones, June 12, 1852, El Destino Plantation Papers, FHSL; *State v Josiah Jacobs,* Spring 1852, Comptroller's Vouchers, Criminal Prosecutions, RG 350, ser. 565, box 6, folder 5, Wakulla County, FSAr; and Proclamation of Thomas Brown, May 11, 1852, Book of Record (Proclamations), RG 156, ser. 13, Book 1, no. 173,

p. 194, FSAr. For the Santa Rosa County victims see Coroner's Inquest over the Body of Martin Williford, 1856, Comptroller's Vouchers, Post Mortem Examinations, RG 350, ser. 565, box 7, folder 5, Santa Rosa County, FSAr; and *Pensacola Gazette,* January 17, 1852.

6. Excellent introductions to these issues and themes can be found in various entries in Charles Reagan Wilson and William Ferris, eds., *Encyclopedia of Southern Culture* (Chapel Hill: University of North Carolina Press, 1989). See especially sections on "Violence," pp. 1469–1513, and "Law," pp. 793–834.

7. One writer who takes this position is Richard Maxwell Brown. See his *Strain of Violence: Historical Studies of American Violence and Vigilantism* (New York: Oxford University Press, 1975); and idem, ed., *American Violence* (Englewood Cliffs, N.J.: Prentice-Hall, 1970). A number of studies of American violence were spawned out of events and issues taking place in the Civil Rights and Vietnam eras. See Richard Hofstadter and Michael Wallace, eds., *American Violence: A Documentary History* (New York: Random House, 1970); Thomas Rose, ed., *Violence in America: A Historical and Contemporary Reader* (New York: Vintage, 1970); and Hugh Davis Graham and Ted Robert Gurr, eds., *Violence in America: Historical and Comparative Perspectives* (Washington, D.C.: U.S. Government Printing Office, 1969).

8. Billington warns that it is easy to overstate the case for frontier and Southern violence. Contemporary "image makers," he claims, "helped saddle the South with this reputation." See *America's Frontier Heritage* (New York: Holt, Rinehart, and Winston, 1966), pp. 69–75, 146–57. See also his *Land of Savagery, Land of Promise: The European Image of the American Frontier in the Nineteenth Century* (New York: Norton, 1981); Philip D. Jordan, *Frontier Law and Order: Ten Essays* (Lincoln: University of Nebraska Press, 1970); and Everett Dick, *The Dixie Frontier: A Social History of the Southern Frontier from the First Transmontane Beginnings to the Civil War* (New York: Knopf, 1948), pp. 140–41. Eugene W. Hollon, though finding much evidence of violence on the Western frontier, thinks the region was a "far more civilized, more peaceful, and safer place than American society is today." See *Frontier Violence: Another Look* (New York: Oxford University Press, 1974), p. x. Similar appraisals can be found in Richard Slotkin, *Regeneration through Violence: The Mythology of the American Frontier* (Middletown, Conn.: Wesleyan University Press, 1973); idem, *The Fatal Environment: The Myth of the Frontier Age of Industrialization, 1800–1890* (New York: Atheneum, 1985); Richard A. Bartlett, *The New Country: A Social History of the American Frontier* (New York: Oxford University Press, 1974); and Arthur Moore, *The Frontier Mind* (New York: McGraw-Hill, 1963).

9. Edward L. Ayers, *Vengeance and Justice: Crime and Punishment in the Nineteenth-Century American South* (New York: Oxford University Press, 1984), p. 12. See also his "A Legacy of Violence," *American Heritage* 42 (October 1991): 102–9. Also on Southern violence see Sheldon Hackney, "Southern Violence," *American Historical Review* 74 (February 1969): 906–25; John Shelton Reed, "Below the Smith and Wesson Line: Southern Violence," in his *One South: An Ethnic Approach to Regional Culture* (Baton Rouge: Louisiana State University Press, 1982), pp. 139–53; William G. Doerner, "The Deadly World of Johnny Reb: Fact, Foible, or Fantasy?" in *Violent Crime: Historical and Contemporary,* ed. James Inciardi and Anne Pottieger (Beverly Hills: Sage, 1978), pp. 91–97; and H. C. Brearly, "The Pattern of Violence," in *The*

Culture of the South, ed. W. T. Couch (Chapel Hill: University of North Carolina Press, 1935), pp. 678–92.

10. Billington, *Land of Savagery,* pp. 268–69.

11. Quoted in Bertram Wyatt-Brown, *Southern Honor: Ethics and Behavior in the Old South* (New York: Oxford University Press, 1982), p. 134.

12. W. J. Cash, *The Mind of the South* (New York: Knopf, 1941), pp. 34–35.

13. Ibid., p. 45.

14. John Hope Franklin, *The Militant South, 1800–1860* (Cambridge: Harvard University Press, 1956), pp. 13, viii–ix, 34–37.

15. One major exception to this is the work of Clement Eaton. See "The Role of Honor in Southern Society," *Southern Humanities Review* 10 (Supplement 1976): 47–58; *The Growth of the Southern Civilization, 1790–1860* (New York: Harper Brothers, 1961); and *The Mind of the Old South* (Baton Rouge: Louisiana State University Press, 1967).

16. Wyatt-Brown, *Southern Honor,* pp. vii–viii. Also on Southern honor see Ayers, *Vengeance and Justice,* pp. 9–33; and idem, "Honor," in Wilson and Ferris, *Encyclopedia of Southern Culture,* pp. 1483–84. On honor with respect to the law see Charles S. Sydnor, "The Southerner and the Laws," *Journal of Southern History* 6 (February 1940): 3–23. Wyatt-Brown has also written persuasively about the way Southern honor affected political relationships with the North and its role in the South's decision to secede from the Union. In addition to the already-cited works see his *Yankee Saints and Southern Sinners* (Baton Rouge: Louisiana State University Press, 1985); William J. Cooper Jr., *The South and the Politics of Slavery, 1828–1856* (Baton Rouge: Louisiana State University Press, 1978); idem, *Liberty and Slavery: Southern Politics to 1860* (New York: Knopf, 1983); and Kenneth S. Greenberg, *Masters and Statesmen: The Political Culture of American Slavery* (Baltimore: Johns Hopkins University Press, 1985).

17. Dickson Bruce Jr., *Violence and Culture in the Antebellum South* (Austin: University of Texas Press, 1979), pp. 5–7, 72.

18. Grady McWhiney, "The Ethnic Roots of Southern Violence," in *A Master's Due: Essays in Honor of David Herbert Donald,* ed. William J. Cooper Jr., Michael J. Holt, and William McCardell (Baton Rouge: Louisiana State University Press, 1985), pp. 115–16. He develops this theme further in *Cracker Culture: Celtic Ways in the Old South* (Tuscaloosa: University of Alabama Press, 1988). McWhiney also thinks that a study of the South's ethnic origins offers a window into the understanding of Southern military tactics in the Civil War. See McWhiney and Perry Jameson, *Attack and Die: Civil War Tactics and the Southern Heritage* (University: University of Alabama Press, 1982). For other aspects of the Celtic heritage as reflected in Southern culture see Forrest McDonald and McWhiney, "The Antebellum Southern Herdsman: A Reinterpretation," *Journal of Southern History* 41 (May 1975): 147–66; idem, "The South from Self-Sufficiency to Peonage: An Interpretation," *American Historical Review* 85 (December 1980): 1095–1118; idem, "Celtic Origins of Southern Herding Practices," *Journal of Southern History* 51 (May 1985): 165–82; Forrest McDonald and Ellen Shapiro McDonald, "The Ethnic Origin of the American People, 1790," *William and Mary Quarterly* 37 (May 1980): 179–99; and McWhiney, "Celtic South," in Wilson and Ferris, *Encyclopedia of Southern Culture,* pp.

1131–32. Also insightful on an ethnic appraisal of Southern violence is Reed, "Below the Smith and Wesson Line."

19. McWhiney, "Ethnic Roots of Southern Violence," 116n. For a discussion of the way the violent life in Ulster prepared the Scotch-Irish for life in the antebellum South, see James Leyburn, *The Scotch-Irish in America: A Social History* (Chapel Hill: University of North Carolina Press, 1962), pp. 147–48, 228.

20. Richard Maxwell Brown, *No Duty to Retreat: Violence and Values in American History and Society* (New York: Oxford University Press, 1991).

21. David J. Bodenhamer and James W. Ely, eds., *Ambivalent Legacy: A Legal History of the South* (Jackson: University of Mississippi Press, 1984), p. 4.

22. *Pensacola Gazette,* January 14, 1837; *Tallahassee Floridian,* January 14, July 22, 1837; *St. Augustine Florida Herald,* July 15, 1837. *Territory v Benita Blaupen,* 1828, Escambia County Case Files; Escambia County, Minutes of the Superior Court, Book 1, pp. 386, 428. John L. Hopkins to Columbus Drew, June 3, 1852, in *Jacksonville Republican,* quoted in *Tallahassee Florida Sentinel,* June 22, 1852; Orange County, Minutes of the Circuit Court, Book A, p. 58.

23. *Jacksonville Florida News,* October 25, 1856; *State v William Stone,* 1856, Comptroller's Vouchers, Criminal Prosecutions, RG 350, ser. 565, box 1, folder 2, Calhoun County, FSAr. *Marianna Florida Whig,* May 12, June 9, 1849; *Tallahassee Floridian and Journal,* May 19, 1949; *Apalachicola Commercial Advertiser,* May 26, 1849.

24. Leon County, Minutes of the Superior Court, Book 3, pp. 179, 214, 215, 216, 231; *Tallahassee Florida Sentinel,* January 28, February 4, 1842. On escape see *Tallahassee Star of Florida,* February 17, 1842; *Tallahassee Florida Sentinel,* February 18, 1842; *Tallahassee Floridian,* February 19, 1842; *St. Augustine News,* March 5, 1842; *St. Augustine Florida Herald and Southern Democrat,* March 4, 1842; and *Pensacola Gazette,* March 5, 1842. On the execution see *St. Augustine News,* March 12, 1842.

25. *St. Augustine Florida Herald,* April 12, July 15, 1837.

26. *Key West Gazette,* April 26, 1831; *Tallahassee Floridian and Advocate,* December 7, 1830; *Territory v Norman Sherwood,* 1831, Monroe County Case Files; Monroe County, Minutes of the Superior Court, 1830–40, pp. 20–21, 38–39, PKYL.

27. *Pensacola Gazette* quoted in *Tallahassee Floridian and Journal,* November 17, 1860; and *Pensacola Observer* quoted in *Fernandina East Floridian,* November 21, 1860. For Duggan's prosecution and conviction see Escambia County, Minutes of the Circuit Court, Book B, p. 90. Jackson Morton to M. S. Perry, July 17, 1861, Correspondence of Madison Starke Perry and John Milton, RG 101, ser. 577, box 1, folder 3, FSAr.

28. Bruce, *Violence and Culture,* p. 93.

29. *State v Henry Edgerton,* 1853, Gadsden County Case Files; Gadsden County, Minutes of the Circuit Court, Book 1, p. 347.

30. Slocumb was eventually captured, and he was prosecuted in the Walton County Superior Court. *Territory v James C. Slocumb,* 1839, Territorial Auditor, Vouchers, RG 352, ser. 584, box 3, folders 2 and 5, FSAr. Mellon, also captured, was prosecuted in the Escambia County Superior Court. He was found guilty of manslaughter and sentenced to thirty-nine lashes and six months in prison. "Trial of Robert Mellon," *Pensacola Gazette,* May 29, 1841; Escambia County, Minutes of

the Superior Court, Book 4, p. 126; *Territory v Robert Mellon,* 1841, Territorial Auditor, Vouchers, RG 352, ser. 584, box 3, folder 1, FSAr.

31. *State v Benjamin Trippe,* Fall 1852, Comptroller's Vouchers, Criminal Prosecutions, RG 350, ser. 565, box 4, folder 3, Leon County, FSAr; Pardon of Benjamin Trippe, November 18, 1852, Book of Record (Proclamations), RG 156, ser. 13, Book 1, no. 208, no. 218, p. 187, FSAr. For Trippe's trial see Leon County, Minutes of the Circuit Court, Book 5, pp. 476, 500. Brown's pardon came through eight days before Trippe was to be executed. See ibid., p. 500.

32. *Jacksonville Florida News,* October 25, 1856. McKinney was indicted in Holmes County and brought to Marianna for trial. *State v William McKinney,* 1856, Comptroller's Vouchers, Criminal Prosecutions, RG 350, ser. 565, box 5, folder 6, Jackson County, FSAr. He was found guilty of manslaughter in the November 1856 term of the Jackson County Circuit Court. His sentence is unknown. Jackson County, Minutes of the Circuit Court, Book C, p. 679.

33. James Piles to Thomas Brown, November 8, 1849, and Petition to Governor Brown, October 22, 1849, Correspondence of Thomas Brown, RG 101, ser. 755, box 2, folder 8, FSAr.

34. Monroe served fifty-two days of a twelve-month sentence before escaping from the Ocala jail. *Ocala Florida Home Companion,* July 12, 1859; *Fernandina East Floridian,* July 14, 1859; Marion County, Minutes of the Circuit Court, Book B, pp. 546, 560; *State v John Monroe,* Fall Term 1859, Comptroller's Vouchers, Criminal Prosecutions, RG 350, ser. 565, box 4, folder 10, Marion County, FSAr.

35. Daniel R. Hundley, *Social Relations in Our Southern States* (New York: H. B. Price, 1860), pp. 224, 239–40; *State v Antoine Collins,* 1854, Escambia County Case Files; *Pensacola Gazette,* October 1, 1853; *Tallahassee Floridian and Journal,* October 15, 1853. For escape see Proclamation for the Arrest of Antoine Collins by Gov. James Broome, January 5, 1854, Book of Record (Proclamations), RG 156, ser. 13, Book 1, no. 236, p. 226, FSAr.

36. All of the preceding trial testimony comes from *Territory v Cornelius Taylor,* 1845, St. Johns County Case Files. From 1821 to the time of the killing, Taylor was involved in a number of slander trials. For an example see *Cornelius Taylor v Josiah Gates,* 1837, Territorial Court of Appeals Case Files, RG 970, ser. 73, box 12, folders 370 and 371, FSAr; and *Cornelius Taylor v Barlolo Olivarez,* 1837; *Same v Philip Solano,* 1837; *Same v Barlolo Olivarez,* 1838; *Same v Philip Solano,* 1838, all in St. Johns County Case Files. To secure his bond, Taylor gave a conditional bill of sale to the St. Johns Circuit Court for all his property in Florida. *St. Augustine News,* June 28, 1845; *St. Augustine Florida Herald and Southern Democrat,* June 24, 1845; *State v Cornelius Taylor,* 1847, Comptroller's Vouchers, Criminal Prosecutions, RG 350, ser. 565, box 5, folders 4 and 6, Orange and St. Lucie Counties, FSAr. Taylor was found not guilty in June 1846. St. Johns County, Minutes of the Circuit Court, Book A, p. 10.

37. Bruce, *Violence and Culture,* p. 93.

38. *Tallahassee Floridian and Journal,* April 30, 1859; Putnam County, Minutes of the Circuit Court, Book 1, pp. 418, 419.

39. *Cedar Keys Telegraph,* quoted in *Fernandina East Floridian,* June 21, 1860.

40. *Territory v Jessee Holton* [Holloman], 1837, Jefferson County Case Files; Jefferson County, Minutes of the Superior Court, Book 1, pp. 452, 497.

41. Subsequently indicted for assault with intent to kill in the April 1839 term of the Jefferson County Superior Court, Barrett jumped bail and forfeited his recognizance. *Territory v Clement B. Barrett,* 1839, Jefferson County Case Files; Jefferson County, Minutes of the Superior Court, Book 1, pp. 361, 384.

42. *Tallahassee Floridian and Journal,* October 13, 1860; *Fernandina East Floridian,* October 18, 31, November 7, 1860.

43. *Territory v Hugh Duncan,* 1838, Jefferson County Case Files. Duncan was indicted for a felony and lodged in the Jefferson County jail, but he escaped. Jefferson County, Minutes of the Superior Court, Book 1, p. 308; Proclamation for the Arrest of Hugh Duncan and Alek, a Slave, in *Tallahassee Floridian,* July 28, 1838.

44. *Territory v Henry Womble et al.,* 1841, Jefferson County Case Files.

45. Wyatt-Brown, *Southern Honor;* Bruce, *Violence and Culture;* Ayers, *Vengeance and Justice;* Franklin, *The Militant South;* Greenberg, *Masters and Statesmen;* Cooper, *Liberty and Slavery.*

46. *Tallahassee Floridian and Journal,* June 16, 1849; *Jacksonville Florida News,* June 9, 1849. At Burleson's trial for cruelty to a slave, he justified his conduct by claiming that he was trying to extract information regarding a poisoning conspiracy among his slaves. See Petition of Daniel Burleson to the General Assembly, November 18, 1850, Nineteenth-Century Florida State Legislature, RG 915, ser. 887, box 5, folder 3, FSAr. Burleson was found not guilty of the above charge. Marion County, Minutes of the Circuit Court, Book A, pp. 64, 107; *State v Henry, a Slave, Property of Daniel Burleson,* 1850, [arrested for administering poison], Comptroller's Vouchers, Criminal Prosecutions, RG 350, ser. 565, box 4, folder 10, Marion County, FSAr.

47. Meadows soon turned himself in to the Marion County authorities, but Burleson remained at large until he was captured one month later in dense woods near Micanopy. *Jacksonville Florida News,* June 16, 1849; *Tallahassee Floridian and Journal,* June 16, July 7, December 22, 1849. Marion County, Minutes of the Circuit Court, Book A, p. 102; *State v Jessee Meadows,* December 1849, Comptroller's Vouchers, Criminal Prosecutions, RG 350, ser. 565, box 4, folder 10, Marion County, FSAr.

Chapter 6

1. *Pensacola Gazette,* February 11, 1826.

2. *Territory v Joseph Mattair,* 1829, St. Johns County Case Files; Alachua, Columbia, and Hillsborough Counties, Minutes of the Superior Court, 1828–35, pp. 55, 77, PKYL.

3. *St. Augustine Florida Herald,* February 10, 1830.

4. Kermit L. Hall, *The Magic Mirror: Law in American History* (New York: Oxford University Press, 1989), p. 35. Florida's Criminal Code of 1828 provided that "a *feme covert* or married woman acting under the threats, command, or coercion of her husband shall not be found guilty of any crime or misdemeanor not punished by death, but the husband shall be prosecuted as principal and receive the same punishment which otherwise would have been inflicted on the wife, if she had been found guilty; provided it shall appear from at the facts and circumstances of the case, that violent threats, commands, and coercion were used." *Acts and Resolutions of the Legislative Council,* 1828, p. 49.

5. Historians have written extensively about the subordinate status of women

in the antebellum South. See Carol Berkin, "Women's Life," in *Encyclopedia of Southern Culture,* ed. Charles Wilson and William Ferris (Chapel Hill: University of North Carolina Press, 1989), pp. 1519–22; Anne G. Jones, "Belles and Ladies," in ibid., pp. 1527–30; Anne Firor Scott, *The Southern Lady: From Pedestal to Politics, 1830–1860* (Chicago: University of Chicago Press, 1970); William J. Cooper Jr. and Thomas E. Terrill, *The American South: A History* (New York: McGraw-Hill, 1991); Francis Butler Simkins, *A History of the South* (New York: Knopf, 1958); Bertram Wyatt-Brown, *Southern Honor: Ethics and Behavior in the Old South* (New York: Oxford University Press, 1982); Dickson D. Bruce Jr., *Violence and Culture in the Antebellum South* (Austin: University of Texas Press, 1979); Barbara Welter, "The Cult of True Womanhood," *American Quarterly* 18 (Summer 1966): 151–74; and Ronald Hogeland, " 'The Feminine Appendage': Feminine Lifestyles in America, 1820–1860," *Civil War History* 17 (June 1971): 101–14.

6. *Key West Key of the Gulf,* July 14, 1860.

7. On divorce see Jane Turner Censer, " 'Smiling through Her Tears': Ante-Bellum Southern Women and Divorce," *American Journal of Legal History* 25 (January 1981): 24–47; Neal R. Feigenson, "Extraterritorial Recognition of Divorce Decrees in the Nineteenth Century," *American Journal of Legal History* 34 (April 1990): 119–67; Lawrence M. Friedman, *A History of American Law* (New York: Simon and Schuster, 1985), pp. 179–84; and Hall, *The Magic Mirror,* pp. 165–67.

8. *Josephine Gagnet v Louis Gagnet,* 1829, Escambia County Case Files.

9. Petition of Ellen Foster to the Legislative Council, 1829, Territorial Legislative Council, Unicameral, RG 910, ser. 876, box 2, folder 3, FSAr; "An Act for the Relief of Ellen Foster," 1831, manuscript copy, ibid., box 3, folder 1. Petition of Mary Rhymes for Divorce, January 17, 1832, ibid., box 3, folder 4; "An Act for the Relief of Mary Rhymes" was passed over Governor DuVal's veto on February 12, 1832. See *Tallahassee Floridian,* March 13, 1832.

10. John C. Richards to Thomas Brown, May 4, 1850, Correspondence of Thomas Brown, RG 101, ser. 755, box 2, folder 8, FSAr. A number of conflicting views reached Governor Brown's desk. John Sammis, a neighbor, thought the husband guilty of extreme cruelty toward his wife. "I feel it my duty to inform you," Sammis wrote Brown, "that so far as his petition charges his wife with misconduct, it is untrue. She is a lady far too good for him. He had degraded himself by low intimacy with his servants and did illtreat his wife." John Sammis to Thomas Brown, February 22, 1850, ibid. Solicitor J. P. Sanderson agreed: "No gentleman of standing will sign Richards' petition. . . . If he was tried again by the same jury several of them have told me personally they would imprison him for three months." J. P. Sanderson to Thomas Brown, February 19, 1850, ibid.

11. *Apalachicola Commercial Advertiser,* May 24, 1843.

12. See *St. Augustine Florida Herald and Southern Democrat,* May 6, June 17, 1842; *St. Augustine News,* June 13, 1842; and Alachua, Hernando, and Hillsborough Counties, Minutes of the Superior Court, 1838–43, pp. 155–58, 170–74, 190–91, 199–201. For Goodman see *Tallahassee Florida Watchman,* September 8, 1838; and *Tallahassee Floridian,* June 2, 1838. For Crawford see *State v William Crawford,* 1852, Comptroller's Vouchers, Criminal Prosecutions, RG 350, ser. 565, box 3, folder 3, Hernando County, FSAr.

13. Proclamation for the Arrest of William J. C. Rogers, August 4, 1856, Book

of Record (Proclamations), RG 156, ser. 13, Book 1, no. 280, p. 267, FSAr; *Jacksonville Florida News,* August 9, 1856. See also *State v William J. C. Rogers,* Comptroller's Vouchers, Criminal Prosecutions, RG 350, ser. 565, box 4, folder 10, Marion County, FSAr; Marion County, Minutes of the Circuit Court, Book B, pp. 129, 139; and Reduction of Jail Sentence and Remission of Fine of William J. C. Rogers, April 9, 1857, Book of Record (Proclamations), RG 156, ser. 13, Book 1, no. 296, p. 285, FSAr.

14. *State v Eliza Goldshier and Daniel Malone,* 1850, Comptroller's Vouchers, Criminal Prosecutions, RG 350, ser. 565, box 5, folder 8, Santa Rosa County, FSAr; *Tallahassee Floridian and Journal,* June 15, 1850.

15. Proclamation for the Arrest of Henry Jourardin, August 31, 1842, Proclamation of Richard Keith Call, Correspondence of the Governors, Letterbooks, RG 101, ser. 32, vol. 1, n.p., FSAr; *Pensacola Gazette,* September 10, 1842; *Tallahassee Star of Florida,* September 1, 1842; *Apalachicola Florida Journal,* September 23, 1842.

16. Joachim Paracune testified before a coroner's inquest that he had seen Crail "frequently beat her with clubs." Another witness declared that Crail always beat Walker "with a board or any other thing he could get hold of." See *Territory v Andrew Crail,* 1829, Escambia County Case Files; Escambia County, Minutes of the Superior Court, Book 1, pp. 419, 421, 422; *Pensacola Gazette,* December 2, 1828, March 10, 1829; *St. Augustine Florida Herald and Southern Democrat,* April 8, 1829; and *Tallahassee Florida Advocate,* March 21, 1829.

17. *State v James O'Conner,* 1859, Jackson County Case Files.

18. *Tallahassee Florida Sentinel,* May 16, 1843.

19. *State v Rachel Drew,* 1846, Jefferson County Case Files; Jefferson County, Minutes of the Circuit Court, Order Book A, pp. 109, 115.

20. Proclamation of John Eaton, April 4, 1835, in Clarence E. Carter, ed., *Territorial Papers of the United States,* 26 vols. (Washington, D.C.: U.S. Government Printing Office, 1934–62), 25:160.

21. Wyatt-Brown, *Southern Honor,* p. 306. See also Robert M. Ireland, "Insanity and the Unwritten Law," *American Journal of Legal History* 32 (April 1988): 157–72; and idem, "The Libertine Must Die: Sexual Dishonor and the Unwritten Law in the Nineteenth-Century United States," *Journal of Social History* 23 (Fall 1989): 27–43.

22. *Key West Register and Commercial Advertiser,* May 28, 1829. *Tallahassee Florida Advocate,* July 11, 1829; *Magnolia Advertiser,* June 26, 1829; *Pensacola Gazette,* July 21, 1829.

23. *Key West Register and Commercial Advertiser,* February 12, 1829; *Tallahassee Floridian and Advocate,* March 14, 1829.

24. *Key West Register and Commercial Advertiser,* September 3, 1829.

25. Ibid.

26. Quoted in ibid., July 23, 1829.

27. Territorial Legislative Council, Unicameral, Session Documents, RG 910, ser. 876, box 2, folder 8, FSAr; Hackley Diary, November 11, 1830, February 10, 18, April 14, 1831, MSL.

28. Henry M. Brackenridge to Caroline Brackenridge, July 27, 1827, Brackenridge Papers, PL.

29. *Pensacola Gazette,* May 16, November 7, 1828; Leon County, Minutes of the Superior Court, Book 1, pp. 39, 60, 62, 75, 85, 101–7, 111.

30. *Jacksonville Courier,* February 25, 1835; *Tallahassee Floridian,* March 28, 1835.

31. *State v David M. Scott,* 1850, Jefferson County Case Files; Jefferson County, Minutes of the Circuit Court, Order Book A, p. 313; Proclamation for the Arrest of David Scott, October 3, 1850, Book of Record (Proclamations), RG 156, ser. 13, Book 1, no. 145, p. 124, FSAr; *Tallahassee Florida Sentinel,* October 8, 1850; *Tallahassee Floridian and Journal,* October 5, 1850.

32. *Tampa Florida Peninsular,* February 27, 1858; *Ocala Florida Home Companion,* March 9, 1858; *Tallahassee Floridian and Journal,* March 6, 1858.

33. John W. Roberts to T. W. Brevard, August 29, 1859, Comptroller's Vouchers, Post Mortem Examinations, RG 350, ser. 565, box 7, folder 3, Hillsborough County, FSAr. See also Coroner's Inquest over the Body of George M. Goodwin, August 25, 1859, ibid.

34. *Fernandina East Floridian,* November 24, 1859. Buckley was hanged on December 16, 1859. Ibid., January 5, 1860; J. M. Hayman to T. W. Brevard, December 29, 1859, State Comptroller Correspondence, RG 350, ser. 554, box 2, folder 5, FSAr.

35. *Newport Wakulla Times,* February 9, 1859; *State v Morris Simms,* 1859, Jackson County Case Files; *Tallahassee Floridian and Journal,* December 6, 1856; *State v G. B. Dixon,* 1856, Comptroller's Vouchers, Criminal Prosecutions, RG 350, ser. 565, box 4, folder 8, Madison County, FSAr.

Chapter 7

1. *Territory v Enoch Hoye,* 1828, Escambia County Case Files; Escambia County, Minutes of the Superior Court, Book 1, pp. 347–49; *Pensacola Gazette,* May 9, 16, 1828.

2. Leslie A. Thompson, *A Manual or Digest of the Statute Law of the State of Florida, of the General and Public Character, In Florida at the End of the Second Session of the General Assembly of the State, on the Sixth Day of January, 1847* (Boston: Charles C. Little and James Brown, 1848), pp. 491–93; John P. Duval, *Compilation of the Public Acts of the Legislative Council of the Territory of Florida Passed Prior to 1840* (Tallahassee: Samuel S. Sibley, 1839), pp. 114–18.

3. See Michael S. Hindus, *Prison and Plantation: Crime, Justice, and Authority in Massachusetts and South Carolina, 1767–1878* (Chapel Hill: University of North Carolina Press, 1980); Edward L. Ayers, *Vengeance and Justice: Crime and Punishment in the Nineteenth-Century American South* (New York: Oxford University Press, 1984); Jack Kenny Williams, *Vogues in Villainy: Crime and Retribution in Antebellum South Carolina* (Columbia: University of South Carolina Press, 1959); and Bertram Wyatt-Brown, "Community, Class, and Snopesian Crime: Local Justice in the Old South," in *Class, Conflict, and Consensus: Antebellum Southern Community Studies,* ed. Orville Vernon Burton and Robert C. McMath Jr. (Westport, Conn.: Greenwood Press, 1982), pp. 173–206.

4. W. D. Barnes to John Milton, October 7, 1861, Correspondence of Madison Starke Perry and John Milton, RG 101, ser. 577, box 1, folder 5, FSAr.

5. *Territory v John Thompson,* 1829, Territorial Auditor, Vouchers, Alachua County, RG 352, ser. 584, box 1, folder 4, FSAr; Alachua, Columbia, and Hillsborough Counties, Minutes of the Superior Court, 1828–35, p. 16, PKYL.

6. *Tallahassee Floridian,* February 2, 1839.

7. Ibid., January 28, 1837, May 17, 1834.

8. *St. Augustine Florida Herald and Southern Democrat,* December 12, 1842; *St. Augustine News,* January 12, 1842, October 8, 1841.

9. *Tallahassee Floridian and Journal,* November 3, 1860; *Pensacola Gazette,* May 11, 1850; *Tallahassee Floridian,* May 20, 1848.

10. *Tallahassee Floridian,* May 17, 1851.

11. *Pensacola Gazette,* June 10, 1828.

12. *Tallahassee Star of Florida,* June 28, 1844; *St. Augustine News,* July 16, 1841; *Tallahassee Floridian,* January 17, 1835.

13. *State v George Walton,* 1846, Escambia County Case Files; Escambia County, Minutes of the Circuit Court, Book A, n.p.; Carraway Smith to Simon Towle, April 20, 1848, and Eben Dorr to Simon Towle, May 4, 1848, State Comptroller Correspondence, RG 350, ser. 554, box 1, folder 3, FSAr; *Tallahassee Southern Journal,* March 10, 1846; *Pensacola Gazette,* February 21, 1846.

14. *Pensacola Gazette,* August 25, 1828.

15. John Hammond Moore, "A South Carolina Lawyer Visits St. Augustine, 1837," *Florida Historical Quarterly* 43 (April 1965): 372–73; see also *St. Augustine Florida Herald,* April 5, 12, 1837.

16. *Tallahassee Star of Florida,* March 29, 1844; *Apalachicola Commercial Advertiser,* April 13, 1844.

17. *Ocala Florida Home Companion,* April 6, 1858; *Tampa Florida Peninsular,* March 29, 1858; *Fernandina Florida News,* March 31, 1858.

18. *St. Augustine News,* October 15, 22, 1842, March 25, 1843.

19. *St. Augustine Florida Herald and Southern Democrat,* February 22, 1843, December 10, 1841; *St. Augustine News,* December 11, 1841.

20. *Jacksonville Florida News,* August 27, 1853.

21. *Pensacola Gazette,* March 5, April 9, 16, 1853; *State v Samuel Piper,* 1853, Escambia County Case Files.

22. Ives Journal, October 27–November 14, 1860, pp. 59–62, SLF.

23. *Tampa Florida Peninsular,* April 24, 1858, and ibid. quoted in *Ocala Florida Home Companion,* May 1, 1858.

24. *Tallahassee Florida Sentinel,* October 3, 1843.

25. *Cedar Keys Telegraph,* July 28, 1860; *St. Augustine Examiner,* August 4, 1860; *Fernandina East Floridian,* July 26, 1860.

26. *Tallahassee Florida Sentinel,* November 5, 1850.

27. *Fernandina East Floridian,* September 6, 1860.

28. Affidavit of Thomas Carrol, January 16, 1845, in *United States v S. P. Fletcher,* 1845, Escambia County Case Files.

29. Postmaster General to William H. Hunt, November 30, 1827, in Clarence E. Carter, ed., *Territorial Papers of the United States,* 26 vols. (Washington, D.C.: U.S. Government Printing Office, 1934–62), 23:940. Hutto was captured, brought to Pensacola, convicted, and sentenced to two years in jail. See *Martin Hutto v Ward and Pittman,* 1828, Escambia County Case Files; Escambia County, Minutes of the

Superior Court, Book 1, pp. 343, 347; *Territory v Martin Hutto,* 1828, Escambia County Case Files; *Pensacola Gazette,* September 7, 1827, January 25, May 9, 23, October 14, November 7, 1828; *Pensacola Florida Argus,* November 11, 1828; Postmaster General to Benjamin Wright, April 12, 1828, in Carter, *Territorial Papers,* 23:1062; and Indictment and Judgment against Martin Hutto, May 1828, in ibid., 24:17–20.

30. Wyatt-Brown, "Community, Class, and Snopesian Crime," p. 176. Wyatt-Brown has suggested that arson and petty thievery, unless they got out of hand, were tolerated: "Class crimes were misdeeds of anonymity and insignificance. By demonstrating the willfulness and disorderliness of the lower ranks, they helped to separate the worthy from the demeaned. They upheld the social order; they did not hurt it." Ibid., p. 177.

31. Thompson, *Digest,* p. 491.

32. "An Act to Amend the Criminal Laws of Force in This State," *Acts and Resolutions of the General Assembly,* 1847, pp. 10–11.

33. *Pensacola Gazette,* May 7, 1825.

34. Ibid., February 20, 1841.

35. *Tallahassee Floridian and Journal,* April 15, 1854.

36. *Jacksonville Florida News,* March 7, 1857.

37. Ibid., May 29, 1852.

38. *Tallahassee Florida Sentinel,* April 22, 1842; *Apalachicola Florida Journal,* November 10, 1842.

39. *Tallahassee Floridian and Journal,* November 17, 1849. For Jackson County see *Marianna Florida Whig,* December 2, 1848; *Tallahassee Floridian,* December 9, 1848; and *Jacksonville Florida Republican,* December 14, 1848. For Columbia County see *Fernandina East Floridian,* September 27, 1860. For Monroe County see *Tallahassee Florida Sentinel,* February 10, 1843.

40. For slaves and arson see Kenneth Stampp, *The Peculiar Institution: Slavery in the Antebellum South* (New York: Vintage, 1956), pp. 127–28; Eugene D. Genovese, *Roll, Jordan, Roll: The World the Slaves Made* (New York: Vintage, 1976), pp. 613–15; Philip J. Schwarz, *Twice Condemned: Slaves and the Criminal Laws of Virginia, 1705–1865* (Baton Rouge: Louisiana State University Press, 1988), pp. 115–18, 210–14; Daniel Flanigan, "The Criminal Law of Slavery and Freedom, 1800–1868" (Ph.D. diss., Rice University, 1973), p. 48.

41. *Tallahassee Florida Sentinel,* March 27, 1849.

42. *State v Rachel, a Slave,* 1849, Escambia County Case Files; Escambia County, Minutes of the Circuit Court, Book A, June Term 1849, n.p.; see also *State v Rachel, a Slave,* 1849, Comptroller's Vouchers, Criminal Prosecutions, RG 350, ser. 565, box 2, folder 2, FSAr.

43. *State v Simon, a Slave,* 1853, Escambia County Case Files; Escambia County, Minutes of the Circuit Court, Book A, February 1853, n.p.; *Tallahassee Floridian and Journal,* August 13, 1853. See also *Simon, a Slave, Plaintiff in Error v The State of Florida,* Term at Marianna, 1853, in *Reports of the Cases Argued and Adjudged in the Supreme Court of Florida,* 9 vols. (Tallahassee: 1845–61), 5:285–301. The case was "abated by the death of the defendant." *State v Simon, a Slave,* June Term 1853, Comptroller's Vouchers, Criminal Prosecutions, RG 350, ser. 565, box 2, folder 3, Escambia County, FSAr.

44. *Pensacola Gazette*, July 27, 1822.

45. Thompson, *Digest*, p. 492. On the Walker case see Jonathan Walker, *Trial and Imprisonment of Jonathan Walker, at Pensacola, Florida, for Aiding Slaves to Escape from Bondage* (1848; reprint, Gainesville: University of Florida Press, 1974).

46. *Tallahassee Floridian*, October 3, 10, 1846; *Jacksonville Florida News*, October 16, 23, 1846.

47. On Stahl see Gadsden County, Minutes of the Circuit Court, Book 1, pp. 232, 244, 267; and Remission of Death Sentence by Thomas Brown, April 26, 1852, Book of Record (Proclamations), RG 156, ser. 13, Book 1, no. 192, p. 171, FSAr. On Evans see Jefferson County, Minutes of the Circuit Court, Book A, pp. 286, 294, 306, 311, 313; *State v Redding Evans*, 1850, Jefferson County Case Files; and Remission of Death Sentence by Thomas Brown, Book of Record (Proclamations), RG 156, ser. 13, Book 1, no. 154, p. 134, FSAr.

48. *Tallahassee Floridian*, June 8, 1839; *Pensacola Gazette*, June 8, 1839.

49. *Pensacola Gazette*, July 14, 1838, August 14, 1841, June 30, 1838.

50. Russell Garvin, "The Free Negro in Florida before the Civil War," *Florida Historical Quarterly* 46 (July 1967): 15–17.

51. *Jacksonville Weekly Republican*, March 24, 1858.

52. *Key West Enquirer*, January 3, 1835.

53. *Tallahassee Floridian and Journal*, December 4, 1852; *Tallahassee Florida Sentinel*, December 7, 1852.

54. *Tallahassee Florida Sentinel*, April 27, June 1, 1852.

55. *Tallahassee Floridian*, April 4, 1840.

56. *Tallahassee Floridian and Journal*, July 7, 1849.

57. *State v Richard Jones*, n.d., Comptroller's Vouchers, Criminal Prosecutions, RG 350, ser. 565, box 4, folder 3, Leon County, FSAr.

58. *Tallahassee Florida Sentinel*, May 14, 1850.

59. *Tallahassee Floridian*, August 8, 1846.

60. Jackson County, Minutes of the Circuit Court, Book C, pp. 227, 232, 233; *State v Martin Davis*, 1853, Jackson County Case Files.

Chapter 8

1. Lawrence M. Friedman, *Crime and Punishment in American History* (New York: Basic Books, 1993), p. 126.

2. "Crimes against Religion, Chastity, Morality, and Decency" included disturbing a religious worship, employing a servant or keeping a store open on the Sabbath, bigamy, incest, adultery and fornication, open lewdness, keeping a lewd house, keeping a gaming house or table, sodomy, and vagrancy. "Offenses against the Public Peace" included riot and affray, libel, placarding or posting one as a coward, and carrying arms secretly. "Offenses against Public Justice" included perjury, bribing a public officer, falsifying any public record, malpractice of jailers, mutilation of documents by an officer, resisting execution of process, rescue, aiding a prisoner to escape from jail, aiding escape from custody, concealing felons, conspiracy to prosecute, barratry, malpractice of justice, threatening letters, and extortion. "Offenses against Trade, Public Highways, and Navigation" included false weights and measures, fraudulent packing, obstructing a public road, and obstruct-

ing a navigable stream. "Malicious and Fraudulent Mischief" crimes were listed as destroying beacons or buoys, firing stacks of fodder, firing woods, burning fences, destroying dams, wounding animals, destroying vessels, driving cattle from a range, and altering landmarks. "Offenses Relative to Slaves and Other Persons of Color" included suffering a slave to trade as free, allowing a slave to hire his own time, providing slaves with false papers, buying from a slave, trading with slaves, selling firearms to slaves, permitting a slave to use firearms, selling liquor to a slave, selling poison to a slave, participating with slaves at an unlawful assembly, permitting a slave to use or operate a ferry, removing slaves held for life of holder, keeping slaves alone on a plantation, and intermarriage or adultery with a slave. See Leslie A. Thompson, *A Manual or Digest of the Statute Law of the State of Florida, of a General and Public Character, in Force at the End of the Second Session of the General Assembly of the State, on the Sixth Day of January 1847* (Boston: Charles C. Little and James Brown, 1848), pp. 494–512.

3. On the concern of order over the rights of the accused see David L. Bodenhamer, "Law and Disorder on the Early Frontier: Marion County, Indiana, 1823–1850," *Western Historical Quarterly* 10 (July 1979): 323–36. The same author contends that in colonial America the "good order of society took precedence over the liberty of the individual." See *Fair Trial: Rights of the Accused in American History* (New York: Oxford University Press, 1992), p. 28. Legal scholar Herbert L. Packer has developed two useful models for the prosecution of crimes in certain jurisdictions. His crime control model is applicable to a jurisdiction that is most concerned with maintaining public order. Prosecution of crimes under this model is more concerned with the suppression of crime than it is with the procedural rights of the accused. The antithesis of this model is the due process model, which is most concerned with protecting the procedural rights of the accused against the coercive power of the state. See *The Limits of Criminal Sanction* (Stanford: Stanford University Press, 1968), pp. 149–246.

4. Friedman, *Crime and Punishment,* p. 13.

5. Thompson, *Digest,* pp. 499–500.

6. *State v Clement Moseley,* 1861, Clay County Case Files; Clay County, Minutes of the Circuit Court, Book 1, p. 34.

7. Thompson, *Digest,* pp. 499–500.

8. Alachua, Columbia, and Hillsborough Counties, Minutes of the Superior Court, 1828–35, pp. 6, 7, 18–19, PKYL.

9. Alachua and Levy Counties, Minutes of the Circuit Court, 1850–57, p. 46, PKYL.

10. Thompson, *Digest,* p. 500.

11. Edward L. Ayers, *Vengeance and Justice: Crime and Punishment in the Nineteenth-Century American South* (New York: Oxford University Press, 1984), p. 117.

12. Friedman, *Crime and Punishment,* pp. 127, 130–31.

13. Alachua and Levy Counties, Minutes of the Circuit Court, 1850–57, pp. 53, 62, 87, PKYL; U.S. Manuscript Census, Population, 1850, Alachua County.

14. Thompson, *Digest,* p. 500.

15. *Territory v Joseph Alton* (three indictments), 1838, Escambia County Case Files. Alton's disorderly house indictment disappeared from the docket. Escambia County, Minutes of the Superior Court, Book 4, pp. 4, 15, 16.

16. *Key West Register and Commercial Advertiser,* July 2, 1929.

17. *State v John Long,* 1857, Jackson County Case Files; Jackson County, Minutes of the Circuit Court, Book D, pp. 21, 45, 80.

18. Escambia County, Minutes of the Circuit Court, Book B, p. 19. *State v Michael McCloskey, William Paisley, Robert Lynn, and William Brown,* 1856, Escambia County Case Files; *State v Same,* 1856, Comptroller's Vouchers, Criminal Prosecutions, RG 350, ser. 565, box 2, folder 4, Escambia County, FSAr.

19. Thompson, *Digest,* p. 499.

20. *Territory v Joseph Kinsey and William Stuart,* 1845, Jefferson County Case Files. No record exists of their fate.

21. *Tallahassee Florida Sentinel,* April 22, 1851.

22. George Pearce, John Curry, William Love, Jeremiah Roberts, William Archer, Jacob Solomon, Elizabeth Roberts, and Melissa Roberts were indicted in the Monroe County Circuit Court. Only Jeremiah Roberts was convicted. Monroe County, Minutes of the Superior and Circuit Court, 1840–70, Book A, n.p.

23. Remission of Fine for Hugh McRae, James Little, Edward Little and William McLeod, February, 15, 1844, Territorial Auditor, Vouchers, RG 352, ser. 584, box 3, folder 6, FSAr.

24. *Territory v Shaw and F. Kallinskin,* 1843, Escambia County Case Files.

25. Lester B. Shippee, ed., *Bishop Whipple's Southern Diary, 1843–1844* (Minneapolis: University of Minnesota Press, 1937), p. 42.

26. *Tallahassee Floridian and Journal,* January 26, 1850.

27. *Pensacola Gazette,* February 23, 1839; *Apalachicola Gazette,* February 23, 1839; *St. Augustine News,* March 16, 1839; *Tallahassee Floridian,* April 20, 1839.

28. *Fernandina News,* April 2, 1858; *Tampa Florida Peninsular,* May 1, 1858.

29. *Apalachicola Florida Journal,* February 4, 1843.

30. *Tallahassee Floridian,* July 22, 1837.

31. *St. Augustine Florida Herald,* October 11, 1832, February 7, 1833.

32. *Tallahassee Floridian,* March 26, 1836.

33. *Tallahassee Star of Florida,* January 5, 1843; *Tallahassee Sentinel,* October 21, 1842.

34. *Jacksonville Florida News,* July 22, 1848.

35. *Pensacola West Florida Times,* March 17, 1857.

36. *St. Augustine News,* February 5, 1841.

37. *Pensacola Gazette,* September 30, 1828.

38. On the popularity of gambling in the South versus the North see Grady McWhiney, "Gambling," in *Encyclopedia of Southern Culture,* ed. Charles Reagan Wilson and William Ferris (Chapel Hill: University of North Carolina Press, 1989), pp. 1224–25. Also on gambling in the South see Bertram Wyatt-Brown, *Southern Honor: Ethics and Behavior in the Old South* (New York: Oxford University Press, 1982), pp. 399–450; and Joan Cashin, *A Family Venture: Men and Women on the Southern Frontier* (New York: Oxford University Press, 1991), pp. 103–4. On gambling and the frontier experience see John Findlay, *People of Chance: Gambling in American Society from Jamestown to Las Vegas* (New York: Oxford University Press, 1986), p. 4; and Philip D. Jordan, *Frontier Law and Order: Ten Essays* (Lincoln: University of Nebraska Press, 1970), pp. 43–61.

39. Findlay, *People of Chance,* p. 52.

40. Timothy Breen, "Horses and Gentlemen: The Cultural Significance of Gambling among the Gentry of Virginia," *William and Mary Quarterly* 34 (April 1977): 239–57; Findlay, *People of Chance*, pp. 22–23. For another excellent discussion of the class nature of gambling see Patricia Click, "The Ruling Passion: Gambling and Sport in Antebellum Baltimore, Norfolk, and Richmond," *Virginia Cavalcade* 39 (Autumn 1989): 62–68, and 39 (Winter 1990): 100–104; and McWhiney, "Gambling," p. 1224.

41. De Tocqueville quoted in Findlay, *People of Chance*, p. 3.

42. Thompson, *Digest*, pp. 501.

43. Ibid.

44. "An Ordinance to Prevent Gambling in the City of Apalachicola," *Apalachicola Gazette*, March 9, 1839.

45. *Tallahassee Floridian*, May 26, 1838.

46. *Apalachicola Gazette*, November 29, 1837.

47. Preston Journal, July 7, 1829, PL.

48. *Pensacola Gazette*, May 19, 1838.

49. Resolution of the Board of Alderman of the City of Pensacola, December 28, 1841, Territorial Legislative Council, Bicameral, RG 910, ser. 877, box 2, folder 3, FSAr.

50. *Tallahassee Floridian*, August 14, December 29, 1832, July 26, 1834; *St. Joseph Times*, September 19, 1840, February 20, 1841. See also Dorothy Dodd, "Horse Racing in Middle Florida, 1830–43," *Apalachee* 3 (1948–50): 20–29.

51. *Tallahassee Florida Sentinel*, May 16, 1843; *Tallahassee Star of Florida*, May 11, 1843.

52. *Tallahassee Floridian and Advocate*, March 13, 1832; *Apalachicola Commercial Advertiser*, October 21, 1843.

53. *State v John Gillison*, Monroe County Case Files; *State v Edward Fox*, 1849, Jefferson County Case Files. Fox was indicted in the October 1849 term of court, but in the next term the solicitor chose not to pursue the case. See Jefferson County, Minutes of the Circuit Court, Book A, pp. 276, 285.

54. Karl H. Grismer, *Tampa: A History of the City of Tampa and the Tampa Bay Region of Florida* (St. Petersburg: St. Petersburg Printing Co., 1950), pp. 125–26.

55. Herbert Asbury, *Suckers Progress: An Informal History of Gambling in America from the Colonies to Canfield* (New York: Dodd, Mead, 1938), pp. 3–19. Also on faro see David R. Johnson, *American Law Enforcement: A History* (Arlington Heights, Ill.: Forum Press, 1981), p. 50; Carl Sifakis, *The Encyclopedia of Gambling* (New York: Facts on File, 1990), pp. 113–15; Jonathan Green, *Gambling Exposed: A Full Exposition of All the Various Arts, Mysteries, and Miseries of Gambling by a Reformed Gambler* (1857; reprint, Montclair, N.J.: Patterson Smith, 1973), pp. 38–39, 110–46, 159–62; and John P. Quinn, *Gambling and Gambling Devices* (1912; reprint, Montclair, N.J.: Patterson Smith, 1969), pp. 44–54.

56. *Territory v Jefferson Sanders*, 1835, Jefferson County Case Files. Sanders's case was dismissed in 1838. See Jefferson County, Minutes of the Superior Court, Book 1, pp. 192, 322. Of the other twelve, eight were dismissed, two were found guilty and fined $10 and $45, one was found not guilty, and one died before his trial. See ibid., pp. 192, 193, 239, 240, 278, 279, 322.

57. *Territory v Joseph Williams, Richard C. Parish, James Hall, Albert Dozier, and Wil-*

liam Clark, 1832, Jefferson County Case Files; Jefferson County, Minutes of the Superior Court, Book 1, pp. 46, 48.

58. *Tallahassee Floridian and Journal,* November 6, 1858.

59. Leon County, Minutes of the Superior Court, Book 3, pp. 66–210. For prosecutions in 1854 see Leon County, Minutes of the Circuit Court, Book 5, pp. 611–33, and Book 6, n.p.

60. *Tallahassee Star of Florida,* March 11, 1843; *Tallahassee Florida Sentinel,* May 16, 1843.

61. Alachua and Levy Counties, Minutes of the Circuit Court, 1850–57, pp. 117–84, PKYL.

62. Hillsborough County, Minutes of the Circuit Court, 1846–54, pp. 379–89, 395–400.

63. *Tallahassee Floridian and Advocate,* August 17, 1831.

64. For Suchet see *Territory v Peter Suchet,* 1838, Escambia County Case Files; Escambia County, Minutes of the Superior Court, Book 3, p. 184. For Collins see *Territory v Antoine Collins,* 1826, Escambia County Case Files; Escambia County, Minutes of the Superior Court, Book 1, pp. 298, 342.

65. *State v Henry Prior, a Negro Slave,* 1852, Escambia County Case Files; Proclamation for the Arrest of Henry Prior, July 10, 1852, Book of Record (Proclamations), RG 156, ser. 13, Book 1, no. 200, p. 179, FSAr; *Pensacola Gazette,* October 16, 1852; *State v Henry Prior,* 1852, Comptroller's Vouchers, Criminal Prosecutions, RG 350, ser. 565, box 2, folder 3, Escambia County, FSAr; Escambia County, Minutes of the Circuit Court, October 1852, Book A, n.p.

66. *St. Augustine Florida Herald and Southern Democrat,* July 11, 1839; *Baltimore (Maryland) Niles Register,* June 22, 1839, p. 265; Alachua, Hernando, and Hillsborough Counties, Minutes of the Superior Court, 1838–43, p. 27.

Chapter 9

1. The historiography of the criminal law of slavery is voluminous, and it is not my purpose to plunge into an extended discussion of the issue here. There are, however, certain studies that should be cited, along with their points of view. Ulrich Bonnell Phillips contends that slave statutes, harsh as they appear, were seldom enforced with rigor. They "describe a hypothetical regime, not an actual one." See *American Negro Slavery* (New York: Appleton and Co., 1918), p. 516. See also pp. 489–56. On slave crime see pp. 454–88. Eugene D. Genovese contends that the law served a "hegemonic function" and was invoked to strengthen the ascendancy of the master class. For Genovese the law seldom functioned efficiently and in the end strengthened the paternalistic nature of slavery. See *Roll, Jordan, Roll: The World the Slaves Made* (New York: Vintage, 1976), pp. 25–49. On slave crime see pp. 599–617. Kenneth Stampp views the law of slavery as a rigid form of race control designed to protect property and ensure the total subjugation of blacks to the will of whites. See *The Peculiar Institution: Slavery in the Antebellum South* (New York: Vintage, 1956), pp. 192–236. On slave crime see pp. 124–32. Also on slavery and the law see Stanley M. Elkins, *Slavery: A Problem in American Institutional and Intellectual Life* (Chicago: University of Chicago Press, 1976), pp. 27–81. Robert William Fogel and Stanley L. Engerman contend that the law was "dualistic" in nature: "Within fairly

wide limits the state, in effect, turned the definition of the codes of legal behavior of slaves, and of the punishment for infractions of these codes over to the planter. . . . The importance of the dual structure of the antebellum South is that the latitude which the state yielded to the planter was quite wide. For most slaves it was the law of the plantation, not of the state, that was relevant. Only a small proportion of the slaves ever had to deal with the law enforcement mechanism of the state. Their daily lives were governed by plantation law." See *Time on the Cross: The Economics of American Negro Slavery* (Boston: Little, Brown, 1974), pp. 128–29. Ira Berlin views laws against blacks as a readily used vehicle for intimidation and demoralization. See *Slaves without Masters: The Free Negro in the Antebellum South* (New York: Pantheon, 1974), pp. 327–40. Perhaps the most important recent work to appear on slave crime, which uses statutes, surviving court records, and extensive use of statistical analysis, is Philip J. Schwarz, *Twice Condemned: Slaves and the Criminal Laws of Virginia, 1705–1865* (Baton Rouge: Louisiana State University Press, 1988). See also Edward L. Ayers, *Vengeance and Justice: Crime and Punishment in the Nineteenth-Century American South* (New York: Oxford University Press, 1984), pp. 106–40; and Michael S. Hindus, *Prison and Plantation: Crime, Justice, and Authority in Massachusetts and South Carolina, 1767–1878* (Chapel Hill: University of North Carolina Press, 1980), pp. 125–62. On blacks and the law see Andrew Fede, *People without Rights: An Interpretation of the Fundamentals of the Law of Slavery in the United States* (New York: Garland, 1992); Mark Tushnet, *The American Law of Slavery, 1810–1860: Considerations of Humanity and Interest* (Princeton: Princeton University Press, 1981); Daniel Flanigan, "The Criminal Law of Slavery and Freedom, 1800–1868" (Ph.D. diss., Rice University, 1973); Robert B. Shaw, *A Legal History of Slavery in the United States* (Potsdam, N.Y.: Northern Press, 1991); Clement Eaton, *The Growth of the Southern Civilization, 1790–1860* (New York: Harper, 1961), pp. 76–97; John Hope Franklin, *From Slavery to Freedom: A History of Negro Americans* (New York: Knopf, 1967), pp. 187–90; Leonard Curry, *The Free Black in Urban America, 1800–1850: Shadows of a Dream* (Chicago: University of Chicago Press, 1981), pp. 112–19; Randall Miller and John Smith, eds. *Dictionary of Afro-American Slavery* (Westport, Conn.: Greenwood Press, 1988), pp. 162, 393; and William J. Cooper Jr. and Thomas E. Terrill, *The American South: A History* (New York: McGraw-Hill, 1991), pp. 208–10. State and local studies have dealt with the crime and punishment of slaves. See James B. Sellers, *Slavery in Alabama* (Tuscaloosa: University of Alabama Press, 1964), pp. 215–65; and Charles S. Sydnor, *Slavery in Mississippi* (Baton Rouge: Louisiana State University Press, 1966), pp. 84–85, 91–92, 107–8. Several excellent works dealing with the history of American law have explored the subject. See Kermit L. Hall, *The Magic Mirror: Law in American History* (New York: Oxford University Press, 1989), pp. 129–42; Lawrence M. Friedman, *A History of American Law* (New York: Simon and Schuster, 1985), pp. 192–201; David J. Bodenhamer and James W. Ely Jr., eds., *Ambivalent Legacy: A Legal History of the South* (Jackson: University of Mississippi Press, 1984); and David J. Bodenhamer, *Fair Trial: Rights of the Accused in American History* (New York: Oxford University Press, 1992), pp. 64–66.

2. The exception to this is Daniel L. Schafer, " 'A Class of People Neither Freemen Nor Slaves': From Spanish to American Race Relations in Florida, 1821–1861," *Journal of Social History* 26 (Spring 1993): 587–609. A number of works deal with slavery and the law in Florida. See Julia Floyd Smith, *Slavery and Plantation Growth*

in Antebellum Florida, 1821–1860 (Gainesville: University of Florida Press, 1973); Jerrell H. Shofner, *History of Jefferson County* (Tallahassee: Sentry Press, 1976); idem, *Jackson County, Florida: A History* (Marianna: Jackson County Heritage Association, 1985); and Clifton Paisley, *The Red Hills of Florida, 1528–1865* (Tuscaloosa: University of Alabama Press, 1989), pp. 176–80. Several articles have dealt with various aspects of slavery and law. See Canter Brown Jr., "Race Relations in Territorial Florida, 1821–1845," *Florida Historical Quarterly* 73 (January 1995): 287–307; Joseph Conan Thompson, "Toward a More Humane Oppression: Florida's Slave Codes, 1821–1861," *Florida Historical Quarterly* 71 (January 1993): 324–38; Thelma Bates, "The Legal Status of the Negro in Florida," *Florida Historical Quarterly* 6 (January 1928): 159–81; Edwin L. Williams, "Negro Slavery in Florida," *Florida Historical Quarterly* 27 (October 1949): 93–110, and 28 (January 1950): 182–204; Russell Garvin, "The Free Negro in Florida before the Civil War," *Florida Historical Quarterly* 46 (July 1967): 1–17; and Ray Granade, "Slave Unrest in Florida," *Florida Historical Quarterly* 55 (July 1976): 18–36.

3. Mark Tushnet contends that "slave law responded to the competing pressures of humanity and interest. . . . [The] concern for humanity arose from one set of social relations whereas the concern for interest arose from another set." See *American Law of Slavery*, p. 6. Carl N. Degler has found that "although by the nineteenth century the text of the law in the southern states . . . defined a slave as chattel property, . . . the law always recognized that a slave was both a human being and a piece of property. The very fact, for instance, that slaves were legally responsible for any crime they committed immediately suggests that their status as chattel property was different from any other piece of property. The courts were quite explicit in their recognition of the humanity of the slave." See *Neither Black Nor White: Slavery and Race Relations in Brazil and the United States* (New York: Macmillan, 1971), p. 27. Also on the debate over the competing concepts of property or persons see Flanigan, "Criminal Law of Slavery and Freedom," pp. 1–11, 73–74; Judith Schafer, "The Long Arm of the Law: Slavery and the Supreme Court of Antebellum Louisiana, 1809–1862" (Ph.D. diss., Tulane University, 1985), pp. 1–23; Ayers, *Vengeance and Justice*, pp. 134–37; and Fede, *People without Rights*, pp. 6–12.

4. Flanigan, "Criminal Law of Slavery and Freedom," p. iii.

5. Those who emphasize the fairness afforded blacks in criminal prosecutions are Daniel Flanigan, "Criminal Law of Slavery and Freedom"; idem, "Criminal Procedure in Slave Trials in the Antebellum South," *Journal of Southern History* 40 (November 1974): 537–64; A. E. Keir Nash, "Fairness and Formalism in the Trials of Blacks in the State and Supreme Courts of the Old South," *Virginia Law Review* 56 (February 1970): 64–100; idem, "The Reason of Slavery: Understanding the Judicial Role in the Peculiar Institution," *Vanderbilt Law Review* 32 (January 1979): 7–221; idem, "The Texas Supreme Court and Trial Rights of Blacks, 1845–1860," *Journal of American History* 58 (December 1971): 622–42; idem, "Negro Rights, Unionism and Greatness on the South Carolina Court of Appeals: The Extraordinary Chief Justice John Belton O'Neall," *South Carolina Law Review* 21 (Spring 1969): 141–90; Meredith Lang, *Defender of the Faith: the High Court of Mississippi, 1817–1875* (Jackson: University of Mississippi Press, 1977); and Arthur Howington, "The Treatment of Slaves and Free Blacks in the State and Local Courts of Tennessee" (Ph.D. diss., Vanderbilt University, 1982). Kermit Hall contends that there is

"danger in making too much of the seeming liberalism (of the equality-within-slavery paradox) of some jurists. Southern appellate judges operated within a proslavery mentality, and the common-law tradition provided a mask that concealed their humanity and that of the slave. The indwelling character of slave law was such that judges, when given a legislative mandate of equality to build upon, could recognize a slave's humanity in a criminal trial without endangering either the master's property rights or the South's economy or the system of racial control. Judges were able as a result to reconcile fairness for slaves (and even a degree of legal equality) with a system of perpetual racial bondage. Too much can also be made of fairness to slaves in the criminal trial courts of the antebellum South." See *The Magic Mirror,* p. 134. David Bodenhamer in general agrees with Hall but adds that the reason for Southern judges' insistence on procedural fairness was their commitment to due process: "Southern jurists were not acting out some charade by insisting that the state follow prescribed procedures when trying accused slaves. These judges could conceive of law's operation in no other way. Due process was too fundamental to the law, even in a code that denied liberty." See *Fair Trial,* p. 65. Others who have generally come down on the negative side of the argument are Michael Hindus, *Prison and Plantation;* idem, "Black Justice under White Law: Criminal Prosecutions of Blacks in Antebellum South Carolina," *Journal of American History* 63 (December 1976): 575–99; Andrew Fede, "Legitimized Violent Slave Abuse in the American South, 1619–1865: A Case Study of Law and Social Change in Six Southern States," *American Journal of Legal History* 29 (April 1985): 93–150; Schwarz, *Twice Condemned;* John C. Edwards, "Slave Justice in Four Middle Georgia Counties," *Georgia Historical Quarterly* 57 (Summer 1973): 265–73; and Royce Shingleton, "The Trial and Punishment of Slaves in Baldwin County, Georgia, 1812–1826," *Southern Humanities Review* 8 (Winter 1974): 67–73.

6. D. Schafer, "A Class of People Neither Freemen Nor Slaves," pp. 592–602; Brown, "Race Relations in Territorial Florida."

7. John P. Duval, *Compilation of the Public Acts of the Legislative Council of the Territory of Florida Passed Prior to 1840* (Tallahassee: Samuel S. Sibley, 1839), pp. 216–28; Leslie A. Thompson, *A Manual or Digest of the Statute Law of the State of Florida, of a General and Public Character, in Force at the End of the Second Session of the General Assembly of the State, on the Sixth Day of January, 1847* (Boston: Charles C. Little and James Brown, 1848), pp. 537–42.

8. Duval, *Compilation,* pp. 218–28; Thompson, *Digest,* pp. 537–45. In 1845, Gabriel, the slave of O. M. Avery, had his conviction for making "abusive and provoking" remarks upon Maximo de Rioboo overturned in the Escambia County Circuit Court. Gabriel had been sentenced to receive five lashes by a justice of the peace, but his master filed an appeal in the circuit court and Gabriel's conviction was overturned. *Maximo de Rioboo v Gabriel, a Slave,* 1845, Escambia County Case Files; Escambia County, Minutes of the Circuit Court, Book A, May Term 1846, n.p.

9. On July 9, 1825, for example, several witnesses testified in the Pensacola municipal court before Mayor John Jerrison that they saw Celestine Ruby, a free black, severely beat Frances, a slave belonging to Marcus Devillers, with an umbrella. Mayor Jerrison bonded Ruby to appear in the next term of the superior court to answer civil process of Frances's owner. Devillers sued Ruby for $700 in damages on the grounds that Frances and her services were lost for three months.

A jury awarded him $70.50. *Territory v Celestine Ruby,* 1825, and *Marcus Devillers v Celestine Ruby,* 1825, Escambia County Case Files.

10. Duval, *Compilation,* p. 227; Thompson, *Digest,* p. 538.

11. Duval, *Compilation,* pp. 228, 219.

12. *Cato v State,* 1860, in *Reports of the Cases Argued and Adjudged in the Supreme Court of Florida,* 9 vols. (Tallahassee: 1845–61) (hereafter cited as *Florida Reports*), 9:173–74. Portions of this statement are also quoted in Hall, *The Magic Mirror,* p. 133, and Bodenhamer, *Fair Trial,* p. 65.

13. "An Act Relating to Crimes and Misdemeanors Committed by Slaves, Free Negroes, and Mulattoes," in Duval, *Compilation,* p. 227. The following are only a few of Florida's distinguished attorneys who represented blacks in capital cases: Samuel Carmack, J. Wayles Baker, Benjamin Wright, Charles Downing, John Milton, William Dilworth, Thomas Baltzell, George T. Ward, Richard K. Call, Walker Anderson, and Ossian Hart.

14. Duval, *Compilation,* pp. 224, 228.

15. See Kenneth Porter, *The Negro on the American Frontier* (New York: Arno Press, 1971); J. Leitch Wright, "A Note on the First Seminole War as Seen by Indians, Negroes, and Their British Advisors," *Journal of Southern History* 34 (November 1968): 565–75; idem, *The Only Land They Knew: The Tragic Story of the Indians of the Old South* (New York: Free Press, 1981); idem, *Creeks and Seminoles: The Destruction and Regeneration of the Muscogulge People* (Lincoln: University of Nebraska Press, 1986); Canter Brown Jr., *Florida's Peace River Frontier* (Orlando: University of Central Florida Press, 1991); idem, "The Sarrazota, or Runaway Negro Plantations: Tampa Bay's First Black Community, 1812–1821," *Tampa Bay History* 12 (Fall/Winter 1990): 5–19; Daniel F. Littlefield, *Africans and Seminoles: From Removal to Emancipation* (Westport, Conn.: Greenwood Press, 1977); and idem, *Africans and Creeks: From the Colonial Period to the Civil War* (Westport, Conn.: Greenwood Press, 1979). For a contemporary view of the question stated from an abolitionist standpoint see Joshua R. Giddings, *The Exiles of Florida: Or the Crimes Committed by Our Government against the Maroons, Who Fled from South Carolina and Other Slave States, Seeking Protection under Spanish Laws* (Columbus, Ohio: Follett, Foster, and Co., 1858).

16. For black and Seminole collaboration during the Second Seminole War see Wright, *Creeks and Seminoles;* John K. Mahon, *History of the Second Seminole War, 1835–1842* (Gainesville: University of Florida Press, 1967); Edwin McReynolds, *The Seminoles* (Norman: University of Oklahoma Press, 1957); Porter, *The Negro on the American Frontier;* and Littlefield, *Africans and Seminoles.*

17. Susan Bradford Eppes, *The Negro of the Old South: A Bit of Period History* (Chicago: Joseph Branch Publishing, 1925), pp. 96–97; *Tallahassee Floridian,* May 17, 1834; ibid., March 29, May 3, 17, November 15, 22, 1834; Territorial Auditor, Vouchers, RG 352, ser. 584, box 1, folder 7, and box 2, folders 1, 3, and 4, FSAr.

18. *Tallahassee Floridian,* July 22, August 26, 1837; *St. Augustine Florida Herald,* August 25, September 6, 1837; Jacob Rhett Motte, *Journey into the Wilderness: An Army Surgeon's Account of Life in Camp and Field during the Creek and Seminole Wars, 1836–1838,* ed. James Sunderman (Gainesville: University of Florida Press, 1953), p. 113.

19. *Apalachicola Gazette,* May 11, 1839.

20. John Jenkins, the master of the steamboat *Ellen,* offered a reward for their capture. *Apalachicola Gazette,* May 10, 1838.

21. *Pensacola Gazette,* April 20, 1839.

22. Ibid., June 22, 1839; *Apalachicola Gazette,* July 17, 1839.

23. Proclamation for the Arrest of Hunter, a Slave, October 16, 1839, in *Tallahassee Floridian,* November 2, 1839; *Apalachicola Gazette,* August 14, 1839; *Territory v Caesar,* January 30, 1840, in Territorial Court of Appeals Case Files, RG 970, ser. 73, box 3, folder 75, FSAr; Certificate of Value for Caesar, April 15, 1842, in *Territory v Caesar, a Slave,* 1839, Territorial Auditor, Vouchers, RG 352, ser. 584, box 3, folder 4, FSAr.

24. *Cedar Keys Telegraph,* September 1, 1860; *Fernandina East Floridian,* August 30, 1860.

25. *Tallahassee Floridian,* December 28, 1833; *Tallahassee Florida Advocate,* November 17, 1829; *Tallahassee Floridian and Journal,* April 16, 1853, and October 27, 1860.

26. Cooper and Terrill, *The American South,* p. 210. Also on the patrol as it functioned in the antebellum South see John Hope Franklin, *The Militant South, 1800–1861* (Cambridge: Harvard University Press, 1956), pp. 70–79; idem, *From Slavery to Freedom,* pp. 189–90; and Stampp, *Peculiar Institution,* pp. 214–15.

27. *Pensacola Gazette,* September 17, 1825.

28. Jackson County, Minutes of the Circuit Court, Book D, pp. 597–98. In 1860 Ely's slave Cato was accused of rape, and another slave, Joe, was shot and killed by John Durden.

29. Escambia County, Minutes of the Superior Court, Book 1, p. 326; Gadsden County GJP, November 15, 1849, Gadsden County Case Files; *Tallahassee Floridian,* June 5, 1832.

30. *State v William D. Moseley,* 1858, Putnam County Case Files. Moseley was indicted three times. He was found guilty in two counts and fined $25 in each case (one of the judgments was overruled, and in a new trial he was found not guilty). His third indictment was quashed. Putnam was indicted once, but his indictment was quashed. Putnam County, Minutes of the Circuit Court, Book 1, pp. 328, 364, 365, 370, 383, 393, 395, 428.

31. *Jacksonville Weekly Republican,* March 24, 1858.

32. Proclamation of the Common Council of Key West, August 2, 1849, Monroe County Case Files.

33. *Apalachicola Gazette,* December 2, 1837; *Apalachicola Commercial Advertiser,* May 23, 1846, February 8, 1849.

34. *Tallahassee Florida Advocate,* October 5, 1830.

35. *Tallahassee Floridian and Journal,* April 16, 1853, December 4, 1852; *Tallahassee Floridian,* October 25, 1837.

36. Thompson, *Digest,* p. 511; Duval, *Compilation,* p. 223.

37. *Tallahassee Floridian and Journal,* December 4, 1852; *Tallahassee Florida Sentinel,* December 7, 1852; Jefferson County, Minutes of the Circuit Court, Book A, p. 455.

38. *Territory v Peter Williamson,* 1829, Escambia County Case Files.

39. *Pensacola Gazette,* March 10, 1829; *Tallahassee Florida Advocate,* March 21,

1829; *St. Augustine Florida Herald,* April 8, 1829; Escambia County, Minutes of the Superior Court, Book 1, pp. 417, 419.

40. Genovese, *Roll, Jordan, Roll,* p. 40.

41. Brown, "Race Relations in Territorial Florida," pp. 299–300, 307. Brown contends further that subsequent laws passed in the 1830s came as much out of the fear of frontier Indian violence as out of the Nat Turner scare or the growing militancy of the abolitionist movement. See ibid., pp. 301–4. For more on the racial implications of the Second Seminole War see Kenneth Porter, "Negroes and the Seminole War, 1835–1842," *Journal of Southern History* 30 (November 1964): 427–50; idem, "Florida Slaves and Free Negroes in the Seminole War, 1835–1842," *Journal of Negro History* 28 (October 1943): 390–421; Mahon, *History of the Second Seminole War;* Wright, *Creeks and Seminoles;* and Littlefield, *Africans and Seminoles.*

42. Address of Gov. Robert R. Reid, January 11, 1841, in *St. Augustine News,* February 5, 1841. Laws regulating the white–free black guardian relationship were passed in 1842, 1848, and 1856. See Garvin, "The Free Negro in Florida before the Civil War," 15–17.

43. Flanigan, "Criminal Procedure in Slave Trials in the Antebellum South," p. 538.

44. *Pensacola Gazette,* October 26, 1827.

45. Leon County, Minutes of the Superior Court, Book 1, p. 76. Also on the case see ibid., pp. 39–41, 46, 61–62, 66, 76; *Pensacola Gazette,* May 16, 1828.

46. See Minor Walker to Samuel H. Duval, in *Territory v Dick, a Negro Slave,* 1840, Territorial Court of Appeals Case Files, RG 970, ser. 73, box 12, folder 376, FSAr.

47. Bill of Indictment of Stepney, and Charge of the Court, in *State v Stepney, a Slave,* 1859, Escambia County Case Files; Escambia County, Minutes of the Circuit Court, Book B, p. 65.

48. *State v Charles, a Slave,* in *Florida Reports,* 1:298–300; *States v Charles, a Slave,* 1847, in Comptroller's Vouchers, Criminal Prosecutions, RG 350, ser. 565, box 3, folder 2, Hamilton County, FSAr.

49. *Pensacola Gazette,* November 27, December 18, 1841; *Territory v Isaac, a Slave,* 1841, Escambia County Case Files; Escambia County, Minutes of the Superior Court, Book 4, pp. 155, 181; *Territory v Isaac, a Slave,* in Territorial Auditor, Vouchers, RG 352, ser. 584, box 3, folder 1, FSAr; Pardon of Isaac by Gov. Richard K. Call, December 8, 1841, in Escambia County Case Files.

50. *Magnolia Advertiser,* October 2, 1829; Alachua, Columbia, and Hillsborough Counties, Minutes of the Superior Court, 1828–35, pp. 22, 24–25, PKYL; Jacob Holbrook to Charles Downing, December 29, 1830 in *Territory of Florida v Monday,* December Term 1829, Alachua County, Territorial Auditor, Vouchers, RG 352, ser. 584, box 1, folder 3, FSAr. In the time between Monday's conviction and the hanging, Judge Joseph L. Smith wrote Gov. William P. DuVal, who was contemplating a pardon, that "evidence was clear and uncontradicted and there appeared nothing in the opinion of the court to mitigate the character of the crime." Joseph L. Smith to William P. DuVal, January 2, 1830, Correspondence of the Territorial Governors, RG 101, ser. 177, box 1, folder 12, FSAr.

51. Flanigan, "Criminal Law of Slavery and Freedom," pp. 47–48.

52. Ibid. See also Peter Bardaglio, "Rape and the Law in the Old South: 'Cal-

culated to Excite Indignation in Every Heart,' " *Journal of Southern History* 60 (November 1994): 763–69; and J. Schafer, "The Long Arm of the Law," pp. 75–78.

53. *State v Cato,* 1860, Jackson County Case Files; *Cato, a Slave, Plaintiff in Error, v the State,* 1860, in *Florida Reports,* 1:162–87; Bill of Indictment of Cato, a Slave, for Rape, Spring Term 1859, U.S. District Court, Northern District, Civil Cases, box 17, bundle entitled Miscellaneous Court Papers, Unidentified Criminal Records, NAEP; *State v Cato,* 1860, Comptroller's Vouchers, Criminal Prosecutions, RG 350, ser. 565, box 2, folder 6, Franklin County, FSAr.

54. Schwarz, *Twice Condemned,* p. 164.

55. *Territory v Simon, a Slave,* 1848, Jefferson County Case Files; Jefferson County, Minutes of the Circuit Court, Book A, pp. 214, 217, 223, 226.

56. *Tallahassee Floridian and Journal,* November 8, 1856; *State v Hall,* 1856, Comptroller's Vouchers, Post Mortem Examinations, RG 350, ser. 565, box 7, folder 4, Madison County, FSAr. *State v Hall,* 1856, ibid., Criminal Prosecutions, box 4, folder 8, Madison County, FSAr.

57. *Fernandina East Floridian,* March 15, May 10, 17, 1860; *Tallahassee Floridian and Journal,* March 10, 21, 1860; Pardon of Moses, Big William, and Cook, January 9, 1861, Book of Record (Proclamations), RG 156, ser. 13, Book 1, p. 367.

58. *Tallahassee Floridian and Journal,* April 7, 1849; *State v Martha, a Slave,* 1849, Comptroller's Vouchers, Criminal Prosecutions, RG 350, ser. 565, box 4, folder 2. Leon County, FSAr; Leon County, Minutes of the Circuit Court, Book 5, pp. 165, 177.

59. Putnam quoted in Thomas Graham, *The Awakening of St. Augustine: The Anderson Family and the Oldest City, 1821–1924* (St. Augustine: St. Augustine Historical Society, 1978), p. 79.

60. *Apalachicola Florida Journal,* November 12, 1842.

61. *Tallahassee Floridian,* October 25, December 6, 1834; Jefferson County, Minutes of the Superior Court, Book 1, pp. 120, 130.

62. *Tallahassee Florida Sentinel,* November 22, 1853; *Tallahassee Floridian and Journal,* November 26, 1853; Leon County, Minutes of the Circuit Court, Book 5, pp. 580, 590; *State v Ned, a Slave,* 1853, in Comptroller's Vouchers, Criminal Prosecutions, RG 350, ser. 565, box 4, folder 3, Leon County, FSAr; Proclamation of Gov. James Broome, May 15, 1854, Book of Record (Proclamations), RG 156, ser. 13, Book 1, no. 238, pp. 227–28, FSAr.

63. *Tallahassee Floridian and Journal,* October 22, 1859; Leon County, Minutes of the Circuit Court, Book 6, p. 295.

64. *Sarah McNeil v Henry Wilson,* 1821, Escambia County Case Files.

65. *Territory v William H. Baker,* 1831, Escambia County Case Files; *Pensacola Gazette,* November 27, 1830; Escambia County, Minutes of the Superior Court, Book 1, pp. 530, 531.

66. Joseph Morris to Thomas Brown, April 17, 1850, Correspondence of Thomas Brown, RG 101, ser. 755, box 1, folder 6, FSAr; Proclamation for the Arrest of Nathaniel Saunders, May 1, 1850, in Book of Record (Proclamations), RG 156, ser. 13, Book 1, no. 131, p. 111, FSAr; *Tallahassee Florida Sentinel,* May 7, 1850, *Tallahassee Floridian and Journal,* May 11, 1850; Madison County, Minutes of the Circuit Court, 1846–54, pp. 225, 227.

67. *State v Guilford Dawkins,* 1850, Jefferson County Case Files; Jefferson County, Minutes of the Circuit Court, Book A, pp. 355, 523.

68. *St. Augustine Ancient City,* July 30, 1853; Orange County, Minutes of the Circuit Court, Book A, p. 79.

69. Affidavit of Duncan M. Bryant, March 4, 1856, in *State v Henry W. Williams,* 1856, Comptroller's Vouchers, Criminal Prosecutions, RG 350, ser. 565, folder 8, FSAr.

70. *Tallahassee Star of Florida,* April 20, 1843; Leon County, Minutes of the Superior and Circuit Court, Book 4, pp. 61, 65.

71. William P. DuVal to William Wilson, November 28, 1829, Territorial Auditor, Vouchers, RG 352, ser. 584, box 1, folder 2, FSAr; *Key West Register and Commercial Advertiser,* February 19, 1829.

72. *Tallahassee Florida Sentinel,* June 4, 1844.

73. Dickson killed Sam, the property of Benjamin A. Dickens. *State v W. D. Dickson,* 1853, Jackson County Case Files. Dickson was indicted but escaped as he was awaiting trial. Jackson County, Minutes of the Circuit Court, Book C, pp. 332, 587. A jury of inquest over the body of Joe, a slave belonging to Horace Ely, found that John Durden shot Joe with a pistol. *State v John Durden,* 1861, Jackson County Case Files; *State v John Durden,* 1861, Comptroller's Vouchers, Criminal Prosecutions, RG 350, ser. 565, box 3, folder 6, Jackson County, FSAr.

74. *Pensacola West Florida Times,* March 17, 1857; *Fernandina East Florida Herald,* October 24, 1860.

Chapter 10

1. Leslie A. Thompson, *A Manual or Digest of the Statute Law of the State of Florida, of a General and Public Character, in Force at the End of the Second Session of the General Assembly of the State, on the Sixth Day of January, 1847* (Boston: Charles C. Little and James Brown, 1848), p. 592.

2. *Acts and Resolutions of the Legislative Council,* 1824, p. 173.

3. Waters Smith and John M. Hanson to Martin Van Buren, January 25, 1825, and Report of the House Committee on Territories, January 26, 1826, in Clarence E. Carter, ed., *Territorial Papers of the United States,* 26 vols. (Washington, D.C.: U.S. Government Printing Office, 1934–62), 23:165–67, 426–28.

4. Thompson, *Digest,* p. 599. A number of Floridians voiced their opposition to this change in the law, which in effect made marshals the executive officer of the superior courts. The law essentially reimposed a previously repealed one. The overall outcome was to "bestow the power of exercising tyranny over the people and of confusing the course of justice." Petition to Congress by the Inhabitants of Pensacola, March 27, 1826, in Carter, *Territorial Papers,* 23:496. The matter continued to be controversial. Territorial delegate David L. White supported the new law of 1826, claiming that under the act "Marshals will generally employ the Sheriffs as Deputies and Assistants, which will make it as valuable to them, as the divided business of the Superior Court." White again defended the arrangement, claiming, "There never was an instance in the judicial history of any country where there were two officers of one court, no matter what accumulation of jurisdiction it possesses. It would be inevitably attended with a conflict of authority, and result in

embarrassment and confusion. In the States where the jurisdiction is distinct and possessed by Federal and State Courts, the question is wholly different. If the Constitution allowed one court to do Federal and State business, no one would ever think of the employment of a Marshal and Sheriff both." See *Pensacola Gazette*, July 1, 1826, March 23, 1827.

5. Governor DuVal to the President, July 21, 1831, in Carter, *Territorial Papers*, 23:540.

6. To the Marshal of the Eastern District of Florida, June 22, 1840, Sanchez Papers, box 2, folder 21, SAHS.

7. Thomas Douglas to Joseph Sanchez, July 14, 1846, ibid., box 1, folder 24.

8. Jesse Carter to Joseph Sanchez, June 20, 1840, ibid., box 1, folder 20.

9. On federal marshals and their duties see Frederick S. Calhoun, *The Lawmen: United States Marshals and Their Deputies, 1789–1989* (Washington, D.C.: Smithsonian Institution Press, 1989); Larry D. Ball, *The United States Marshals in the New Mexico and Arizona Territories, 1846–1912* (Albuquerque: University of New Mexico Press, 1978); idem, *Desert Lawmen: The High Sheriffs of New Mexico and Arizona, 1846–1912* (Albuquerque: University of New Mexico Press, 1992), pp. 48–50; Frank Richard Prassel, *The Western Peace Officer: A Legacy of Law and Order* (Norman: University of Oklahoma Press, 1972), pp. 220–43; and David R. Johnson, *American Law Enforcement: A History* (Arlington Heights, Ill.: Forum Press, 1981), pp. 96–100.

10. Thompson, *Digest*, p. 60.

11. Lawrence M. Friedman, *Crime and Punishment in American History* (New York: Basic Books, 1993), p. 67.

12. The best way to find information on sheriffs is to use the census in conjunction with the following three sources: "Roster of State and County Officers Commissioned by the Governor of Florida, 1845–1868," prepared by Florida Historical Records Survey, Division of Community Service Programs, Works Progress Administration, Jacksonville: Florida Historical Records Survey, February 1941; *The Florida Sheriff: Yearbook of the Florida Sheriffs Association* (1958), pp. 23–88; and RG 151, Office of the Secretary of State, ser. 259, Lists of Territorial, State, and County Officers, 1827–1923, 1960, and ser. 1284, State and County Directories, 1845–61, FSAr.

13. U.S. Manuscript Census, Population, 1850, Calhoun County, Florida.

14. Ibid., Franklin County.

15. Peter Gautier to the Secretary of State, April 30, 1838, in Carter, *Territorial Papers*, 25:504–5.

16. *Tallahassee Floridian and Journal*, June 26, 1858.

17. Leon County sheriffs were Alfred A. Fisher (1845–51), Haley T. Blocker (1851–57), and Richard Saunders (1857–67). Gadsden County sheriffs were Benjamin C. West (1845–49), Samuel B. Love (1849–55), and James M. Smith (1855–63). See "Roster," pp. 128, 188–89. For sheriffs in Alachua, Duval, Escambia, Hamilton, and St. Johns Counties, see appendix 3.

18. John Babb to Col. Henry J. Coffman, October 26, 1837, Fox Papers, USC.

19. For examples of some of these see Philip D. Jordan, *Frontier Law and Order: Ten Essays* (Lincoln: University of Nebraska Press, 1970), pp. 162–63.

20. David L. Brownell to T. W. Brevard, April 16, 1860, State Comptroller Correspondence, RG 350, ser. 554, box 2, folder 6, FSAr.

21. J. C. Stewart to T. W. Brevard, December 31, 1859, ibid., box 2, folder 5.

22. During the nineteenth century almost all law enforcement officers and some civil service personnel operated on the fee system. See Prassel, *Western Peace Officer,* pp. 119–20, 191, 223–25, 264–65; Ball, *United States Marshals,* pp. 6, 11; Ball, *Desert Lawmen,* p. 7; and Leonard White, *The Jacksonians: A Study in Administrative History, 1829–1861* (New York: Macmillan, 1954), pp. 388–91.

23. John P. Duval, *Compilation of the Public Acts of the Legislative Council of the Territory of Florida Passed Prior to 1840* (Tallahassee: Samuel S. Sibley, 1839), pp. 210–15.

24. Leslie A. Thompson to Romeo Lewis, April 30, 1832, Territorial Auditor, Vouchers, RG 352, ser. 584, box 1, folder 7, FSAr.

25. Charles Austin to William Wilson, December 14, 1833, Territorial Auditor, Vouchers, RG 350, ser. 584, box 1, folder 7, FSAr. In 1846 the state comptroller outlined the duties and responsibilities of sheriffs, county commissioners, and others involved in tax collecting and the settling of delinquent accounts. See N. P. Bemis to Sheriffs, August 24, 1846, Sanchez Papers, box 1, folder 31, SAHS.

26. Charles Evans to the President, April 20, 1841, in Carter, *Territorial Papers,* 26:301.

27. *Pensacola Gazette,* September 15, 1838.

28. B. Frisbee to Theodore W. Brevard, March 23, 1857, State Comptroller Correspondence, RG 350, ser. 554, box 2, folder 2, FSAr.

29. See "An Act for the Apprehension of Criminals and the Punishment of Crimes and Misdemeanors," section 7, in Duval, *Compilation,* pp. 162–63.

30. James H. Johnson to Theodore Brevard, August 21 and September 10, 1857, State Comptroller Correspondence, RG 350, ser. 554, box 2, folder 2, FSAr.

31. Affidavit of William Harvey, Coroner of Jackson County, November 20, 1854, Nineteenth-Century Florida State Legislature, RG 915, ser. 887, box 6, folder 2, FSAr.

32. *Tallahassee Floridian,* April 20, 1833.

33. William A. Forward to Arthur Wright, May 26, 1855, and Arthur Wright to Theodore W. Brevard, October 22, 1855, Comptroller's Vouchers, Criminal Prosecutions, RG 350, ser. 565, box 1, folder 6, Columbia County, FSAr.

34. Cobb was eventually indicted for resisting process, but after he spent more than twelve months at large the district attorney decided to drop the prosecution. Affidavit of R. L. Cotton, August 11, 1827 in *Territory v Isaac Cobb,* 1828, in Escambia County Case Files; Escambia County, Minutes of the Superior Court, Book 1, pp. 344, 432.

35. *State v Charles Brightly,* 1851, Escambia County Case Files; Escambia County, Minutes of the Circuit Court, Book A, n.p.

36. *Territory v William Mimms,* 1827, Escambia County Case Files; Escambia County, Minutes of the Superior Court, Book 1, pp. 325, 343, 406.

37. *Tallahassee Floridian and Journal,* April 2, 1859.

38. See *Pensacola Gazette,* October 12, 1844, June 28, 1845; *State v William Watson,* 1844, Comptroller's Vouchers, Criminal Prosecutions, RG 350, ser. 565, box 3, folder 6, Jackson County, FSAr. See also Proclamation for the Arrest of James Avant and William Watson, September 19, 1844, in Correspondence of the Governors, Letterbooks, RG 101, ser. 32, vol. 2, n.p., FSAr.

39. Proclamation for the Arrest of William H. Watson, alias James Black, January 5, 1849, in Book of Record (Proclamations), RG 156, ser. 13, Book 1, no. 92, p. 74, FSAr; *Marianna Florida Whig,* January 12, 1849; *Tallahassee Florida Sentinel,* January 9, 1849; *Tallahassee Floridian and Journal,* January 6, 1849; *Jacksonville Florida News,* April 15, May 13, June 3, 1848, January 13, 1849; *Pensacola Florida Democrat,* January 18, 1849.

40. *Jacksonville Florida News,* March 31, 1855.

41. *Fernandina News,* April 28, 1858; *Tallahassee Floridian and Journal,* April 24, 1858.

42. Thompson, *Digest,* pp. 494, 496.

43. *Pensacola Gazette,* May 30, 1828.

44. *Territory v George Taylor,* 1845, Jefferson County Case Files. The results of Taylor's prosecution remain unknown.

45. W. D. Barnes to T. W. Brevard, March 25 and May 21, 1860; David J. Brownell to T. W. Brevard, March 20, 1860, all in State Comptroller Correspondence, RG 350, ser. 554, box 2, folder 6, FSAr.

46. Jordan, *Frontier Law and Order,* p. ix.

Chapter 11

1. "An Act Concerning Criminals," in John P. Duval, *Compilation of the Public Acts of the Legislative Council of the Territory of Florida Passed Prior to 1840* (Tallahassee: Samuel S. Sibley, 1839), p. 166.

2. *Territory v Fluendo Caldez,* 1831, Monroe County Case Files; Monroe County, Minutes of the Superior Court, 1830–40, pp. 67, 77–78, 124, 233, PKYL; Bill of Costs to Philip J. Fontane for Guarding Caldez, December 23, 1834, Territorial Auditor, Vouchers, RG 352, ser. 584, box 2, folder 3, FSAr; *Key West Gazette,* May 4, 1831.

3. Benjamin Hagler to Thomas Brown, May 18 and 22, 1850, Correspondence of Thomas Brown, RG 101, ser. 755, box 1, folder 6, FSAr; *Tallahassee Florida Sentinel,* June 4, 1850.

4. "An Act for the Apprehension of Criminals and the Punishment of Crimes and Misdemeanors," in Duval, *Compilation,* pp. 161–63.

5. James D. Westcott to P. W. Bower, September 27, 1831, Correspondence of the Secretary of State, RG 150, ser. 24, vol. 1, p. 76, FSAr.

6. James Broome to E. F. Kendrick, April 3, 1854, Correspondence of the Governors, Letterbooks, RG 101, ser. 32, vol. 5, p. 286, FSAr.

7. J. B. Love to Thomas Brown, June 28, 1851, Correspondence of Thomas Brown, RG 101, ser. 755, box 2, folder 1, FSAr; Proclamation for the Arrest of Thomas Boatright, June 30, 1851, Book of Record (Proclamations), RG 156, ser. 13, Book 1, no. 173, p. 152, FSAr; *Tallahassee Floridian and Journal,* July 12, 1851.

8. James M. Gilchrist to Thomas Brown, October 10, 1850, Correspondence of Thomas Brown, RG 101, ser. 755, box 1, folder 6, FSAr; Proclamation for the Arrest of James Riggins, October 12, 1850, Book of Record (Proclamations), RG 156, ser. 13, Book 1, no. 144, p. 125, FSAr; *Tallahassee Floridian and Journal,* October 19, 1850; *Tallahassee Florida Sentinel,* October 15, 1850.

9. Thomas Broxson to James Broome, February 13, 1856, Correspondence of James Broome, RG 101, ser. 777, box 2, folder 1, FSAr.

10. For Huguenin see Proclamation of Richard K. Call, June 30, 1837, in *Tallahassee Floridian,* July 22, 1837. For King see Proclamation for the Arrest of Simeon King, June 23, 1851, Book of Record (Proclamations), RG 156, ser. 13, Book 1, no. 170, p. 149, FSAr; Joseph D. Morris to Thomas Brown, June 19, 1851, Correspondence of Thomas Brown, RG 101, ser. 755, box 2, folder 1, FSAr; *Tallahassee Florida Sentinel,* June 24, 1851; and *Tallahassee Floridian and Journal,* June 28, 1851. For O'Neil see Proclamation for the Arrest of Daniel O'Neil, September 14, 1860, Book of Record (Proclamations), RG 156, ser. 13, Book 1, pp. 355–56, FSAr; and *Tallahassee Floridian and Journal,* September 15, 1860. For Goodman see Proclamation for the Arrest of Jessee Goodman, June 2, 1838, in *Tallahassee Florida Watchman,* September 8, 1838; and *Tallahassee Floridian,* June 2, 1838. For Ellison see Proclamation of James Ellison, March 31, 1859, Book of Record (Proclamations), RG 156, ser. 13, Book 1, no. 325, p. 319, FSAr; and *Tallahassee Floridian and Journal,* April 2, 1859. For the Selphs see Proclamation for the Arrest of Charmack and William Selph, October 5, 1854, Book of Record (Proclamations), RG 156, ser. 13, Book 1, no. 250, p. 239, FSAr; *Tallahassee Floridian and Journal,* October 7, 1854; and *Jacksonville Florida News,* October 14, 1854. For Adams see *Tallahassee Floridian and Journal,* September 24, 1859.

11. For Bembry see *Tallahassee Floridian,* August 8, 1835. For Riggins see Proclamation for the Arrest of James Riggins, October 12, 1850, Book of Record (Proclamations), RG 156, ser. 13, Book 1, no. 144, p. 125, FSAr; *Tallahassee Floridian and Journal,* October 19, 1850; and *Tallahassee Florida Sentinel,* October 15, 1850. For Huguenin see *Tallahassee Floridian,* July 22, 1837. For Dozier see *Tallahassee Floridian,* September 10, 1836; and Proclamation of Richard K. Call, September 7, 1836, Correspondence of the Governors, Letterbooks, RG 101, ser. 32, vol. 1, n.p., FSAr. For Barkwell's advertisement see *Tallahassee Florida Watchman,* September 8, 1838; and *Tallahassee Floridian,* July 21, 1838.

12. For Jourardin see Proclamation for the Arrest of Henry Jourardin, August 31, 1842, Correspondence of the Governors, Letterbooks, RG 101, ser. 32, vol. 2, n.p., FSAr; *Pensacola Gazette,* September 10, 1842; and *Tallahassee Star of Florida,* September 1, 1842. For Passmore see *Quincy Sentinel,* January 1, 1841; *Tallahassee Floridian,* December 26, 1840; *St. Joseph Times,* January 23, 1841; and *St. Augustine Florida Herald and Southern Democrat,* April 20, 1840. For Gill see Proclamation for the Arrest of King Gill, February 15, 1840, Correspondence of the Governors, Letterbooks, RG 101, ser. 32, vol. 2, n.p., FSAr; and *St. Augustine Florida Herald and Southern Democrat,* April 20, 1840. For Fountain see *Tallahassee Floridian,* September 10, 1836. For Hall see *Tallahassee Floridian and Journal,* March 26, 1853. For Meridith see Proclamation for the Arrest of Bryant Meridith, July 18, 1840, Correspondence of the Governors, Letterbooks, RG 101, ser. 32, vol. 2, n.p., FSAr; *Tallahassee Floridian,* July 25, 1840; and *St. Joseph Times,* August 14, 1840.

13. Proclamation for the Arrest of Benjamin Wood, in *Pensacola Gazette,* October 12, 1844; *St. Joseph Times,* March 23, 1839.

14. *Tallahassee Floridian and Journal,* March 29, 1859.

15. F. L. Villepigue to A. H. Bush, August 2, 1860, Correspondence of the Secretary of State, RG 150, ser. 24, Letterbook 2, n.p., FSAr.

16. William P. DuVal to David Floyd, January 4, 1831, Territorial Auditor, Vouchers, RG 352, ser. 584, box 1, folder 6, FSAr; Leon County, Minutes of the Superior Court, Book 1, p. 266.

17. Petition of William Blount to the General Assembly, July 11, 1845, box 1, folder 2, and Deputy Marshal H. R. Taylor to Legislative Council, n.d., box 1, folder 5, Nineteenth-Century Florida State Legislature, RG 915, ser. 887, FSAr.

18. *Tallahassee Floridian and Journal,* October 13, 1860; *Fernandina East Floridian,* October 18, 31, November 7, 1860.

19. *Jacksonville Florida News,* December 25, 1846, January 8, 1847; *Tallahassee Florida Sentinel,* December 22, 1846, January 5, 1847; *Tallahassee Floridian,* December 19, 1846. Later authorities learned that a Jefferson County jury had acquitted Clyde of murder in 1845, but the public outcry against him was so great that he was nearly lynched. According to an affidavit, Clyde deposed that a number of citizens had threatened to lynch him should he be "acquitted of the felony of which he stood charged." The threats came while Clyde was a prisoner in the Leon County jail. Among those who threatened Clyde was John Grantham, who forewarned Clyde that "if he were not hanged by the law, he would be hanged at any rate, and that he would not be permitted to remain in the Country." Clyde asked that Grantham be brought in and be required to give a peace bond. Affidavit of John C. Clyde, April 25, 1845, in *Territory v John Grantham,* 1845 (Grantham's Peace Bond also included), Jefferson County Case Files.

20. *Jacksonville Florida News,* January 8, 1847.

21. *Merriam-Webster's Collegiate Dictionary,* 10th ed. (Springfield, Mass.: Merriam-Webster, Inc., 1993), p. 230. On comity, extradition, and rendition see Edward Smith and Arnold Zurcher, *Dictionary of American Politics* (New York: Barnes and Noble, 1968), pp. 72, 378; Paul Finkelman, *An Imperfect Union: Slavery, Federalism, and Comity* (Chapel Hill: University of North Carolina Press, 1981), pp. 6–9. See also "Act in Relation to Fugitives from Justice," in Duval, *Compilation,* p. 166.

22. Proclamation of Richard K. Call, July 2, 1844, Correspondence of the Governors, Letterbooks, RG 101, ser. 32, vol. 2, n.p., FSAr.

23. Powell was suspected of being a member of a gang committing crimes in the Lake City area. "A Citizen of Florida" wrote a letter to the editor of the *St. Augustine News,* describing Powell's crime: "This notorious individual, in the darkness of night, concealed himself upon one of the roads leading to this place, and attempted the assassination of one of our citizens." *St. Augustine News* quoted in *Tallahassee Floridian,* February 21, 1846; A. H. Cole to William D. Moseley, April 27, 1846, Correspondence of William D. Moseley, RG 101, ser. 679, box 2, folder 9, FSAr. See also Proclamation of Gov. William D. Moseley, May 1, 1846, ibid.; Book of Record (Proclamations), RG 156, ser. 13, Book 1, no. 30, p. 24, FSAr; and *Tallahassee Southern Journal,* June 2, 1846.

24. *Tallahassee Florida Intelligencer,* July 29, 1826; *Pensacola Gazette,* August 18, 1826.

25. "Grand Exhibition of Natural Magic," *St. Joseph Times* quoted in *Pensacola Gazette,* March 2, 1839.

26. *Pensacola Gazette,* February 16, 23, March 2, 1839; *Augustine News,* February 16, March 16, 1839; *Apalachicola Gazette,* February 23, 1839; *Tallahassee Floridian,* April 20, 1839.

27. John Milton to Thomas Brown, December 18, 1849, Correspondence of Thomas Brown, RG 101, ser. 755, box 3, folder 5, FSAr.

28. P. B. Woolen to James Broome, December 15, 1853, Correspondence of James Broome, RG 101, ser. 777, box 3, folder 2, FSAr.

29. Proclamation for the Arrest of Bennett L. Caro, March 13, 1848, Book of Record (Proclamations), RG 156, ser. 13, Book 1, no. 69, pp. 54–55, FSAr; Proclamation for the Arrest of George Lang, May 3, 1844, Correspondence of the Governors, Letterbooks, RG 101, ser. 32, vol. 2, n.p., FSAr. John Branch to the Governor of North Carolina, November 19, 1844, ibid.; *Territory v George Thomas,* 1844, Territorial Auditor, Vouchers, RG 352, ser. 584, box 3, folder 6, FSAr.

30. C. A. Price to James E. Broome, January 15, 1855, Correspondence of James Broome, RG 101, ser. 777, box 3, folder 4, FSAr; see also Proclamation to the Governor of South Carolina, January 27, 1855, Book of Record (Proclamations), RG 156, ser. 13, Book 1, no. 262, pp. 250–51, FSAr.

31. Proclamation for the Arrest of John Henderson, October 5, 1846, Book of Record (Proclamations), RG 156, ser. 13, Book 1, no. 5, p. 4, FSAr; *Tallahassee Florida Sentinel,* October 14, 1845; *Tallahassee Star of Florida,* October 10, 1845; *Tallahassee Floridian,* November 1, 1845; *Pensacola Florida Democrat,* January 23, 1846. Thomas Genois to Charles Evans, March 4, 1846; Charles Evans to William Moseley, March 10, 1846, Correspondence of William D. Moseley, RG 101, ser. 679, box 2, folder 9, FSAr; *State v John Henderson,* 1846, Comptroller's Vouchers, Criminal Prosecutions, RG 350, ser. 565, Escambia County, box 2, folder 2, FSAr; *State v John Henderson,* 1846, Escambia County Case Files.

32. William Hopkins to Thomas Brown, June 18, 1850, Correspondence of Thomas Brown, RG 101, ser. 755, box 1, folder 6, FSAr; Proclamation to the Governor of South Carolina for the Arrest of Simon Taylor, 1850, Book of Record (Proclamations), RG 156, ser. 13, Book 1, no. 138, p. 118, FSAr; Proclamation for the Arrest of Simon Taylor, December 31, 1840, in *Tallahassee Floridian,* January 9, 1841; *Pensacola Gazette,* January 16, 1841; *Tallahassee Florida Sentinel,* March 25, 1851; *Tallahassee Floridian and Journal,* March 29, 1851; *State v Simon Taylor,* 1850, Comptroller's Vouchers, Criminal Prosecutions, RG 350, ser. 565, box 4, folder 2, Leon County, FSAr; Leon County, Minutes of the Circuit Court, Book 5, p. 389.

33. On May 2, 1844, the Leon County Grand Jury presented that evidence was addressed before them that the bank had not only suspended specie payments but that assignments of its assets had been made in New York: "*Not for the benefit of those who have been plundered here, but it is believed to carry out the scheme of fraud originally concocted!*" Leon County, Minutes of the Superior and Circuit Court, Book 4, pp. 203–4. See also ibid., pp. 203, 205, 249, 334, 348, 518; Richard K. Call to William C. Houck, Governor of New York, July 25, 1844, Correspondence of the Governor, Letterbooks, RG 101, ser. 32, vol. 2, n.p., FSAr; *Tallahassee Florida Sentinel,* May 28, 1844.

34. William C. Houck to Richard Keith Call, June 21, 1844; Richard K. Call to William Houck, July 25, 1844, Correspondence of the Governors, Letterbooks, RG 101, ser. 32, vol. 2, n.p., FSAr.

35. *St. Augustine Florida Herald and Southern Democrat,* October 31, 1843; *St. Augustine News,* October 7, 23, November 4, 1843, January 20, 1844. The St. Johns and Mosquito County Grand Jury demanded that "proper authorities demand [the

runaways] from . . . the Queen of Great Britain" so that they may be returned and "brought to trial and suffer such punishment as by our laws they may be found to have incurred." *St. Augustine News,* December 2, 1843; *Tallahassee Florida Sentinel,* October 17, 1843; *Baltimore (Maryland) Niles Register,* December 9, 1843; *Apalachicola Commercial Advertiser,* March 11, 1844; Secretary of State to Joseph Browne, November 25, 1843, in Clarence E. Carter, ed., *Territorial Papers of the United States,* 26 vols. (Washington, D.C.: U.S. Government Printing Office, 1934–62), 26:792–93.

Chapter 12

1. *Apalachicola Gazette,* November 25, 1837; Clarence E. Carter, ed., *Territorial Papers of the United States: Territory of Florida,* 26 vols. (Washington, D.C.: U.S. Government Printing Office, 1934–62), 26:18.

2. William F. Steele to the Secretary of State, May 1822, in Carter, *Territorial Papers,* 22:447–48.

3. William Sebree to Secretary of State, May 1, 1823, in ibid., 22:677.

4. *St. Augustine East Florida Herald,* March 29, 1823; *Pensacola Floridian,* November 15, 1823.

5. *St. Augustine News,* May 1, 1840.

6. Judge Webb to Secretary of the Treasury, April 9, 1829, in Carter, *Territorial Papers,* 24:183–85.

7. Presentment of the Grand Jury of the Southern District, May 9, 1829, in ibid., 24:215–16.

8. Judge Marvin to Delegate Levy, November 20, 1841, in ibid., 26:403. See also Presentment of the Grand Jury of Monroe County, May Term 1841, in ibid., 26:404–5. That same year the territorial legislature also passed a resolution to request an appropriation for a jail at Key West. They claimed their city was "exposed to the aggression of the wicked and lawless," who were often "set at large . . . or make their escape on account of the insufficiency of the jail." *Tallahassee Star of Florida,* April 7, 1842.

9. *Tallahassee Floridian,* May 26, 1838.

10. Ibid., November 9, 1839; *Tallahassee Floridian and Journal,* December 20, 1851.

11. *St. Augustine Florida Herald and Southern Democrat,* December 31, 1840.

12. *St. Augustine News,* January 29, 1841; *St. Augustine Florida Herald and Southern Democrat,* February 5, 1841.

13. *Pensacola Gazette,* October 26, 1827.

14. *Tallahassee Floridian,* October 25, 1837.

15. Ibid., May 26, 1838.

16. Monroe County, Minutes of the Superior Court, 1830–40, pp. 354–55, PKYL.

17. *Pensacola Gazette,* June 24, 1848; *Newport Gazette,* February 16, 1847; Clay County, Minutes of the Circuit Court, Book 1, p. 38.

18. *Jacksonville Florida News,* September 24, 1847. The Marion County Board of County Commissioners announced that it would begin accepting "sealed proposals for a contract to erect a jail at Ocala." "Proposal for Building a Jail," *Ocala Argus,* February 26, 1848.

19. Hillsborough County, Minutes of the County Commissioners, pp. 27, 29.

20. *Tallahassee Florida Sentinel,* November 18, 1845; Jefferson County, Minutes of the County Commissioners, pp. 7, 20–21; Jefferson County, Minutes of the Circuit Court, Book A, pp. 24, 26, 43, 45, 63.

21. *Jacksonville Courier,* January 1, 1835; *St. Augustine News,* June 1, 1839; Duval County, Minutes of the County Court, Book 1, pp. 33–35, 41, 54, 57, SLF.

22. *Apalachicola Gazette,* April 13, 20, 1839.

23. Report of the Committee on Claims, 1845, Nineteenth-Century Florida State Legislature, RG 915, ser. 887, box 1, folder 2, FSAr.

24. Escambia County, Minutes of the Superior Court, Book 1, p. 137.

25. *Pensacola Gazette,* August 21, 1824.

26. Ibid., June 8, 15, 1827.

27. Ibid., June 8, 1827.

28. Monroe County, Minutes of the Superior Court, 1830–40, pp. 26–29, PKYL; Southern District of Florida, Minutes of the U.S. District Court, 1828–37, Carta 1, pp. 8–9, 39–40, RG 21, NAEP; *Key West Register and Commercial Advertiser,* June 4, 1829.

29. Monroe County, Minutes of the Superior Court, 1830–40, pp. 241–45, PKYL; *Key West Enquirer,* January 3, April 11, 1835. "Cactus," a correspondent to the above journal, noted that the jail in Jackson square presented a "very jail-like appearance externally—We have not seen the interior arrangement." Ibid., November 8, 1834; Account Current with William Whitehead, One of the Jail Commissioners Appointed to Superintend the Building of a Jail at Key West in the Southern Judicial District, April 1, 1835, Territorial Auditor, Vouchers, RG 352, ser. 584, box 2, folder 4, FSAr.

30. Monroe County GJP, May 1841, Monroe County Case Files.

31. Monroe County GJP, November 1849, Monroe County Case Files. See also Monroe County, Minutes of the Superior and Circuit Court, Book A, pp. 415–16; see Monroe County GJP, November 1850, Monroe County Case Files.

32. *Ocala Florida Home Companion,* December 22, 1857.

33. *St. Augustine Florida Herald,* October 25, 1838.

34. *Apalachicola Commercial Advertiser,* March 10, 1858.

35. *Tallahassee Florida Sentinel,* November 18, 1845; *Tallahassee Floridian and Journal,* November 22, 1845.

36. *Tallahassee Florida Sentinel,* November 5, 1850; *Tallahassee Floridian and Journal,* November 9, 1850.

37. Gadsden County, Minutes of the Circuit Court, Book 1, p. 336; *Tallahassee Florida Sentinel,* March 22, 1853.

38. *St. Augustine Ancient City,* November 15, 1851.

39. Jackson County, Minutes of the Circuit Court, Book D, pp. 120, 596.

40. Petition to Madison Starke Perry, n.d., Correspondence of Madison Starke Perry and John Milton, RG 101, ser. 577, box 1, folder 1, FSAr.

41. Affidavit of Drs. Randolph and Gamble, August 30, 1849, Correspondence of William D. Moseley, RG 101, ser. 679, box 2, folder 1, FSAr; Proclamation of William D. Moseley, August 31, 1849, Book of Record (Proclamations), RG 156, ser. 13, Book 1, no. 102, p. 82, FSAr.

42. Pardon of Leonidus McNeal, September 19, 1846, Book of Record (Procla-

mations), RG 156, ser. 13, Book 1, no. 40, p. 30, FSAr; Pardon of Isaac Kent, December 14, 1848, ibid., Book 1, no. 87, p. 69.

43. Ibid., Book 1, no. 23, p. 19.

44. Joseph Finegan to James E. Broome, December 9, 1856, Correspondence of James Broome, RG 101, ser. 777, box 3, folder 2, FSAr.

45. *Apalachicola Commercial Advertiser,* August 1, 1840.

46. Affidavit of Dr. A. J. Baldwin, February 6, 1858, in Coroner's Inquest over the Body of Henry Hawkins, August 4, 1857, Comptroller's Vouchers, Criminal Prosecutions, RG 350, ser. 565, box 1, folder 8, Duval County, FSAr.

47. Jackson County, Minutes of the Circuit Court, Book D, p. 298.

48. Leon County, Minutes of the Superior and Circuit Court, Book 4, pp. 340–41.

49. Leon County, Minutes of the Circuit Court, Book 6, pp. 89, 119.

50. On May 7, 1838, Gadsden County jailer L. J. Bell offered a $30 reward for the capture of Michael Killala, an escaped prisoner sent to Quincy from Apalachicola. See *Tallahassee Floridian,* May 19, 1838. Also breaking free was John Davis, indicted for murder in Monroe County. Judge James Webb had ordered that Davis be transported to the Middle District for confinement. See Order of Judge James Webb, May 5, 1837, in *Territory v John Davis,* 1837, Monroe County Case Files. Three Franklin County prisoners also escaped. Asa Ferris, Simpson Vaughn, and David Wooden, all "mariners," were charged in the murder of John Butterworth in Franklin. See Proclamation of Richard Keith Call, July 13, 1837, in *Tallahassee Floridian,* July 22, 1837.

51. Gadsden County, Minutes of the Circuit Court, Book 1, p. 66; *Tallahassee Floridian and Journal,* June 1, 1850; *Tallahassee Florida Sentinel,* June 4, 1850. In 1853 the grand jury presented that the "county jail, its decaying timbers and horrid condition presents little obstacle to the escape of prisoners. . . . Even if their flight is provided against, the same causes combine with the negligence with which the jail is kept operates to produce an atmosphere which is revolting to humanity. To expose even the condemned criminal to such an atmosphere is bad enough, much less one who is awaiting trial and may prove innocent." Gadsden County, Minutes of the Circuit Court, Book 1, p. 336; *Tallahassee Florida Sentinel,* March 22, 1853. The next year the grand jury reported that the "gaol . . . is altogether unfit for the use for which it is intended." In the fall of 1857 the grand jury "earnestly reiterated [the] sentiments expressed" in previous presentments regarding the "unfitness, and foul state" of the jail. They "again call[ed] attention to the county commission" that the jail "remains in the dilapidated and decayed condition." Gadsden County GJP, Fall 1857, Gadsden County Case Files.

52. Order of Judge J. Wayles Baker, March 13, 1861, in *State v Jacob Wilder,* Gadsden County Case Files.

53. David S. Rogers to G. W. Glenn, July [?], 1832, Microfilm 144-K, MSL. For Rogers's trial and controversial appeal process see *Tallahassee Floridian,* May 1, 8, 15, June 19, July 31, August 14, 1832, November 9, 23, 1833; *St. Augustine Florida Herald,* July 12, September 13, 1832, November 28, 1833.

54. Proclamation for the Arrest of Charmack Selph and Proclamation for the Arrest of William Selph, in *Tallahassee Floridian and Journal,* October 7, 1854; *Jacksonville Florida News,* October 14, 1854; Book of Record (Proclamations), RG 156,

ser. 13, Book 1, no. 251, pp. 239–40, FSAr. *State v William and Charmack Selph,* 1854, Comptroller's Vouchers, Criminal Prosecutions, RG 350, ser. 565, box 3, folder 3, Hernando County, and box 4, folder 3, Leon County, FSAr.

55. *Tallahassee Floridian and Journal,* February 24, April 7, 1855.

56. *Jacksonville Standard,* March 24, April 21, 1859. Also indicted were William Tyler and John and Eli Prescott. Orange County, Minutes of the Circuit Court, Book A, p. 146.

57. *Ocala Florida Home Companion* quoted in St. Augustine *Examiner,* March 31, 1860; *Fernandina East Floridian,* January 5, 1860. See also *State v Aaron Jernigan et al.,* 1859, Comptroller's Vouchers, Criminal Prosecutions, RG 350, ser. 565, box 4, folder 10, Marion County, FSAr. Of the seven men indicted for murder, only William Tyler was tried. He was convicted for manslaughter, sentenced to thirty days in jail, and fined $200. Orange County, Minutes of the Circuit Court, Book A, pp. 171, 174, 190–91.

58. *Tallahassee Floridian and Journal,* March 26, April 2, November 26, 1859; *Jacksonville Standard,* March 3, 1859; Proclamation for the Arrest of James Ellison, March 31, 1859, Book of Record (Proclamations), RG 156, ser. 13, book 1, no. 325, p. 319, FSAr. James Ellison was captured in Georgia, but the man who apprehended him had difficulty collecting the reward. See F. L. Villepigue to A. H. Bush, August 2, 1860, Correspondence of the Secretary of State, RG 150, ser. 24, Letterbook 2, n.p., FSAr.

59. *Tallahassee Floridian,* February 19, 1842; *St. Augustine News,* March 5, 1842; *Tallahassee Florida Sentinel,* February 18, 1842; *St. Augustine Florida Herald and Southern Democrat,* March 4, 1842; *Tallahassee Star of Florida,* February 17, 1842.

60. *Key West Enquirer,* November 22, 1834, July 25, 1835; *Jacksonville Courier,* September 10, 1836; *Pensacola Gazette,* January 9, 1836; *Territory v James Simonds,* 1835, Monroe County Case Files; Monroe County, Minutes of the Superior Court, 1830–40, pp. 234, 239, 272, 338–39, PKYL.

61. *Pensacola Democrat,* January 30, 1846.

62. *Madison Southern Messenger* quoted in *St. Augustine Examiner,* May 12, 1860.

63. The fugitives were Moses Townsend, Spencer Townsend, William Saffold, and John McDowell. Jefferson County GJP, November 29, 1834, Jefferson County, Minutes of the Superior Court, Book 1, p. 133; *Tallahassee Floridian,* December 6, 1834.

64. Jefferson County, Minutes of the Superior Court, Book 1, pp. 199–200; *Territory v Will McCardell,* 1837, Jefferson County Case Files.

65. Proclamation for the Arrest of Hugh Duncan and Alek, in *Tallahassee Floridian,* July 28, 1838.

66. Order of Judge Thomas Randall, January 10, 1837, in *Territory v Samuel Barrington,* 1837, Jefferson County Case Files. Barrington was convicted of a misdemeanor and fined $25 in the November 1837 term of court. Jefferson County, Minutes of the Superior Court, Book 1, pp. 217, 238.

67. Proclamation for the Arrest of James Huguenin, in *Tallahassee Floridian,* July 22, 1837. Petitioners in Gadsden County wrote to the legislative council in favor of Withers, asking the body to pass a special law to revoke his fine. They claimed that the evidence at his trial demonstrated that Withers was "only guilty of an Error of judgement as a disposition to be *lenient* and not guilty of any evil intention or dis-

position to aid in the escape of the prisoner." Petition of the Citizens of Gadsden County to the Senate and House of Representatives of Florida, November 1, 1838, Territorial Legislative Council, Bicameral, RG 910, ser. 877, box 1, folder 2, FSAr.

68. *Tallahassee Floridian,* November 13, 1847; *Tallahassee Southern Journal,* November 22, 1847; *Jacksonville Florida News,* November 26, 1847.

69. *Jacksonville Florida News,* June 3, 1848; *St. Augustine Florida Herald and Southern Democrat,* May 27, 1848.

70. Isaac Bronson to David L. Yulee, June 1, 1848, Attorney General's Papers, Letters Received, Florida, 1821–61, RG 60, box 1, NA.

71. St. Johns County, Minutes of the Circuit Court, Book A, p. 63. In a surprising move, Gov. William Moseley remitted Eubank's fine. See Pardon of James Rogers, July 1848, Book of Record (Proclamations), RG 156, ser. 13, book 1, no. 78, pp. 62–63, FSAr.

72. *Jacksonville Florida News,* November 10, 1855.

Chapter 13

1. Marxist historian Eric J. Hobsbawm has cast those who participated in gangs as "social bandits." See *Primitive Rebels* (Manchester, England: Glencoe, 1959). Others have followed his lead to imply that some sort of "Robin Hood" phenomenon was at work. This interpretation gives these lawbreakers a kind of hero status. See Richard White, "Outlaw Gangs of the Middle Border: American Social Bandits," *Western Historical Quarterly* 12 (October 1981): 387–408; Kent L. Steckmesser, "Robin Hood and the American Outlaw," *Journal of American Folklore* 79 (April 1966): 348–55; and Paul Kooistra, *Criminals as Heroes: Structure, Power, and Identity* (Bowling Green, Ohio: Bowling Green State University Press, 1989). There is some evidence of this phenomenon in Florida and elsewhere in the South after the Civil War, when railroad companies and banks—often the victims of gangs—were viewed as preying off the public. But this was less so in the antebellum era. There is little evidence to suggest that gangs and their members ever achieved a heroic status. On the contrary, gang members were the most hated and feared persons in Florida in these years.

2. The most reliable and informed treatment of lynching in the Old South is still Clement Eaton, "Mob Violence in the Old South," *Mississippi Valley Historical Review* 29 (December 1942): 351–70; and idem, *The Growth of the Southern Civilization, 1790–1860* (New York: Harper, 1961), pp. 75–77. See also Richard M. Brown, *Strain of Violence: Historical Studies of American Violence and Vigilantism* (New York: Oxford University Press, 1975); idem, "The American Vigilante Tradition," in *Violence in America: Historical and Comparative Perspectives,* ed. Hugh Davis Graham and Ted Robert Gurr (Washington, D.C.: U.S. Government Printing Office, 1969), 1:121–80; and idem, "The History of Vigilantism in America," in *Vigilante Politics,* ed. H. Jon Rosenbawm and Peter C. Sederberg (Philadelphia: University of Pennsylvania Press, 1976), pp. 79–109.

3. On Florida's postwar experience with vigilantism see Jerrell H. Shofner, *Nor Is It Over Yet: Florida in the Era of Reconstruction, 1863–1877* (Gainesville: University of Florida Press, 1974); Canter Brown Jr., *Florida's Peace River Frontier* (Orlando: University of Central Florida Press, 1991), pp. 239–54; and Robert Ingalls, *Urban*

Vigilantes in the New South: Tampa, 1882–1936 (Knoxville: University of Tennessee Press, 1988).

4. On September 19, 1835, the *Key West Enquirer* reported that "from the disclosures of a man named Murrel at present in a Tennessee Penitentiary, . . . there is every reason to believe that the intended insurrection in Mississippi was but part of an extensive conspiracy" extending "throughout the slave holding states. Confederates are scattered in every direction." The *Richmond Enquirer* claimed to have a partial list of some 456 of Murrell's conspirators, 16 of them Floridians. James Lal Penick Jr., after extensive study, has determined that Murrell's vast nationwide organization was a hoax, the creation of Virgil A. Stewart, his captor, the author of *A History of the Detection, Conviction, and the Designs of John A. Murrell,* published in 1835. The book went through many editions and was widely read throughout the South. See Penick, *The Great Western Land Pirate: John A. Murrell in Legend and History* (Columbia: University of Missouri Press, 1981); and idem, "John A. Murrell: A Legend of the Old Southwest," *Tennessee Historical Quarterly* 48 (Fall 1989): 174–83. For the scare in Mississippi see Edwin A. Miles, "The Mississippi Slave Insurrection Scare of 1835," *Journal of Negro History,* 42 (January 1957): 48–60; and Eaton, "Mob Violence in the Old South," pp. 359–361.

5. *Tallahassee Floridian,* November 4, 1835; *St. Augustine Florida Herald,* September 10, 1835; *Jacksonville Courier,* September 3, 10, 1835.

6. Judge Reid's reference came during a trial in the Alachua County Superior Court involving two slaves accused of murdering a white man. Robert R. Reid Charge to the Jury, August 9, 1837, in *St. Augustine Florida Herald,* August 25, 1837. For Cotton's lynching see *Tallahassee Floridian,* November 14, 1835.

7. Thomas J. Hodson to Eugene Hodson, August 13, 1846, Hodson Letters, SLF.

8. *Tallahassee Florida Sentinel,* August 18, 1846.

9. Ibid., August 11, 18, 1846; *Tallahassee Floridian,* August 1, 1846.

10. *Tallahassee Floridian,* October 10, 1846.

11. *Tallahassee Southern Journal,* September 22, 29, 1846. Proclamation for the Arrest of Young and Clifton in Book of Record (Proclamations), RG 156, ser. 13, Book 1, no. 39, p. 29, FSAr; *Tallahassee Floridian,* October 3, 1846; *Tallahassee Florida Sentinel,* September 8, 1846. John Black and Thomas Smith were also hanged. *Jacksonville Florida News,* October 16, 23, 1846; *Tallahassee Floridian,* October 3, 10, 1846; *Baltimore (Maryland) Niles Register,* October 24, 1846, p. 122. Ten men were indicted on charges of slave stealing, robbery, and murder, including the proprietor of the stage line, Reuben Scott. (His indictment was quashed.) Holloman, Flowers, Smith, and Black were the only ones found guilty. See *State v Jessee Robinson, Thomas Smith, John Black, Dempsey Tidwell, John, a slave, Alvin Flowers, Samuel Holloman, William Carruthers, Sam, a slave, and Reuben Scott,* 1846, Comptroller's Vouchers, Criminal Prosecutions, RG 350, ser. 565, box 3, folder 1, Gadsden County, FSAr.

12. *Tallahassee Floridian,* October 10, 1846. See also ibid., October 31, 1846; and *Jacksonville Florida News,* November 13, 1846.

13. *Pensacola Gazette,* June 28, 1845.

14. Ibid.

15. *Tallahassee Florida Sentinel,* August 4, 1846; *Tallahassee Floridian,* August 1, 8, 1846.

16. *Tallahassee Florida Sentinel,* August 4, 1846. Four years earlier, authorities near Irwinton (Eufala), Alabama, had broken up a gang of "Murrellites" organized in military fashion. John L. Scott, a member of the gang, confessed at his trial that the gang had so many members that a special handshake grip was devised "by which they might be enabled immediately to recognize each other." The editor thought that the remnants of this gang had come to Florida to resume like activities. See *Irwinton (Alabama) Shield* quoted in *Tallahassee Florida Sentinel,* May 13, 1842. See also ibid., August 4, 1846.

17. Hatheway Diary, n.p., MSL.

18. *Territory v David Burney, William Burney, and Harrison Adams,* 1843, Jefferson County Case Files; Proclamation for the Arrest of William Burney and David Burney, July 17, 1843, in Correspondence of the Governors, Letterbooks, RG 101, ser. 32, vol. 2, n.p., FSAr. Georgia Gov. George Crawford's Proclamation was issued on February 26, 1844, ibid.; *Tallahassee Florida Sentinel,* October 21, 1843; *Tallahassee Star of Florida,* August 11, 1843; *Pensacola Gazette,* August 5, 1843. The Burneys were never apprehended. Minutes of the "Public Meeting for the Protection of Property and Upholding the Cause of Justice," *Tallahassee Floridian,* November 22, 1845; *Tallahassee Florida Sentinel,* November 25, 1845.

19. *State v Stephen Yeomans,* 1845, Jefferson County Case Files; Jefferson County, Minutes of the Circuit Court, Book A, p. 12; *Pensacola Gazette,* January 24, 1846; *Baltimore (Maryland) Niles Register,* January 17, 1846.

20. *Apalachicola Commercial Advertiser,* May 9, 1846; *Baltimore (Maryland) Niles Register,* June 6, 1846.

21. *Tallahassee Florida Sentinel,* May 5, 1846. For other impassioned appeals against lynching see Judge William Marvin's Charge to the Dade and Monroe County Grand Jury, in *Tallahassee Florida Sentinel,* November 26, 1841; "Lynch's Law," *Pensacola Gazette,* May 31, 1828; "Stoppage of Laws," *Tallahassee Florida Sentinel,* May 13, 1842; and Judge Robert Reid's Charge to the Alachua, Hillsborough, and Columbia Counties Superior Court in *St. Augustine Florida Herald,* August 25, 1837.

22. *Tallahassee Florida Sentinel,* June 9, November 28, 1846.

23. For an example see "A Citizen of Columbia" to the editor of the *News,* February 10, 1846, in *Tallahassee Floridian,* February 21, 1846. The undersigned defended the decision of citizens in Columbia County to form a vigilance committee on the grounds that "life has been assaulted under the canopy of darkness, stores have been broken open, and rifled of their contents, our moral atmosphere has been darkened by scenes of midnight revelry and debauchery, that would reflect, if possible, disgrace upon the inmates of a brothel." Moreover, he insisted that the editor of the *News,* "remote from the theatre of commotion," had no right to label those involved a band of "*quasi* deputy sheriffs."

24. Eliza Bailey to Burton Bailey, September 23, 1848, Bellamy-Bailey Papers, PKYL.

25. *Jacksonville Florida News,* September 16, 1848.

26. Ibid., October 28, 1848, June 16, 1849; *Tallahassee Southern Journal,* November 6, 1848; *Tallahassee Floridian and Journal,* June 16, 1849.

27. *Jacksonville Florida News,* May 10, 1851. Hardin's most daring exploit in Florida was the robbery of the Jacksonville Hotel in 1848. A party of community leaders offered $100 for his arrest. See "$100 Reward for John B. Hardin, Escaped

from the Duval County Jail," in ibid., January 13, 1849; *Jacksonville Florida Republican,* December 14, 1848. For the events leading up to his capture see *Tallahassee Floridian and Journal,* April 26, May 3, 1851; *Pensacola Gazette,* April 19, 1851. Hardin admitted that he "richly deserved death, for he had been a villain all his life." He declared that he had twenty wives and had killed at least sixteen other men. "He refused any further confession, as he would implicate many heads of families who passed as respectable and would thereby leave many widows and orphans." Hardin, a witness noted, "met death without a shudder; was as cool as a cucumber." *Jacksonville Florida News,* June 14, 1851; *Pensacola Gazette,* May 31, 1851; *Tallahassee Floridian and Journal,* June 14, 1851.

28. "A Descent among the Murrellites," *Jacksonville Florida News,* August 11, 1855.

29. *Tallahassee Floridian and Journal,* November 21, 1857.

30. Ibid., January 8, 1859.

31. The *Tampa Florida Peninsular,* though silent at the time, one and a half years later admitted the existence of a regulating band in the Tampa area. Editor A. Delaunay insisted that this extrajudicial activity was necessary because the town was "infested with gamblers, black-legs, thieves, robbers, and cutthroats of every shade of high and low degree" with whom the civil authorities were powerless to deal. "The first law of nature was resumed. The ordinary process being powerless." *Tampa Florida Peninsular,* January 21, 1860. Subsequent reminiscences of persons in later years suggest that regulators were indeed active. See *Tampa Sunland Tribune,* September 1, 1877; James McKay, "History of Tampa of the 'Olden Days,' " *Tampa Daily Times,* December 18, 1923; Mrs. N. M. Jones, "Early Days in Florida—Some Interesting Incidents in the History of Polk County," *Bartow Courier-Informant,* October 5, 1905; "Peace River Reminiscences," in ibid., September 21, 1890; G. W. Hendry, "Fort Meade's Later History," *Fort Meade Leader,* June 12, 1913; *Jacksonville Florida Times-Union,* July 27, September 28, 1891; and S. Hammock, "The Simon Hammock Settlement," *Tampa Guardian,* April 21, 1886.

32. *Tampa Florida Peninsular,* April 17, 1858. I wish to thank Canter Brown Jr., who shared many of his materials with me. Much of the discussion of the regulator movement in the Tampa Bay area owes immeasurably both to these materials and to extensive conversations with him.

33. *Tampa Florida Peninsular,* May 1, 1858; *Ocala Florida Home Companion,* May 4, 11, 1858; *Tallahassee Floridian and Journal,* May 8, 1858.

34. " 'Veritas,' to Mr. Editor," *Newport Wakulla Times,* June 23, 1858. Historian Canter Brown Jr. has depicted this controversy as the result of a political dogfight between James Magbee and Henry Crane, late editor of the *Tampa Florida Peninsular,* for the control of the Democratic Party in Tampa. See Brown, *Florida's Peace River Frontier,* p. 126.

35. S. T. Bowen to Editor, June 24, 1858, in *Savannah Daily Republican,* June 30, 1858.

36. "The Tampa Affair," *Savannah Daily Republican,* July 14, 1858; *New York Tribune,* July 3, 1858; *New York Times,* July 3, 1858.

37. "The Early Pioneer Days, Captain Watson Tells of His Return from the Indian Wars, How Tampa Treated Cut-Throats," *Jacksonville Florida Times-Union,* September 28, 1891.

38. *Tallahassee Florida Sentinel,* November 26, 1841.

39. Locomotive, "The Cause and the Remedy," *Tampa Florida Peninsular,* May 1, 1858.

40. "Regulating Clubs," *Tallahassee Floridian and Journal,* July 31, 1858.

41. *St. Augustine Examiner,* April 28, 1860.

42. On the "Calhoun County War" see "Calhoun County in a State of Insurrection," *St. Augustine Examiner,* October 20, 1860; "Civil War in Calhoun—Quiet Restored," *Tallahassee Floridian Journal,* October 13, 1860; ibid., November 17, 1860; "Horrible Murders in Calhoun County, Florida—County in a State of Insurrection," *Fernandina East Floridian,* October 18, 1860; and "Calhoun Difficulties Settled," ibid., October 31, 1860. See also Abstract of Accounts in favor of J. B. Stone, Clerk of the Circuit Court of Calhoun County, Comptroller's Vouchers, Criminal Prosecutions, RG 350, ser. 565, box 1, folder 2, Calhoun County, FSAr.

43. Eaton, "Mob Violence in the Old South," p. 367.

44. Judge James King promptly returned from his dinner and issued a warrant for their arrest, but they were never apprehended. *Ocala Florida Home Companion,* April 13, 1858. State criminal prosecution records contain the schedule of costs of Such or Jack, a slave accused of killing Leroy Hogens in Nassau County in 1858. The account states that the "prisoner was rescued from the court while on his trial and was found dead the next morning." See *State v Such or Jack, a Slave,* 1858, in Comptroller's Vouchers, Criminal Prosecutions, RG 350, ser. 565, box 5, folder 2, Nassau County, FSAr.

45. *Fernandina East Floridian,* December 19, 1860.

46. *Tallahassee Floridian and Journal,* November 10, 1860; *Tampa Florida Peninsular,* October 20, 27, November 3, 1860; *Fernandina East Floridian,* October 18, 1860.

47. *Fernandina East Floridian,* March 8, 22, 29, 1860; *St. Augustine Examiner,* February 25, March 24, 1860; *Tallahassee Floridian and Journal,* March 21, 1860; *Cedar Keys Telegraph,* March 3, September 1, 1860; *Tampa Florida Peninsular,* February 25, March 24, 1860.

48. *Cedar Keys Telegraph,* March 3, 1860.

49. Ives Journal, April 26, 1861, p. 104, SLF; *St. Augustine Examiner,* May 4, 1861.

50. *Fernandina East Floridian,* November 21, December 6, 1860.

51. "Insurrection in Madison," *St. Augustine Examiner,* December 1, 1860. One month earlier, Washington Ives of Lake City recorded in his diary that "tonight there was great excitement, the militia was called out, to suppress a supposed revolt of slaves." The cause: sixty slaves were missing from a nearby plantation, and another slave "confessed knowing about Lincoln's election as a thing to free him." Ives Journal, November 20, 1860, p. 64, SLF.

52. *Micanopy Peninsular Gazette* quoted in *St. Augustine Examiner,* September 29, 1860.

53. *Tallahassee Floridian and Journal,* November 3, 1860; *St. Augustine Examiner,* November 3, 1860.

54. *St. Augustine Examiner,* November 10, 1860.

55. Calvin L. Robinson, "Memoirs of Calvin L. Robinson," n.d., pp. 1–4, PKYL.

56. *Fernandina East Floridian,* August 2, 9, 1860.

57. Ibid.

58. Ives Journal, September 8, 1860, p. 47, SLF.

59. For these references see ibid., May 8, 22, September 21, 29, October 23, December 7, 11, 29, 1860, January 12, 13, 1861, pp. 15, 19, 50–52, 58, 68, 73, 76; *Fernandina East Floridian,* September 27, 31, 1860.

60. Calvin L. Robinson, "Memoirs of Calvin L. Robinson," PKYL; George E. Buker, *Jacksonville: Riverport-Seaport* (Columbia: University of South Carolina Press, 1992), pp. 60–63.

61. It is no simple coincidence that violence attributed to the regulators broke out in the same areas where it emerged before the Civil War. See Brown, *Strain of Violence,* p. 308. Also on violence in Florida during Reconstruction see Shofner, *Nor Is It Over Yet,* pp. 225–42; Brown, *Florida's Peace River Frontier,* pp. 195–214, 239–54. Ralph L. Peek, "Lawlessness in Florida, 1868–1871," *Florida Historical Quarterly* 40 (October 1961): 164–85; and Janet Snyder Matthews, *Edge of Wilderness: A Settlement History of Manatee River and Sarasota Bay* (Tulsa, Okla.: Caprine Press, 1983), pp. 315–65.

Chapter 14

1. For Jackson County, 108 to 48 (1851–65); for Gadsden County, 57 to 10 (1849–55); for Leon County, 410 to 104 (1826–33, 1841–66); for Jefferson County, 243 to 66 (1828–41, 1846–61); and for Madison County, 93 to 11 (1846–54).

2. For Monroe County, 137 to 57 (1828–53); for Hillsborough County, 83 to 30 (1846–66); and for Escambia County, 323 to 126 (1822–66).

Appendix 1

1. *Territory v Benjamin Donica,* 1827, Escambia County Case Files; *Pensacola Gazette,* June 22, 1827.

2. *Pensacola Gazette,* September 30, 1828; *Pensacola Florida Argus,* September 28, 1828.

3. Walker, Crail's victim, was his common-law wife. She was described as a "worthless female." *Pensacola Gazette,* March 10, 1829; *St. Augustine Florida Herald and Southern Democrat,* April 8, 1829; *Tallahassee Florida Advocate,* March 21, 1829.

4. Sherwood killed Wilson, his "friend and partner," as the latter was trying to break up a fight between Sherwood and someone else. Richard Hackley noted that Sherwood "said nothing at the gallows" but "died stubbornly and did not even change color." *Key West Gazette,* April 26, 1831; Hackley Diary, December 16, 1830, MSL.

5. *Tallahassee Floridian,* July 12, August 14, 1832.

6. *St. Augustine Florida Herald,* February 6, 1834.

7. *Charleston Courier,* January 5, 1836.

8. *Tallahassee Weekly True Democrat,* August 13, 1915.

9. *St. Augustine Florida Herald,* July 15, 1837.

10. *Tallahassee Star of Florida,* February 17, 1842; *Pensacola Gazette,* March 5, 1842; *St. Augustine News,* March 12, 1842.

11. Both Hastings and Greer "exhibited great calmness and resignation in their last moments." They made "solemn and impressive addresses to the spectators, and fully admitted the justice of the sentence they were about to suffer." *St. Augustine*

News, June 13, 1842; *St. Augustine Florida Herald and Southern Democrat,* June 17, 1842.

12. Ibid.

13. Everhart was described as a "cold-blooded and inhumane monster" and "the most hardened villain that has ever *stretched a rope.*" *Apalachicola Commercial Advertiser,* May 24, 1843; *Tallahassee Florida Sentinel,* June 20, 1843.

14. *Tallahassee Floridian,* October 3, 10, 1846; *Jacksonville Florida News,* October 3, 10, 1846.

15. Ibid.

16. Jacobs killed Cherry in a drunken brawl at the Bemis distillery in Newport. He met his "fate with firmness and resignation." *Tallahassee Florida Sentinel,* June 22, 1852.

17. Burns assassinated Alston as the latter was on a "Sunday walk" with his wife. The murder occurred in Jackson County, and the venue was changed to Washington County. Burns, described as having a "particularly ugly and distasteful" appearance, claimed that the deceased had continually threatened him. *Tallahassee Floridian and Journal,* June 12, 1852.

18. *Fernandina East Floridian,* January 5, 1860.

19. Sailors were part of the "crew of the *Enterprise* [and] have been convicted at Key West of the murder of Capt. Morantes, and have been sentenced to execution." Ibid., December 22, 1859.

20. O'Connor was convicted and sentenced to hang on June 29. He escaped while he waited to hear about an appeal to the Florida Supreme Court. He was captured on September 20, 1860. See ibid., September 6, October 11, 1860.

21. *Pensacola West Florida Times,* March 17, 1857; *Fernandina East Floridian,* October 24, 1860.

22. Ammons killed McQuagg in a drunken brawl. His main defense was that McQuagg called his recently deceased mother a "rogue." It is not known whether his sentence was actually carried out, although his appeal failed. "Nothing appearing why sentence of death should not again be passed upon him said Judge, in open court, do sentence the said Ammons to be executed at such time and place as the court may deem fit and proper, and that said court so cause sentence to be carried into execution." *John Ammons v State,* 1861, in *Reports of the Cases Argued and Adjudged in the Supreme Court of Florida,* 9 vols. (Tallahassee, 1845–61): 9:559.

23. The crime was committed under "circumstances of brutal barbarity." Monday was chased by a posse, wounded, and almost lynched. Alachua, Columbia, and Hillsborough Counties, Minutes of the Superior Court, 1828–35, pp. 22, 24–25, PKYL; *Territory v Monday, a Slave,* 1829, Territorial Auditor, Vouchers, RG 352, ser. 584, box 1, folder 3, FSAr.

24. Leon County, Minutes of the Superior Court, Book 1, p. 76.

25. Certificate of Value for Joe and Crittenden, December 15, 1834, Territorial Auditor, Vouchers, RG 352, ser. 584, box 1, folder 7, FSAr.

26. An Act for the Relief of Paul McCormick of Leon County, 1836, Legislative Council, Unicameral, RG 910, ser. 876, box 5, folder 3, FSAr.

27. *St. Augustine Florida Herald,* July 15, 1837.

28. *Pensacola Gazette,* January 5, 1839.

29. Ibid., May 25, 1839.

30. Ibid., June 15, 1839.

31. Caeser was convicted of throwing Herrin into a creek and then taking after "him in a boat and beating him in the water with a paddle and drowning Herrin." Certificate of Value for Caeser, April 15, 1842, Territorial Auditor, Vouchers, RG 352, ser. 584, box 3, folder 4, FSAr.

32. Will admitted that he killed Mrs. Senterfeit at the instigation of a female slave. *Pensacola Gazette,* May 22, 1841.

33. Anthony was found guilty of felony in Hamilton County. He was ordered to be jailed in Leon County and was executed by the marshal there. *Territory v Anthony, a Slave,* 1843, Territorial Auditor, Vouchers, RG 352, ser. 584, box 3, folder 4, FSAr.

34. *Jacksonville Florida News,* September 23, 1848.

35. Jefferson County, Minutes of the Circuit Court, Book A, pp. 217, 223.

36. *State v Arnold,* 1850, Comptroller's Vouchers, Criminal Prosecutions, RG 350, ser. 565, box 1, folder 2, Calhoun County, FSAr.

37. *State v Abraham, a Slave,* 1852, ibid., box 1, folder 5, Columbia County.

38. *State v Joe, a Slave,* 1853, ibid., box 1, folder 2, Calhoun County.

39. *State v Hall,* 1856, ibid., box 4, folder 8, Madison County.

40. *State v Bill Jones, a Slave,* 1856, ibid., box 5, folder 9, Santa Rosa County.

41. Alachua and Levy Counties, Minutes of the Circuit Court, 1850–57, pp. 513–14, 532, PKYL.

42. *Fernandina East Floridian,* May 10, 17, 1860.

43. Ibid., March 29, 1860.

44. Cotton was lynched by the "Livingston Committee" on suspicion of inciting a slave revolt. *Tallahassee Floridian,* November 14, 1835.

45. Avant was the accused leader of an outlaw gang. *Pensacola Gazette,* June 28, 1845.

46. Yeomans was an accused gang leader. Ibid., January 24, 1846; *Baltimore (Maryland) Niles Register,* January 17, 1846.

47. Jewel was accused of operating a gang to perpetrate slave stealing and murder. *Apalachicola Commercial Advertiser,* May 9, 1846; *Baltimore (Maryland) Niles Register,* June 6, 1846.

48. Hardin was accused of murder, slave stealing, and bigamy. He was caught in company with a slave accomplice, and they were lynched together. *Mobile (Alabama) Tribune* quoted in *Jacksonville Florida News,* June 14, 1851; *Pensacola Gazette,* May 31, 1851; *Tallahassee Floridian and Journal,* June 14, 1851.

49. Locke and Sheldon were accused of stealing horses and jewelry in Tampa. *Tampa Florida Peninsular* April 24, 1858; *Ocala Florida Home Companion,* May 11, 1858; *Tallahassee Floridian and Journal,* May 8, 1858.

50. Haywood was "hanged near the racetrack by some person or persons unknown." *Tampa Florida Peninsular,* May 1, 1858.

51. S. T. Bowen, in a letter to the *Savannah Republican* dated June 24, 1858, reported that the four men were lynched on the grounds of their Know-Nothing political affiliation. But the lynching cannot be verified. Several newspapers proclaimed the story a "hoax." See *Tallahassee Floridian and Journal,* July 10, 1858.

52. An unspecified number of thieves were lynched after robbing a train. Ibid., January 8, 1859.

53. Dick was convicted of rape and was lynched as he was waiting for news of his appeal. *Territory v Dick, a Slave,* 1840, Territorial Court of Appeals Case Files, RG 970, ser. 73, box 12, folder 376, FSAr.

54. The victim was caught in company with John B. Hardin, who was accused of murder, slave stealing, and bigamy. They were lynched together. *Mobile (Alabama) Tribune* quoted in *Jacksonville Florida News,* June 14, 1851; *Pensacola Gazette,* May 31, 1851; *Tallahassee Floridian and Journal,* June 14, 1851.

55. Convicted of arson and sentenced to hang, Simon was lynched as he was waiting for word of his appeal. *State v Simon, a Slave,* 1853, Comptroller's Vouchers, Criminal Prosecutions, RG 350, ser. 565, box 2, folder 3, Escambia County, FSAr.

56. Jack or Such was hanged by regulators as a jury was deliberating his guilt in a trial for the murder of a white man named Leroy Hogens. See *Ocala Florida Home Companion,* April 13, 1858; *State v Such or Jack, a Slave,* in Comptroller's Vouchers, Criminal Prosecutions, RG 350, ser. 565, box 5, folder 2, Nassau County, FSAr.

57. Adam was convicted of murder and lynched while he was waiting for word of his appeal. *Tampa Florida Peninsular,* January 21, 1860.

58. The three slaves were accused in the murder of their master, Dr. W. J. Keitt. They were tried and executed by a "committee of twelve free-holders" appointed by a large meeting of the citizens. *Fernandina East Floridian,* March 8, 22, 29, 1860; *St. Augustine Examiner,* February 25, March 24, 1860; *Cedar Keys Telegraph,* March 3, September 1, 1860; *Tampa Florida Peninsular,* February 25, March 24, 1860; *Tallahassee Floridian and Journal,* March 21, 1860.

59. Hemp was accused of killing his master, Albert Clark. *Tampa Florida Peninsular,* October 20, 27, November 3, 1860; *Tallahassee Floridian and Journal,* November 10, 1860; *Fernandina East Floridian,* October 18, 1860.

60. They were accused of plotting to murder their master. *Fernandina East Floridian,* December 19, 1860.

61. Seven slaves were accused in the murder of Richard Plummer at Cunningham Creek, near Mandarin. A crowd apprehended them and, in a curious mix of legal and extralegal procedures ("with counsel on both sides"), determined them to be guilty. Three were hanged and four were given a total of 310 lashes. *St. Augustine Examiner,* May 4, 1861; Ives Journal, April 26, 1861, SLF.

Appendix 2

1. *Acts and Resolutions of the Legislative Council,* 1824, pp. 278–80.

2. Ibid., pp. 252–54.

3. Ibid.

4. Early settlers in Alachua attended superior court in St. Augustine until 1828. *Acts,* 1824, pp. 278–80; 1825, p. 65; 1828, p. 211.

5. Brevard County (previously St. Lucie) was created in 1844. St. Lucie's settlers attended court first in St. Augustine and then (one year later) in the Orange County Circuit Court in Mellonville. See *Acts,* 1844, p. 33; Orange County, Minutes of the Circuit Court, Book A; *St. Augustine Ancient City,* October 12, 1850.

6. The site for the Calhoun County seat changed often. When the county was created in 1838, St. Joseph—just selected as the county seat of Franklin County one year earlier—fell within the area encompassed by the new Calhoun County. Thus

St. Joseph became the de facto county seat, but it soon proved inadequate because its isolated location on the coast made it unpopular with many settlers. In 1845 the legislative council directed that the superior court meet in Iola until a courthouse could be erected. *Acts,* 1845, p. 53. In 1848 a county election selected Panther's Head as the site for the new courthouse, but, as a petition stated soon thereafter, "It however turned out that there were two places in said county known by that name, and it became impossible to determine which of them was balloted for—Consequently, the question is still left open and unsettled." It was requested that Abe Springs Bluff on the Chipola River be selected because it was a place "conveniently central to population and geography." Petition of the Citizens of Calhoun County to the Legislature, 1848, Nineteenth-Century Florida State Legislature, RG 915, ser. 887, box 4, folder 6, FSAr. In 1856 another petition asked that elections be held for a new site on the basis of the "great disadvantage and inconvenience of a majority of the legal voters of said county." Ibid., box 7, folder 4. Later the county site changed to Blountstown.

7. From 1832 until approximately 1833 Columbia County settlers attended court in Newnansville. Alachua, Columbia, and Hillsborough Counties, Minutes of the Superior Court, 1828–35, PKYL; *Acts,* 1832, p. 34.

8. In 1843 the legislative council directed that the superior court meet at Lancaster. *Acts,* 1843, p. 46. In 1845 the county seat was changed to Alligator. Ibid., 1845, p. 50.

9. When Dade County was created in 1836, several settlers complained that there were not enough permanent settlers to constitute a pool of unbiased jurors, arguing also that Jacob Housmann, a prominent land owner and wrecker, had essentially taken over the county's justice system. In 1836 a new law required that superior court be held in Dade County, and it was promptly annulled by act of Congress. The next legislative council reenacted the law. There the matter stood until 1850, when the general assembly consolidated Monroe and Dade Counties, "making them a district for judicial purposes." The measure directed that "all records and papers belonging to Dade Circuit Court shall be transferred to Monroe County." *Acts,* 1836, p. 19; 1841, p. 23; *Tallahassee Florida Sentinel,* December 3, 1841; *Acts and Resolutions of the General Assembly,* 1850, pp. 140–41.

10. In 1844 the legislative council established the Dade County seat at Miami. See *Acts and Resolutions of the Legislative Council,* 1844, p. 17.

11. The first court met in Franklin County in 1832. *Acts,* 1832, p. 103. In 1836 St. Joseph was chosen to replace Apalachicola as county seat, but, when Calhoun County was created the next year, it fell within the new boundaries of that county. Ibid., 1836, pp. 1–2.

12. Early settlers in Gadsden County attended superior court in Tallahassee until 1827. Ibid., 1824, p. 278; 1825, p. 65; 1827, p. 153.

13. From 1827 to 1830 settlers of Hamilton County attended court in Monticello. The legislative council decreed that the first superior court would meet in December 1830. Ibid., 1828, pp. 211, 209; Jefferson County, Minutes of the Superior Court, Book 1.

14. In 1836 the legislative council established Wallburg as the county seat. *Acts,* 1836, p. 11. Later the county seat was changed to Jasper.

15. Created in 1843, Hernando County became Benton County in 1844, only

to become Hernando County again in 1850. Residents attended superior court in Newnansville, but by 1845 regular sessions of the court were held in the county. Ibid., 1845, p. 50; Alachua, Hernando, and Hillsborough Counties, Minutes of the Superior Court, 1838–43, PKYL; Alachua, Hillsborough, Benton, and Marion Counties, Minutes of the Superior and Circuit Court, 1844–50, PKYL.

16. DeSoto was mentioned in *Acts,* 1852, p. 126. Bayport is listed as county site in ibid., 1854, p. 84. Two years later it was decided to move the county seat to a site closer to the center of the county. Ibid., 1856, p. 62. At least courts were held near Pierceville. Finally, a new county seat, Brooksville, was established at that location in 1856. See Richard J. Stanaback, *A History of Hernando County, 1840–1976* (Brooksville, Fla.: Action '76 Steering Committee, 1976), pp. 22–27.

17. Between 1834 and 1845 Hillsborough County settlers attended court in Newnansville. Alachua, Columbia, and Hillsborough Counties, Minutes of the Superior Court, 1828–35, PKYL; Alachua, Hernando, and Hillsborough County, Minutes of the Superior Court, 1838–43, PKYL; Alachua, Hillsborough, Benton, and Marion Counties, Minutes of the Superior and Circuit Court, 1844–50, PKYL.

18. The name was changed to Cerro Gordo in 1860. *Acts,* 1860, p. 172.

19. The first superior court in Jackson County met in 1824 at "such place as shall be appointed by the judges of the county court." Ibid., 1824, p. 278. By 1828 superior courts were meeting at the new county courthouse in Marianna. Ibid., 1828, p. 209.

20. The first superior court in Jefferson County was held in 1828. Ibid., 1827, p. 28.

21. The general assembly directed that court would be held there until a permanent site could be selected. Ibid., 1856, p. 49.

22. Before 1850, Levy County settlers attended court in Newnansville. Ibid., 1845, pp. 55–56; *St. Augustine Ancient City,* October 12, 1850; Alachua and Levy Counties, Minutes of the Circuit Court, 1850–57, PKYL.

23. From 1827 until approximately 1838, settlers in Madison County attended court in Monticello. Jefferson County, Minutes of the Superior Court, Book 1. *Acts,* 1828, p. 211. The first mention of Madison County having its own superior court was in the 1839 laws. See ibid., 1839, p. 17.

24. Early Marion County settlers attended court in Newnansville. In 1844 the legislative council decreed that the superior court would be held in Marion County that May, but the court records reveal that the first session of the Marion County Superior Court was not held until 1848. See ibid., 1844, p. 45–46; Alachua, Hillsborough, Benton, and Marion Counties, Minutes of the Superior and Circuit Court, 1844–50, PKYL.

25. Settlers in Monroe County attended superior court in St. Augustine until 1828. See *Acts,* 1824, pp. 278–80.

26. Nassau County's early settlers attended court in Jacksonville. Ibid., 1824, p. 278. In 1829 the legislative council set the first meeting of the Nassau County Superior Court as March 1830. Ibid., 1829, p. 75. Numerous maps, official documents, and newspapers list the county seat as Nassau C. H., Nassau Court House, Court House, or simply C. H. See ibid., 1833, pp. 51–52; *Tallahassee Floridian,* August 28, 1847; *Jacksonville Florida News,* April 23, 1847. Later, Fernandina was selected as county seat.

27. The legislature stipulated that the court would meet at William Roberts's store until a permanent site could be selected. *Acts,* 1858, p. 38.

28. In 1845 Mosquito County became Orange County. Ibid., 1845, p. 56.

29. Orlando became the county seat of Orange County in 1857.

30. Santa Rosa County was created out of a section of Escambia County in 1842, and superior courts began meeting immediately at Milton. *Acts,* 1842, pp. 3–4.

31. Sumterville became the Sumter County seat in 1858.

32. The legislature stipulated that court meet at William Hines's house until the "necessary buildings may be erected." *Acts,* 1858, p. 38.

33. The legislature directed that court meet at David Bryant's house until the "necessary buildings may be erected." Ibid., 1856, p. 49.

34. Enterprise, the Volusia County seat, previously fell within the boundaries of Mosquito County. In 1843 the town was named the county seat. See ibid., 1843, p. 17. The next year the legislative council decreed that a superior court would meet in Mosquito County. See ibid., 1844, p. 37. Finally, Orange County court minutes indicate that the Volusia Circuit Court sometimes met in Mellonville and Orlando.

35. Wakulla County was created in 1843 out of Leon County, and superior courts began meeting immediately. See ibid., 1843, p. 29.

36. Before 1830, Walton County settlers attended the Escambia County Superior Court in Pensacola. The first superior court for the county was held in 1830. Ibid., 1829, pp. 157–58.

37. Washington County settlers attended court in Marianna until 1833. See ibid., 1828, p. 210. The first evidence of a court meeting in Washington County dates to 1833. See ibid., 1833, p. 50.

38. Roaches Bluff, cited in *Tallahassee Floridian,* August 28, 1847. Later, court was held at Mossy Hill Meeting House. *Acts,* 1848, p. 69. Other county sites for court meetings were William A. Lofton's home near St. Andrews Bay, the Holmes Valley Post Office, Staple's Landing (on Holmes Creek), and Vernon. I wish to thank Brian R. Rucker for his assistance in this matter.

Bibliography

A Note on Sources

Newspapers, court records, official documents of the territorial and statehood periods, and manuscript collections helped to preserve the record of Florida's criminal justice system. Newspapers for Pensacola, St. Augustine, and Tallahassee are the most extensive, but files also exist for Jacksonville, St. Joseph, Quincy, Apalachicola, Marianna, Key West, Fernandina, Ocala, Cedar Key, Newnansville, and Tampa. Newspapers offer detailed descriptions of crimes. Editors often published letters received from eyewitnesses, and editorial comment was sometimes included. Still, for political and other reasons, newspapers often gave biased accounts of criminal conduct, especially if the people involved were politicians or had strong political connections.

Many editors, reluctant to alienate a large portion of their readership, made it a policy not to notice crimes committed in their locale, giving only vague references to a robbery, affray, or melee if it occurred in the general vicinity. Difficulties of a potentially political nature were sometimes avoided. Some feared that reporting the facts would prejudice potential jurors in sparsely settled districts where adequate numbers of grand and petit jurors were difficult to obtain. Some editors claimed that extensive notice of lawbreaking had the effect of increasing crime.

Even so, crime topics fascinated readers and occupied much space in antebellum Florida's newspapers. Readers of the local press were treated to extensive coverage of crimes committed in other districts, while crimes committed in the immediate area received only vague reference. In sparsely settled regions most residents knew what was going on in the immediate area but hungered for exciting news from other districts. Editors often published letters from other towns detailing a murder, trial, or public execution. Consequently, to learn about a murder that occurred in Tallahassee, readers might have to consult newspapers in Pensacola or St. Augustine.

Criminal court records are an invaluable source for the study of criminal behavior. Three major types have been used. First, the minute books of the superior and circuit courts can usually be found at the county seats. Minute books are the official record of criminal prosecution within a district, but they are largely restricted to the simple recording of indictments, pleas, and verdicts. They provide information regarding the number and type of indictments and conviction rates in particular districts.

Minute books also reveal the names of grand and petit jurors and the attorneys in the case. Clerks, grand jurors, or judges, if they wished, could have presentments or a judge's charge to the jury included in the official record. Rules regarding such inclusion were vague and varied from county to county. To say the least, the researcher is never quite sure what he or she will find. But the extensive use of court minutes has its pitfalls. There are certain seductive qualities about these records. There is a kind of natural inclination to leap into a kind of mania for quantitative analysis in an effort to "prove" long-term trends or themes regarding such things as the frequency of crime, which types of crime were most prosecuted, the efficiency of prosecution, and even which types of crimes society found most threatening. Surviving court minutes give only a rough estimate of crime. This is so because of gaps in the record, clerical mistakes of the court officials, and, of course, because a large number of crimes simply went unrecorded.

Minute books can be significantly supplemented with case files, also housed at the county seats. At the time of a case's adjudication, a file was created that included all pertinent paperwork. These "bundles," filed with the county clerk, contain bills of indictment, summons, warrants, affidavits, pleas, bonds, decrees, the judge's charges to the jury, the coroner's inquests, and, most important of all, actual trial testimony. Case files from many counties have escaped courthouse fires, rats and moths, and even destruction by county officials themselves. Where available, criminal prosecutions can be traced through minute books, case files, and newspapers.

Also important to the researcher are grand jury presentments. These "state of the county" reports, recorded after every court session, addressed many matters. They made observations and recommendations concerning the conduct of judges, officers of the court, and law enforcement officials; the condition of jails, courthouses, and roads; the treatment and supervision of slaves; and the need for additional laws.

Presentments also noted community practices that led to crime, especially violations of the liquor laws. Virtually no issue or problem—local, state, or national—escaped comment. Grand jury presentments were often recorded in minute books or could be found among loose documents included among case files. Presentments were usually published in newspapers and were easily converted into petitions to be sent to the legislative council, general assembly, Congress, or even the president.

The third major source of this study are official territorial, state, and federal documents concerning law enforcement. In the territorial period most criminal prosecutions were paid for by the federal government. Clerks, district attorneys, and marshals had to submit their accounts to the territorial auditor's office in Tallahassee for reimbursement. In both the territorial and the statehood periods, county law enforcement officials worked on the fee system. Schedules of the costs to prosecute each criminal case had to be made out before fees were paid. Many cases also required extra expenses. Sometimes special guards had to be requisitioned and extra distances traveled. All additional expenditures had to be carefully recorded, certified by a judge, and forwarded to the territorial auditor before officials could be reimbursed.

After the territorial period, the state assumed full financial responsibility for violations of its own criminal code. Accounts were certified or rejected by the state comptroller. (Prosecutions brought before federal court and under federal law were still paid for by the federal government.) The Florida State Archives has preserved these financial records. Included in this data are the schedules submitted by county law enforcement officials for each criminal prosecution. Also included is correspondence to authorities in Tallahassee regarding special problems encountered in a specific case, or justification for particular claims disallowed by the comptroller. Financial records provide a relevant source in recording law enforcement in nineteenth-century Florida.

Among the official documents is correspondence directed to the governor's office concerning pardons. Citizens, prosecutors, other attorneys, and even the criminals themselves often wrote to the governor on the merits of a case. A governor made decisions based largely on the information he received. These decisions were not only a choice of life or death, but most likely involved either the remission of fines, the curtailment of a jail sentence, or the tempering of some form of corporal punishment. The volume of this sort of material in any governor's correspondence suggests that deciding whether to pardon occupied a large measure of his time. The official papers of the legislative council and general assembly also include many similar appeals.

The Florida State Archives also houses minute books and case files of the Territorial Court of Appeals and the Florida Supreme Court. Most of the litigation involves civil matters, but several criminal cases also exist. Because these tribunals did not accept appeals in criminal cases unless specific errors were made in the lower court, their records are important for studying the criminal appeals process.

The Florida volumes of Clarence Carter's *Territorial Papers of the United States* compiled, annotated, and published important documents from the National Archives regarding the territory of Florida. Of special interest to scholars are letters and petitions discussing the organization of the courts, the appointment of officials, or the particular difficulties federal appointees encountered in the administration of justice. The National Archives in Washington and its annex at East Point, Georgia, also contain court records and case files of the federal courts created after statehood. Also included are miscellaneous records of the U.S. marshals, district attorneys, and judges of the federal courts.

The last primary sources in this study are personal family papers. Despite obvious biases, manuscripts often offer vivid accounts of locations and events and descriptions of the society as seen by the observer. They also reveal the opinions and passions of the criminal and victim alike.

Primary Sources

Manuscripts

Florida Historical Society, University of South Florida, Tampa, Florida
Call (Richard Keith) Papers
El Destino Plantation Papers
Fleming (Francis P.) Papers
White (Pleasents Woodson) Papers
Florida State Archives, R. A. Gray Building, Tallahassee, Florida
Bauskett (William) Manuscript Collection

Call (Richard Keith) Letters and Journal
Prince (Henry) Diary, 1836–42
"Roster of State and County Officers Commissioned by the Governor of Florida, 1845–68." Jacksonville: Florida Historical Records Survey, Works Progress Administration, February 1941.
Stephens Family Papers
Yulee (David) Correspondence
John C. Pace Library, University of West Florida, Pensacola, Florida
Brackenridge (Henry Marie) Papers
Keep Family Papers
Preston (David) Journal
Yonge Family Papers
William R. Perkins Library, Duke University, Durham, North Carolina
Branch Family Papers
Campbell Family Papers
MacRae (Hugh) Papers
Meek (Alexander Beaufort) Papers
Reed (A. M.) Papers
Vinton (John Rogers) Papers
St. Augustine Historical Society, St. Augustine, Florida
Sanchez (Joseph S.) Papers
Smith (Edmund Kirby) Papers
South Caroliniana Library, University of South Carolina, Columbia, South Carolina
Fox (John) Papers
McGehee (John C.) Papers
Miscellaneous Manuscripts
Southern Historical Collection, University of North Carolina, Chapel Hill, North Carolina
Branch Papers
Cathell (Henry L.) Diary
Croom (Hardy Bryan) Papers
Davidson Papers
Gaston (William) Papers
Hagner (Peter) Papers
Hentz Family Papers
Hubbard Family Papers
L'Engle (Edward McCrady) Papers
Parish Family Papers
Parkhill (John) Papers
Philips (James Jones) Papers
Simpson (Leah and Rebecca) Papers
Smith (Edmund Kirby) Papers
Stephens (Marcus Cicero) Papers
Swann Family Papers
Weedon-Whitehurst Papers

Wirt Papers
State Library of Florida, Dorothy Dodd Room of Florida History, R. A. Gray Building, Tallahassee, Florida
Hodson (Thomas J.) Letters
Ives (Washington) Journal (Diary) and Papers
Miscellaneous Territorial Papers
Reid (Robert Raymond) Diary
Spaulding (D. A.) Papers, 1854–59
Tappan (John S.) Papers
Territorial Financial Papers
Vann, Enoch J., "Reminiscences of a Georgia-Florida-Pinewoods-Cracker Lawyer"
Robert Manning Strozier Library, Florida State University, Tallahassee, Florida
Bradford (Edward) Papers
Byrd (F. A.) Collection
Eppes (Susan Bradford) Collection
Fairbanks Collection
Hackley (Richard) Diary
Hatheway (Frank) Diary
Hollingsworth Papers
Pine Hill Plantation Papers
St. Augustine Papers
Territorial Florida Account Sheets
Walker Papers
Wilson (William) Letters
U.S. Military Academy Library, U.S. Military Academy, West Point, New York
Anderson (James W.) Papers
Tidball (John) Papers
P. K. Yonge Library of Florida History, University of Florida, Gainesville, Florida
Anderson (James Patton) Papers
Call (Richard Keith) Correspondence
Bellamy-Bailey Papers
Davenport (William) Papers
Dow (Warren Q.) Diary
DuVal (William Pope) Letters
Fairbanks (George R.) Papers
Hazzard (George) Papers
Hentz, Charles A., "My Autobiography"
Keenan-Brown Papers
Keene (Otis) Diary
Kirby (Reynold) Diary
Lang (David) Papers
Levy [Yulee] (David) Papers
McLean (James) Papers
Miscellaneous Manuscripts (cited individually)

Robinson, Calvin L., "Memoirs of Calvin L. Robinson"
Stephens Papers
Yonge (Chandler Cox) Papers

Federal Documents, Unpublished

National Archives, Washington, D.C.
Attorney General's Papers, Appointment Papers, Florida, 1853–69, RG 60, General Records of the Department of Justice.
Attorney General's Papers, Letters Received, Florida, 1821–61, RG 60, General Records of the Department of Justice.
Letters Sent by the Department of Justice: General and Miscellaneous, 1818–1904, RG 60, General Records of the Department of Justice.
Letters Sent by the Department of Justice Concerning Judiciary Expenses, 1849–84, RG 60, General Records of the Department of Justice.
Registers of the Records of the Proceedings of the U.S. Army, General Court-Martial, 1809–90, RG 153.
National Archives, East Point, Georgia
Northern District of Florida, U.S. District Court Minutes, 1846–57, Book 3 (Tallahassee), RG 21.
Northern District of Florida, U.S. District Court Minutes, 1847–67, Book 4 (Apalachicola), RG 21.
Northern District of Florida, General Execution Docket, 1847–62, Book 1, RG 21.
Northern District of Florida, U.S. District Court, Criminal Case Files, 1856–60, Box 15, RG 21.
Northern District of Florida, Civil Case Papers and Miscellaneous Criminal Papers of Ambrose Crane and S. W. Spencer (Indian War Claims), 1856–60, Box 17, RG 21.
Northern District of Florida, Miscellaneous Court Records, 1821–60, Box 19, RG 21.
Southern District of Florida, Minutes of the U.S. District Court, 1828–37, Carta 1, RG 21.
Southern District of Florida, Minutes of the U.S. District Court, 1828–41, Carta 2, RG 21.
Southern District of Florida, Minutes of the U.S. District Court, 1841–46, Carta 3, RG 21.
Southern District of Florida, Minutes of the U.S. District Court, 1856–65, Carta 4, RG 21.
U.S. Census
U.S. Manuscript Census, Population, 1850, for the following counties: Alachua, Calhoun, Columbia, Dade, Duval, Escambia, Franklin, Gadsden, Hamilton, Hernando, Holmes, Jackson, Jefferson, Leon, Levy, Madison, Marion, Monroe, Nassau, Orange, Putnam, St. Johns, Santa Rosa, Wakulla, Walton, Washington.
U.S. Manuscript Census, Population, 1860, for the following counties: Alachua, Calhoun, Columbia, Dade, Duval, Escambia, Franklin, Gadsden, Hamilton, Hernando, Holmes, Jackson, Jefferson, Leon, Levy, Madi-

son, Marion, Monroe, Nassau, Orange, Putnam, St. Johns, Santa Rosa, Wakulla, Walton, Washington, Brevard, Clay, Lafayette, Manatee, Sumter, Taylor, Volusia.

U.S. Manuscript Census, Slave, 1850, for the following counties: Alachua, Calhoun, Columbia, Dade, Duval, Escambia, Franklin, Gadsden, Hamilton, Hernando, Holmes, Jackson, Jefferson, Leon, Levy, Madison, Marion, Monroe, Nassau, Orange, Putnam, St. Johns, Santa Rosa, Wakulla, Walton, Washington.

U.S. Manuscript Census, Slave, 1860, for the following counties: Alachua, Calhoun, Columbia, Dade, Duval, Escambia, Franklin, Gadsden, Hamilton, Hernando, Holmes, Jackson, Jefferson, Leon, Levy, Madison, Marion, Monroe, Nassau, Orange, Putnam, St. Johns, Santa Rosa, Wakulla, Walton, Washington, Brevard, Clay, Lafayette, Manatee, Sumter, Taylor, Volusia.

Federal Documents, Published

Carter, Clarence E., ed. *The Territorial Papers of the United States*. 26 vols. Washington D.C.: U.S. Government Printing Office, 1934–62. Vols. 22–26 cover the Florida Territory.

U.S. Bureau of the Census. *A Century of Population Growth from the First Census of the United States to the Twelfth, 1790–1900*. Washington, D.C.: U.S. Government Printing Office, 1909.

———. *Statistics of the United States in 1860*. Washington, D.C.: U.S. Government Printing Office, 1866.

U.S. Congress. *Seventh Census, 1850*. Washington, D.C.: Robert Armstrong, 1853.

———. *Eighth Census, 1860*. Washington, D.C.: U.S. Government Printing Office, 1864.

State Documents, Unpublished

Florida State Archives, R. A. Gray Building, Tallahassee, Florida
- RG 101, Correspondence of the Governors
  - Ser. 32, Letterbooks, 1836–1909, vols. 1–6.
  - Ser. 177, Correspondence of the Territorial Governors, 1825–36.
  - Ser. 577, Correspondence of Madison Starke Perry and John Milton, 1857–68.
  - Ser. 679, Correspondence of William D. Moseley, 1845–49.
  - Ser. 755, Correspondence of Thomas Brown, 1849–53.
  - Ser. 777, Correspondence of James Broome, 1853–57.
- RG 150, Department of State
  - Ser. 24, Correspondence of the Secretary of State.
  - Ser. 392, Court Appearance Bonds.
- RG 151, Office of the Secretary of State
  - Ser. 259, Lists of Territorial, State, and County Officers, 1827–1923, 1960.
  - Ser. 1284, State and County Directories, 1845–61.
- RG 156, Office of the Governor

Ser. 13, Book of Record (Proclamations), Books 1–2.
RG 350, State Comptroller
Ser. 28, Tax Rolls, 1828–73.
Ser. 554, Correspondence, 1845–1904.
Ser. 559, Daybooks, 1831–80, vols. 1–2.
Ser. 564, Warrant Books, 1845–62, vols. 1–9.
Ser. 565, Criminal Prosecutions, Vouchers, Post Mortem Examinations, 1846–62.
Ser. 567, Abstracts of Warrants Issued, vols. 1–3.
RG 352, Territorial Auditor of the Public Accounts
Ser. 491, Reports from the Clerks of the Superior Courts, 1831–45.
Ser. 582, Auditor's Office, Letterbooks, 1832–45.
Ser. 583, Auditor's Office, Warrants, 1823–45.
Ser. 584, Auditor's Office, Vouchers, 1823–46.
RG 650, Department of Legal Affairs
Ser. 632, Attorney General's Opinions, 1859–1913.
RG 910, Florida Territorial Legislative Council
Ser. 876, Records of the Legislative Council, Unicameral, 1822–38.
Ser. 877, Records of the Legislative Council, Bicameral, 1839–45.
RG 915, Nineteenth-Century Florida State Legislature
Ser. 74, Gubernatorial Appointment Nominations for County Offices, 1825–73.
Ser. 415, Official Journals, Senate, 1839–1905.
Ser. 416, Official Journals, House, 1837–1905.
Ser. 887, Records of the Nineteenth-Century State Legislature, 1845–1911.
RG 970, Supreme Court
Ser. 49, Supreme Court Case Files, 1846–1900.
Ser. 73, Territorial Court of Appeals Case Files, 1825–46.
Ser. 985, Minutes of the Territorial Court of Appeals, 1825–46.

State Documents, Published

Acts and Resolutions of the General Assembly. 1845–61.
Acts and Resolutions of the Legislative Council. 1822–45.
Duval, John P. *Compilation of the Public Acts of the Legislative Council of the Territory of Florida Passed Prior to 1840*. Tallahassee: Samuel S. Sibley, 1839.
House and Senate Journals. 1845–61.
Journal of the Proceedings of a Convention of Delegates to Form a Constitution for the People of Florida, Held at St. Joseph, December, 1838. St. Joseph, 1839.
Journal of the Proceedings of the Convention of the People of Florida, Begun and Held at the Capital in the City of Tallahassee on Thursday, January 3, 1861. Tallahassee, 1861.
Long, Richard. *Laws of the United States Relative to the Territory of Florida Passed by Congress Prior to 1838*. Tallahassee: Samuel S. Sibley, 1837.
Reports of the Cases Argued and Adjudged in the Supreme Court of Florida. Vols. 1–9. Tallahassee, 1845–61.
Thompson, Leslie A. *A Manual or Digest of the Statute Law of the State of Florida,*

of a General and Public Character, in Force at the End of the Second Session of the General Assembly of the State, on the Sixth Day of January, 1847. Boston: Charles C. Little and James Brown, 1848.

County Court Records, Unpublished

Clay County (Green Cove Springs, Florida)
Circuit Court Minutes, 1859–86, Book 1.
Case Files, 1858–61.
Escambia County (Pensacola, Florida)
Superior Court Minutes, 1822–33, Book 1.
Superior Court Minutes, 1833–38, Book 3.
Superior Court Minutes, 1838–42, Book 4.
Superior Court Minutes, 1842–45, Book 5.
Circuit Court Minutes, 1846–54, Book A.
Circuit Court Minutes, 1855–66, Book B.
Case Files, 1822–60.
Gadsden County (Quincy, Florida)
Circuit Court Minutes, 1849–55, Book 1.
Circuit Court Minutes, 1859–66, Book 3.
County Court Minutes, 1832–37.
Case Files, 1845–60.
Hamilton County (Jasper, Florida)
Criminal–Common Law Docket (Superior Court), 1839–45.
Circuit Court Minutes, 1855–67, Book 2.
County Commissioners' Minutes, 1846–63, Book B.
Case Files, 1837–60.
Hillsborough County (Tampa, Florida)
Circuit Court Minutes, 1846–54.
Circuit Court Minutes, 1854–66.
County Commissioners' Minutes, 1846–63.
County Court Minutes, 1836–45.
Jackson County (Marianna, Florida)
Circuit Court Minutes, 1851–57, Book C.
Circuit Court Minutes, 1857–61, Book D.
Circuit Court Minutes, 1861–67, Book E.
Case Files, 1850–60.
Jefferson County (Monticello, Florida)
Superior Court Minutes, 1828–41, Book 1.
Circuit Court Minutes, 1846–54, Book A.
Circuit Court Minutes, 1854–70, Book B.
County Commissioners' Minutes, 1845–69.
County Court Minutes, 1840–45, Book A.
Case Files, 1826–60.
Leon County (Tallahassee, Florida)
Superior Court Minutes, 1824–33, Book 1.
Superior Court Minutes, 1841–43, Book 3.
Superior and Circuit Court Minutes, 1843–47, Book 4.

Circuit Court Minutes, 1847–55, Book 5.
Circuit Court Minutes, 1855–69, Book 6.
Case Files, 1828–60.
Madison County (Madison, Florida)
Circuit Court Minutes, 1846–54.
County Commissioners' Minutes, 1859–74.
Manatee County (Bradenton, Florida)
Circuit Court Minutes, 1858–86, Book 1.
County Commissioners' Minutes, 1856–69.
Marion County (Ocala, Florida)
Circuit Court Minutes, 1848–55, Book A.
Circuit Court Minutes, 1855–61, Book B.
Circuit Court Minutes, 1861–73, Book C.
Monroe County (Key West, Florida)
Superior and Circuit Court Minutes, 1840–70, Book A.
Case Files, 1822–60 (Monroe County Public Library).
Orange County (Orlando, Florida)
Circuit Court Minutes, 1847–83, Book A.
Putnam County (Palatka, Florida)
Circuit Court Minutes, 1850–59, Book 1.
Circuit Court Minutes, 1859–83, Book 2.
Case Files, 1850–60.
St. Johns County (St. Augustine, Florida)
Circuit Court Minutes, 1846–60, Book A.
County Court Minutes, 1827–45 (St. Augustine Historical Society)
Case Files, 1822–60.
Volusia County (Deland, Florida)
Case Files, 1854–61.
Court Records in Florida Historical Society Library, University of South Florida, Tampa, Florida
Alachua County, Superior and Circuit Court Minutes, 1840–49.
Hillsborough County, County Court Records, 1850–83.
Court Records in State Library of Florida, Dorothy Dodd Room of Florida History, R. A. Gray Building, Tallahassee, Florida
Duval County, County Court Minutes, n.d.
Leon County, County Court Minutes, 1825–33.
Court Records in P. K. Yonge Library of Florida History, University of Florida, Gainesville, Florida
Alachua County, County Court Minutes, 1833–45.
Alachua, Columbia, and Hillsborough Counties, Superior Court Minutes (District Court of East Florida at Newnansville), 1828–35.
Alachua, Hernando, and Hillsborough Counties, Superior Court Minutes (District Court of East Florida at Newnansville), 1838–43.
Alachua, Hillsborough, Benton, and Marion Counties, Superior and Circuit Court Minutes (District Court of East Florida at Newnansville), 1844–50.
Alachua and Levy Counties, Circuit Court Minutes (District of East Florida), 1850–57.

Monroe County, Superior Court Minutes (Southern District of Florida), 1830–40.

Florida Antebellum Newspapers

Alligator Columbia Democrat, 1858
Apalachicola Apalachicolian, 1840–41
Apalachicola Commercial Advertiser, 1840–51, 1858–59
Apalachicola Courier, 1839–40
Apalachicola Florida Journal, 1840–44
Apalachicola Gazette, 1836–40
Apalachicola Star of the West, 1848
Apalachicola Watchman of the Gulf, 1843
Cedar Keys Telegraph, 1859–60
Fernandina East Floridian, 1959–61
Fernandina Florida News, 1858–59
Fernandina Peninsula, 1863–64
Jacksonville Courier, 1835–36
Jacksonville East Florida Advocate, 1839–40
Jacksonville Florida News, 1846–57
Jacksonville Florida Republican, 1848–56
Jacksonville Florida Union, 1860
Jacksonville St. Johns Mirror, 1861
Jacksonville Southern Confederacy, 1861
Jacksonville Standard, 1859–60
Jacksonville Tropical Plant, 1844
Jacksonville Weekly Republican, 1858
Key West Enquirer, 1834–36
Key West Gazette, 1831–32, 1845
Key West Key of the Gulf, 1856–60
Key West New Era, 1862
Key West Register and Commercial Advertiser, 1829
Key West South Floridian, 1838–39
Madison Southern Messenger, 1858
Magnolia Advertiser, 1828–30
Marianna Florida Whig, 1847–52
Micanopy Cotton States, 1861–64
Newnansville Florida Dispatch, 1860
Newport Gazette, 1846–48
Newport Wakulla Times, 1858–59
Ocala Argus, 1848
Ocala Conservator, 1851–52
Ocala Florida Home Companion, 1857–60
Ocala Florida Mirror, 1853
Ocala Southern Sun, 1854
Palatka Whig Banner, 1846–47
Pensacola Florida Argus, 1828
Pensacola Florida Democrat, 1846–51, 1856

Pensacola Floridian, 1821–24
Pensacola Gazette, 1821–60
Pensacola Live Oak, 1857
Pensacola Neutral, 1848
Pensacola West Florida Times, 1857
Quincy Republic, 1859
Quincy Sentinel, 1839–41
Quincy Times, 1848
St. Augustine Ancient City, 1850–56
St. Augustine East Florida Herald, 1823–28
St. Augustine Examiner, 1859–62
St. Augustine Florida Gazette, 1821
St. Augustine Florida Herald, 1829–37
St. Augustine Florida Herald and Southern Democrat, 1838–42
St. Augustine News, 1838–47
St. Joseph Times, 1839–41
Tallahassee Florida Advocate, 1827–29
Tallahassee Florida Courier, 1831
Tallahassee Florida Intelligencer, 1826
Tallahassee Florida Sentinel, 1841–60
Tallahassee Florida Watchman, 1837–38
Tallahassee Floridian, 1831–48
Tallahassee Floridian and Advocate, 1829–31
Tallahassee Floridian and Journal, 1849–61
Tallahassee Southern Journal, 1846–49
Tallahassee Star of Florida, 1839–45
Tampa Florida Peninsular, 1856–61
Tampa Herald, 1854

Secondary Sources

On Florida

Akerman, Joe. *Florida Cowman: A History of Florida Cattle Raising*. Kissimmee: Florida Cattleman's Association, 1976.

Bates, Thelma. "The Legal Status of the Negro in Florida." *Florida Historical Quarterly* 6 (January 1928): 159–81.

Black, Hugo L. "Richard Fitzpatrick's South Florida, 1822–1844, Key West Phase." *Tequesta* 40 (1980): 41–77.

Boyd, Joseph, and Randall O. Reder. "A History of the Supreme Court of Florida." *University of Miami Law Review* 35 (September 1981): 1019–66.

Boyd, Mark F. "The Seminole War: Its Background and Onset." *Florida Historical Quarterly* 30 (July 1951): 3–115.

Brevard, Caroline Mays. *A History of Florida from the Treaty of 1763 to Our Own Times*. 2 vols. Deland: Florida State Historical Society, 1924–25.

Brinton, Daniel. *Notes on the Floridian Peninsula: Its Literary History, Indian Tribes, and Antiquities*. Philadelphia: Joseph Sabin, 1859.

Brown, Canter, Jr. *Florida's Peace River Frontier*. Orlando: University of Central Florida Press, 1991.

———. *Fort Meade, 1849–1900*. Tuscaloosa: University of Alabama Press, 1995.

———. "Race Relations in Territorial Florida, 1821–1845." *Florida Historical Quarterly* 73 (January 1995): 287–307.

———. "The Sarrazota, or Runaway Negro Plantations: Tampa Bay's First Black Community, 1812–1821." *Tampa Bay History* 12 (Fall/Winter 1990): 5–19.

Browne, Jefferson. *Key West: The Old and New*. St. Augustine: Record Co., 1912.

Buker, George E. *Jacksonville: Riverport-Seaport*. Columbia: University of South Carolina Press, 1992.

Campbell, James T. "The Charles Hutchinson Letters from Territorial Tallahassee, 1839–1843." *Apalachee* 4 (1950–56): 13–18.

de Castelnau, Francis. "Comte de Castelnau in Middle Florida, 1837–1838. Notes Concerning Two Itineraries from Charleston to Tallahassee." Translated by Arthur Seymour. *Florida Historical Quarterly* 26 (April 1948): 300–324.

———. "Essay on Middle Florida, 1837–1838." Translated by Arthur Seymour. *Florida Historical Quarterly* 26 (January 1948): 199–255.

Catteral, Helen Tunncliff, ed. "Florida Cases." In idem, *Judicial Cases Concerning American Slavery and the Negro*. 5 vols., 1929–37. Washington: Carnegie Institution of Washington, 3:107–25.

Covington, James W. "The Armed Occupation Act of 1842." *Florida Historical Quarterly* 40 (July 1961): 41–52.

———. *The Seminoles of Florida*. Gainesville: University Press of Florida, 1993.

Cox, Merlin, and Charles Hildreth. *History of Gainesville, Florida, 1854–1979*. Gainesville: Alachua County Historical Society, 1981.

Davis, Mary Lamar. "Tallahassee through Territorial Days." *Apalachee* 1 (1944): 47–61.

Davis, Thomas Frederick. *A History of Jacksonville, Florida, and Vicinity, 1513 to 1924*. St. Augustine: Florida Historical Society, 1925.

Davis, William Watson. *Civil War and Reconstruction in Florida*. New York: Columbia University Press, 1913.

Denham, James M. "The Florida Crackers before the Civil War as Seen through Travelers' Accounts." *Florida Historical Quarterly* 72 (April 1994): 453–68.

———. "From a Territorial to a Statehood Judiciary: Florida's Antebellum Courts and Judges." *Florida Historical Quarterly* 73 (April 1995): 443–55.

———. " 'The Peerless Wind Cloud': Thomas Jefferson Green and the Tallahassee-Texas Land Company." *East Texas Historical Journal* 29 (Fall 1991): 3–14.

———. "The Read-Alston Duel and Politics in Territorial Florida." *Florida Historical Quarterly* 68 (April 1990): 427–46.

———. " 'Some Prefer the Seminoles': Violence and Disorder among Soldiers and Settlers in the Second Seminole War, 1835–1842." *Florida Historical Quarterly* 70 (July 1991): 38–54.

Dillon, Rodney. "South Florida in 1860." *Florida Historical Quarterly* 60 (April 1982): 440–54.

Dodd, Dorothy. "The Corporation of Tallahassee, 1826–1860." *Apalachee* 3 (1948–50): 80–95.

———. *Florida Becomes a State*. Tallahassee: Florida Centennial Commission, 1945.

———. "Florida in 1845." *Florida Historical Quarterly* 24 (July 1945): 3–29.

———. "Horse Racing in Middle Florida, 1830–43." *Apalachee* 3 (1948–50): 20–29.

———. "Jacob Housman of Indian Key." *Tequesta* 8 (1948): 3–20.

Doherty, Herbert J. "Antebellum Pensacola, 1821–1861." *Florida Historical Quarterly* 37 (January 1959): 337–56.

———. "The Code Duello in Florida." *Florida Historical Quarterly* 29 (April 1951): 243–52.

———. "Political Factions in Territorial Florida." *Florida Historical Quarterly* 28 (October 1949): 131–42.

———. *Richard Keith Call: Southern Unionist*. Gainesville: University of Florida Press, 1961.

———. "The Whigs of Florida." *University of Florida Monographs* 1 (Winter 1959).

Douglas, Marjory Stoneman. *Florida: The Long Frontier*. New York: Harper and Row, 1967.

Douglas, Thomas. *Autobiography*. New York: Caukins and Stiles, 1856.

Dovell, J. E. *Florida: Historic, Dramatic, Contemporary*. New York: Lewis Historical Publishing Co., 1952.

Eppes, Susan Branford. *The Negro of the Old South: A Bit of Period History*. Chicago: Joseph Branch Publishing, 1925.

———. *Through Some Eventful Years*. Macon, Ga.: J. W. Burke Co., 1926.

Eriksen, John M. *Brevard County: A History to 1955*. Tampa: Florida Historical Society Press, 1994.

Farris, Charles D. "The Courts of Territorial Florida." *Florida Historical Quarterly* 19 (April 1941): 346–67.

Fernald, Edward A., and Elizabeth D. Purdum, eds. *Atlas of Florida*. Gainesville: University Press of Florida, 1992.

The Florida Sheriff: Yearbook of the Florida Sheriffs Association (1958): 23–88.

Garvin, Russell. "The Free Negro in Florida before the Civil War." *Florida Historical Quarterly* 46 (July 1967): 1–17.

George, Paul S., ed. *A Guide to the History of Florida*. Westport, Conn.: Greenwood Press, 1989.

Giddings, Joshua R. *The Exiles of Florida: Or the Crimes Committed by Our Government against the Maroons, Who Fled from South Carolina and Other Slave States, Seeking Protection under Spanish Laws*. Columbus, Ohio: Follett, Foster, and Co., 1858.

Graham, Thomas. *The Awakening of St. Augustine: The Anderson Family and the Oldest City, 1821–1924*. St. Augustine: St. Augustine Historical Society, 1978.

Granade, Ray. "Slave Unrest in Florida." *Florida Historical Quarterly* 55 (July 1976): 18–36.

Grismer, Karl H. *Tampa: A History of the City of Tampa and the Tampa Bay Region of Florida*. St. Petersburg: St. Petersburg Printing Co., 1950.

Groene, Bertram. *Antebellum Tallahassee*. Tallahassee: Heritage Foundation, 1971.

———. "Justice Samuel Douglas as Governor Marvin Remembered Him." *Florida Historical Quarterly* 49 (January 1971): 268–77.

———. "Lizzy Brown's Tallahassee." *Florida Historical Quarterly* 46 (October 1969): 155–75.

Hall, Kermit L., and Eric W. Rise. *From Local Courts to National Tribunals: Federal District Courts of Florida, 1821–1990*. Brooklyn, N.Y.: Carlson Publishing Co., 1991.

Hanna, Alfred Jackson. *A Prince in Their Midst: The Adventurous Life of Achille Murat on the American Frontier*. Norman: University of Oklahoma Press, 1946.

Hanna, Kathryn Abbey. *Florida: Land of Change*. Chapel Hill: University of North Carolina Press, 1948.

Harper, Roland. "Antebellum Census Enumerations in Florida." *Florida Historical Quarterly* 6 (July 1927): 42–52.

Housewright, Wiley L. *A History of Music and Dance in Florida, 1565–1865*. Tuscaloosa: University of Alabama Press, 1991.

Ingalls, Robert P. "Lynching and Establishment Violence in Tampa, 1858–1935." *Journal of Southern History* 53 (November 1987): 613–44.

———. *Urban Vigilantes in the New South: Tampa, 1882–1936*. Knoxville: University of Tennessee Press, 1988.

Kearney, Kevin E., ed. "Autobiography of William Marvin." *Florida Historical Quarterly* 36 (January 1958): 179–222.

Knauss, James Owens. *Florida Territorial Journalism*. Deland: Florida State Historical Society, 1927.

———. "St. Joseph: An Episode in the Economic and Political History of Florida." *Florida Historical Quarterly* 6 (July 1927): 178–95.

———. "William Pope Duval." *Florida Historical Quarterly* 11 (January 1933): 95–139.

Long, Ellen Call. *Florida Breezes, Or Florida New and Old*. 1883. Reprint, Gainesville: University of Florida Press, 1962.

Mahon, John K. *History of the Second Seminole War, 1835–1842*. Gainesville: University of Florida Press, 1967.

Maloney, Walter C. *A Sketch of the History of Key West, Florida*. 1876. Reprint, Gainesville: University of Florida Press, 1968.

Martin, Richard. *The City Makers*. Jacksonville: Convention Press, 1972.

Martin, Sydney Walter. *Florida during Territorial Days*. Athens: University of Georgia Press, 1944.

———. "Richard Keith Call." *Florida Historical Quarterly* 21 (April 1943): 332–51.

Matthews, Janet Snyder. *Edge of Wilderness: A Settlement History of Manatee River and Sarasota Bay*. Tulsa, Okla.: Caprine Press, 1983.

McDuffie, Lillie B. *The Lures of the Manatee: A True Story of South Florida's Glamorous Past*. Bradenton, Fla.: Oliver K. Fletcher, 1961.

McMurtrie, Douglas. "The Beginnings of Printing in Florida." *Florida Historical Quarterly* 23 (October 1944): 63–96.

McReynolds, Edwin. *The Seminoles*. Norman: University of Oklahoma Press, 1957.

Moore, John Hammond. "A South Carolina Lawyer Visits St. Augustine, 1837." *Florida Historical Quarterly* 43 (April 1965): 361–78.

Mormino, Gary. "Florida Slave Narratives." *Florida Historical Quarterly* 66 (April 1988): 399–419.

Mormino, Gary, and Anthony P. Pizzo. *Tampa: The Treasure City*. Tulsa, Okla.: Centennial Heritage Press, 1983.

Motte, Jacob Rhett. *Journey into the Wilderness: An Army Surgeon's Account of Life in Camp and Field during the Creek and Seminole Wars, 1836–1838*. Edited by James F. Sunderman. Gainesville: University of Florida Press, 1953.

Ordonez, Margaret. "Plantation Self-Sufficiency in Leon County: 1824–1860." *Florida Historical Quarterly* 60 (April 1982): 428–39.

Ott, Eloise Robinson. "Ocala Prior to 1868." *Florida Historical Quarterly* 6 (October 1927): 85–110.

Otto, John Sollomon. "Florida's Cattle-Raising Frontier: Hillsborough County." *Florida Historical Quarterly* 63 (July 1984): 71–83.

———. "Hillsborough County (1850): A Community in the South Florida Flatwoods." *Florida Historical Quarterly* 62 (October 1983): 180–93.

———. "Open Range Cattle-Herding in Southern Florida." *Florida Historical Quarterly* 65 (January 1987): 317–34.

Paisley, Clifton. *The Red Hills of Florida, 1528–1865*. Tuscaloosa: University of Alabama Press, 1989.

Parker, Susan R. "Men without God or King: Rural Settlers of East Florida, 1784–1790." *Florida Historical Quarterly* 69 (October 1990): 135–55.

Pearce, George F. *The U.S. Navy in Pensacola from Sailing Ships to Naval Aviation, 1828–1930*. Pensacola: University Presses of Florida, 1980.

Peek, Ralph E. "Lawlessness in Florida, 1868–1871." *Florida Historical Quarterly* 40 (October 1961): 164–85.

Peters, Virginia Bergman. *The Florida Wars*. Hamden, Conn.: Archon Books, 1979.

Phillips, Rebecca. "A Diary of Jesse Talbot Bernard: Newnansville and Tallahassee." *Florida Historical Quarterly* 18 (October 1939): 115–26.

Pizzo, Anthony P. *Tampa Town, 1824–1886: Cracker Village with a Latin Accent*. Miami: Hurricane House, 1969.

Porter, Kenneth. "Florida Slaves and Free Negroes in the Seminole War, 1835–1842." *Journal of Negro History* 28 (October 1943): 390–421.

———. "Negroes and the Seminole War, 1835–1842." *Journal of Southern History* 30 (November 1964): 427–50.

Porter, Louise M. *The Chronological History of the Lives of St. Joseph*. Chattanooga: Great American Publishing Co., 1975.

Portier, Michael. "From Pensacola to St. Augustine in 1827: A Journey of the Rt. Reverend Michael Portier." *Florida Historical Quarterly* 26 (October 1947): 135–66.

Rawick, George P., ed. *The American Slave: A Composite Autobiography*. 41 vols. Vol. 16, *Florida Narratives*. Westport, Conn.: Greenwood Press, 1972–79.

Reid, Robert Raymond. "Diary of Robert Raymond Reid." In *The Bench and the Bar of Georgia: Memoirs and Sketches*, vol. 2, edited by Stephen Franks Miller, 182–237. Philadelphia: Lippincott, 1858.

Rerick, Rowland H. *Memoirs of Florida*. Edited by Francis P. Fleming. 2 vols. Atlanta: Southern Historical Association, 1902.

Rivers, Larry E. "Dignity and Importance: Slavery in Jefferson County, Florida, 1827–1860." *Florida Historical Quarterly* 61 (April 1983): 404–30.

———. "Slavery and the Political Economy of Gadsden County, Florida, 1823–1861." *Florida Historical Quarterly* 70 (July 1991): 1–19.

———. "Slavery in Microcosm: Leon County, Florida, 1824–1860." *Journal of Negro History* 46 (February 1981): 235–45.

Rogers, Ben F. "Florida by Nineteenth-Century Travelers." *Florida Historical Quarterly* 34 (October 1955): 177–89.

Rogers, William W. *Outposts on the Gulf: Saint George Island and Apalachicola from Early Exploration to World War II*. Pensacola: University of West Florida Press, 1986.

Schafer, Daniel L. " 'A Class of People Neither Freemen Nor Slaves': From Spanish to American Race Relations in Florida, 1821–1861." *Journal of Social History* 26 (Spring 1993): 587–609.

Shofner, Jerrell H. *Daniel Ladd: Merchant Prince of Frontier Florida*. Gainesville: University Presses of Florida, 1978.

———. *History of Jefferson County*. Tallahassee: Sentry Press, 1976.

———. *Jackson County, Florida: A History*. Marianna: Jackson County Heritage Association, 1985.

———. *Nor Is It Over Yet: Florida in the Era of Reconstruction, 1863–1877*. Gainesville: University of Florida Press, 1974.

Smith, Julia Floyd. *Slavery and Plantation Growth in Antebellum Florida, 1821–1860*. Gainesville: University of Florida Press, 1973.

———. "Slave Trading in Antebellum Florida." *Florida Historical Quarterly* 50 (January 1972): 252–61.

Stanaback, Richard J. *A History of Hernando County, 1840–1976*. Brooksville, Fla.: Action '76 Steering Committee, 1976.

———. "Postal Operations in Territorial Florida, 1821–1845." *Florida Historical Quarterly* 52 (October 1973): 157–74.

Stanley, J. Randall. *A History of Gadsden County*. Quincy: Gadsden County Historical Commission, 1948.

———. *A History of Jackson County*. Marianna: Jackson County Historical Society, 1950.

Tebeau, Carlton. *A History of Florida*. Coral Gables: University of Miami Press, 1971.

Thompson, Arthur W. "Jacksonian Democracy on the Florida Frontier." *University of Florida Monographs* 6 (Winter 1961).

Thompson, Joseph Conan. "Toward a More Humane Oppression: Florida's Slave Codes, 1821–1861." *Florida Historical Quarterly* 71 (January 1993): 324–38.

Thrift, Charles T. *The Trail of the Florida Circuit Rider*. Lakeland: Florida Southern College Press, 1944.

Walker, Jonathan. *Trial and Imprisonment of Jonathan Walker, at Pensacola, Florida, for Aiding Slaves to Escape from Bondage*. 1848. Reprint, Gainesville: University of Florida Press, 1974.

Warner, Lee H. *Free Men in the Age of Servitude: Three Generations of a Black Family*. Lexington: University of Kentucky Press, 1992.

Waters, Robert Craig, ed. *The Florida Supreme Court: A Reference Manual*. Tallahassee: The Supreme Court of Florida, 1995.
Wethering, Wade. "The *Florida Peninsular*'s View of Slavery, 1855–1861." *Tampa Bay History* 12 (Fall/Winter 1990): 46–71.
Williams, Edwin L. "Negro Slavery in Florida." *Florida Historical Quarterly* 27 (October 1949): 93–110; 28 (January 1950): 182–204.
Willoughby, Lynn. *Fair to Middlin': The Antebellum Cotton Trade of the Apalachicola River Valley*. Tuscaloosa: University of Alabama Press, 1993.
Womack, Miles. *Gadsden: A Florida County in Word and Picture*. Quincy: Gadsden County Bicentennial Committee, 1976.
Wright, J. Leitch. "A Note on the First Seminole War as Seen by Indians, Negroes, and their British Advisors." *Journal of Southern History* 34 (November 1968): 565–75.
Yelton, Susan. "Newnansville: A Lost Florida Settlement." *Florida Historical Quarterly* 53 (January 1975): 319–31.

Other Works

Asbury, Herbert. *Sucker's Progress: An Informal History of Gambling in America from the Colonies to Canfield*. New York: Dodd, Mead, 1938.
Ayers, Edward L. "A Legacy of Violence." *American Heritage* 42 (October 1991): 102–9.
———. *Vengeance and Justice: Crime and Punishment in the Nineteenth-Century American South*. New York: Oxford University Press, 1984.
Ball, Larry D. *Desert Lawmen: The High Sheriffs of New Mexico and Arizona, 1846–1912*. Albuquerque: University of New Mexico Press, 1992.
———. *The United States Marshals in the New Mexico and Arizona Territories, 1846–1912*. Albuquerque: University of New Mexico Press, 1978.
Bardaglio, Peter. "Rape and the Law in the Old South: 'Calculated to Excite Indignation in Every Heart.' " *Journal of Southern History* 60 (November 1994): 749–72.
Bartlett, Richard A. *The New Country: A Social History of the American Frontier, 1776–1890*. New York: Oxford University Press, 1974.
Beattie, J. M. *Crime and the Courts in England, 1660–1800*. Princeton: Princeton University Press, 1985.
———. "The Pattern of Crime in England, 1660–1800." *Past and Present* 62 (February 1974): 47–95.
Bedau, Hugo Adam, ed. *The Death Penalty in America*. New York: Oxford University Press, 1982.
Berlin, Ira. *Slaves without Masters: The Free Negro in the Antebellum South*. New York: Pantheon, 1974.
Billington, Ray Allen. *America's Frontier Culture: Three Essays*. College Station: Texas A&M University Press, 1977.
———. *America's Frontier Heritage*. New York: Holt, Rinehart, and Winston, 1966.
———. *Land of Savagery, Land of Promise: The European Image of the American Frontier in the Nineteenth Century*. New York: Norton, 1981.

Bishop, Joel Prentiss. *Commentaries on the Criminal Law.* 2 vols. Boston: Little, Brown, 1856.

Blassingame, John W. *The Slave Community: Plantation Life in the Antebellum South.* New York: Oxford University Press, 1979.

Bodenhamer, David J. "Criminal Justice and Democratic Theory in Antebellum America: The Grand Jury Debate in Indiana." *Journal of the Early Republic* 5 (Winter 1985): 481–502.

———. "Criminal Punishment in Antebellum Indiana: The Limits of Reform." *Indiana Magazine of History* 82 (December 1986): 358–75.

———. "The Efficiency of Criminal Justice in the Antebellum South." *Criminal Justice History* 3 (1983): 81–95.

——— *Fair Trial: Rights of the Accused in American History.* New York: Oxford University Press, 1992.

———. "Law and Disorder on the Early Frontier: Marion County, Indiana, 1823–1850." *Western Historical Quarterly* 10 (July 1979): 323–36.

———. "Law and Lawlessness in the Deep South: The Situation in Georgia, 1830–1860." In *From the Old South to the New: Essays on the Transitional South,* edited by Walter J. Fraser and Winifred Moore, 109–19. Westport, Conn.: Greenwood Press, 1981.

———. *The Pursuit of Justice: Crime and Law in Antebellum Indiana.* New York: Garland, 1986.

Bodenhamer, David J., and James W. Ely Jr., eds. *Ambivalent Legacy: A Legal History of the South.* Jackson: University of Mississippi Press, 1984.

Brearly, H. C. "The Pattern of Violence." In *The Culture of the South,* edited by W. T. Couch, 678–92. Chapel Hill: University of North Carolina Press, 1935.

Breen, Timothy. "Horses and Gentlemen: The Cultural Significance of Gambling among the Gentry of Virginia." *William and Mary Quarterly* 34 (April 1977): 239–57.

Brown, Elizabeth. "Frontier Justice: Wayne County, 1796–1836." *American Journal of Legal History* 16 (April 1972): 126–53.

Brown, Richard Maxwell. "The American Vigilante Tradition." In *Violence in America: Historical and Comparative Perspectives,* edited by Hugh Davis Graham and Ted Robert Gurr, 1:121–80. Washington, D.C.: U.S. Government Printing Office, 1969.

———. "The History of Extra-Legal Violence in Support of Community Values." In *Violence in America: A Historical and Contemporary Reader,* edited by Thomas Rose, 86–95. New York: Vintage, 1970.

———. "The History of Vigilantism in America." In *Vigilante Politics,* edited by H. Jon Rosenbaum and Peter C. Sederberg, 79–109. Philadelphia: University of Pennsylvania Press, 1976.

———. "Legal and Behavioral Perspectives on American Vigilantism." In *Law in American History,* edited by Donald Fleming and Bernard Bailyn, 93–144. Boston: Little, Brown, 1972.

———. *No Duty to Retreat: Violence and Values in American History and Society.* New York: Oxford University Press, 1991.

———. "The Paradox of American Violence." In *Violence in America: Historical *and Comparative Perspectives,* edited by Hugh Davis Graham and Ted Robert Gurr, 475–90. Beverly Hills: Sage, 1979.

———. "Southern Violence—Regional Problem or National Nemesis?: Legal Attitudes toward Southern Homicide in Historical Perspective." *Vanderbilt Law Review* 32 (January 1979): 225–50.

———. *Strain of Violence: Historical Studies of American Violence and Vigilantism.* New York: Oxford University Press, 1975.

———, ed. *American Violence.* Englewood Cliffs, N.J.: Prentice-Hall, 1970.

Browning, Frank, and John Gerassi. *The American Way of Crime.* New York: Putnam, 1980.

Bruce, Dickson D., Jr. *Violence and Culture in the Antebellum South.* Austin: University of Texas Press, 1979.

Buck, Paul H. "The Poor Whites in the Antebellum South." *Mississippi Valley Historical Quarterly* 31 (November 1925): 41–54.

Burton, Orville Vernon. *In My House There Are Many Mansions: Family and Community in Edgefield, South Carolina.* Chapel Hill: University of North Carolina Press, 1985.

Calhoun, Frederick S. *The Lawmen: United States Marshals and Their Deputies, 1789–1989.* Washington: Smithsonian Institution Press, 1989.

Cash, W. J. *The Mind of the South.* New York: Knopf, 1941.

Cashin, Joan. *A Family Venture: Men and Women on the Southern Frontier.* New York: Oxford University Press, 1991.

Censer, Jane Turner. " 'Smiling through Her Tears': Ante-Bellum Southern Women and Divorce." *American Journal of Legal History* 25 (Spring 1981): 24–47.

Chapin, Bradley. *Criminal Justice in Colonial America, 1606–1660.* Athens: University of Georgia Press, 1983.

Click, Patricia. "The Ruling Passion: Gambling and Sport in Antebellum Baltimore, Norfolk, and Richmond." *Virginia Cavalcade* 39 (Autumn 1989): 62–68; 39 (Winter 1990): 100–104.

Clinton, Catherine. *The Plantation Mistress: Woman's World in the Old South.* New York: Pantheon Books, 1982.

Collins, Bruce. *White Society in the Antebellum South.* New York: Longman, 1985.

Cooper, William J., Jr., and Thomas E. Terrill. *The American South: A History.* New York: McGraw-Hill, 1991.

———. *Liberty and Slavery: Southern Politics to 1860.* New York: Knopf, 1983.

———. *The South and the Politics of Slavery, 1828–1856.* Baton Rouge: Louisiana State University Press, 1978.

Coulter, E. Merton. "Four Slave Trials in Elbert County Georgia." *Georgia Historical Quarterly* 41 (September 1956): 237–46.

———. "Hangings as a Socio-Penal Institution in Georgia and Elsewhere." *Georgia Historical Quarterly* 57 (Spring 1973): 17–55.

Curry, Leonard. *The Free Black Man in Urban America, 1800–1850: Shadows of a Dream.* Chicago: University of Chicago Press, 1981.

Cutler, James Elbert. *Lynch-Law: An Investigation into Lynching in the United States.* London: Longmans, Green, 1905.

Davis, David. *Homicide in American Fiction, 1798–1860: A Study in Social Values.* Ithaca, N.Y.: Cornell University Press, 1957.

———. "The Movement to Abolish Capital Punishment in America, 1787–1861." *American Historical Review* 63 (October 1957): 23–46.

Degler, Carl N. *Neither Black Nor White: Slavery and Race Relations in Brazil and the United States*. New York: Macmillan, 1971.

Denham, James M. "New Orleans, Maritime Commerce, and the Texas War for Independence, 1836." *Southwestern Historical Quarterly* 97 (January 1994): 511–34.

Dick, Everett. *The Dixie Frontier: A Social History of the Southern Frontier from the First Transmontane Beginnings to the Civil War*. New York: Knopf, 1948.

Dobash, Russell, and Emerson Dobash. "Community Response to Violence against Wives: Charivari, Abstract Justice, and Patriarchy." *Social Problems* 28 (June 1981): 563–81.

Dodd, Donald B., and Wynelle S. Dodd. *Historical Statistics of the South, 1790–1970*. Tuscaloosa: University of Alabama Press, 1973.

Doerner, William G. "The Deadly World of Johnny Reb: Fact, Foible, or Fantasy?" In *Violent Crime: Historical and Contemporary Issues,* edited by James Inciardi and Anne Pottieger, 91–97. Beverly Hills: Sage, 1978.

Durden, Robert F. *The Self-Inflicted Wound: Southern Politics in the Nineteenth Century*. Lexington: University of Kentucky Press, 1985.

Eaton, Clement. "Class Differences in the Old South." *Virginia Quarterly Review* 33 (Summer 1957): 356–70.

———. *The Freedom of Thought Struggle in the Old South*. New York: Harper, 1964.

———. *The Growth of the Southern Civilization, 1790–1860*. New York: Harper, 1961.

———. *A History of the Old South*. New York: Macmillan, 1966.

———. *The Mind of the Old South*. Baton Rouge: Louisiana State University Press, 1967.

———. "Mob Violence in the Old South." *Mississippi Valley Historical Review* 29 (December 1942): 351–70.

———. "The Role of Honor in Southern Society." *Southern Humanities Review* 10 (Supplement 1976): 47–58.

———. *The Waning of the Southern Civilization*. New York: Pegasus, 1969.

Edwards, John C. "Slave Justice in Four Middle Georgia Counties." *Georgia Historical Quarterly* 57 (Summer 1973): 265–73.

Ekirch, A. Roger. *Bound for America: Transportation of British Convicts to the Colonies, 1718–1775*. New York: Oxford University Press, 1987.

Elkins, Stanley M. *Slavery: A Problem in American Institutional and Intellectual Life*. Chicago: University of Chicago Press, 1976.

Elliot, Mabel. "Crime and the Frontier Mores." *American Sociological Review* 9 (April 1944): 185–92.

Ely, James W., Jr. "Regionalism and Legal History of the South." In *Ambivalent Legacy: A Legal History of the South,* edited by David J. Bodenhamer and James W. Ely Jr., 3–29. Jackson: University of Mississippi Press, 1984.

Fede, Andrew. "Legitimized Violent Slave Abuse in the American South, 1619–1865: A Case Study of Law and Social Change in Six Southern States." *American Journal of Legal History* 29 (April 1985): 93–150.

———. *People without Rights: An Interpretation of the Fundamentals of the Law of Slavery in the United States*. New York: Garland, 1992.

Feigenson, Neal R. "Extraterritorial Recognition of Divorce Decrees in the Nineteenth Century." *American Journal of Legal History* 34 (April 1990): 119–67.

Feldberg, Michael. *The Turbulent Era: Riot and Disorder in Jacksonian America*. New York: Oxford University Press, 1980.

Filler, Louis. "Movements to Abolish the Death Penalty in the United States." In *Capital Punishment,* edited by Thorsten Sellin, 104–21. New York: Harper and Row, 1967.

Findlay, John. *People of Chance: Gambling in American Society from Jamestown to Las Vegas*. New York: Oxford University Press, 1986.

Finkelman, Paul. *An Imperfect Union: Slavery, Federalism, and Comity*. Chapel Hill: University of North Carolina Press, 1981.

Flanigan, Daniel. "Criminal Procedure in Slave Trials in the Antebellum South." *Journal of Southern History* 40 (November 1974): 537–64.

Flynt, J. Wayne. *Dixie's Forgotten People: The South's Poor Whites*. Bloomington: University of Indiana Press, 1979.

———. *Poor But Proud: Alabama's Poor Whites*. Tuscaloosa: University of Alabama Press, 1989.

Fogel, Robert William, and Stanley L. Engerman. *Time on the Cross: The Economics of American Negro Slavery*. Boston: Little, Brown, 1974.

Franklin, John Hope. *From Slavery to Freedom: A History of Negro Americans*. New York: Knopf, 1967.

———. *The Militant South, 1800–1861*. Cambridge: Harvard University Press, 1956.

Friedman, Lawrence M. *Crime and Punishment in American History*. New York: Basic Books, 1993.

———. *A History of American Law*. New York: Simon and Schuster, 1985.

———. "The Law between the States: Some Thoughts on Southern Legal History." In *Ambivalent Legacy: A Legal History of the South,* edited by David J. Bodenhamer and James W. Ely Jr., 30–46. Jackson: University of Mississippi Press, 1984.

Gastil, Raymond D. "Homicide and a Regional Perspective." *American Sociological Review* 36 (April 1971): 412–27.

Genovese, Eugene D. *Roll, Jordan, Roll: The World the Slaves Made*. New York: Vintage, 1976.

———. "Slavery in the Legal History of the South and the Nation." *Texas Law Review* 59 (May 1981): 969–98.

Gorn, Elliot J. " 'Gouge and Bite, Pull Hair and Scratch': The Social Significance of Fighting in the Southern Backcountry." *American Historical Review* 90 (February 1985): 18–43.

Graham, Hugh Davis, and Ted Robert Gurr, eds. *Violence in America: Historical and Comparative Perspectives*. 2 vols. Washington, D.C.: U.S. Government Printing Office, 1969.

Green, Jonathon. *Gambling Exposed: A Full Exposition of All the Various Arts, Mysteries, and Miseries of Gambling by a Reformed Gambler*. 1857. Reprint, Montclair, N.J.: Patterson Smith, 1973.

Greenberg, Douglas. *Crime and Law Enforcement in the Colony of New York, 1691–1776*. Ithaca, N.Y.: Cornell University Press, 1976.

Greenberg, Kenneth S. *Masters and Statesmen: The Political Culture of American Slavery*. Baltimore: Johns Hopkins University Press, 1985.

———. "The Nose, the Lie, and the Duel in the Antebellum South." *American Historical Review* 95 (November 1990): 57–74.

Grossberg, Michael. *Governing the Hearth: Law and Family in the Nineteenth Century*. Chapel Hill: University of North Carolina Press, 1986.

Grund, Francis. *The Americans in Their Moral, Social, and Political Relations*. Boston: Marsh, Cooper, and Lynn, 1837.

Hackney, Sheldon. "Southern Violence." *American Historical Review* 74 (February 1969): 906–25.

Hall, John A. " 'A Rigour of Confinement Which Violates Humanity': Jail Conditions in South Carolina during the 1790s." *Southern Studies* 24 (Fall 1985): 285–94.

Hall, Kermit L. *The Magic Mirror: Law in American History*. New York: Oxford University Press, 1989.

———. *The Politics of Justice: Lower Federal Judicial Selection and the Second Party System, 1829–61*. Lincoln: University of Nebraska Press, 1979.

———. "The 'Route to Hell' Retraced: The Impact of Popular Elections on the Southern Appellate Judiciary, 1832–1920." In *Ambivalent Legacy: A Legal History of the South*, edited by David J. Bodenhamer and James W. Ely Jr., 229–56. Jackson: University of Mississippi Press, 1984.

Haskins, George L. "Court Records and History." *William and Mary Quarterly* 5 (October 1948): 547–52.

Haunton, Richard H. "Law and Order in Savannah, 1850–1860." *Georgia Historical Quarterly* 56 (Spring 1972): 1–24.

Henderson, Dwight. *Congress, Courts, and Criminals: The Development of the Federal Criminal Law, 1801–1829*. Westport, Conn.: Greenwood Press, 1985.

Hibbert, Christopher. *The Roots of Evil: A Social History of Crime and Punishment*. Boston: Little, Brown, 1963.

Hindus, Michael S. "Black Justice under White Law: Criminal Prosecutions of Blacks in Antebellum South Carolina." *Journal of American History* 63 (December 1976): 575–99.

———. *Prison and Plantation: Crime, Justice, and Authority in Massachusetts and South Carolina, 1767–1878*. Chapel Hill: University of North Carolina Press, 1980.

Hobsbawm, Eric J. *Bandits*. New York: Pantheon Books, 1981.

———. *Primitive Rebels*. Manchester, England: Glencoe, 1959.

Hobson, Fred. "The Savage South: An Inquiry into the Origins, Endurance, and Presumed Demise of an Image." *Virginia Quarterly Review* 61 (Summer 1985): 377–95.

Hoffer, Peter C., and William B. Scott, eds. *Criminal Proceedings in Colonial Virginia: [Records of] Fines, Examinations of Criminals, Trials of Slaves etc. from*

March 1710 [1711] to [1754] Richmond County. Athens: University of Georgia Press, 1984.

Hofstadter, Richard, and Michael Wallace, eds. *American Violence: A Documentary History*. New York: Random House, 1970.

Hogan, William Ransom. *The Republic of Texas: A Social and Economic History*. Norman: University of Oklahoma Press, 1946.

Hogeland, Ronald. " 'The Feminine Appendage': Feminine Lifestyles in America, 1820–1860." *Civil War History* 17 (June 1971): 101–14.

Hollon, Eugene W. *Frontier Violence: Another Look*. New York: Oxford University Press, 1974.

Howington, Arthur F. "Violence in Alabama: A Study of Late Antebellum Montgomery." *Alabama Review* 27 (July 1974): 213–31.

Hull, N. E. H. *Female Felons: Women and Serious Crime in Colonial Massachusetts*. Urbana: University of Illinois Press, 1987.

Hundley, Daniel R. *Social Relations in Our Southern States*. New York: H. B. Price, 1860.

Hunt, William R. *Distant Justice: Policing the Alaska Frontier*. Norman: University of Oklahoma Press, 1987.

Ireland, Robert M. *The County Courts in Antebellum Kentucky*. Lexington: University of Kentucky Press, 1972.

———. "Homicide in Nineteenth-Century Kentucky." *Register of the Kentucky Historical Society* 81 (Spring 1983): 134–53.

———. "Insanity and the Unwritten Law." *American Journal of Legal History* 32 (April 1988): 157–72.

———. "Law and Disorder in Nineteenth-Century Kentucky." *Vanderbilt Law Review* 32 (January 1979): 281–300.

———. "The Libertine Must Die: Sexual Dishonor and the Unwritten Law in the Nineteenth-Century United States." *Journal of Social History* 23 (Fall 1989): 27–43.

Johnson, David R. *American Law Enforcement: A History*. Arlington Heights, Ill.: Forum Press, 1981.

Johnson, Guion Griffis. *Antebellum North Carolina: A Social History*. Chapel Hill: University of North Carolina Press, 1937.

Jordan, Philip D. *Frontier Law and Order: Ten Essays*. Lincoln: University of Nebraska Press, 1970.

Kealey, Linda. "Patterns of Punishment: Massachusetts in the Eighteenth Century." *American Journal of Legal History* 30 (April 1986): 163–86.

Keller, William F. *The Nation's Advocate: Henry Marie Brackenridge and Young America*. Pittsburgh: University of Pittsburgh Press, 1956.

Kolchin, Peter. *American Slavery, 1619–1877*. New York: Hill and Wang, 1993.

Kooistra, Paul. *Criminals as Heroes: Structure, Power, and Identity*. Bowling Green, Ohio: Bowling Green State University Press, 1989.

Lack, Paul. "Law and Disorder in Confederate Atlanta." *Georgia Historical Quarterly* 66 (Summer 1982): 171–95.

Lang, Meredith. *Defender of the Faith: The High Court of Mississippi, 1817–1875*. Jackson: University of Mississippi Press, 1977.

Laurence, John. *A History of Capital Punishment*. New York: Citadel Press, 1960.

Leyburn, James G. *Frontier Folkways*. New Haven: Yale University Press, 1935.

———. *The Scotch-Irish in America: A Social History*. Chapel Hill: University of North Carolina Press, 1962.

Littlefield, Daniel F. *Africans and Creeks: From the Colonial Period to the Civil War*. Westport, Conn.: Greenwood Press, 1979.

———. *Africans and Seminoles: From Removal to Emancipation*. Westport, Conn.: Greenwood Press, 1977.

Masur, Louis P. *Rites of Execution: Capital Punishment and the Transformation of American Culture, 1776–1865*. New York: Oxford University Press, 1989.

McCardell, John. *The Idea of a Southern Nation: Southern Nationalists and Southern Nationalism, 1830–1860*. New York: Norton, 1979.

McDade, Thomas. *The Annals of Murder: A Bibliography of Books and Pamphlets on American Murders from Colonial Times to 1900*. Norman: University of Oklahoma Press, 1961.

McDonald, Brenda. "Domestic Violence in Colonial Massachusetts." *Historical Journal of Massachusetts* 14 (January 1986): 53–64.

McDonald, Forrest. "The Ethnic Factor in Alabama History: A Neglected Dimension." *Alabama Review* 31 (October 1978): 256–65.

McDonald, Forrest, and Ellen Shapiro McDonald. "The Ethnic Origins of the American People, 1790." *William and Mary Quarterly* 37 (April 1980): 179–99.

McDonald, Forrest, and Grady McWhiney. "The Antebellum Southern Herdsman: A Reinterpretation." *Journal of Southern History* 41 (May 1975): 147–66.

———. "Celtic Origins of Southern Herding Practices." *Journal of Southern History* 51 (May 1985): 165–82.

———. "The South from Self-Sufficiency to Peonage: An Interpretation." *American Historical Review* 85 (December 1980): 1095–1118.

McGrath, Roger. *Gunfighters, Highwaymen, and Vigilantes: Violence on the Frontier*. Berkeley: University of California Press, 1984.

McIlwaine, Sheilds. *The Southern Poor-White from Lubberland to Tobacco Road*. Norman: University of Oklahoma Press, 1939.

McWhiney, Grady. *Cracker Culture: Celtic Ways in the Old South*. Tuscaloosa: University of Alabama Press, 1988.

———. "The Ethnic Roots of Southern Violence." In *A Master's Due: Essays in Honor of David Herbert Donald,* edited by William Cooper Jr., Michael J. Holt, and John McCardell, 112–37. Baton Rouge: Louisiana State University Press, 1985.

McWhiney, Grady, and Perry Jameson. *Attack and Die: Civil War Tactics and the Southern Heritage*. University: University of Alabama Press, 1982.

Mellen, Paul. "Coroner's Inquests in Colonial Massachusetts." *Journal of the History of Medicine and Allied Sciences* 40 (October 1985): 462–72.

Miles, Edwin A. "The Mississippi Slave Insurrection Scare of 1835." *Journal of Negro History* 42 (January 1957): 48–60.

Miller, Randall, and John Smith, eds. *Dictionary of Afro-American Slavery*. Westport, Conn.: Greenwood Press, 1988.

Monkkonen, Eric. "The Quantitative Historical Study of Crime and Criminal Justice." In *History and Crime: Implications for Criminal Justice Policy,* edited by James A. Inciardi and Charles F. Faupel, 55–74. Beverly Hills: Sage, 1980.

Moore, Arthur. *The Frontier Mind*. New York: McGraw-Hill, 1963.

Moore, John Hebron. "Local and State Governments of Antebellum Mississippi." *Journal of Mississippi History* 44 (May 1982): 104–34.

Moore, Waddy W. "Some Aspects of Crime and Punishment on the Arkansas Frontier." *Arkansas Historical Quarterly* 23 (Spring 1964): 50–64.

Murat, Achille. *America and the Americans*. New York: W. H. Graham, 1849.

———. *A Moral and Political Sketch of the United States of North America*. London: Effingham Wilson, 1833.

Nash, A. E. Keir. "Fairness and Formalism in the Trials of Blacks in the State Supreme Courts of the Old South." *Virginia Law Review* 56 (February 1970): 64–100.

———. "A More Equitable Past?: Southern Supreme Courts and the Protection of the Antebellum Negro." *North Carolina Law Review* 48 (February 1970): 197–242.

———. "Negro Rights, Unionism, and Greatness on the South Carolina Court of Appeals: The Extraordinary Chief Justice John Belton O'Neall." *South Carolina Law Review* 21 (Spring 1969): 141–90.

———. "The Reason of Slavery: Understanding the Judicial Role in the Peculiar Institution." *Vanderbilt Law Review* 32 (January 1979): 7–221.

———. "The Texas Supreme Court and the Trial Rights of Blacks, 1845–1860." *Journal of American History* 58 (December 1971): 622–42.

Newby, I. A. *Plain Folk in the New South: Social Change and Persistence, 1880–1915*. Baton Rouge: Louisiana State University Press, 1989.

Oakes, James B. *The Ruling Race: A History of American Slaveholders*. New York: Knopf, 1982.

Otto, John Solomon. *Southern Frontiers, 1607–1860: The Agricultural Evolution of the Colonial and Antebellum South*. Westport, Conn.: Greenwood Press, 1989.

Owens, Leslie Howard. *This Species of Property: Slave Life and Culture in the Old South*. New York: Oxford University Press, 1976.

Owsley, Frank L. *Plain Folk of the Old South*. Baton Rouge: Louisiana State University Press, 1949.

Packer, Herbert L. *The Limits of Criminal Sanction*. Stanford: Stanford University Press, 1968.

Parramore, Tom. "Gouging in Early North Carolina." *North Carolina Journal of Folklore* 22 (May 1974): 55–62.

Penick, James Lal, Jr. *The Great Western Land Pirate: John A. Murrell in Legend and History*. Columbia: University of Missouri Press, 1981.

———. "John A. Murrell: A Legend of the Old Southwest." *Tennessee Historical Quarterly* 48 (Fall 1989): 174–83.

Phillips, Ulrich Bonnell. *American Negro Slavery*. New York: Appleton and Co., 1918.

———. *Life and Labor in the Old South*. Boston: Little, Brown, 1929.

Pitt-Rivers, Julian. "Honor." In *International Encyclopedia of the Social Sciences,* edited by David L. Sills, 6:503–11. New York: Macmillan, 1968.

Pleck, Elizabeth. *Domestic Tyranny: The Making of American Social Policy against Family Violence from Colonial Times to the Present*. New York: Oxford University Press, 1987.

———. "Wife Beating in Nineteenth-Century America." *Victimology* 4 (Fall 1979): 60–74.

Porter, Kenneth. *The Negro on the American Frontier*. New York: Arno Press, 1971.

Prassel, Frank Richard. *The Western Peace Officer: A Legacy of Law and Order*. Norman: University of Oklahoma Press, 1972.

Prude, Jonathon. "To Look Upon the 'Lower Sort': Runaway Ads and the Appearance of Unfree Laborers in America, 1750–1800." *Journal of American History* 78 (June 1991): 129–59.

Quinn, John P. *Gambling and Gambling Devices*. 1912. Reprint, Montclair, N.J.: Patterson Smith, 1969.

Redfield, H. V. *Homicide North and South: Being a Comparative View of Crime against the Person in the Several States of the United States.* Philadelphia: Lippincott, 1880.

Reed, John Shelton. "Below the Smith and Wesson Line: Southern Violence." In *One South: An Ethnic Approach to Regional Culture,* edited by John Shelton Reed, 139–53. Baton Rouge: Louisiana State University Press, 1982.

———. "To Live and Die in Dixie: A Contribution to the Study of Southern Violence." *Political Science Quarterly* 86 (September 1971): 429–43.

Richardson, Simon Peter. *The Lights and Shadows of Itinerant Life: An Autobiography*. Nashville: Barbie and Smith, 1901.

Robertson, James I. "Frolics, Fights, and Firewater in Frontier Tennessee." *Tennessee Historical Quarterly* 17 (June 1958): 97–111.

Rorabaugh, W. J. *The Alcoholic Republic: An American Tradition*. New York: Oxford University Press, 1979.

Rose, Thomas, ed. *Violence in America: A Historical and Contemporary Reader*. New York: Vintage, 1970.

Rousey, Dennis. "Caps and Guns: Police Use of Deadly Force in Nineteenth-Century New Orleans." *American Journal of Legal History* 28 (January 1984): 41–66.

Rowe, G. S. "*Femes Covert* and Criminal Prosecution in Eighteenth-Century Pennsylvania." *American Journal of Legal History* 32 (April 1988): 138–56.

———. "Women's Crime and Criminal Administration in Pennsylvania, 1763–1790." *Pennsylvania Magazine of History and Biography* 109 (July 1985): 335–68.

Saunders, Robert M. "Crime and Punishment in Early National America: Richmond, Virginia, 1784–1820." *Virginia Magazine of History and Biography* 86 (January 1978): 33–44.

Schlachter, Gail, ed. *Crime and Punishment in America: A Historical Bibliography*. Santa Barbara, Calif.: ABC-Clio Information Service, 1984.

Schwarz, Philip J. *Twice Condemned: Slaves and the Criminal Laws of Virginia, 1705–1865*. Baton Rouge: Louisiana State University Press, 1988.

Scott, Anne Firor. *The Southern Lady: From Pedestal to Politics, 1830–1930*. Chicago: University of Chicago Press, 1970.

Sellers, James B. *Slavery in Alabama*. Tuscaloosa: University of Alabama Press, 1964.

Semmes, Raphael. *Crime and Punishment in Early Maryland*. Baltimore: Johns Hopkins Press, 1938.

Shaw, Robert B. *A Legal History of Slavery in the United States*. Potsdam, N.Y.: Northern Press, 1991.

Shingleton, Royce. "The Trial and Punishment of Slaves in Baldwin County, Georgia, 1812–1826." *Southern Humanities Review* 8 (Winter 1974): 67–73.

Shippee, Lester B., ed. *Bishop Whipple's Southern Diary, 1843–1844*. Minneapolis: University of Minnesota Press, 1937.

Sifakis, Carl. *The Encyclopedia of American Crime*. New York: Smithmark, 1992.

———. *The Encyclopedia of Gambling*. New York: Facts on File, 1990.

Simkins, Francis Butler. *A History of the South*. New York: Knopf, 1958.

Slotkin, Richard. *The Fatal Environment: The Myth of the Frontier Age of Industrialization, 1800–1890*. New York: Atheneum, 1985.

———. *Regeneration through Violence: The Mythology of the American Frontier, 1600–1860*. Middletown, Conn.: Wesleyan University Press, 1973.

Smith, Albert Colby. "Southern Violence Reconsidered: Arson as Protest in Black-Belt Georgia, 1865–1910." *Journal of Southern History* 51 (November 1985): 527–64.

Smith, Edward, and Arnold Zurcher. *Dictionary of American Politics*. New York: Barnes and Noble, 1968.

Smith, Stephen. "Arkansas Advocacy: The Territorial Period." *Arkansas Law Review* 31 (Fall 1977): 449–76.

Spindell, Donna J., and Stuart W. Thomas Jr. "Crime and Society in North Carolina, 1663–1740." *Journal of Southern History* 49 (May 1983): 223–44.

Stampp, Kenneth. *The Peculiar Institution: Slavery in the Antebellum South*. New York: Vintage, 1956.

Steel, Edward. "Criminality in Jeffersonian America—A Sample." *Crime and Delinquency* 18 (April 1972): 154–59.

Steckmesser, Kent L. "Robin Hood and the American Outlaw." *Journal of American Folklore* 79 (April 1966): 348–55.

Sydnor, Charles S. *Slavery in Mississippi*. Baton Rouge: Louisiana State University Press, 1966.

———. "The Southerner and the Laws." *Journal of Southern History* 6 (February 1940): 3–23.

Tachau, Mary K. Bonsteel. *The Federal Courts in the Early Republic: Kentucky, 1789–1816*. Princeton: Princeton University Press, 1978.

Thompson, Bruce E. "Reforms in the Penal System in Mississippi, 1820–1850." *Journal of Mississippi History* 7 (January 1945): 51–74.

Tushnet, Mark. "The American Law of Slavery, 1810–1860: A Study in the Persistence of Legal Autonomy." *Law and Society* 10 (Fall 1979): 119–84.

———. *The American Law of Slavery, 1810–1860: Considerations of Humanity and Interest*. Princeton: Princeton University Press, 1981.

———. "Approaches to the Study of the Law of Slavery." *Civil War History* 25 (December 1979): 329–37.

Tyrrell, Ian R. "Drink and Temperance in the Antebellum South: An Overview and Interpretation." *Journal of Southern History* 48 (November 1982): 485–510.

Wade, Richard C. *Slavery in the Cities: The South, 1820–1860*. New York: Oxford University Press, 1964.

———. *The Urban Frontier: The Rise of the Western Cites, 1790–1830*. Cambridge: Harvard University Press, 1959.

Walker, Samuel. *Popular Justice: A History of American Criminal Justice*. New York: Oxford University Press, 1980.

Watson, Alan D. "The Constable in Colonial North Carolina." *North Carolina Historical Review* 68 (January 1991): 1–16.

Welter, Barbara. "The Cult of True Womanhood." *American Quarterly* 18 (Summer 1966): 151–74.

White, Leonard. *The Jacksonians: A Study in Administrative History, 1829–1861*. New York: Macmillan, 1954.

White, Richard. "Outlaw Gangs of the Middle Border: American Social Bandits." *Western Historical Quarterly* 12 (October 1981): 387–408.

White, Walter. *Rope and Faggot*. New York: Arno Press, 1969.

Williams, Jack Kenny. "Crime and Punishment in Alabama, 1819–1840." *Alabama Review* 6 (January 1953): 14–30.

———. "The Criminal Lawyer in Ante-Bellum South Carolina." *South Carolina Historical Magazine* 56 (July 1955): 138–51.

———. *Dueling in the Old South: Vignettes of Social History*. College Station: Texas A&M University Press, 1980.

———. *Vogues in Villainy: Crime and Retribution in Antebellum South Carolina*. Columbia: University of South Carolina Press, 1959.

———. "White Lawbreakers in Antebellum South Carolina." *Journal of Southern History* 21 (August 1955): 360–73.

Wilson, Charles Reagan, and William Ferris, eds. *Encyclopedia of Southern Culture*. Chapel Hill: University of North Carolina Press, 1989.

Wood, Gordon S. *The Creation of the American Republic, 1776–1787*. Chapel Hill: University of North Carolina Press, 1969.

Wooster, Ralph A. *The People in Power: Courthouse and Statehouse in the Lower South, 1850–1860*. Knoxville: University of Tennessee Press, 1969.

Wright, A. J. *Criminal Activity in the Deep South, 1700–1930: An Annotated Bibliography*. Westport, Conn.: Greenwood Press, 1989.

Wright, J. Leitch. *Creeks and Seminoles: The Destruction and Regeneration of the Muscogulge People*. Lincoln: University of Nebraska Press, 1986.

———. *The Only Land They Knew: The Tragic Story of the Indians of the Old South*. New York: Free Press, 1981.

Wunder, John R. *Inferior Courts, Superior Justice: A History of the Justices of the Peace on the Northwest Frontier, 1853–1889*. Westport, Conn.: Greenwood Press, 1979.

Wyatt-Brown, Bertram. "Community, Class, and Snopesian Crime: Local Justice in the Old South." In *Class, Conflict, and Consensus: Antebellum Southern Community Studies*, edited by Orville Vernon Burton and Robert C. McMath Jr., 173–206. Westport, Conn.: Greenwood Press, 1982.

———. *Honor and Violence in the Old South*. New York: Oxford University Press, 1986.

———. "The Ideal Typology and Antebellum Southern History: A Testing of a New Approach." *Societas—A Review of Social History* 5 (Winter 1975): 1–29.

———. *Southern Honor: Ethics and Behavior in the Old South*. New York: Oxford University Press, 1982.

———. *Yankee Saints and Southern Sinners*. Baton Rouge: Louisiana State University Press, 1985.

Younger, Richard D. *The People's Panel: The Grand Jury in the United States, 1634–1941*. Providence: Brown University Press, 1963.

Master's Theses and Doctoral Dissertations

Atkins, Emily Harvard. "A History of Jacksonville, Florida, 1816–1902." Master's thesis, Duke University, 1941.

Bodenhamer, David J. "Crime and Criminal Justice in Antebellum Indiana: Marion County as a Case Study." Ph.D. diss., Indiana University, 1977.

Bonkrude, Hardeen. "Crime and Its Treatment in Minneapolis and St. Anthony to 1880." Ph.D. diss., University of Minnesota, 1971.

Chatham, Katherine. "Plantation Slavery in Middle Florida." Master's thesis, University of North Carolina, 1938.

Denham, James M. "Dueling in Territorial Middle Florida." Master's thesis, Florida State University, 1983.

———. " 'A Rogues Paradise': Violent Crime in Antebellum Florida." Ph.D. diss., Florida State University, 1988.

Flanigan, Daniel. "The Criminal Law of Slavery and Freedom, 1800–1868." Ph.D. diss., Rice University, 1973.

Fouracker, Warren G. "The Administration of Robert Raymond Reid." Master's thesis, Florida State University, 1949.

Graham, Thomas. "Antebellum Tallahassee Newspapers, 1845–1861." Master's thesis, Florida State University, 1967.

Gratiot, Adolf. "Criminal Justice on the Kentucky Frontier." Ph.D. diss., University of Pennsylvania, 1952.

Hill, Dorothy. "Joseph M. White: Florida's Territorial Delegate, 1825–1837." Master's thesis, University of Florida, 1950.

Howington, Arthur. "The Treatment of Slaves and Free Blacks in the State and Local Courts of Tennessee." Ph.D. diss., Vanderbilt University, 1982.

Jackson, Jesse J. "The Negro and the Law in Florida, 1821–1921." Master's thesis, Florida State University, 1960.

Keith, Rebecca. "The Humanitarian Movement in Florida, 1821–1861." Master's thesis, Florida State University, 1951.

Kerr, Derek Noel. "Petty Felony, Slave Defiance, and Frontier Villainy: Crime and Criminal Justice in Louisiana, 1770–1803." Ph.D. diss., Tulane University, 1983.

Kirkland, Herbert Donald. "A City Is Born: From Choya to Antebellum Jacksonville." Master's thesis, Florida State University, 1969.

Landers, Jane. "Black Society in Spanish St. Augustine, 1784–1821." Ph.D. diss., University of Florida, 1988.

Lavin, Jack Cardwell. "The Temperance Movement in Antebellum Florida." Master's thesis, Florida State University, 1967.

Lisenby, Julie Anne. "The Free Negro in Antebellum Florida." Master's thesis, Florida State University, 1967.

Nolan, Patrick Bates. "Vigilantes on the Middle Border: A Study of Self-Appointed Law Enforcement in the States of the Upper Mississippi from 1840 to 1880." Ph.D. diss., University of Minnesota, 1971.

Owens, Harry P. "Apalachicola before 1861." Ph.D. diss., Florida State University, 1966.

Schafer, Judith. "The Long Arm of the Law: Slavery and the Supreme Court of Antebellum Louisiana, 1809–1862." Ph.D. diss., Tulane University, 1985.

Smith, Albert Colby. "Down Freedom's Road: The Contours of Race, Class, and Property in Crime in Black-Belt Georgia, 1866–1910." Ph.D. diss., University of Georgia, 1982.

Thompson, Arthur W. "David Levy Yulee: A Study of Nineteenth-Century American Thought and Enterprise." Ph.D. diss., Columbia University, 1954.

Thurston, William. "A Study of Maritime Activity in Florida in the Nineteenth Century." Ph.D. diss., Florida State University, 1972.

Williams, Edwin L. "Florida in the Union, 1845–1861." Ph.D. diss., University of North Carolina, 1951.

Index

Index

Index

Index

Index

Index

Index

About the Author

James M. Denham is Associate Professor of History at Florida Southern College, Lakeland, Florida. He received his bachelor's, master's, and doctorate degrees from Florida State University. A specialist in Florida history, Denham has published numerous articles in the *Florida Historical Quarterly* and other journals. In 1992, Denham was the recipient of the Florida Historical Society's Arthur W. Thompson prize. He also served two years on the speakers bureau of the Florida Humanities Council and in 1990 won the Governor's Distinguished Professor Award.